The Earthscan Reader in Population and Development

Edited by Paul Demeny and Geoffrey McNicoll

Earthscan Publications Ltd

First published in the UK 1998 by
Earthscan Publications Limited

Copyright © Paul Demeny and Geoffrey McNicoll, 1998; see pages vii and viii
for individual chapters

A catalogue record for this book is available from the British Library

ISBN: 1 85383 275 8 paperback
      1 85383 474 2 hardback

Typesetting and page design by PCS Mapping & DTP, Newcastle upon Tyne

Printed and bound by Biddles Ltd, Guildford and Kings Lynn

Cover design by Andrew Corbett

For a full list of publications please contact:
Earthscan Publications Limited
120 Pentonville Road
London N1 9JN
Tel. (0171) 278 0433
Fax: (0171) 278 1142
Email: earthinfo@earthscan.co.uk
WWW: http://www.earthscan.co.uk

Earthscan is an editorially independent subsidiary of Kogan Page Limited
and publishes in association with WWF-UK and the International Institute
for Environment and Development.

Contents

Part IV Resources and the Environment

Part V Futures

Sources and Acknowledgements

Earthscan and the editors would like to thank the authors and copyright holders for permission to reprint contributions appearing in this volume.

Chapter 1: United Nations *The Population Debate: Dimensions and Perspectives, Volume 1* New York, 1975, pp425–433.

Chapter 2: *Population and Development Review* volume 17, number 1, March 1991, pp105–114. © The Population Council.

Chapter 3: Reproduced, with permission, from the *Annual Review of Sociology* volume 3, 1977, pp163–178. © Annual Reviews, Inc.

Chapter 4: Theodore W Schultz *The Economics of Being Poor* Oxford, Blackwell, 1993, pp290–295. Originally published in *Journal of Political Economy* volume 82, number 2, part 2, March/April 1974, ppS2–S10. © Theodore W Schultz. Reproduced with permission of the authors and the publishers.

Chapter 5: *Population and Development Review* volume 6, number 2, June 1980, pp225–255. © The Population Council.

Chapter 6: Albert O Hirschman *The Strategy of Economic Development* New Haven, Yale University Press, 1958, pp176–182. © Yale University Press.

Chapter 7: William H McNeill *The Pursuit of Power: Technology, Armed Force, and Society Since AD1000* Chicago, University of Chicago Press, 1982, pp309–316. © William H McNeill. Reproduced with permission of the author and the publisher.

Chapter 8: *International Social Science Journal* volume 26, number 2, 1974, pp302–314. © UNESCO.

Chapter 9: *American Economic Review* volume 78, number 1, March 1988, pp1–13. © American Economic Association. Reproduced by permission.

Chapter 10: G McNicoll and M Cain (eds) *Rural Development and Population: Institutions and Policy* (supplement to *Population and Development Review*, volume 15, 1989) New York, The Population Council and Oxford University Press, pp61–76. © Amartya Sen.

Chapter 11: *Scientists and World Affairs* Proceedings of the Twenty-Second Pugwash Conference on Science and World Affairs, 7–12 September 1972, London, nd, pp279–288.

Chapter 12: *Feminist Studies* volume 9, number 2, summer 1983, pp261–284. © Nancy Folbre.

Chapter 13: *Eugenics Quarterly* volume 2, number 1, March 1955, pp32–39.

Chapter 14: Ronald D Lee et al (eds) *Population, Food and Rural Development* Oxford, Clarendon Press, 1988, pp101–117. © IUSSP.

Chapter 15: Kerstin Lindahl-Kiessling and Hans Landberg (eds) *Population, Economic Development, and the Environment* Oxford, Oxford University Press, 1994, pp211–230. © Oxford University Press.

Chapter 16: Papers of the East–West Population Institute, number 37, Honolulu, East–West Population Institute, 1976. © Norman B Ryder.

Chapter 17: G McNicoll and M Cain (eds) *Rural Development and Population: Institutions and Policy* (supplement to *Population and Development Review*, volume 15, 1989) New York, The Population Council and Oxford University Press, pp45–60. © Ester Boserup.

Chapter 18: *Population and Development Review*, volume 16, number 1, March 1990, pp93–106. © The Population Council.

Sources and Acknowledgements

Chapter 19: Just Faaland (ed) *Population and the World Economy in the 21st Century* New York, St Martin's Press, 1982, pp206–228. © The Norwegian Nobel Institute.

Chapter 20: *Population Bulletin* volume 13, number 4, May 1957, pp61–75. © Population Reference Bureau.

Chapter 21: *Economic Development and Cultural Change* volume 19, number 4, July 1971, pp545–559. © The University of Chicago. Reproduced with permission of the University of Chicago Press.

Chapter 22: Francis Graham-Smith (ed) *Population – The Complex Reality: A Report of the Population Summit of the World's Scientific Academies* London, The Royal Society, and Golden, Colorado, North American Press, 1994, pp85–92. © The Royal Society.

Chapter 23: Kingsley Davis and Mikhail S Bernstam (eds) *Resources, Environment and Population: Present Knowledge, Future Options* (supplement to *Population and Development Review* volume 16, 1990) New York, The Population Council and Oxford University Press, 1991, pp315–322. © The Population Council.

Chapter 24: Robert Goodland et al (eds) *Environmentally Sustainable Economic Development: Building on Brundtland* Paris, UNESCO, 1991, pp29–38. © UNESCO.

Chapter 25: Kingsley Davis and Mikhail S Bernstam (eds) *Resources, Environment and Population: Present Knowledge, Future Options* (supplement to *Population and Development Review* volume 16, 1990) New York, The Population Council and Oxford University Press, 1991, pp408–421. © The Population Council.

Chapter 26: F A Hayek *The Fatal Conceit: The Errors of Socialism* (from *The Collected Works of F A Hayek, Volume 1*) Chicago, University of Chicago Press, 1988, pp121–134. © Estate of F A Hayek. Reproduced with permission of the publisher and the estate of the author.

Chapter 27: *Scientific American* March 1994, pp36–42. Reprinted with permission. © 1994 by Scientific American, Inc. All rights reserved.

Chapter 28: Reproduced by permission of the publishers from *Population in an Interacting World* edited by William Alonso, Cambridge, Massachusetts, Harvard University Press, pp78–94. © 1987 by the President and Fellows of Harvard College.

Chapter 29: Kingsley Davis and Mikhail S Bernstam (eds) *Resources, Environment and Population: Present Knowledge, Future Options* (supplement to *Population and Development Review* volume 16, 1990) New York, The Population Council and Oxford University Press, 1991, pp72–75. © The Population Council.

Chapter 30: William H McNeill *Population and Politics Since 1750* Charlottesville, Virginia, University Press of Virginia, 1990, pp49–71. Reprinted courtesy of the University Press of Virginia. © Rector and Visitors of the University of Virginia.

Chapter 31: *Journal of the American Medical Association* volume 260, number 5, August 5 1988, pp684–685. © American Medical Association. Reproduced by permission.

Chapter 32: Fred Hoyle *A Contradiction in the Argument of Malthus* Hull, University of Hull Publications, 1963. © F Hoyle.

Introduction

The growth of populations and of economies are major forces for change in the contemporary world. Both have their own determinants, particularly in the advance of human knowledge and technological prowess and in the elaboration of cultural patterns and social institutions. Both have consequences – for the natural world, for the political order, and for human wellbeing. Each also impinges on the other. This, in the broadest terms, is the subject known as population and development.

The scale and recency of this growth can be captured in a few numbers. In the early 1800s, with industrialization barely underway, the world population stood at one billion; as late as 1930 it had reached just two billion; by 1990, it had passed five billion, and by the end of the 20th century it will have passed six billion. While dramatic enough to be described as an 'explosion', this growth in population seems almost modest in comparison to the expansion of the global economy in the same period. An index of gross world product (at constant prices – though the calculations required are complicated and inherently somewhat dubious over these time intervals) set at 1 in 1820, reaches 5 in 1929, 40 in 1990, and will likely have exceeded 50 by 2000.

Declining mortality began the population explosion; declining fertility, now in train, will eventually halt it. Economic development hastens both of these declines, yielding the affluence of the consumer society and its mixture of environmental gains and losses. But rapid population growth in turn slows the pace of development and may exacerbate the environmental damage inflicted along the way; in the end, it perhaps limits what development is able to deliver. For the world as a whole, the demographic future will influence the course of change both in international relations and in major global ecosystems.

These are the relationships and issues that are the subject of this Reader. Although complex and in part still poorly understood, they are often treated simplistically in popular debate. In contrast, the voluminous technical literature on the subject is in large part inaccessible to non-specialists – full of the formalisms and abstruse statistical procedures of present-day academic social science. In between these two genres, however, there is a literate middle ground where sophisticated but intelligible analysis and argument can be conducted. The Reader is situated on that ground.

The selections, grouped in five parts, are chosen for readability as well as for insight. They emphasize recent contributions – the earliest from 1955 and two-thirds of them dating from after 1980. The authors in most cases are social scientists, mainly economists and sociologists. The treatment of the subject is deliberately aimed to emphasize continuities of problems and issues across rich and poor countries rather than distinguishing 'Third World' countries as a particular category for which special theories need to be sought. Some attention is given to policy questions, but for the most part in passing rather than as a major focus. The diversity of stances covered in the selections, however, clearly implies that policy consensus in this field is not readily attained.

In common usage the scope of population and development is often construed fairly narrowly – to comprise the demographic changes associated with economic development and the economic determinants and consequences of population change. These relationships, moreover, are studied predominantly at just two levels: family and nation. There are significant research questions in the subject thus defined, but they allow only highly contingent answers. The resulting literature tends to be dryly academic. A set of readings restricted to those bounds would not be short of material but would have excluded from its range issues of potentially great interest and import. The more expansive view of population and development that is adopted here takes account of the social, biological, and physical surrounds of populations and economies – in particular, the political systems through which they are (in some measure) governed, their natural and built environments, and the ecological systems within which they are embedded.

Surprisingly, some of the most basic questions in population and development remain beset by controversy, sometimes on matters that would seem to be empirically resolvable. Intensive research attention to them over several decades has not produced closure. The continuing debate over the consequences of rapid population growth for economic development is a prime case in point; the net effects are variously seen as strongly detrimental, neutral, or even supportive. In the political and environmental spheres there is also scant agreement on the role of population. Controversy attaches to the weighting of the forces that have led to the long-run decline in human mortality, as among public health measures, mass education, and economic advances; and to the long-run decline in fertility, as between falling demand for children and the effects of anti-natalist programmes. Lack of closure in such cases variously reflects limitations on data, differing modelling strategies, and divergences in values and ideology. The selections in this Reader, while avoiding polar positions, allow some of the main contending voices to be heard.

Part I

The Dynamics of Transition

Economic development can be described in terms of structural transformations in the economy and society that take place along with growth in per capita income. Such transformations include those in the structure of production, consumption, investment, and trade; and in income distribution, labour allocation, education, and urbanization. Systematic comparative study of these patterns of change originates in classic work by Colin Clark and Simon Kuznets (see Clark 1940, Kuznets 1966) and has been continued in many subsequent studies (see, in particular, Chenery and Syrquin 1975 and Chenery et al 1986). 'Demographic transition', the transformation from from high to low birth and death rates, belongs in the same list – indeed, in terms of its direct effect on human wellbeing and its social and economic implications, it is among the most important structural changes associated with development.

Each of these dimensions of change, as a subject for study and theorizing, also has its own intellectual history. Our interest is in the population case. A general association of population growth with prosperity was a theme of classical economics. In Malthus's writings this link was reinterpreted as a threat to prosperity – calling for individual or family level behavioural responses to curtail fertility if the 'positive' check of higher mortality was to be avoided. For Malthus, the acceptable response was postponement of marriage; for most subsequent writers on the subject (the so-called Neomalthusians) it was birth control. Malthus's own scepticism that most people would choose to limit their family size proved wholly unfounded: as it turned out, sustained income growth seemed almost invariably to bring about lower rates of fertility.

The phenomenon of demographic transition gained close attention only with the pervasive mortality and fertility declines of the 20th century. Theories of demographic transition were devised based on the European and American experience – cast in fairly broad terms, since it was soon found that the detailed course of population change varied by culture, historical background, and political circumstances. Notable contributions included Landry (1934), Notestein (1953), Banks (1954), Davis (1963), United Nations (1973), Caldwell (1976), Dyson and Murphy (1985), and Coale and Watkins (1986). Initial expectations were that the same transition experience would apply to the developing countries in the years after World War II, as modernization progressed. Rapidly falling mortality, mainly from adoption of relatively cheap public health measures, and resulting unprecedented rates of population growth in these countries soon led many observers to doubt that the predicted fertility reponse would come quickly enough to avoid hindering the development effort – hence the widespread advocacy and adoption of government-supported (and often government-run) birth control programmes. However, with varying delays and with some assistance from those programmes, the fertility decline indeed began in most of these countries and in many of them progressed faster than in the Western experience.

The literature on demographic transition is now vast. Kuznets's 1975 overview, in this Part, sketches the principal relationships; a comprehensive account of the subject is given by Chesnais (1992). Didier Blanchet, in this Part, presents a graphical discussion of the analytical complications that result from the fact that population–development relationships are two-way. For further studies and references, see Easterlin (1980), Birdsall (1988), and Coleman and Schofield (1986). As the diversity of transition experience became apparent, researchers no longer sought all-embracing theory. They recognized that mortality and fertility do not necessarily respond to similar forces – nor fertility to mortality. Hence we find separate treatment of mortality decline (the 'epidemiological transition' in disease patterns; the 'health transition' in health outcomes) and fertility decline. There is even, by some accounts, a 'mobility transition' in patterns of migration.

The dramatic and virtually worldwide experience of mortality decline is discussed by Samuel H. Preston, in this Part. There has been a vigorous debate on the relative significance of the various contributing factors in bringing about this decline as among improvements in public health and in general economic wellbeing, health education, and advances in and wider availability of medical services (see McKeown 1976; Preston 1975; Caldwell 1986; Caldwell et al 1990).

Fertility decline, similarly, is a striking and nearly worldwide phenomenon, and weighting the factors behind it has proven contentious. At a broad level those factors are unmysterious; principally, a falling 'demand' for children traceable to a host of actual and anticipated changes in the family economy, educational and labour market opportunities, and related normative images of family and society. Also contributing to fertility decline are lessened child mortality, greater knowledge and availability of modern contraceptive methods, and, in some situations, strong government efforts to promote smaller families. Two selections in this section discuss effects of development on fertility: T.W. Schultz on the increasing value of human time, and John C. Caldwell on mass education. A fuller treatment of fertility determinants is given in Parts II and III.

Urbanization is a demographic consequence or concomitant of development, warranting treatment alongside other demographic changes. In addition, the radical changes in lifestyle and in economic opportunities that it brings are important influences on fertility and mortality trends. Historical urbanization is discussed in de Vries (1984) and Wrigley (1987), contemporary patterns in Todaro (1976) and Gugler (1996).

The effects of population growth on development, to the surprise of many, have been controversial among social scientists. The aggregate income data, at least until the 1980s, have not supported a significant negative effect. Globally, moreover, the years of fastest economic and demographic growth coincide (see Maddison 1995 – whose estimates were drawn on in the Introduction). However, aggregate data are difficult to interpret in the presence of offsetting effects and reverse causation, and research attention has tended to shift to delineating particular routes of impact. Negative effects were traced through the simple dilution of resources under population growth and through effects of changing dependency rates on savings and public expenditures (Coale and Hoover 1958, National Academy of Sciences 1971). Countervailing positive effects – especially on productivity – are suggested by Hirschman (in this Part), Boserup (1965), Clark (1977), and Simon (1981, 1986). Reviews of the subject, variously positioned but tending toward a middle ground and showing the difficulty of arriving at straightforward conclusions, are presented in Kuznets (1973), Cassen (1976, 1994), McNicoll (1984), National Research Council (1986), Johnson and Lee (1987), Kelley (1988), Dasgupta (1995), and Ahlburg et al (1996).

Whatever the economic data show, few would dispute that both the size and rate of growth of populations have profound effects on human societies and their governance and on their environment. If these outcomes are distinguished from effects on 'development', that is because development has come to be construed narrowly, mainly in terms of incomes. Demographic effects on the social order are treated in a historical context by Glass and Revelle (1972), Tilly (1978), Goldstone (1991), McNeill (in this Part), and in several selections in Part V. Environmental consequences are discussed in Part IV.

REFERENCES

Ahlburg, Dennis A., Allen C. Kelley, and Karen Oppenheim Mason (eds.) (1996) *The Impact of Population Growth on Well-being in Developing Countries*, Springer-Verlag, Berlin.

Banks, J.A. (1954) *Prosperity and Parenthood: A Study of Family Planning among the Victorian Middle Classes*, Routledge and Kegan Paul, London.

Birdsall, Nancy (1988) 'Economic approaches to population growth and development', in *Handbook of Development Economics*, H.B. Chenery and T.N. Srinivasan (eds.),Vol. I, North Holland, Amsterdam.

Boserup, Ester (1965) *The Conditions of Agricultural Growth*, Allen and Unwin, London.

Caldwell, John C. (1976) 'Toward a restatement of demographic transition theory', *Population and Development Review* 2: pp321–366.

Caldwell, John C. (1986) 'Routes to low mortality in poor countries', *Population and Development Review* 12: pp171–220.

Caldwell, John C. et al (eds.) (1990) *What We Know about Health Transition: The Cultural, Social and Behavioural Determinants of Health*, Health Transition Centre, Australian National University. 2 vols, Canberra.

Cassen, Robert. (1976) 'Population and development: A survey', *World Development* 4: pp785–830.

Cassen, Robert (ed.) (1994) *Population and Development: Old Debates, New Conclusions*, Transaction Publishers, New Brunswick.

Chenery, Hollis, Sherman Robinson, and Moshe Syrquin (1986) *Industrialization and Growth: A Comparative Study*, Oxford University Press, for the World Bank, New York.

Chenery, Hollis and Moshe Syrquin (1975) *Patterns of Development, 1950-1970*, Oxford University Press, for the World Bank, London.

Chesnais, Jean-Claude (1992) *The Demographic Transition: Stages, Patterns, and Economic Implications*, translated by Elizabeth and Philip Kreager, Clarendon Press, Oxford.

Clark, Colin (1940) *The Conditions of Economic Progress*, Macmillan, London.

Clark, Colin (1977) *Population Growth and Land Use*. 2nd ed, Macmillan, London.

Coale, Ansley J. and Edgar M. Hoover (1958) *Population Growth and Economic Development in Low-Income Countries*, Princeton University Press, Princeton.

Coale, Ansley J. and Susan Cotts Watkins (eds.) (1986) *The Decline of Fertility in Europe*, Princeton University Press, Princeton.

Coleman, David and Roger Schofield (eds.) (1986) *The State of Population Theory: Forward from Malthus*, Blackwell, Oxford.

Dasgupta, Partha (1995) 'The population problem: theory and evidence', *Journal of Economic Literature* 33: pp1879–1902.

Davis, Kingsley (1963) 'The theory of change and response in modern demographic history', *Population Index* 29: pp345–366.

de Vries, Jan (1984) *European Urbanization 1500–1800*, Harvard University Press, Cambridge, Massachusetts.

Dyson, Tim and Mike Murphy (1985) 'The onset of fertility transition', *Population and Development Review* 11: pp399–440.

Easterlin, Richard A. (ed.) (1980) *Population and Economic Change in Developing Countries*, University of Chicago Press, Chicago.

Glass, David V. and Roger Revelle (eds.) (1972) *Population and Social Change*, Arnold, London.

Goldstone, Jack A. (1991) *Revolution and Rebellion in the Early Modern World*, University of California Press, Berkeley.

Gugler, Josef (1996) *The Urban Transformation of the Developing World*, Oxford University Press, New York.

Johnson, D. Gale and Ronald D. Lee (eds.) (1987) *Population Growth and Economic Development: Issues and Evidence*, University of Wisconsin Press, Madison.

Kelley, Allen C. (1988) 'Economic consequences of population change in the Third World', *Journal of Economic Literature* 26: pp1685–1728.

Kuznets, Simon (1966) *Modern Economic Growth: Rate, Structure, and Spread*, Yale University Press, New Haven.

Kuznets, Simon (1973) *Population, Capital, and Growth: Selected Essays*, Norton, New York.

Landry, Adolphe (1934) *La Révolution démographique*, Sirey, Paris.

Maddison, Angus (1995) *Monitoring the World Economy 1820–1992*, Organisation for Economic Co-operation and Development, Paris.

McKeown, Thomas (1976) *The Modern Rise of Population*, Academic Press, New York.

McNicoll, Geoffrey (1984) 'Consequences of rapid population growth: an overview and assessment', *Population and Development Review* 10: pp177–240.

National Academy of Sciences (1971) *Rapid Population Growth: Consequences and Policy Implications*, (1971) Prepared by a Study Group of the Office of the Foreign Secretary, National Academy of Sciences, Johns Hopkins University Press, Baltimore.

National Research Council (1986) *Population Growth and Economic Development: Policy Questions*, National Academy Press, Washington, DC.

Notestein, Frank W. (1953) 'Economic problems of population change', in *Proceedings of the Eighth International Conference of Agricultural Economists*, Oxford University Press, New York.

Preston, Samuel H. (1975) 'The changing relation between mortality and level of economic development', *Population Studies* 29: pp231–248.

Simon, Julian L. (1981) *The Ultimate Resource*, (new edition, 1996), Princeton University Press, Princeton.

Simon, Julian L. (1986) *Theory of Population and Economic Growth*, Blackwell, Oxford.

Tilly, Charles (ed.) (1978) *Historical Studies of Changing Fertility*, Princeton University Press, Princeton.

Todaro, Michael P. (1976) *Internal Migration in Developing Countries: A Review of Theory, Evidence, Methodology, and Research Priorities*, International Labour Organisation, Geneva.

United Nations. (1973) *Determinants and Consequences of Population Trends*, United Nations, New York.

Wrigley, E.A. (1987) *People, Cities and Wealth: The Transformation of Traditional Society*, Blackwell, Oxford.

Chapter 1

Population Trends and Modern Economic Growth

Simon Kuznets

Birth and growth, youth and maturity, senescence and death, frame – somewhat differently for males and females – the life-span of an individual as a member of society. Demographic processes and structures, while resting on a biological base, have far-reaching social implications. Fertility, growth, mortality, and the resulting sex and age distributions of changing numbers, condition the division of labour in society and the sequential roles – economic and social – of the demographically distinct groups. Conversely, economic and social processes and structures have far-reaching demographic consequences, affecting fertility, family formation and the life-cycle of dependence, education, maturity, occupation and retirement.

The economic growth process of a given historical epoch, characterized usually by distinctive major sources of increased capacity, must have specific effects on the demographic processes and structures. These effects are associated with the *opportunities*, economic and social, provided by the epoch's sources of growth and development, and with the *requirements* that the current material and social technology imposes. Modifications of the basic demographic processes, introduced by economic growth and social development, then become the bases that condition the further stages in the economic and social growth process.

The discussion below concentrates, for greater relevance, on the interrelations between *modern* economic growth as exemplified by the process in the currently developed countries over the last one and a half to two centuries, and the major trends in their demographic processes. But a similar interplay between population and economic growth (including concomitant social development) could be traced for pre-modern stretches of history in the presently developed countries, or for those regions of the world in the recent past that have been relatively free of the impact of modern economic growth.

INTERRELATIONS BETWEEN POPULATION TRENDS AND MODERN ECONOMIC GROWTH

The major demographic trends observed in the developed countries (largely Europe, the European offshoots overseas, and Japan) over the long period since they entered modern economic growth are familiar and do not call for lengthy discussion.[1] Of prime importance was the marked reduction in mortality, which raised life expectancy at birth from 40 years or below to close to 70 years. It had major impacts on the mortality of infants and young children, on the mortality (and associated morbidity) from infections and related diseases, and on mortality in the cities, which had previously suffered from much higher death rates than the countryside. This reduction in mortality was accompanied, but not simultaneously, by a decline in fertility. The crude birth rates declined (in the older countries of Europe) from over 30 to 1,000 to well below 20, a trend that largely reflected intramarital fertility and was a result of decisions by the families to limit the number of children. It was not the result of any genetic changes, or of involuntary reaction by the human species to changes in the material conditions associated with economic growth. The combination of low mortality with low fertility – while still allowing for a much greater long-term rate of natural increase than that over the preceding centuries of high birth and death rates – was new and unique. It had to be new because the opportunities for reducing the death rates to the low levels attained were new and unparalleled in the past.

The above comments may suggest both a close timing relation between modern economic growth and the downward trends in mortality and fertility; and a distinction between the long-term trends in mortality and fertility, in that the element of human choice and decision was absent in the former and of great importance in the latter. Neither suggestion is valid. In many European countries crude death rates declined in the 18th century and were in their low 20s by the second quarter of the 19th century – *preceding* the initiation of modern economic growth by several decades. By contrast, in many countries there was no further decisive decline of death rates until late in the 19th century, with most of the reduction concentrated in the current century – several decades after modern economic growth was initiated. Urban death rates were substantially higher than rural even in the first decade of the 20th century, in the European countries and in the United States. Likewise, in the older European countries (but not in the United States), fertility did not begin to decline until well into the last quarter of the 19th century – with a substantial lag after the initiation of their modern economic growth. Despite the connection between the delay in the decline of birth rates and the delay in the decline of mortality (and the latter provides only a partial explanation), and despite the connection between the delay in the decline of mortality and the effects of rapid urbanization on the aggregate death rate, it still remains true that the timing of the broad association between modern patterns of mortality and fertility and modern economic growth, is *not* close. The economic growth processes undoubtedly provided opportunities for reducing mortality and raised the inducements and requirements for lower fertility. But the opportunities were not so free of obstacles, nor the inducements and requirements so dominant in the early stages of the industrialization process, as to effect a prompt response in the demographic trends.

Nor was a strong element of social, or even individual, decision absent from

---

1 The summary of population trends presented is clearly selective, and cannot be viewed as an adequate survey. In addition to many United Nations sources, ranging from the 1953 report, *The Determinants and Consequences of Population Trends*, to the two major population bulletins, no. 6, 1962 (on mortality), and no. 7, 1963 (on fertility), to the background papers, prepared for the 1965 World Population Conference, on mortality (by C.C. Spicer) and on fertility (by George W. Roberts), and to *The World Population Situation in 1970* (1971), I found particularly helpful the summary by Glass and Grebenik (1965).

the proximate factors that made for the reduction of mortality, and for the delay in its decline in the 19th century. Granted that for an individual, the decision to postpone death is not usually a matter of choice, the views on mortality – particularly of children – changed slowly. The acceptance of their death as 'usual' or even as an offset to the 'improvidence of the poor' persisted. But it was the socially determined implemented decision that was more telling. If the reduction in death rates before World War II was due, as has recently been argued, to better nutrition and living conditions, and to public health and sanitation measures, far more than to advances in medical care and knowledge,[2] the role of social decisions becomes patent. The provision of means of subsistence and of housing, of generally improved living conditions, reflects policies on income distribution, prices of necessities, housing and treatment of the poor. Public health measures, involving political decisions on uses of funds and on regulation of the private sector and of individuals, clearly rested on a social consensus that was slow in coming. A delay in the latter would have delayed even further the decline in the urban, and hence aggregate, death rates. The long struggles of the public health reformers through much of the 19th century clearly indicate that even when the sources of high mortality were known, much effort had to be expended to secure the social decisions needed to reduce their impact.

The opportunities and pressures produced by modern economic growth led to decisions important in the reductions of the death rate and crucial in the declines of the birth rates, and affected family formation, location and migration, and the life cycle sequence of education, occupation, and retirement. For a better understanding of these we note some distinctive features of modern economic growth. The reference must perforce be brief and simple. But the features are sufficiently conspicuous and persistent, and many of them amply documented, to minimize misunderstanding.[3]

First, the permissive basis for the great rise in per capita product, combined with high rates of population growth, was the rapid increase in our tested knowledge of natural processes, applied to problems of production technology. This increase took the form of successive technological innovations, which in their turn spread into mass use raised product and productivity. They also led to further knowledge concerning the properties of nature and to invention of additional tools, which facilitated new discoveries – and thus led to further applications. The reinforcing connections between discoveries, inventions, innovations, applications, further learning, more discovery, and so on, permitted the sustained pressure toward higher production levels. But the key link in this chain was the mass application of innovations for wide use – which meant that knowledge was directed toward agreed-upon useful ends, among which the provision of goods for ultimate consumption was paramount. It was hardly an accident that innovations relating to final consumption and consumer goods were just as prominent as those relating to producer goods; and that the growth of consumption per capita was almost as great as that of total product per capita. This orientation of knowledge to useful ends and of production to ultimate consumption obviously has

---

2 See McKeown, Brown, and Record (1972); and on public health in Great Britain, most of the issue of *Population Studies* 17, no. 3, March 1964.
3 For a summary of the characteristics of modern economic growth see my Nobel Memorial lecture, 'Modern economic growth: findings and reflections' (Kuznets 1972a). A more detailed discussion is given in the earlier monographs, *Modern Economic Growth: Rate, Structure, and Spread* and *Economic Growth of Nations* (Kuznets 1966, 1971).

bearing on mortality – life and health being prime consumption goods. It also has bearing on fertility, in that the orientation toward greater consumption for the existing and next generations would, other conditions being equal, lead to the choices of fewer children. These implications will become clearer as we consider some other distinctive features of modern economic growth, closely connected with the one just noted.

Second, a high rate of growth of product per capita, fed by successive technological innovations and their mass application, was, perforce, accompanied by rapid changes in the production structure of the country undergoing modern economic growth – the structure of the sectors in which the active economic members of the population were engaged – with consequent changes in the occupations and the geographic location of these participants. These rapid changes in the country's production structure were partly due to shifts in domestic demand, reflecting different income elasticities of demand for various goods; partly to the tendency of the focus of innovations to shift from one sector to another, as the potentials of economic advantage of new applications shifted; and partly to the effects of innovations in transport, communication and the natural resource advantage among nations. *Industrialization* – the movement of output, capital, and labour shares from agriculture to industry – has been the most prominent of these changes in production structure; but the shifts within the non-agricultural sector, particularly of labour toward the service- rather than commodity- producing industries, have been equally important. One implication of these rapid shifts in production structure for our theme is that they widen the possibility of intergenerational breaks – with sons being attached to industries, occupations, and locations different from those of their fathers, to a far greater extent than in a more slowly changing, traditional, economy. The effect on formation of families and, in general, on the ties of authority of the older over the younger generation, is obvious. Moreover, it is reinforced by other aspects of this shift in production structure that have markedly influenced population trends.

One of the two most relevant aspects is the sharp rise in the proportions of capital and labour engaged in large-scale, nonpersonal enterprises – as contrasted with the decline in the proportions attached to small-scale, personal, or family units. The other is the sharp rise in the educational and other skill requirements of labour. The rise in the size of the productive plant was associated with the economies of scale of modern technology. These economies were the results of technological properties of new sources of industrial power, of better controls over precision in fabrication and of major improvements in intraplant communication – technological and social. The growth of the large-scale enterprise (the economic, not the production, unit) was also facilitated by the revolutionary changes in communication, and by the organizational innovations feasible with a technology the rules of which could be overtly formulated and easily and widely communicated – impossible on the basis of earlier personal master–apprentice relations. The requirements for more formal education and greater skills were partly a direct consequence of the larger scale of productive units and enterprises, which demanded adequate communication and understanding within the organization; partly a reflection of the increasing reliance of society on the production of new knowledge as a source of further growth; and partly a result of the need for *formal* education as the basis for judging the equipment of would-be participants – given the system of recruitment into economic activity associated with modern economic growth, to be touched upon below.

The rapid shifts in production structure, the emergence of large-scale production plants and economic enterprises, and the rise in educational requirements of the economically active groups in the population had striking effects on the location of population, internal migration, family formation, and the typical life cycle of an individual or family unit. Describing these population trends as consequences or corollaries of modern economic growth, or responses by individuals and families to changing opportunities and changing conditions of exploiting these opportunities associated with economic growth, is partly a semantic problem. The important point is the *coherence* between the economic growth and the population trends, a basis for evaluating the current situation in both developed and developing countries.

Industrialization was associated with intensive modern urbanization because the former was accompanied by a rise in the scale of the productive unit to a point where the economies of scale demanded concentration of production and large bodies of workers, and induced the formation of new or larger cities. Even without economies of scale, the movement away from agriculture would have furthered urbanization: the emergence of specialized crafts in the Middle Ages led to some urbanization in the European countries, even though the scale of handicraft production and trade was relatively small. But it was primarily the rapidly rising scale of modern technology and the successful resolution of the problems of communication and organization that powered the movement toward the cities and their rapid rate of growth in the nineteenth and twentieth centuries, *pari passu* with the accelerated rate of growth of product and population. An additional, and key, permissive factor lay in the marked rise in labour productivity in agriculture, which made it possible for a small fraction of the labour force (well below 10 per cent in recent years) to produce enough agricultural goods to satisfy, at a high per capita level, the other nine-tenths of the population. The rapid movement, suggested by these fractions, to high levels of urbanization, is clearly a product of modern technology and economic growth – much of it in response to economic scales of production and enterprise. And the recent emergence of dormitory suburbs in the developed industrialized countries, an attempt at adjustment permitted by greater affluence, only confirms the element of economic pressure involved in the urbanization process in earlier decades.[4]

Given the parameters of modern economic growth, particularly those of the growth of sectoral demand for labour, and the more limited parameters of population growth, rapid urbanization and rapid structural changes within the production system could not have occurred without vast internal migration. With modern economic growth characterized by rapid structural changes, which imply wide differences in the growth rates of the various parts of the structure, the disparities between differential rates of population increase and differential rates of growth of demand for labour were bound to become wide. When the demand for labour in some new industries grew between 5 and 10 per cent per year, and that in the older industries located elsewhere hardly grew at all, the differential in natural increase rates could not accommodate itself to such disparities. In addition, there was, through most of the period, a higher rate of natural increase

---

4 For a summary of data on urbanization and discussion of concepts see United Nations (1969), and the references there to historical studies. Current worldwide data on the structure of labour force by sectoral attachment can be found in International Labour Office (1971). Historical data on industrial attachment of labour force are given in Bairoch et al (1968).

in the countryside – where additional employment opportunities were limited – than in the cities – in which such opportunities grew more rapidly. Urbanization reflected only the major disparities between rates of natural increase and rates of growth of employment opportunities, and the internal migration implicit in it was only part of the stream augmented by intercity and interregional flows. (In some countries, the United States for example, immigration contributed to the adjustment by its differential flow into those regions where demand for labour was particularly active.) Such vast internal migration and immigration is important for our theme. It broke the ties between the participant in economic activity and his family origins; it made the migrant more receptive to economic opportunities; it changed the conditions of life and work, with whatever effects they may have had on family formation and fertility; and it reinforced the increasing separation between family and economic activity, which has been a most important consequence of modern economic growth.

Migration only reinforced the separation between the family and economic activity that was imposed by the increase in scale of production and of the economic enterprise. Unlike a farm, a handicraft shop, a small store, or an individual service activity, a modern large-scale plant cannot be contained within a household. A large economic enterprise, demanding large amounts of fixed capital and with a perpetuating future not dependent on any one person's or family's life, cannot be effectively operated as a personal or a family firm. It demands an overt, impersonal and effective organization in which the roles, responsibilities and privileges are explicitly formulated and legally enforceable. The control and organization of large-scale production demand that it be separated from the household. The individual participants must perform their tasks within the plant or the office, away from their families and households. They thus become members of a group whose practices and discipline have only limited contact with the life of the individual participant as a member of a household or a family. As a result, a large volume of economic activity formerly carried on within the households of traditional farmers, craftsmen, shopkeepers, has been removed from family activity. Moreover, the function of the family as an institution transmitting economic experience and skills from one generation to the next has been severely limited. And while the process began with the removal of market-oriented activities from most families, it was followed by mechanization of household services, by professionalization and hence removal from the family of many educational services, and by the shift out of the family and into the organized labour markets of an increasing proportion of domestic labour resources that previously had provided services within the family.

The removal of the full-time economic activity from the family and household and the resulting separation between the production plant and the home were accompanied, and eventually reinforced, by the revolutionary changes in the practice and criteria of recruitment of individuals into economic activity. Given the large scale of the modern plant and enterprise, the large numbers of active participants involved, and the migrant origin of much of the available labour, it was impossible to recruit on the basis of personal knowledge of candidates and their family origins (although this approach was followed in the recruitment of unskilled immigrants through the ethnic compatriot boss system in some early phases of U.S. growth). Furthermore, the requirements of rising education and other skills to handle effectively rather complex production tasks involving costly capital equipment, made personal knowledge of an applicant far less important than knowledge of his testable equipment, whether it was manual dexterity, ability to relate to people, or general or professional formal education. The large numbers and the large economic magnitudes involved in adequate resolution of recruiting and staffing problems warranted a concerted and prolonged effort to develop an effective classification of the production tasks within the plant and enterprise, and to formulate criteria of satisfactory selection. These were bound to replace the traditional type of recruitment based on personal knowledge of workers and of their family antecedents. The shift from recruitment on the basis of status, closely connected with family origins and warranted in earlier times by lack of better ways for judging the suitability of individuals for their economic tasks, to recruitment on the basis of a person's objectively tested capacity for performance, specifically formulated to a well-defined range of production tasks, was a revolutionary change in the modernization of society in adjustment to modern economic growth. And it had far-reaching effects on population and the life cycle of its members. Economic activity and preparation for it occupy much of the life of an individual, from childhood through maturity; and major changes in conditions of entry, and implicitly in the criteria for rise *within* the economic system, that occurred in the shift in recruitment, were bound to have multiple and far-reaching consequences.

One immediate consequence was the rise in the level of formal education and the spread of formal certification. The educational system became increasingly involved in screening individuals, and in channelling them to more advanced levels roughly on the basis of ability – even if qualified by parental position and by surviving patterns of discrimination. A growing proportion of the labour force underwent longer periods of general and professional training, which was supplemented at later stages of the occupational career. And a rapidly increasing share of economic positions was contingent upon formal certification, with respect either to educational levels attained, or to specialized skills, or to both. Thus, the trend within the labour force away from entrepreneurial and self-employment to employment status was accompanied by the trends to higher levels of formal and specialized education, professionalization of occupations, and an extension of certification. For our theme, the main bearing of these trends is the increased investment in *human* (as distinct from material) capital, prolongation of the period of education that kept the younger generation out of both economic and household activity, in separate schools. This contributed further to the shift of the transmission of knowledge and experience between generations from the family and household to the non-family, non-personal institutions.

The distinctive characteristics of modern economic growth noted above – rapid changes in production structure, urbanization and vast internal migration (and immigration), the shifts of requirements and conditions of participation in economic activity and the associated increase of emphasis on education and training, and testable criteria of individual performance – all had profound influences on fertility, family formation, and the life cycle of learning, work, and retirement. These influences were not limited to the urban populations whose proportions in the total were rapidly growing. They extended also to the rural populations that were sending many of their younger generation to the cities and the conditions of whose life were also thoroughly affected by the higher educational and other requirements of modern economic growth. In fact, the declines in rural fertility in a country like the United States were, at least before World War II, relatively as great as those for urban fertility – although the differentials tended to persist.

The decline in birth rates was clearly associated with the greatly increased costs of children, resulting partly from the withdrawal of their labour from the family milieu, and partly from the requirement for a longer and more expensive span of education and training. Both of these costs were directly connected with the rearing of the next generation to economic maturity, and with the upward mobility of the parental generation itself. These trends toward greater costliness of children were reinforced by the shift to urban life, and the competitive pressures of a rising standard of consumption, in the cities and in the countryside. The resulting decline in the size of the family was reinforced by the separation of generations. Correspondingly, a trend developed toward the conjugal (or nuclear) family, characterized by 'the relative exclusion of a wide range of affinal and blood relatives from its everyday affairs', and effectively limited to parents and their children largely below the adult ages, and free from more extended family ties in the choice of mates, in the process of family formation and in the choice of location.[5] And, too, the life cycle of learning, work, and retirement changed markedly. The age of entry into the labour force in the developed countries rose substantially, associated largely with the prolongation of the period of formal education; and the age of retirement from full-time economic activity dropped sharply, reflecting the more widespread employee status combined with the increased obsolescence of human skills and facilitated by institutional provisions for supporting the retired population. Since all these demographic trends can be viewed as responses, in a greater or lesser degree, to the requirements for effective and productive economic activity under the shifting conditions of modern economic growth, when realized, they contributed significantly to the high growth rates of the developed countries. It is difficult to envisage modern economic growth without the reduced birth rates, the greater investment in human capital represented by education and training, the smaller family, and the concentration of the labour force in the prime ages between the late entry and early retirement.

The condensed summary of the interrelations between population trends and modern economic growth must be concluded with a brief reference to four major qualifications. They are reminders of omissions to be kept in mind in evaluating the bearing of the past interrelations on the present and future.

First, the coherence between the opportunities and requirements of modern economic growth and the response of the population trends should not be viewed as an easy and smooth process, characterized by close timing and a relatively close relation between the economic and demographic parameters. The movement away from agriculture should not be viewed only as a response of labour to greater opportunities in industry and the cities; it could just as well have been the result of the push from the countryside produced by a shrinking market for agricultural products combined with advanced agricultural technology and institutions that displaced farm labour. The rapid changes in production structure stressed above meant not only greater opportunities in the rapidly growing sectors but also declining opportunities and technological unemployment in the slowly growing sectors; and the adjustment was never a simple and prompt transfer of displaced resources. And, as already indicated, the decline of both death and birth rates lagged for decades behind industrialization in many currently developed countries. In other

---

5 The term 'conjugal' and the quotation are from Goode (1963), p8. This monograph presents an interesting analysis of the conjugal family as an 'ideal type' concept, toward which the evolution of family in modern times tended to converge.

words, much of modern economic growth took place *before* the modern demographic patterns emerged; also, before the wide spread of literacy and education. The process was long, with leads and lags, and disparities in adjustment; and like all processes of change in economic and social performance and institutions, it was subject to distortions and changes in pace. Thus, the demographic patterns that developed did not, in their timing, closely conform to those in economic growth. While, in general, birth and death rates are lower in the developed than in the developing countries, *within* the group of developed countries general indexes like per capita product, and birth and death rates, are not closely associated.

Second, the duration of the processes, the interrelations of which are our theme, is partly due to the *gradual* spread, particularly of population trends, among the different social and economic groups within a developed country. The economic and social differentials among birth and death rates could not be considered in our brief summary; but it is clear that the transition to lower birth and death rates, in response to greater opportunities provided by economic growth, could not occur simultaneously and at the same rate for all economic and social groups.[6] Some of the trends in the differential aspects of death and birth rates have significant bearing on changing inequalities in economic position and material welfare. At least the older countries (as distinct from the European offshoots overseas) may have experienced for a while a *widening* of the economic and social differentials in fertility, with possible widening of inequality in size distribution of income. But this topic requires more intensive study than is feasible here; and is mentioned only because of its possible bearing on the prospects in developing countries, once their transition to lower fertility levels begins.

Third, modern economic growth spread gradually and began at different dates in the currently developed countries – these dates (rough approximations only) ranging from the late 18th century in pioneering England, to the 1840s for several European countries and the United States, to the 1880s in Japan, and to the 1930s for the USSR (after an initial spurt in Russia in the 1890s). The international aspects of modern economic growth could not be covered in this summary. Yet, needless to say, they affected population trends – not only through international migration, which was particularly open and responsive, for the European countries of origin, during the 19th and early 20th centuries, but also through the international demonstration effect of the declines in death and birth rates. The innovations in economic and social policies, and later in health technology, made in the pioneer countries, could spread to others, at lesser cost and input than required by the pioneers – just as the economic advance of the pioneer developed countries could be followed, at lesser cost, by other countries that were sufficiently prepared to take advantage of the opportunities. The reduction in birth rates and the shift to the conjugal family, once emerged in the pioneer developed country, could become readily known and even adopted as a desirable model by a growing segment of the population in the follower countries.

Fourth and last, the interrelations between economic growth and population trends are, as already indicated, only part of the network of factors determining demographic patterns; and, more relevant here, the connections between economic growth and population trends are not only direct but operate through what, from one standpoint, may be viewed as intermediate variables. Yet each of the latter may have a life and effect of its own, both on population and on economic

---

6 A recent summary is given by Johnson (1960).

growth. To illustrate: modern economic growth has been associated with the increasing importance of the national sovereign state, which serves as the arbiter of conflicts generated by rapid economic growth, as the referee of the social and legal innovations stimulated by the latter, and as the regulator of any difficulties stemming from the conflict between private and social interests in a complex market economy. The existence of this effective political and social institution meant that policies relating to both mortality and fertility could be adopted that would not have been possible otherwise. Another illustration: the greater urbanization, the formation of large cities, created a condition of anonymity among the inhabitants that was unknown in the rural and small-town surroundings. This condition – a direct result of urbanization, not of economic processes – affected the consumption and living patterns and family formation patterns. Or consider the effects of the power of science and tested knowledge on the diminution of authoritarian religious belief, and hence on the teachings of religious institutions and their doctrines regarding life and death. In this case, modern economic growth affects ideology indirectly through the demonstration of the power bestowed on man by tested knowledge that accepts no authority except that of observation, experiment, and the canons of scientific inference. In short, both economic growth and modern population trends are parts of the whole modernization process that occurred in the developed countries over the last one and a half to two centuries; and the two have interacted not only directly, but also via other institutional and ideological variables.

BEARING ON CURRENT PROBLEMS

The bearing of the preceding discussion on current problems can be put in general terms. Modern economic growth has provided opportunities for a great reduction in death rates and inducements and requirements for a marked reduction in birth rates; for a small, mobile family unit; and for a great change in the life cycle of education, occupation, and retirement. But with successive innovations and the rapid structural changes underlying the high aggregate rate of modern growth, the response to opportunities and the adjustment to displacement and changing requirements was neither prompt nor smooth, if only because of technological unemployment, and a push toward migration even before the pull became dominant. Differentials in birth rates, death rates, and migration may have widened inequality in the distribution of income before institutional adjustments produced a shift toward equality; and, as exemplified by ecological and other correlates, all the demographic consequences of modern economic growth could not be easily forecast or forestalled if found undesirable. Current social problems – that is, current developments that seem socially undesirable and call for remedial policy action – are largely the results of past growth, in which unforeseen consequences of past desirable attainments have grown to dimensions sufficient to demand attention. Recognition of a current social problem is thus a judgement, in terms of accepted criteria (which may change over time), of undesirable consequences of some past positive achievement. Of course, a current problem that originated in past positive achievement is still a problem calling for action, but relating it to its origin places it in the proper perspective and within a fairly wide group of similar problems that may have been overcome. And the ways in which the latter have been resolved deserve scrutiny, imitation, or rejection.

[...]

In the light of the preceding discussion, it is obvious that the problem [of rapid population growth in the less developed regions] is associated with the rapid decline in the death rates – a positive attainment, made possible in large part by modern economic growth. The high level of technological capacity in production as well as in the medical arts, the ability to establish rapid communication with, and penetration into, the economically less developed world, and the basic philosophy of the value of material welfare and of health, all contributed to this achievement. Although obvious, this comment needs to be made in order to stress that the problem originated in the effective spread of a major *positive* contribution. To be sure, the difficulties could have been avoided by an equally prompt response of birthrates. But the slowness of the adjustment should not blind us to the magnitude of the positive attainment, realized and projected. And it can be argued that such a decline in death is an indispensable prerequisite for modern economic growth; and that it is also a prerequisite for the decline in birth rates, in so far as they are determined by a given size of *surviving* family desired by the parental generation.

The second comment stems from our discussion of the connection between modern economic growth and the decline in birth rates in the developed countries. We stressed the changed inducements and requirements of the modern economy that made fewer children, with greater investment in their education and training, and a smaller family, more attractive; and suggested that, in general, economic growth and modernization removed the need for a large family by shifting many of its economic, educational, and protective functions to impersonal business or public enterprise, educational institutions, and the state. These institutional-change corollaries of modern economic growth, components in the general modernization process, took time to evolve, and the decline in birth rates was both delayed and drawn out – particularly in the countries that entered modern economic growth first. The relevant question here for the less developed regions of today is whether the economic, political, and social institutions have been restructured, and the ideological views of society changed, to place emphasis on greater investment in fewer children, to provide political and social stability combined with internal social mobility that would enhance the interest of the parental generation in smaller families.

An answer to this question demands more knowledge of the changing social and political institutions of the less developed regions than is at hand. The temptation to give a negative answer is great, but is not fully valid. Modernization has been initiated and substantial reduction in birth rates has been realized in several less developed countries. Yet, to point up the difficulties in establishing political stability, we need only mention the internal conflicts in such major countries of Asia as Pakistan, Indonesia, and the Philippines, and of sub-Saharan Africa as the Congo, Nigeria, and Ghana, and the spread of military dictatorships in much of Latin American and other less developed regions. The absence of political stability makes it impossible to generate a restructuring of economic and social institutions, which are often likely to sharpen the conflict between traditional and modern interests. The comment is made, despite limitations in our knowledge, in order to emphasize the connection between declines in birth rates and the necessary transformation of economic and social institutions that would *assure* the interest of the parental generation in fewer children and in greater investment in human capital. A social and economic structure that provides no rewards for fewer children, with slight prospect of a better future for them and their parents, would scarcely encourage low birth rates. This is not to minimize the effects of recent improvements in the technology of birth control in response to the recognition of a more acute need for them, nor of relevant changes in public attitudes and governmental policies – all of which may be needed to implement fully the interest in smaller families once it is established. However, far-reaching reductions in birth rates require an economic and social milieu that would not reward reliance on a genetic lottery, that is, on a large number of surviving children, for lack of assurance that greater investment in fewer numbers would yield appreciable benefits – to the parental and to the younger generation.

Third, once birth rates begin to drop in the developing countries, the reduction is likely to be evident first among some groups, usually those in the modern advanced types of professional and modern occupations and those in the upper-income brackets; and will only later spread to the more traditional, and lower-income, occupations. It may, therefore, for a time, have the effect of maintaining, or even widening, the already wide inequalities in income. The pressures on national unity and on tolerance of continuing inequalities, of failure of significant benefit from whatever economic growth takes place, are thus likely to become great – particularly because the spread of economic growth to the less developed regions is accompanied by the spread of modern views on the presumptive power of modern technology to bestow material benefits on all humanity, and the demonstration effects of widespread high standards of consumption elsewhere. This means that, with respect to population, the developing societies must take account not only of the overall difficulty of raising aggregate income per capita when the total rate of population growth is so high, but also of the need to change the economic and social conditions of the large population groups at the lower rungs of the economic ladder to assure their interest in fewer children and smaller families.

This suggests the fourth and most general comment on the problem under consideration, in the light of our earlier discussion of interrelations between population growth and modern economic growth in their historical perspective. The adjustment that has to be made to the rapid decline in the death rates in the less developed countries is much greater and more pressing in many important respects than were the similar adjustments of the birth rates in developed countries in the past. Not only is the current growth rate of population in the less developed regions so much higher than that of the older developed countries in their long-term past. Not only are the economic levels and reserves of the less developed regions so much lower than those of most currently developed countries in their premodern past. Not only may the tolerance of economic deprivation and inequalities have been lowered with the spread of modern economic growth and modern views on the importance of equality of economic opportunity and on assurance of a minimum of material benefit for all groups. There is also a greater awareness of the connections between demographic trends and the conditions of economic advance in the age of modern technology and modern economic growth; and of the role that can be played by a more enlightened policy than the laissez-faire and pronatalist policy which prevailed in the currently developed countries in the past.

The above comment should not be interpreted to mean that no economic advance would be possible in the less developed regions of today, without striking reductions in birth rates. After all, despite the high growth rates of population, per capita product of the less developed economies grew over 1950s and 1960s at a rate of about 1 per cent per year (after all adjustments), which meant a rise over the two decades of about a third.[7] But while this record looks good in comparison with the past, it is far short of that shown by the developed economies over the period. More important, it raises questions as to whether such a gain can be maintained with continuation, and indeed the projected acceleration, in the rate of population growth. Whatever the answer, the historical perspective suggests that a more deliberate population policy might consider not only the spread of knowledge of birth control technology, but also the ways in which the given institutional framework affects incentives on the part of a large proportion of people to shift toward greater investment in human capital and fewer children. This means exploring changes in economic, political, and social institutions that would enhance the interest of an increasing proportion of the population in the modern type of family – given the attainment of death rates low enough to approximate modern levels.

As indicated above, the comments on the current problem of high rates of population growth in the less developed countries are illustrative. More intensive consideration was impossible, partly for lack of knowledge and partly for lack of space. In general, inferences from the past for the present and the future can only be suggestive. We could have illustrated the relevance of the historical perspective to the problems of demographic adjustment in the *developed* countries – which are, however, quite different in range and emphasis from those stressed for the current problem for the less developed regions. It was not feasible to do so here. Yet I would like to conclude by stressing the differences in the specific implications of the population adjustment problems between the developed and less developed regions, which are marked – as are those even among some sub-regions within each of the two groups. This means that the historical perspective would have to be translated into rather different implications for the two groups of countries, or for some sub-regions within each. Thus, although we are all inhabitants of one planet and members of world humanity, the population problems of the various regions are rather different. This has its favourable aspects, in that we are not all caught in the same bind that constrains many less developed countries, and resources can be transferred. But it also has its unfavourable aspects, in the sense that our interests and concern differ. But regardless of the implications for policy, in order to achieve better understanding, our interpretation of the historical perspective must be geared to the different problems of the several societies and regions. And the very analysis of what we can learn from the past must be refined and tested, if it is to serve as a basis for more intelligent treatment of current population problems.

REFERENCES

Bairoch, P et al (1968) *The Working Population and Its Structure*, Brussels: Institut de Sociologie, Université Libre de Bruxelles.

Glass, D V and E Grebenik (1965) 'World population, 1800–1950', in *The Cambridge Economic History of Europe*, ed H J Habakkuk and M Postan, vol VI, Cambridge:

---

7 Estimates, including the various adjustments, are discussed in my paper, 'Problems in comparing recent growth rates for developed and less developed countries' (Kuznets 1972b).

Cambridge University Press.

Goode, William J (1963) *World Revolution and Family Patterns*, New York: The Free Press.

International Labour Office (1971) *Labour Force Projections, 1965-1985*, parts I-V Geneva.

Johnson, Gwendolyn Z (1960) 'Differential fertility in European countries', in *Demographic and Economic Change in Developed Countries*, ed Ansley J Coale, Princeton: Princeton University Press, for the National Bureau of Economic Research.

Kuznets, Simon (1966) *Modern Economic Growth: Rate, Structure, and Spread*, New Haven: Yale University Press.

— (1971) *Economic Growth of Nations: Total Output and Production Structure*, Cambridge, Massachusetts: Harvard University Press.

— (1972a) 'Modern economic growth: findings and reflections', in Les Prix Nobel en 1971 (Stockholm); reprinted in *American Economic Review*, June 1973.

— (1972b) 'Problems in comparing recent growth rates for developed and less developed countries', *Economic Development and Cultural Change* 20, no 2, pp185-209.

McKeown, T, R G Brown, and R G Record (1972) 'An interpretation of the modern rise of population in Europe', *Population Studies* 26, no 3, pp345-382.

United Nations (1953) *The Determinants and Consequences of Population Trends*, New York.

— (1969) *Growth of the World's Urban and Rural Population, 1920-2000* New York.

— (1971) *The World Population Situation in 1970*, New York.

Chapter 2

Relationships between Population Growth and Economic Growth

Didier Blanchet

Dennis Hodgson (1988) has identified three schools of thought concerning the relationship between population and development in Third World countries. By order of appearance since World War II, he characterized these three schools as follows:

- *Transition theory* views industrialization as a necessary prerequisite for fertility decline. Economic development is first a factor in accelerating population growth. This relationship temporarily reduces the potential for increasing per capita welfare, since increases in total production are partially offset by increases in population numbers. Sooner or later, however, population trends reverse as fertility decline sets in, and economic growth thereafter proceeds unhindered.
- *'Orthodoxy'*, as it dominated population debates until recently, views demographic trends as 'determinants of economic trends [and views] rapid population growth as a cause of continued underdevelopment. Lowering fertility becomes a way of facilitating structural change' (Hodgson 1988, p.542). The outcome postulated by transition theory is not assured. Laissez faire regarding population matters is therefore not sufficient, and fertility declines must be induced by deliberate state intervention, if not by coercion.
- *'Revisionism'* holds that population growth is a neutral phenomenon with respect to economic development, or is even beneficial to it because of constant or increasing returns to scale, or, in a more modern and more interesting formulation, because of endogenous technical progress attributable to, and more than compensating for, population growth. In this case, any justification for deliberately seeking to induce a decline in the rate of population growth disappears. People looking for ways to accelerate development should consider causes of backwardness other than population growth, such as faulty economic organization or political instability. Pushing the logic of this line of argument further, population growth should be encouraged since it is a stimulus to economic growth – defined throughout this note as an increase in per capita income. While this position is rarely held concerning developing countries, it is implicit behind most population-ist statements concerning developed countries.

In the same article, Hodgson describes the empirical evidence that has favoured the emergence of the last school of thought. This evidence relies on the only data source that is available to test relationships between demographic change and economic growth at aggregate levels – the-country-by-country time series of population growth rates and growth rates of per capita gross domestic product. Now, it is well known that plotting the one series against the other for almost any period of time fails to exhibit the negative association postulated by orthodoxy. In other words, higher population growth rates do not seem to imply lower rates of income growth.

Interpretations of this familiar result depend on one's preferred paradigm. Adherents of orthodoxy often choose to disregard it, on grounds of the poor quality of data or the inappropriateness of applying simple regression analysis to highly heterogeneous data sets. On the other hand, revisionists cite this finding as crucial support of their views. An article by Julian Simon (1989) provides an illustration of this position.

It is true, as Simon shows, that arguments used by orthodoxy are often questionable. Applied literally, some of them amount to denying any role to empirical evidence in the discussion of demographic-economic relationships or of relationships between macro-economic growth and any other measurable phenomena – a position that is hard to accept. But conceding this point does not mean that empirical correlation results can be taken at face value.

This note argues for a middle course between uncritical acceptance and total rejection of the correlations. This approach relies on transition theory. Transition theory can explain a lack of association or even a positive association between population growth and economic growth at the onset of demographic transition, because it assumes that population growth is, at least partially, driven by economic change, resulting in simultaneity bias. The possibility of such bias in this context is well recognized by statisticians. Simon rules it out in the article cited above. This note seeks to show that, in fact, such bias can exist. We will do so by recourse to a simple graphical exposition.

This illustration has other applications. It can account for a variety of patterns of association between population growth and economic growth, including the re-emergence of a negative correlation at a later stage of development – a phenomenon documented by several analysts of recent data.[1] We will also suggest that transition theory lends support to an intermediate position concerning the need for policies aimed at slowing population growth. While it does not imply that these policies are an absolute necessity, it suggests they may be useful in accelerating the transition process and thus in promoting economic development.

IMPLICIT ASSUMPTIONS OF COMPETING MODELS

Key facets of the analytic structure of demographic-economic models[2] are illustrated in Figure 1. The three approaches characterized above can be considered as three parametrizations of a more general model that exhibits the following

---

1 For example, Chesnais (1985) and United Nations (1988).
2 The most comprehensive view is provided by Lee (1986). To follow his presentation, we insist here on the role of technology as the key variable explaining development, although other factors such as capital accumulation also play an obvious role in the process.

		Technological change	
		Exogenous	Endogenous
Population growth	Exogenous	'Orthodoxy'	'Revisionism'
	Endogenous	'Transition theory'	'General model'

Figure 1 *A classification of demographic-economic paradigms*

assumptions concerning the relationship between population growth and economic growth.

1. Returns to scale are decreasing, given the state of technology.
2. Population growth is endogenous, with each of the three components of population growth – mortality, fertility, and migration – being affected by the level of income per capita, among other variables.
3. Technological progress is endogenous, progress being determined by the level of income per capita, by total production, and either directly by population size or by the rate of population growth, depending on the formulation of the particular model.

To put things simply, the orthodox position amounts to dropping the assumption of endogeneity of both population growth and technological progress (assumptions 2 and 3). It retains only assumption (1). Decreasing returns to scale should manifest themselves through simple negative regressions of growth rates of per capita product on the rates of population growth. Yet, as noted above, this does not happen. When so caricatured, the orthodox position is not supported by the data.

The revisionist position, while generally accepting assumptions (1), gives the major role to (3) and neglects (2) on the grounds that it refers to a weak and very long-run relationship. In this model formulation, the relationship implied by (1) is compensated by the relationship implied by assumption (3). This explains why assumption (1) is not borne out by the empirical record.[3]

---

3 Compensation, however, may prove inadequate if the positive impact of population pressure is not instantaneous.

Finally, transition theory embraces the first two assumptions and generally ignores the third, viewing technological progress as exogenous, as did most economic growth models at the time the theory was formulated. Concerning assumption (2), transition theory holds that it has a particular form. Instead of the monotonic positive association between the rate of population growth and the level of per capita income posited in the transitional models of the Malthusian trap,[4] the theory assumes that this relationship is positive in an initial phase, because better economic conditions imply lower mortality and, often, also higher fertility (due to better health). Then, after a critical point, a second phase emerges in which this relationship turns negative, as gains in life expectancy become harder to attain and also have a lesser impact on the rate of population growth, and rising levels of income per capita lead to fertility decline. The reasons for this downturn of fertility as a response to a higher standard of living are not well established, but this is another debate.

DEVELOPMENT PATHS ACCORDING TO TRANSITION THEORY

The best model, of course, would incorporate all three assumptions in their most general forms (thus occupying the lower right quadrant in the fourfold classification shown in Figure 1). But our aim here is to show the potential explanatory power of the pure transition model. Can this model explain the absence of relationship (1) in the observed empirical record? There is some disagreement here, and a few technical considerations intrude at this point.

Demographic-economic Take-off

In a model where population growth would affect and simultaneously be affected by economic growth, we know that we can observe neither casual relationship directly. What we observe is a mix of them, which is different from the two relationships taken separately. But does this apply here? At first sight, the answer is no, since the two relationships involved are:

- A relationship linking the *growth rate* of per capita income to the *growth rate* of population in a manner that would correspond to assumption (1), which is the relationship we are trying to ascertain empirically.
- A relationship that corresponds to assumption (2), linking *population growth* to the level of per capita income.

The two relationships are not symmetrical. Because the second involves the level of income and not its growth rate, we do not have a model of closed feedback, but rather what is called a recursive model. In such a model, theoretically, the relationship corresponding to assumption (1) will be observed without any bias.

---

4 See Nelson (1956). Malthusian trap models have been criticized by Kuznets (1967), Preston (1975), Simon (1980), and others. As stated very suggestively by Samuel Preston, the trap, if any exists, closes so slowly that escaping from it is nearly unavoidable. As will be seen, our presentation takes this point into account.

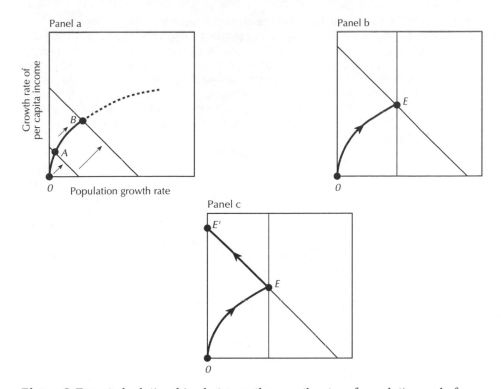

Figure 2 *Expected relationships between the growth rates of population and of per capita income according to transition theory*

This is the position argued by Simon (1989).[5]

Recursivity is not a sufficient condition, however, for this last proposition to be valid. Some additional assumptions are necessary. The most important is that the exogenous perturbations that affect relationship (1) do not present any regular trend or fluctuation over time. Technological progress is one of these potential perturbations. Using long-run historical series, Ronald Lee (1989) presented a systematic account of how the observation of decreasing returns to scale of a given state of technology is biased under various assumptions about the exogenous fluctuations of technology. Relying only on informal analysis, we will arrive at similar results in the special case of progressive acceleration of technical progress, which can be hypothesized for the onset of demographic-economic transition in a typical developing country.

Let us sketch out some stylized theoretical sequences of events of this transition in a graph where the population growth rate is indicated on the horizontal axis and the growth rate of per capita income is on the vertical (Figure 2). Assume an initial equilibrium where both population and standard of living are stationary,[6] represented by point 0. Then assume that technological progress becomes

---

5 See the earlier allusions to this point in Lee (1983), and the discussion of it in the recent survey on population and economic development by Kelley (1989).
6 The results will not be different if we start from an initial equilibrium where population growth is already positive.

slightly positive (panel a). This will result in a quasi-equivalent increase in per capita income, since the rate of population growth will remain near zero, reflecting the fact that the change in income is too slight to produce a significant change in demographic parameters. We thus move to point A. Then, if technological progress continues over time, we will move upward on the vertical axis. But, since improvements in the standard of living end up being more than marginal, the rate of population growth will also begin to rise, so that we start moving to the right on the horizontal axis. On the whole, we move on the graph as shown by the solid arrow (towards point B).

Clearly, the relationship between economic growth and population growth in the initial phase of the transition is not negative. This result can be interpreted in another way. For a given level of technological progress, decreasing returns to scale imply that the growth rates of population and of GNP per capita are negatively related: a more rapid rate of population growth implies lower growth in the standard of living. This negative relationship is the one depicted in panel a by any of the different oblique lines with negative slopes. Now, the basic point here is that we do not stay on the same line throughout the process: we are moving on lines which are themselves moving upwards, so that observed points will be along the OAB path. This will be true whether we observe data for one country at successive periods or for various countries at different stages of the process at one point in time.

After Take-off: Some Potential Scenarios

If we assume that population growth and technological progress can both continue without limits, it can be shown analytically that we will go on moving in the same direction. The observed relationship between per capita income growth and population growth will be forever positive, as shown in panel a of Figure 2.[7]

If we drop these two unrealistic assumptions and consider that both technological progress and the rate of population growth have some limits, we see that the further evolution will be constrained by the two straight lines shown in panel b of the figure. The vertical line corresponds to the maximum possible level of the rate of population growth, after which the demographic growth response will come to a halt. The oblique line shows the negative impact of population growth on per capita income growth once the level of technological progress is stabilized at its upper limit.

Assume that the two straight lines intersect at a point E with positive values of the economic and the demographic growth rates. If there is no second phase of the demographic transition, that is, if there is no downturn of population growth at some level of development – this intersection will be a stable long-run equilibrium. Thus, the path followed by the country will be as shown in panel b of Figure 2. Once point E is reached, population and per capita income should both start expanding at constant rates (there may be various ways to arrive at this equilibrium; panel b represents the case of a smooth convergence).

What happens now if, after a certain level of development is reached, the rate of population growth declines – that is, if there is a second phase of the demographic transition? We will now move leftwards on the horizontal axis, and,

---

7 See a fuller analytical account of this result in Blanchet (1989).

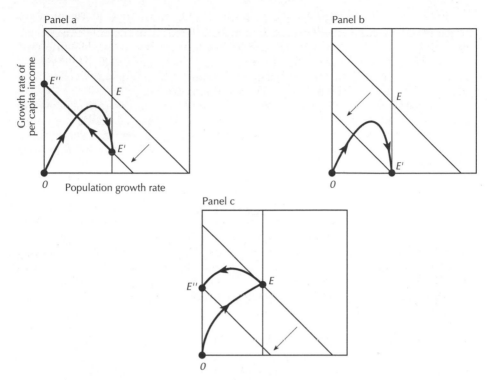

Figure 3 *Development paths reflecting economic setbacks during the demographic transition*

since we are constrained to move along the oblique line, the evolution will follow the path shown in panel c of Figure 2. After some level of development is reached – that corresponding to point *E* – we again observe the negative relationship between the rate of population growth and the rate of income growth. Assuming no negative rates of population growth, stability will be attained at point *E'*.

Last, what happens if technological change also slows down after some point? A slowdown can happen for structural reasons – for example, because development starts with a phase of rapid expansion due to existing backwardness, hence the possibility of technology imports; once these opportunities are exhausted, technological progress will be less rapid. A slowdown can also be caused by external factors – for example, due to economic recession in the developed countries. In both cases, the oblique line will shift downward after having reached its maximal position. Three possible stylized development paths are shown in Figure 3.

In one scenario, represented in panel a, a moderate reversal of the rate of per capita income growth occurs *before* the country has entered the second phase of the demographic transition. This implies that, instead of continuing toward the equilibrium point *E*, the system is driven to the new equilibrium *E'*. Income growth slows down but, since it remains positive, eventually a standard of living is reached at which fertility starts decreasing. Beyond that point, the development path moves along the lower oblique line up to the new equilibrium *E''*.

A second situation (shown in panel b) is similar to the first except that the downturn of per capita income growth is more severe. Then, the long-run equilibrium *E'* is an equilibrium in which the level of income per capita is stationary. This pattern corresponds to one of the familiar variants of the Malthusian trap model. In that model, the level of income during the take-off fails to increase sufficiently to lead to an ultimate reversal of population trends.

In a third scenario (depicted in panel c), the decline in the rate of economic growth takes place *after* the entry into the second phase of the demographic transition – that is, after population growth has started to decline. The ultimate equilibrium *E''* is analogous to that obtained in panel a, but it is reached through a different path.

CONCLUSION

We do not mean to suggest that the actual development paths for any country will exhibit the stylized patterns shown in Figures 2 and 3. First, we must recall that all of the so-called equilibrium points may be largely temporary, especially when they involve continuous demographic or economic expansion. Second and above all, transition paths to these points will be more complicated than suggested, owing to shocks and random changes on both the demographic and the economic components of the system.[8] But it remains true that mechanisms of the demographic transition can play a significant role in shaping the observed relationships between population growth and economic growth, even if we assume that the feedback which exists between the two variables is recursive rather than purely simultaneous. This does not preclude the possibility that a more direct positive impact of population growth on economic growth is also at work. The point is simply that this is not the only possible explanation for our empirical observations.

Now, if we give priority to the transition model over the revisionist one, the empirical problem remains: which of the potential paths described above best approximates the actual pattern of development? Optimists and non-interventionists will argue that occurrence of an evolution of the type shown in panel b of Figure 3 is not a realistic expectation, hence we should wait for the natural (and satisfactory) outcome of the demographic transition process described in panels a and c of that figure. Pessimists or interventionists will say that population policy aimed at inducing or accelerating fertility change is useful because it is the only way to ensure avoidance of a Malthusian trap and because it will speed up and improve the outcome of the types of evolution described in panels a and c of Figure 3. One element not taken into account here that could favour this last position is the inertia of population growth, due to age-structural effects. Population growth can continue at a rapid rate long after economic conditions have become less favourable, because a young structure induces, all else equal, a large excess of births over deaths. Introducing this kind of age dependence in the model would

---

8 For example, if population change were in fact the mixed result of both exogenous and endogenous determination, this could explain why the correlation between observed growth rates of population and per capita income is zero rather than positive. Note also that sufficiently large shocks could imply negative growth rates for some countries over some periods of time, a possibility not considered in Figures 2 and 3

be particularly useful, although it would preclude the use of the simple graphical tools we relied upon here.

REFERENCES

Blanchet, Didier (1989) 'Croissance de la population et du produit par tête au cours de la transition démographique: Un modéle malthusian peut-il rendre compte de leurs relations?' *Population* 44, no 3, pp613–29.

Chesnais, Jean-Claude (1985) 'Progrès économique et transition démographique dans les pays pauvres: Trente ans d'expérience (1950–1980)', *Population* 40, no 1, pp11–28.

Hodgson, Dennis (1988) 'Orthodoxy and revisionism in American demography', *Population and Development Review* 14, no 4, pp541–69.

Kelley, Allen C (1989) 'Economic consequences of population change in the Third World', *Journal of Economic Literature* 25, pp1685–728.

Kuznets, Simon (1967) 'Population and economic growth', *Proceedings of the American Philosophical Society* 111, no 3, pp170–93.

Lee, Ronald D (1983) 'Economic consequences of population size, structure and growth', *IUSSP Newsletter*, no 17.

— (1986) 'Malthus and Boserup: A dynamic synthesis', in *The State of Population Theory: Forward from Malthus*, ed David Coleman and Roger Schofield, Oxford: Basil Blackwell, pp96–130.

— (1989) 'Population autoregulation: Malthusian systems in stochastic settings', presented at the INED/ESPE seminar 'Reconstruction of Past Populations and their Dynamics', Junc.

Nelson, Richard R (1956) 'A theory of the low-level equilibrium trap in underdeveloped economics', *American Economic Review* 46, pp894–908.

Preston, Samuel H (1975) 'The changing relation between mortality and the level of economic development', *Population Studies* 29, no 2, pp231–248.

Simon, Julian L (1980) 'There is no low-level fertility and development trap', *Population Studies* 34, no 3, pp476–86.

— (1989) 'On aggregate empirical studies relating population variables to economic development', *Population and Development Review* 15, no 2, pp323–32.

United Nations (1988) *World Population Trends and Policies: 1987 Monitoring Report*, New York: United Nations, DIESA (Population Studies No 103).

Chapter 3

Mortality Trends

Samuel H Preston

MAGNITUDE OF MORTALITY CHANGES

Identifying precisely the average length of life is still impossible for slightly more than half of the world's population, since registration of death remains badly incomplete in many countries. The data problems are magnified when attention shifts to earlier eras of human history. But even for these periods, substitute sources of information permit the estimation of life expectancy within a reasonably narrow range. For prehistoric populations, the only source of information is skeletal remains. The various estimates based on such data are summarized in Acsádi and Nemeskéri (1970). Their summary suggests that life expectancy in prehistoric populations was probably in the range of 18–25 years. Hunter-gatherer populations and others at an early developmental stage were almost certainly clustered into groups too small to sustain the acute infectious diseases that were later to present a persistent scourge among more densely settled groups (Cockburn 1963). For this reason, the native populations of the New World were totally unprepared for the diseases brought by European colonists. Some have suggested that the absence of acute infectious diseases resulted in a higher life expectancy in typical hunter-gatherer populations than among more densely settled early agriculturalists, but the data used in support of this claim have been inadequate (Dumond 1975). Inappropriate nutritional practices, exposure, birth traumas, chronic infectious diseases, diseases with a non-human reservoir, and violence formed a sufficiently potent combination that acute infectious diseases did not have to be invoked in order to severely abbreviate life.

Life expectancy among Romans at the height of empire was probably somewhere between 20 and 30 years (Acsádi and Nemeskéri 1970, Petersen 1976). Confidence in the estimate range is enhanced by the availability of burial inscriptions to support analysis of skeletal remains. For periods beginning around the 14th and 15th centuries, mortality estimates become available that are based upon genealogical records kept by the European aristocracy. The earliest data, referring to persons born into British ducal families between 1330 and 1479, suggest that male life expectancy at birth was 24 years and female, 32.9 years (Hollingsworth 1957). The wide sex difference seems largely attributable to the greater incidence of violent death among males. The interesting feature of these estimates is the relatively minor improvement that seems to have occurred since the Roman era and even since prehistoric times, despite the highly privileged nature of the group supplying data. Peller's (1965) estimates of mortality among European aristocracy are consistent with the British series at comparable early dates. Both series show marked increases for cohorts born after 1700 and before 1780 to a life expectancy of about 37 years among the European aristocracy and 46 years among the British.

There are probably many reasons for this improvement in mortality during the 18th century, but two stand out as most important: a decline in death rates from plague and an improvement in methods of agricultural production. Potatoes and corn introduced from the New World were the first significant changes in medieval agriculture (Dovring 1966). Improved methods of production, especially rotation of crops, also increased yields. Improved methods of bulk transportation facilitated the shipment of produce from an area of surplus to one of deficit. The net result was that the ancient correlation between the price of grain and death rates had essentially disappeared from England by 1700 (Flinn 1970). Reasons for plague's decline are more mysterious. The last major plague in England occurred in 1666 and in France in 1720. An improvement in housing quality in England has been held partially responsible (Shrewsbury 1970), but the disease also lost severity in other countries where no changes in housing or living standards had occurred (Cipolla 1965). The most plausible explanation is that natural immunity evolved among the rat or human population, coupled with the gradual displacement throughout Europe of an indoor rat by an outdoor rat, on which the most effective flea vector in the spread of the plague had great difficulty in over-wintering (Hirst 1953).

The abrupt disappearance of plague from Europe is only one of many possible illustrations of the exogenous role that mortality played in pre-industrial populations. To be sure, death rates in part followed the crop cycle, but they also had a cycle of their own that was not dependent upon human activity (Chambers 1972, Habakkuk 1971). Lee (1976) shows very cleverly that time-series relations between population and economic processes in England can best be understood by assuming that mortality variations were largely exogenous to economic activity, which was itself forced to respond to changing mortality conditions and the cumulative population pressure that they imposed or relieved.

A more gradual improvement in mortality from the middle of the 18th to the end of the 19th centuries in England has been ascribed principally to improvements in living standards that followed the agricultural and, at a longer distance, the industrial revolutions. McKeown and Brown (1955) and McKeown and Record (1962) argue that public health and medical measures deployed during this period were largely ineffective and occasionally harmful. However, they have almost certainly underestimated the importance of smallpox inoculation and vaccination (Razzell 1969). According to Razzell, smallpox may have accounted for as many as 20–25 per cent of English deaths in 1700, and the dramatically effective Sutton method of inoculation that was widely diffused after 1760 reduced this fraction to insignificance by 1900. Others have suggested that practices in the hospitals examined by McKeown and colleagues were unrepresentative of those in effect throughout England (Flinn 1970).

A new era in mortality history began around 1880, when life expectancy in northern and western Europe was in the mid-40s, in southern and eastern Europe, in the mid-30s, and in Africa, Asia, and Latin America, in the mid-20s. Gains in the average length of life in the subsequent 90 years exceeded all of the gains that had apparently been made since prehistoric times. Life expectancy at birth in populations of European descent in 1965–1970 was about 70–71 years, and in less developed countries, about 50 years: 60 in Latin America, 50 in Asia, and 43 in Africa (World Health Organization 1974). The reader may consult a number of excellent reviews of mortality declines that focus on the period since 1880 (United Nations 1963, 1973, 1974; Stolnitz 1974; Arriaga 1967; World Health Organization 1974).

As in the case of earlier eras, there has been considerable dispute about the causes of the rapid mortality declines since 1880. The sheer speed of mortality decline, together with a few examples of obviously effective governmental programmes, has convinced most demographers that the decline was primarily produced by social policy measures with an unprecedented scope or efficacy (Davis 1956, Coale, and Hoover 1958, Stolnitz 1974). But this interpretation has been widely disputed by specialists in international health (Fredericksen 1961, 1966a, b; Marshall, Brown and Goodrich 1971), and occasionally by others (McKeown 1965, Sharpston 1976). The counterclaim is usually that intervention programmes have been ineffective or insufficiently widespread, especially in less developed countries, to have radically altered mortality. Advances in living standards, especially in nutrition, are promoted as the leading competing explanation.

Preston (1975) has attempted to resolve the dispute as it pertains to the period since 1930. He has calculated the quantitative relation between measures of life expectancy and per capita national income for nations of the world in the 1930s and again in the 1960s. A very apparent shift in the relation occurs; for the income ranges where most of the world's population is located, life expectancy was 10–12 years higher in the 1960s than it was in the 1930s. Since the country distribution of world income is known with moderate precision for these periods, it is possible with the computed relations to assign a certain fraction of the mortality gains since the 1930s to changes in incomes and a certain fraction to factors exogenous to national income. Results of this exercise suggest that gains in living standards were responsible for only about 20 per cent of the gain in mortality during the period, with exogenous factors accounting for the remainder. Probably the most important of these exogenous factors were remarkably effective and inexpensive anti-malarial programmes embodying post-war technical innovations, and widespread campaigns to prevent or treat airborne diseases that also utilized primarily post-war technical developments. These campaigns were facilitated by a stabilized international political order and by the activity therein of international humanitarian agencies, especially the World Health Organization and the Rockefeller Foundation. Virtually all of the advances were predicated on the germ theory of disease, whose acceptance around 1880 is almost certainly the major reason why the subsequent period is so distinct from all preceding periods in its pace of mortality change.

Many analysts have stressed the role of more developed countries in the mortality declines enjoyed by less developed countries. Financially, however, their role appears to be very minor. Preston (1976) estimates that only about 2 per cent of the total health expenditure in less developed countries (LDCs) in 1970 was financed by aid from bilateral or multilateral sources. The annual budget of the World Health Organization, the largest source of international health aid, was less than that of Massachusetts General Hospital in 1970 (Goodman 1971, p223). But more developed countries (MDCs) were critically important in two other respects. First, the development of low-cost methods of disease control occurred almost exclusively in labouratories of MDCs; second, small-scale projects sponsored by

MDCs served to demonstrate the feasibility and remarkable cost-effectiveness of applying these methods to health problems of LDCs.

DIFFERENTIALS IN MORTALITY CHANGE

Not all groups shared equally in the decline. In terms of absolute changes in death rates, children under 5 and adults above 40 have typically enjoyed the largest declines. The reason is simply that these are the ages that are most vulnerable to infectious diseases, and hence they have profited the most from technical advances against these causes of death. The older childhood ages, where infectious diseases were virtually the only causes of death, have experienced the largest proportionate gains. Life-expectancy gains for females have in virtually every country outstripped those for males. In Western countries in the 19th century, female life expectancy exceeded that of males by about 2–3 years. The difference is now on the order of 7–8 years. Two factors appear to be responsible for the widening gap. First, males and females of the same age are about equally vulnerable to infectious diseases, but males die at a faster rate from degenerative causes, especially from cardiovascular diseases. The decline of the relatively neutral infectious diseases has left the typical degenerative disadvantage for males more starkly exposed. Madigan (1957) has supported this argument by showing that among American brothers and sisters of Catholic orders whose styles of living were very similar and largely constant over time, the same changes in sex-mortality differentials occurred during the 20th century as occurred in the American population as a whole. The implication is that changing styles of living were not responsible for the widening sex differentials in mortality, and that the differentials were in some sense innate. However, others have shown that this is an incomplete explanation. A second factor that appears to be involved in the widening differentials is an increasing masculinity of mortality from the degenerative diseases themselves (Enterline 1961; Retherford 1975). Very consistently among Western nations, male death rates from cardiovascular disease and cancer have risen slightly since 1930, while female rates from these causes have fallen decisively (Preston and Weed 1976). Declines are expected because of improved living standards and medical measures and a reduced incidence of infectious diseases (for example, rheumatic heart disease). Among males, however, the expected declines have been more than counterbalanced by other factors. Probably the most important of these influences are declines in daily on-the-job exercise levels and increases in cigarette smoking, both of which are on other grounds expected to be more consequential for males (Preston 1970). In a broad sense, socio-economic modernization has almost certainly been more beneficial to women's health than to men's, although the relative male disadvantage seems to reflect deliberate choices facilitated by affluence.

In general, the decline of infectious diseases has allowed greater play to the style-of-life factors that influence mortality from chronic diseases. In addition to cigarette smoking and lack of exercise, these factors include a diet high in animal fat, excessive alcohol consumption, obesity, and a hard-driving, time-oriented personality (Cairns 1975, Breslow and Enstrom 1974, Belloc 1973). Belloc (1973) has classified individuals according to seven health practices believed to be related to chronic disease mortality (smoking, exercise, etc). She finds that the average life expectancy of men aged 45 with good scores was 11 years higher than that of men with poor ones. These differences are probably reflected in mortality varia-tions among geographic areas and social groups. For example, Lyon et al (1976) demonstrate significantly lower mortality from a wide variety of cancers in the state of Utah and particularly among Mormons in that state.

Social differentials in mortality have changed in a complex way as overall levels have declined. Despite their typically lower incomes, rural residents in 19th-century Europe systematically enjoyed lower mortality levels than urban residents (United Nations 1973; Davis 1973). Cities were a more effective arena for spread-ing infectious diseases by virtue of their frequent personal interactions and because common resources, especially water supplies, were more readily befouled in large agglomerations. The superimposition of the rural–urban dimension on classical differentials by standards of living produced a muddled picture of class mortality differentials. Among classically urban occupations, it seems clear that class differentials favoured the higher-status groups (Matthiessen 1972; Antonovsky 1967).

The advent of public sanitation programmes and the spread of weapons to combat infectious diseases have effectively neutralized the health disadvantages of urban areas. Metropolitan areas in the United States in 1960 had age-adjusted death rates that were only 5 per cent above those of non-metropolitan areas (Kitagawa and Hauser 1973). Rural districts in England and Wales recorded a life expectancy at birth that was only one year higher than that of urban districts in 1967 (Keyfitz and Flieger 1971, pp474–76). In LDCs, on the other hand, public health programmes and medical expenditures have been disproportionately directed towards large urban areas (World Bank 1975). The result is that urban areas typically have lower mortality rates than do rural ones (Johnson 1964; Davis 1973).

Antonovsky (1967) considers in great detail the nature of changes in social-class mortality differentials during the past two centuries. Several empirical generalizations are tentatively offered: that class differentials first widened and then contracted as public health measures and access to advanced medical care gradually diffused through the social strata; and that we may be entering a period of widening differentials again as methods of reducing mortality from chronic diseases are similarly diffused. But the size of mortality differentials is quite diffi-cult to measure in a way that permits inter-population comparisons. Their size depends in large part on the measure chosen (slope, ratio, difference), the degree of detail and internal validity in the occupational classification, and the per centiles represented by classes for which mortality data are available. The longest series of occupational class differentials is available for England and Wales. The series shows a distinct contraction in the ratio of mortality rates of lower to those of higher classes between 1910–1912 and 1949–1953 (Antonovsky 1967, p63). By the later period, mortality rates were, for all practical purposes, identical among the classes except for labourers, who showed death rates roughly 14 per cent above average.

Social inequalities in the distribution of life appear to be considerably greater in the United States. By far the largest and most complex study of class mortality differentials ever conducted was based on a matching of 62,487 death certificates for 1960 with corresponding forms from the 1960 US Census of Population (Kitagawa and Hauser 1973). The purpose of the record linkage was to provide nationwide statistics on death rates according to the detailed socio-economic characteristics appearing on census schedules. This procedure improves upon those of past studies in two respects: it resolves the inconsistencies of definition and reporting for characteristics such as occupation that appeared on both the death certificate and the census schedule; and it provides for the first time death rates according to such characteristics as family income and parity that appear only in the census. The advantages of record linkage were reduced, however, by the 27 per cent non-match rate, which not only introduced ambiguity into the results, but also seems to have circumscribed the analytic procedures that could be employed. Educational attainment serves as the basic indicator of social class, since it is essentially invariant after age 25 and is not influenced by illness itself (unlike income or occupation). Kitagawa and Hauser's figures reveal a very large differential in mortality by educational attainment for all ages of women and for men below age 65. The largest differential occurs for white women aged 25–64, among whom those with less than five years of schooling have death rates slightly more than double those of college graduates. According to the 1960 rates, white women aged 25 with one or more years of college will live, on average, 9.6 years longer than those with less than five years of schooling; for white males the difference is 3.2 years. For both sexes, a majority of the advantage of the college-educated is attributable to their lower rates of death from cardiovascular-renal diseases, among which arteriosclerotic and degenerative heart disease makes the largest contribution. For males, accidents contribute 23 per cent and lung cancer 11 per cent.

Why American class differentials in mortality are larger than British differentials cannot be judged because the appropriate studies have not been conducted. One would surmise that differences in the health-care delivery system were largely responsible, but many factors could be involved. Mortality studies, once among the most technically advanced in the social sciences, have lagged far behind much of the rest of sociology. Multivariate studies of the influence of particular individual and ecological factors on mortality are still confined almost exclusively to tabular presentations involving, at most, three variables. The problem is partly the nature of the dependent variable: death is so infrequent, a once-in-a-lifetime event, that very large studies are required in order to supply a sufficiently large number of cases for significant results to emerge. At the moment, we don't know whether the high mortality of lower-class American adults reflects primarily problems of physical development when they were children; poor nutrition, housing, or clothing; restricted access to health care; crowded living areas; unhealthy jobs; or greater frequency of emotional difficulties.

[...]

CONCLUSION

Life expectancy at birth for the world population has increased from about 20–25 years in the prehistoric era to about 50–55 years today. The majority of this advance has occurred in the short space of time since 1880. Prior to that time, much of the improvement that occurred was probably a result of gains in standards of living. Since then, it seems primarily attributable to advances in medical knowledge and to the embodiment of those advances in government programmes of death control. All nations and groups have shared in these gains, but they have been largest for the very young and the very old, for females, for urbanites, and for the most disadvantaged social groups.

These declines are singlehandedly responsible for the vast acceleration of population growth rates during this century, and their differential distribution has modified population composition. As a result of mortality declines, the weight of world numbers has shifted more rapidly toward LDCs, toward urban areas, toward persons outside of labour-force age, and toward the offspring of lower classes. The principal economic-demographic response to the mortality reduction has been an expanded growth rate of total production. The demographic pressure has in some instances been eased by induced declines in fertility and by international migration. Nevertheless, there are instances where mortality decline has apparently led to widescale economic devastation.

For individuals, the mortality decline has meant a longer and more predictable future and a much more stable social network. Many fewer people will lead lives that are truncated before the major stages of education, work, and family building are completed. The longer projected length of life has probably induced a more planful approach to life and greater investments in one's personal future. The reduced incidence of death and its common postponement until the major functions of life are performed is probably in part responsible for the recession of fatalism and the emergence of a heightened sense of personal efficacy that commonly accompany socio-economic modernization.

REFERENCES

Acsádi, G and J Nemeskéri (1970) *History of Human Life Span and Mortality*, Akad Kiado, Budapest.

Antonovsky, A (1967) *Social class, life expectancy, and overall mortality, Milbank Memorial Fund Quarterly* 45, no 2, pp31–73.

Arriaga, E (1967) *Mortality Decline and Its Demographic Effects in Latin America* Institute of International Studies, Berkeley, University of California.

Belloc, N B (1973) 'Relationship of health practices and mortality', *Prev Med* 2, pp67–81.

Breslow, N E and J E Enstrom (1974) 'Geographic correlations between cancer mortality rates and alcohol-tobacco consumption in the United States', *Journal of the National Cancer Institute* 53, no 3, pp631–39.

Cairns, J (1975) 'The cancer problem', *Scientific American* 233, no 5, pp64–78.

Cipolla, C M (1965) 'Four centuries of Italian economic development', in *Population in History*, ed D V Glass and D E C Eversley, London: Arnold.

Chambers, J D (1972) *Population, Economy, and Society in Pre-Industrial England*, Oxford University Press, London.

Coale, A J and E M Hoover (1958) *Population Growth and Economic Development in Low-Income Countries*, Princeton, Princeton University Press, NJ.

Cockburn, A (1963) *The Evolution and Eradication of Infectious Diseases*, Johns Hopkins University Press, Baltimore.

Davis, K (1956) 'The amazing decline of mortality in underdeveloped areas', *American Economic Review* 46, pp305–18.

– (1973) 'Cities and mortality', in *Proceedings of the International Population Conference, Liège* International Union for the Scientific Study of Population, vol 3, Liège, Belgium.

Dovring, F (1966) 'The transformation of European agriculture', in *The Cambridge Economic History of Europe*, ed H J Habbakkuk and M Postan, Cambridge University Press, Cambridge.

Dumond, D E (1975) 'The limitation of human population: a natural history', *Science* 187, pp 713–21.

Enterline, P E (1961) 'Causes of death responsible for recent increases in sex mortality differentials in the United States', *Milbank Memorial Fund Quarterly* 34, no 2, pp 312–25.

Flinn, M W (1970) *British Population Growth, 1700–1850,* Macmillan, London.

Fredericksen, H (1961) 'Determinants and consequences of mortality trends in Ceylon', *Public Health Reports* 76, pp659–63.

— (1966a) 'Determinants and consequences of mortality and fertility trends', *Public Health Reports* 81, pp715–27.

— (1966b) 'Dynamic equilibrium of economic and demographic transition', *Economic Development and Cultural Change* 14, pp316–22.

Goodman, N M (1971) *International Health Organizations and Their Work,* Churchill-Livingstone, Edinburgh.

Habakkuk, H J (1971) *Population Growth and Economic Development since 1750,* Humanities Press, New York.

Hirst, L F (1953) *The Conquest of Plague: A Study of the Evolution of Epidemiology,* Oxford University Press, London.

Hollingsworth, T H (1957) 'A demographic study of British ducal families', *Population Studies* 11, no 1, pp4–26.

Johnson, G (1964) 'Health conditions in rural and urban areas of developing countries', *Population Studies* 17, pp293–309.

Keyfitz, N and W Flieger (1971) *Population: Facts and Methods of Demography,* Freeman, San Francisco.

Kitagawa, E M and P M Hauser (1973) *Differential Mortality in the United States: A Study in Socioeconomic Epidemiology,* Harvard University Press, Cambridge, Massachusetts.

Lee, R (1976) 'An historical perspective on economic aspects of the population explosion: the case of preindustrial England', in *Conference on Population and Economic Change in Less Developed Countries, Philadelphia, 1976* [Published as *Population and Economic Change in Developing Countries,* ed R A Easterlin, University of Chicago Press, 1980, Chicago].

Lyon, J L; M R Klauber; J W Gardner; C R Smart (1976) 'Cancer incidence in Mormons and non-Mormons in Utah, 1966–1970', *New England Journal of Medicine* 294, no 3, pp129–33.

Madigan, F C (1957) 'Are sex mortality differentials biologically caused?' *Milbank Memorial Fund Quarterly* 35, no 2, pp202–23.

Marshall, C L; R E Brown; C H Goodrich (1971) 'Improved nutrition vs public health services as major determinants of world population growth', *Clin Pediatr* 10, pp363–68.

Matthiessen, P (1972) 'Application of the Brass-Sullivan method to historical data: differential child mortality in Copenhagen in the 1870's', *Population Index* 38, no 4, pp403–9.

McKeown, T (1965) 'Medicine and world population', in *Public Health and Population Change,* ed, M C Sheps and J C Ridley, University of Pittsburgh Press, Pittsburgh.

McKeown, T and R G Brown (1955) 'Medical evidence related to English population changes in the 18th century', *Population Studies* 9, pp119–41.

McKeown, T and R G Record (1962) 'Reasons for the decline of mortality in England and Wales during the 19th century', *Population Studies* 16, pp94–122.

Peller, S (1965) 'Births and deaths among Europe's ruling families since 1500', in *Population in History,* ed D V Glass and D E C Eversley, London: Arnold.

Petersen, W (1976) *Population,* Macmillan 3rd ed, New York.

Preston, S H (1970) *Older Male Mortality and Cigarette Smoking: A Demographic Analysis,* Institute of International Studies, University of California, Berkeley.

— (1975) 'The changing relation between mortality and level of economic development', *Population Studies* 29, no 2, pp 231–48.

— (1976) 'Causes and consequences of mortality declines in less developed countries during the 20th century', in *Conference on Population and Economic Change in Less Developed Countries, Philadelphia, 1976* [Published as *Population and Economic Change in Developing Countries*, ed R A Easterlin, University of Chicago Press, 1980, Chicago].

Preston, S H and J Weed (1976) 'Causes of death responsible for international and intertemporal variation in sex mortality differentials', *World Health Statistical Reports* 29, no 3, pp144–88.

Razzell, P E (1969) 'Population change in 18th century England: a reappraisal', in *Population in Industrialization*, ed M Drake, Methuen, London.

Retherford, R D (1975) *The Changing Sex Differential in Mortality*, Greenwood, Westport, Conn.

Sharpston, M J (1976) 'Health and the human environment', *Finance and Development* 13, no 1, pp24–28.

Shrewsbury, J F D (1970) *A History of Bubonic Plague in the British Isles*, Cambridge University Press, Cambridge.

Stolnitz, G J (1974) 'International mortality trends: some main facts and implications', Background paper for United Nations World Population Conference, Bucharest (E/CONF 60/CBP/17).

United Nations, Department of Economic and Social Affairs (1973) *The Determinants and Consequences of Population Trends*, 2nd ed, vol 1 New York.

United Nations, Population Branch (1963) *Population Bulletin of the United Nations* no 6, New York.

United Nations, Population Division (1974) 'Recent population trends and future prospects' World Population Conference Paper E/CONF 60/3 New York.

World Bank (1975) *Health: Sector Policy Paper,* Washington, DC.

World Health Organization (1974) 'Health aspects of population trends and prospects', Working Paper No 8 for the World Population Conference, Bucharest.

Chapter 4

Population Effects of the Value of Human Time

Theodore W Schultz

Two decidedly different population equilibria can now be formulated. They may be viewed as two extreme types with respect to the state of economy. The foundation of the first equilibrium is a consequence of increases in the price of the services of natural resources relative to the services of labour (wages). The foundation of the second equilibrium is determined by increases in the price of human time relative to that of materials. The supply of time for consumption becomes the limiting factor. The per capita income implication of the first is subsistence and that of the second a high standard of living.

The first type, as it was envisaged by early English economists, has long been a standard part of economics. It assumes that the supply of land is fixed and that diminishing returns increase the price of food as a consequence of population growth. Gains in productivity from capital are exhausted by this process. This concept can, of course, be extended to encompass the results of the recent macro-system models that purport to show the limits of the earth in accommodating population growth. These models are not restricted solely by the availability of land to produce food, since they also include the physical limits set by the availability of minerals, energy, and space for people. The fertility behaviour of people in these models is crudely Malthusian; population growth stops as a consequence of the inevitable food, energy, and space limitation. Within the Ricardian framework, this concept is a logical conception of a population equilibrium. It is a dismal view of human behaviour that has long been important in social thought.

The foundation of the second concept is the high price of human time relative to the price of the services of material factors and goods. This concept rests on the proposition that the state of the economy is such that the value of services of natural resources and of intermediate material products is small relative to the value of services of human agents. Accordingly, the contribution of materials to human satisfactions is small compared to that of human agents. In such an economy, the opportunity cost of bearing children is high and the investment in their human capital is large. The welfare implications of this concept are unmistakably optimistic because the gains in productivity from the accumulation of human and non-human capital are transformed into high standards of living supported by high per capita income. Advances in useful knowledge, embodied in human and non-human capital, have gradually destroyed the assumption of the fixed supply of the 'original properties of the soil' In the process, it is the scarcity of human time and its high value that dominate, and it is the 'fixed supply of human time' consisting of 24 hours per day and of a man's lifetime that become the critical factor in analysing the economic behaviour of people, including their fertility.

There is an abundance of evidence which shows that the price of human time accounts for most of the costs in a modern economy. The upward tendency of real wages and salaries, including fringe benefits, of earnings forgone by mature students, and of the value of the time of housewives relative to the price of materials is well documented.[1] Economic theory implies, and we observe, that material goods are substituted for human time by firms and by households. Received theory, however, is silent on the effects of the high and rising price of human time on pure consumption, although consumption obviously entails time. *The ultimate economic limit of affluence (economic growth) is not in the scarcity of material goods but in the scarcity of human time for consumption.*[2]

The critical postulate assumes that there is a dynamic process that determines the increases in the price of human time relative to the price of services of the non-human factors and that this process tends toward an equilibrium. The dynamic part is the economic key to the following four issues:

1. the relative increase in investment in human capital augmenting the quality of human beings;
2. the relatively high price of all labour-intensive goods and other sources of labour-intensive satisfactions, including children, thus leading to the substitution of quality for numbers of children;
3. the relatively cheap material goods that are not labour-intensive;
4. the scarcity of the time for consumption, setting the ultimate limit to the satisfactions that can be derived from materials provided by economic growth.

Although it is obvious that the economic value of human time is high in affluent countries that have a modern economy, it is not obvious why these economies have developed the demand for and supply of human abilities that have such a high value, in terms of earnings and satisfactions that people derive from them.

My approach to a persistent secular increase in the economic value of human time consists of supply and demand developments that determine the rise of the price of human time in the context of the modernizing processes. The developments explaining the increases in the supply of the quality attributes of human agents are fairly clear, whereas the developments underlying the increases in the demand for these quality attributes are less clear. Recent advances in economic analysis[3] provide parts of the theory for determining the supply of these quality attributes. They treat the useful abilities that people acquire as forms of human capital. The investment in these abilities is taken to be in response to favourable investment opportunities, and thus the increases in the supply depend on current expenditures (sacrifices) made by individuals, families, and public bodies on education, health, job training, as well as for information, and geographical migra-

---

1 Evidence, for example, on long-term changes in wages and salaries relative to rent paid for the services of farmland in the United States shows that the total real compensation per hour at work of all manufacturing-production workers increased between 1929 and 1970 more than four times as much as did the rent on farm real estate per acre, similarly adjusted (see Schultz, 1972a).
2 The approach outlined in this paragraph and a considerable part of the argument that follows appear in Schultz (1973).
3 Ibid; see also Schultz (1972b).

tion to take advantage of better jobs or of better consumption opportunities. These expenditures (sacrifices) are presumably made deliberately with an eye to future satisfactions and earnings. The theories of the allocation of time and household production are of special importance in analysing the incentives and responses of people in acquiring education and job training, in enhancing their health, in searching for information, and in altering their fertility, including the substitution of quality for numbers of children. Thus, these supply responses to the increases in the economic incentives associated with modernization are not hard to comprehend. The human capital literature abounds with studies dealing with aspects of these supply responses.

But these human capital studies have not explained the secular increases in the demand for these quality attributes of human agents. The clue to this unresolved puzzle is concealed in two basic factual issues. The first is that diminishing returns to capital have not occurred generally, despite the vast accumulation of capital in the advanced economies. The second issue is the relatively high rate at which the formation of human capital has occurred. Of the two concerns the first is fundamental, and the resolution of it provides a solution for the second. The key to both is in that part of the economic process that increases the stock of useful knowledge.[4] It is the acquisition, adoption, and efficient utilization of this knowledge that has provided *decisive new sources of investment opportunities* that have maintained the growth process and have kept the returns to capital from diminishing over time. Furthermore, these additions to the stock of knowledge have been relatively more favourable in increasing the investment opportunities in the quality attributes of human agents than in the quality components of material agents of production. The investment incentives that are revealed by the inequalities in these investment opportunities, as they occur over time, are the mainspring in this process.

In an all-inclusive view of these investment opportunities, the knowledge-producing sector must be included. It is not a trivial sector in modern countries, nor is it exogenous. Research is an organized activity that requires specific, expensive, scarce resources. Although research is costly, recent studies, many of them devoted to analysing the rates of return to investment in organized agricultural research, show high rates of return.

With respect to this investment process, economists could have been spared much aimless wandering had they perceived the implications of the concept of capital as Marshall saw it. His predecessors had formulated the concept of the 'state of the productive arts', and they then proceeded to develop the core of economic theory under the assumption that these arts remained constant. It was an ingenious simplification and their theory was in general relevant to a wide array of problems of their day. But industrialization undermined this simplifying assumption, and Marshall saw it clearly and cogently. In his treatment of the agents of production, he extended the concept of labour to include work with our heads. It should be noted with care that his concept of capital:

---

4 Simon Kuznets, in his Nobel Prize lecture, which appeared in the June 1973 *American Economic Review* under the title 'Modern economic growth: findings and reflections', also attributed a major role to the additions in knowledge in this context. He argued that the last two centuries have been periods during which there has occurred 'enormous accumulation in the contribution to the stock of useful knowledge by basic and applied research' (p251).

consists in great part of knowledge and organization; and of this some part is private property and the other part is not. Knowledge is our most powerful engine of production... *Organization aids knowledge...The distinction between public and private property in knowledge and organization is of great and growing importance: in some respects of more importance than that between public and private property in material things.*[5]

In not seeing the implications of Marshall's remarkable insights, economists have wandered for years in the wilderness of capital confined to material goods.

Thus, in a nutshell, the persistent increase in the demand for the high-quality services of human agents is a function of the additions to the stock of useful knowledge.[6] The complexities of the additions to this knowledge have been much greater in recent, modern economic growth than during early, relatively simple industrialization. The rate at which the stock of useful knowledge has increased has also been higher than the rate at which it grew during the early stages of industrialization.

This approach has broad integrative power in that it provides a unifying principle for a consistent explanation of the allocation of investment resources encompassing both human and non-human capital as modernization proceeds. From it we derive important empirical implications that can be tested. It implies that the value of human time increases relative to the cost of investment resources.[7] It implies that the relative share of national income accruing to labour increases over time.[8] It implies that there is a special premium for the allocative ability of both males and females in managing firms (Welch 1970) and households, and in allocating their own time, including investments in themselves. It also implies that as the value of the time of mothers increases, fertility declines (Nerlove 1974). These implications are derived from the process, as the economy arrives at this equilibrium.

The concept of a general economic equilibrium in this context is useful, however, as an analytical guide. It is an assumed economic state towards which this modernization process tends. Given this state, there are no inequalities among investment opportunities. The high price of human time is stable in the sense that it is no longer increasing relative to other factor service prices. There is no incentive to make additional investments in human capital or in the knowledge-producing sector, as a consequence of the completion of the modernization process, and advances in knowledge no longer augment the productivity of human time within firms and households; presumably, virtually all of the value added in production is contributed by the input of human time. The basic economic constraint that determines this equilibrium is the increasing scarcity of human time for consumption. The underlying logic can be put simply: modernization

---

5 Marshall (1930), book 4, chapter 1, pp138–9; the emphasis is mine.

6 The argument in support of this summary statement appears in Schultz (1972a, 1973), chapters 1 and 2; Chapter 12 treats the 'Allocation of resources to research'.

7 A simplified approach to this implication is to treat the cost of investment resources as constant under the assumptions that the 'normal' long-term real rate of interest remains constant and that, from an increasing amount of capital embodied in human beings, people derive earnings and satisfactions commensurate with the going rate of interest.

8 As the earnings from the increasing stock of human capital rise relative to income acquired from property assets.

increases the consumption stream; consumption requires human time; advances in knowledge, whether they are embodied in material capital or in human capital, are ultimately severely limited in the extent to which they can alleviate the scarcity of human time for consumption.

REFERENCES

Kuznets, Simon (1973) 'Modern economic growth: findings and reflections', *American Economic Review* June.

Marshall, Alfred (1930) *Principles of Economics* (8th ed). Macmillan, London.

Nerlove, Marc (1974) 'Household and economy: towarda new theory of population and economic growth', *Journal of Political Economy* 82, no 2, Part II, ppS200–S218.

Schultz, Theodore W (1971) *Investment in Human Capital: The Role of Education and Research*. Free Press, New York.

– (1972a) 'The increasing economic value of human time', *American Journal of Agricultural Economics* 54, pp843–50.

– (1972b) *Human Resources*, Fiftieth Anniversary Colloquium 6th, Atlanta, 1971. National Bureau of Economic Research, New York.

– (1973) 'Explanation and interpretations of the increasing value of human time', Woody Thompson lecture to the Midwest Economics Association, Chicago, 5th April.

Welch, Finis (1970) 'Education in production', *Journal of Political Economy* 78, pp35–59.

Chapter 5

Mass Education and Fertility Decline

John C Caldwell

THE ARGUMENT

Education has its impact on fertility through at least five mechanisms:

First, it reduces the child's potential for work inside and outside the home. This occurs not merely because certain hours are subtracted from the day by school attendance and homework, but, perhaps more importantly, for two other reasons. The child is frequently alienated from those traditional chores that he feels to be at odds with his new learning and status. Parents, other adults, and even siblings may share some of these feelings and either fail to enforce traditional work or positively discourage it. Parents may feel that the child should retain all its energies for succeeding at school; they may feel that traditional familial work does not befit a person who is headed for non-traditional employment and status; they may be apprehensive of alienating the affection of a child who is so demonstrably going to be successful in the new, outside world.

Second, education increases the cost of children far beyond the fees, uniforms, and stationery demanded by the school. Schools place indirect demands on families to provide children with better clothing, better appearance (even extending to feeding), and extras that will enable the child to participate equally with other school children. But costs go beyond this. School children demand more of their parents than do their illiterate siblings fully enmeshed in the traditional family system and morality. They ask for food and other things in the house in a way that is unprecedented, and they ask for expenditures outside. Their authority is the new authority of the school, and their guides are the non-traditional ways of life that have been revealed. Parents regard the school child as a new and different type of child with greater needs, and fear alienating him. Parents are aware that such alienation has been made likelier because the educated child is less likely to need familial employment, and the new morality from the school (and from the outside world to which the school has provided an introduction and a feeling of membership) makes it less likely that he will as completely heed the teachings of family morality.

Third, schooling creates dependency, both within the family and within the society. In the absence of schooling, all members of the family are clearly producers-battlers in the family's struggle for survival. Children may get a disproportionately small share of the returns, but that is because they must have patience and wait, and they owe something for parental guidance and even for the gift of life. With schooling, it becomes clear that the society regards the child as a future rather than a present producer, and that it expects the family to protect the society's investment in the child for that future. Family relationships tend to adjust to this expectation. Reinforcing changes occur in the wider society: legislation to protect children typically accelerates in the first years of universal schooling. All these changes make children less productive and more costly both to the family and to society. These changes also mean that children no longer really share responsibility for the family's survival in the present.

Fourth, schooling speeds up cultural change and creates new cultures. In the West, values of the school were clearly middle-class values, and the schools imposed as many of these on the working class as they could. However, schools induced changes in all classes, partly because, by their nature and their very existence, their agenda was so obviously that of the broad society and its economy – its capitalist economy – and not that of family production and the morality that sustained that production.

Fifth, in the contemporary developing world, the school serves as a major instrument – probably the major instrument – for propagating the values, not of the local middle class, but of the Western middle class. Little is taught or implied that is at odds with Western middle-class values, while traditional family morality is disdained or regarded as irrelevant and as part of that other non-school, pre-school – even anti-school – world.

The first two postulates are widely accepted, partly because they can be seen to operate even without the recognition of a major restructuring of family morality. But it is probably the last three that have the most impact in changing family economies from a situation in which high fertility is worthwhile to one in which it is disastrous. Indeed, the significance of the changes in terms of altering the impact of fertility on parental prerogative may well be in ascending order as listed.

Several points about the nature of education should be made. The important engine of demographic change seems to be formal schooling rather than the widespread attainment of literacy without mass schooling, as occurred in the West prior to the mid-19th century. Furthermore, demographic change is unlikely if the movement toward mass schooling is confined largely to males, as has been the case in parts of the Middle East. The impact of education in the West was not identical with its impact in the contemporary developing world; in the former, the importation of a different culture was a far less important aspect (and so education may have taken longer to reverse the wealth flow and required greater economic change to do so). Finally, the first generation of mass schooling usually appears to be enough to initiate fertility decline. If it does not, the second generation should prove conclusive. Educated parents tend to concede that the demands of educated children are fundamentally right, even if irritating and impoverishing. Educated mothers usually see to it that their children obtain a larger share of the family pie, and justify this to their husbands or the older generation. It seems improbable – and has yet to be demonstrated – that any society can sustain stable high fertility beyond two generations of mass schooling.

[...]

THE CONTEMPORARY DEVELOPING WORLD

Mass schooling, also as the spread of an idea, has come to much of the developing world at an earlier stage, in terms of economic structure, than it did in much of the West. It has probably much greater implications for changing family relationships and declining fertility than it had in the West. In the latter, a somewhat different culture was transmitted from one part of society to another, and ultimately certain aspects of middle-class culture were intensified and taught to the whole society. In the developing world, not only is a foreign culture being imported, but this is being done at a time when that culture has moved far toward egalitarianism within the family and toward numerous adjustments to low fertility.

The two major strains in developing-world education – the objective of instilling moral values and the importation of these values from Western culture – have their origins in the earliest colonial efforts to provide such education. In early British India, views on the role of education were often very explicit. In 1792 Charles Grant wrote that education should be used 'to improve native morals' (Carnoy 1974, p96). Macaulay, in his 1835 Minute, asserted, 'We must at present do our best to form a class who may be interpreters between us and the millions whom we govern – a class of persons Indian in blood and colour, but English in tastes, in opinions, in morals and in intellect.' Marx in the same year wrote, 'England has to fulfil a double mission in India: one destructive and the other regenerating – the annihilation of old Asian society and the laying of the material foundations of Western society in Asia (Lannoy 1971, pp237–8).

In Africa there was even less doubt about promoting new moralities, for missionaries, who formed the backbone of the schooling system until the 1960s, 'had come to Africa primarily to convert and civilize the heathen and to stop the slave trade' (Carnoy 1974, p130). A more sympathetic observer of the missionaries comments, with regard to initiation and other rites de passage that were the hallmark of family morality in that they established differentiations by age and sex:

> *The age at which children went to school, the prevalence of mission boarding schools, and features of the initiation rites which were dangerous to health and objectionable on Christian moral grounds caused the missionaries to clash with this traditional training. The result was that it was largely abandoned by Christians.*

And again, more generally:

> *When the former training of children and young people in African societies is compared with the modern school systems now operating, certain features of the traditional patterns appear to have been abandoned, notably those which showed the close correlation between the training of personality and character and the integration and cohesion of family, clan and tribal units (Read 1970, pp274–5).*

Sutton explained the 'civilizing' role of education:

> *This missionary impulse made education in Western forms ancillary to religious purpose. Enough had to be taught to make Christian ideas comprehensible and to combat practices and beliefs that were regarded as barbarous or heathenish (Sutton 1965, p61).*

Ogunsheye, reporting somewhat ruefully on the schooling of his own people, the Yoruba of Nigeria, noted an 'inevitable emphasis on English traits and individuals'; the 'British put the foremost emphasis on character training' (Ogunsheye 1965, p130). Clearly, neither the character nor the traits were those found in traditional familial roles.

Musgrove (1952) reported of the school in which he taught in Uganda following World War II that it consciously taught European values and that it saw as part of this process the adoption of European clothing, food, and habits of punctuality. Giraure (1975) reported of the school at which he was a pupil during the 1960s in Papua New Guinea that a thorough-going effort was made to change his culture. He was given a new European name in the mission school and then required to speak only English while attending the government school. Ultimately, 'we looked with horror upon the village life...the children returned...having little in common with the people among whom they were to live. The result was and still is chaos...juvenile delinquency...the breakdown of village traditions and life' (Giraure 1975, pp103–4). Quotations of this kind, detailing the dismantling of the pre-existing system of family relationships, would not be so telling if any participants ever told a different tale. One might anticipate the different tale with independence, but it is not so, for new nations see prosperity being built on the foundation provided by the destruction of traditional society. In modern India, where the educated are identified by 'their dress, speech and manners', schooling 'is now intended as a prime means of innovation, rather than as the great instrument for conservation' (Mandelbaum 1970, pp414, 508). In its crudest form, this goal is stated approvingly by a Westerner:

> In Burma the object of education is not in doubt: education is to serve as one of the means of social transformation from a raw material producing society where the bulk of the people had a narrow, peasant, traditional view to a diversified, somewhat industrialized society able to absorb and use the most modern of scientific knowledge: it is to build a modern nation of responsible citizens (Nash 1970, pp301–2).

There has always been some resistance or doubt. In India in the late 18th century, Warren Hastings and others in the East India Company banned missionary education on the grounds that it was unsettling to society. In post-World War II Uganda, schoolboys remained suspicious of European motives in providing education.[1] There is, in fact, an interesting question of why the demand for the schooling of children exists, given that it destroys a family structure of which the older generation has always approved and a family economy that brought them benefits in proportion to the number of children they had. Is education seen as a means to further social justice and mobility, the stability of the political order, and national strength, as it was in the West, or are there other attractions?

The earliest attractions toward Western education were varied. One element was virtue, because education had traditionally been a training for priestly duties. This element remains a potent force in India, where the trends toward more education and toward Sanskritization can have similar roots and appearance. Another was magical power – the ability to transcribe words into marks on paper that someone else could convert back again in another place and time. In the villages of western Uganda in the 1950s, where literacy was greatly respected, the descrip-

---

1 On India, see Carnoy (1974), p89; on Uganda, Musgrove (1952), p248.

tions "reader' and 'Christian' [were] still convertible terms'.[2] In a more down-to-earth sense, Africans wanted education in order to learn and manipulate the European secret of power.[3] Jobs became increasingly important, first because they brought cash, or extra revenue, to supplement the family economy; then because individuals were deserting that economy and fending for themselves rather than for relatives; and finally because the family economy could not stand either this desertion or the competing forms of production and collapsed.[4] Pride in children's achievements can also play a significant role (Fakhouri 1972, p100), although in India a father with an unmarriable educated daughter 'may be accused of sacrificing his daughter's chances in life to a mistaken whim intended to glorify his own name' (Mandelbaum 1970, pp108–9). On the other hand, in South Asia and even in South-west Asia, there is a growing awareness that only an educated daughter can secure that desirable addition to the family – an educated son-in-law with a job in the modern sector – and that a large dowry on its own may no longer be sufficient. In South Asia even a rural family often feels the need for one educated son simply to cope with the bureaucrats.[5]

The present position of education is complex and uncertain. While traditional family morality persists and the wealth flow is from the younger to the older generation, an while the educated are paid far more or have far greater access to power than the uneducated, the temptation for parents to educate their children and so obtain access to the wealth of the economy's modern sector can be immense. Yet the same education may clearly destroy the moral system that alone can guarantee the older generation large and continuing returns. It does not necessarily do so in one generation in the absence of universal education. The traditional morality can show surprising resilience, as among the Yoruba (Caldwell 1976a, 1976b, 1977), and the education of children can bring parents high rewards and can buttress high fertility.

How education can endanger the traditional system is clear enough even from the syllabuses and textbooks, and has been shown vividly by a study of infant and primary school textbooks in Ghana, Nigeria, and Kenya (Caldwell and Caldwell 1980). These books are important because they are used in schools attended by a much larger proportion of the community than are secondary schools. They are important also because they are first read when the children are young and impressionable, and when they most uncritically accept the teacher and school as new authority figures and often as superior ones with regard to knowledge about the modern world that many of the pupils will increasingly aspire to join. The messages are all the more potent because they are most often found in reading primers, where the substance or attitudes are taken for truth, rather than in specialized books on society, which might be expected to point to some areas of controversy or doubt.

In the books that we studied, we found no support for such basic African traditional institutions as polygyny, unstable marriage, the condemnation of sterile women or women who repeatedly lose children, bewitchment, and, most

---

2 On India, see Mandelbaum (1970), pp500–20. On education as magical power, see Yates (1971), pp161–7, on the Congo Free State and the Belgian Congo; and Deng (1972), pp153–4, on the Dinka of south-western Sudan. On Uganda, see Musgrove (1952), p244.
3 Sutton (1965), p62.
4 Yates (1971), pp161–7.
5 Mandelbaum (1970), pp109 and 247.

importantly, the attitude that the needs of the family have priority over those of the community.

There was in Kenya alone, in a new series of tales from a traditional viewpoint,[6] some support (at least in stories of the past) for bride price, arranged marriage, initiation, and violence in tribal warfare. However, concessions are made to the traditional family authority structure and to the age-old upward direction of the wealth flow. Where arranged marriage and bride price exist, they merely confirm a love match already in existence – rather like the expression of parental approval of an engagement. And where a tribal conflict is plotted and carried out, it is the young man who does it while leaving his father in ignorance rather than disobeying him (Mbugua 1971). Initiation is handled by laying stress almost solely on the joy of attaining manhood.

The school reading books generally assume that children are dependents; that the husband must farm (or work in an office) while his wife undertakes the domestic work and the children give first place to their schoolwork; that priority should be given to nation-building, citizenship, and honesty in the larger society; that children should do jobs at home to be 'good' rather than as an enforceable duty to the family; that fathers are kindly and understanding rather than distant and awesome; and that parents are closer to children, and that husbands are usually closer to wives, than they are to other relatives. Children are portrayed at play; nuclear families are portrayed eating together. Drumming and traditional dance, if covered, are divorced from traditional religious rites. Extended family residence, when mentioned, coexists with nuclearization.[7] An East African first reader unintentionally brings out the magnitude of the changes with its portrayal of a family in a traditional setting behaving like members of the Western middle class; children with toys, father entertaining his young daughter, mother dapper in a clean dress (*New Link Reader* 1973, p64). The chief thrust of school-books in independent countries is exemplified by the introductory 'Note to the Teacher' in a widely used Ghanaian series:

> The chief aim in teaching citizenship education is to help young people become well-informed, hard-working, selfless, honest and responsible citizens. With citizens such as these, a nation will be sufficiently equipped to achieve success and moral prosperity (Mensah 1975).

These messages – often presented as African traditions – are remote from the family morality and lifestyle still practised by the great majority of citizens. Yet the textbooks never give any indication that this is so: African names are used for persons, objects, and ceremonies; the illustrations show African huts, animals, and bush. But the message is contemporary Western and, if fully acted out, would certainly mean that high fertility would prove economically oppressive and that family size would eventually decline.[8]

---

6 The original impetus came from sessions for secondary school children written by Kenyan playwrights at the request of Radio Kenya. Other works of this type are published by Longman.

7 As a Nigerian textbook about a Yoruba family puts it: 'My grandparents live in the compound with us but in a separate house. Their house is where the elders in our village meet from time to time' (Olayomi 1970).

8 The message is the same among the Indians of rural Peru, where 'the curriculum was oriented to life in an urban metropolis, which had little meaning to the Indian child other than, perhaps, to alienate him from an agrarian existence ... the impact the school has had seems to be in the direction of creating a hiatus between the values of the Indian child and his parents' (Epstein 1971, pp192–3).

It should be noted that syllabuses with Western messages were not merely imposed by colonialist. There has always been a strong local demand for colonial educational systems and for syllabuses identical with those in the metropolitan centres; it is partly a question of not accepting the second-best and partly one of students gaining unchallenged access to further education in the metropolises. Newly independent nations felt competitive pressures for closely paralleling the West in the nature and message of schools, and their efforts were strongly supported by international organizations. Carnoy claims, 'In the nonindustrialized country, the school is an institution that not only keeps the individual from self-definition, but keeps the entire society from defining itself. The schools are an extension of the metropole structure.[9] That definition will in fact never hold, for schools are mechanisms for creating a Westernized global society. They do this largely unwittingly, for most educationalists take learning to be virtue, and do not distinguish the various brands of virtue. In any case, really new workable institutions are extremely difficult to create. The West has an educational model that will inevitably be used, partly because it exists and is widely known; partly because it produces usable textbooks or textbook prototypes, syllabuses, teachers and organizational models; and partly because it is associated with successful economic development.

THE IMPACT OF SCHOOLING ON THE DEVELOPING-WORLD FAMILY SYSTEM

The main message of the school is not spelled out in textbooks. It is assumed by teachers, pupils, and even parents. They all know that school attendance means acceptance of a way of life at variance with the strictly traditional. Many schoolchildren no longer realize just how great that variance is or just what strictly traditional behaviour is.

Masemann (1974) reported that the hidden syllabus in the Ghanaian girls' school where she taught was the Western way of life, and said of the typical pupil:

> *She learns how to play marital, parental and occupational roles through experiencing many aspects of school life that are never made explicit in a formal curriculum... When the students write about the kind of life they expect to lead after marriage, they mention co-operation between husband and wife in financial matters, solidarity of the married couple in conflict with kin, shared responsibility for children... They feel ... competent to 'live a modern life' and they have every intention of doing so.'[10]*

Several points should be noted. First, if they achieve the degree of solidarity and co-operation within marriage that they anticipate, and if they focus this on their children to the relative exclusion of their kin, then the upward wealth flow to their

---

9 Compare Carnoy (1974), p72.
10 Masemann continued: 'She is also expected to bring up her children with scheduled meal-times and bed-times, quite unlike the more relaxed demand-feeding and sleeping times of the more uneducated mothers. This attitude to schedule is part of the constellation of values attached to a modern industrial society, and students are expected to be socialized into valuing time as a commodity which can be wasted or put to good use and which can be turned into money' (1974; quotations are from pp483, 486, and 494).

own parents will be greatly diminished, and the net flow over a lifetime almost certainly reversed. Second, although it is not discussed by Masemann, these students may already be making ever-stronger demands for financial support from their parents (and possibly other kin) over the strict minimum needed to keep them at school Third, these changes in family emotional and economic relationships have not been economically determined; the economic effects – profound ones for the society and its fertility – have been purely the result of attitudinal changes arising from the intentional and unintentional Westernizing impact of their schooling.

Most developing-world societies are very much aware that schooling leads to profound social change. At early stages this is usually anticipated with apprehension.[11] Although tempted by the money and influence following in the wake of education, traditional families often remained justifiably apprehensive of schooling, especially for girls. In the Congo Free State during the late 19th century, 'local people objected strenuously to sending children to the mission station because they "came back changed"'. Among the Dinka of the Sudan, over half a century later, 'girls' education was especially abhorred because that implied turning them into town-women, immoral and unsuited for marriage'.[12] The Dinka are not Muslim in religion, but their views are still echoed over much of the Islamic world and beyond it into village India.

There is widespread agreement that schooling at advanced levels is first and foremost a process of Westernization. Tilman (1976) wrote of the Malay College in Kuala Kangsar, Malaysia, that 'by the time of graduation, its students had been thoroughly socialized into an upper-class English cultural environment', while Kirk-Greene (1965) reported much the same for the highly educated Hausa élite of northern Nigeria, and Sutton (1965) more generally for those receiving higher education in Africa. However, the same process, although less extreme, occurs from the first days at school; the Wisers observed the effects of vestigial elementary schooling in a small village on India's Gangetic Plain 50 years ago: 'The boys who know nothing beyond village routine are content. Those who have gone to school are restless. They have disassociated learning from the work their fathers have to offer them.' They also reported a landowner chasing an Untouchable boy, obligated to do him services under the jajmani system, away from their classes, not because the boy had anything else to do at that time of night, but because the jajman was well aware of the alien influences transmitted by schooling and the likelihood that new attitudes would begin to change ancient lines of authority and obligation (Wiser and Wiser 1971, pp42, 98). In Latin America, the Westernizing influence of schooling is likely to make Indian students adopt as models the lifestyles of the mestizos or ladinos. This was the major conclusion of Epstein's

---

11 However, Margaret Mead (1956) presented a different picture of the situation on Manus Island half a century ago: 'When people did not understand, when the old women shrieked at each other in the style of long ago, when middle-aged men beat their wives, when there was a poor attendance at church, when discussion in meetings was rambling and petty, the enthusiasts for the New Way would comfort themselves and each other, saying, "When the schoolboys grow up it will be different These others, they grew up in the old bad ways It is not their fault that they fly into rages, they do not know how to speak in a meeting or how to treat their wives and children But when the children grow up it will be different"' (pp421–2). The rages had, of course, been a method whereby the aged retained their ancient authority; the beatings of wives and children ensured patriarchal rights; but the family as the main organizational unit could be said to be waning when it was more important to exert influence in meetings or to attend church.

12 On the Congo, see Yates (1971), p170; on the Dinka, see Deng (1972), p153.

research in rural Peru and of Redfield's in rural Guatemala. The latter, reviewing a long period of contact with the same village, wrote:

> *As I look at the school in the little village where I once was resident, it appears to me to play a greater part in changing the culture of the people than in handing it on from one generation to the next, although its influence in the direction of change is indirect.*[13]

In one sense, the attack on family morality begins with, or is paralleled by, an attack on the theology that supports and justifies it. This is obvious and widely felt in Muslim societies. An imam in southern Thailand explained that 'education made a man unreligious; literacy enables a man to disobey God. Civilization is antireligious' (Fraser 1966, p84). 'Civilization' in this sense is Westernization, culturally as well as theologically. This is less obvious in the case of more ancient religions, although these are more intimately connected with ancestral spirits and the morality of gerontratic control. Greenfield and Bruner (1966, p84) found that illiterate children in West Africa, like their ancestors, explained a wider range of phenomena in 'magical' terms – as being ordained by persons other than those present at the experiment. However, 'the school suppresses this mode of thinking with astonishing absoluteness. There is not one instance of such reasoning among either bush or city Senegalese children who have been in school seven months or longer.'

Schools destroy the corporate identity of the family, especially for those members previously most submissive and most wholly contained by the family: children and women. In Mexico,

> *Going to school has in addition awakened new desires in children by removing them from the limited sphere of parental influence. They are no longer content to stay within patio walls at the beck and call of their mother; they urgently want to be with friends and to play after school. Play always has been, and still is, considered a possible source of danger and a waste of time by parents (Lewis 1960, p76).*

These problems are widespread in the developing world, with concern over the danger to the family system outweighing concern over the specific loss of time. Playing is but a symptom of a greater assault on the family's corporate identity. Literate culture often lays stress on behavioural patterns inimical to the family system, such as in its encouragement of differentiation and solitariness, whereas the oral tradition does not.[14] Indeed, in West Africa the main limitation on the extension of rural housing seems to be not lack of labour or capital, but the lack of demand in non-literate households for space peripheral to the centre of family activities. In India, too, education, especially when it is extended, can provide an

> *initial psychological impetus: a sense of individuality with a desire for greater independence...[However,] the initiative for leaving the joint family often comes from the wife, whereas psychological conditioning sometimes prevents the husband from himself contemplating such a move (Lannoy 1971, p125).*

The wife (the daughter-in-law in the joint family) has, of course, much more to gain by such a move, and may attempt it less because she has acquired a feeling of individuality than because she has received from education a new cultural

---

13 Epstein (1971), pp193–8; Redfield (1970), pp287–300; the quotation is from p289.
14 Compare Goody and Watt (1963), pp336–337.

backing and a new cultural status that justifies her break with family tradition both in her own eyes and in those of her relatives-in-law. Education in India may place a man at a distance not only from his family but also from its alliances and the factions to which it adheres, thus eroding another of the values of high fertility (Caldwell 1981; Mandelbaum 1970, p247).

Schooling means revolt against non-Western family relationships, although research has tended to concentrate much more on the erosion of agreement on the wife's role than on that of the child – perhaps partly because the latter is taken so much for granted. Omari (1960, pp203–5, 208), surveying secondary school pupils in Ghana over 20 years ago, found that 1 per cent of girls desired a traditional marriage, while 86 per cent 'thought polygamy definitely backward' and 94 per cent believed 'love in marriage most important'. Only 45 per cent were certain that they would obey their parents' arrangements for marriage. 'With increase in education the women fail to see the need for sharing a husband with another – apart from the fact that the thought runs anomalous to the Western ideas they have imbibed at school and abroad.' The strongest reaction against the education of girls in the Congo Free State and the Belgian Congo arose from the fear that girls who had been to school would revolt against arranged marriage and marriage to polygamists (Yates 1971, pp168–9). The Christian church everywhere has battled polygyny, making it clear in Africa, when protesters pointed to the fact that the Old Testament recorded the institution without condemning it, that modern Christian morality means Western morality. In India there is the 'fear that [a woman] will not make a proper, dutiful wife because of her schooling' (Mandelbaum 1970, p108). This paper has concentrated on the direct impact of schooling on child-parent emotional economic relationships whether or not husband-wife relationships have changed. Nevertheless, in the most traditional families the position of the wife of the younger generation – that is, the mother of non-adult children – is not very different from that of the children; a change in her role is almost certain to effect a change in theirs (although the fact that children have been to school usually does not affect the role of an illiterate mother).

Fundamentally, the school attacks the traditional family's economic structure by weakening the authority of the old over the young (and of the male over the female). In Africa, where the mission and the school were for long almost indistinguishable, Yates said of the Congo that, 'of course, missionary dominance meant a decrease of African political authority' and quoted the Prefect Apostolic as reported in 1905: 'They [the Chiefs] sense as if by instinct that if we are successful it will mark the end of their despotic domination...they do not want us to speak of God, of Christ and especially of monogamy.' Clignet argues that this was inevitable because of the extent to which, both in the West and in the developing world, schools have been expected to act *in loco parentis*. Schools attacked parental authority partly by providing new authority models from the West or from Westernized local people who seemed to epitomize the cultural patterns taught or implied. Indeed, the models, by their behaviours, provided much of the implicit teaching. In Burma, 'The teacher is the repository of knowledge... They would never challenge [him]'; in Masemann's school in Ghana, the teacher was the role model; throughout Africa when schools first appeared, 'the newly educated looked to Europeans... for advancement and for models of behaviour'.[15] The real

15 Yates (1971), p170, quoting Prefect Apostolic Leon Derikx at Gumbari, 30 July 1905, reported in *Mouvement des Missions Catholiques au Congo*, March 1906, p83; Remi Clignet (1975), p89. On Burma, see Nash (1970), p307. On Africa, Masemann (1974), pp492–3, and Sutton (1965), p66.

position is more complex even than this, for a major stabilizing force in traditional society has been the superior wisdom of the old, both occult and from long experience. The school provides the young with knowledge and skills that the old do not possess, while usually also attacking the value of traditional knowledge. This alone, during the attainment of mass schooling in the 19th-century West and the contemporary developing world, weakens family authority.

A SYNTHESIS

In spite of much sophisticated analysis of 'the global economy', we have hardly begun to discuss the parallel and related creation of a 'global society'. The movement toward a global economy makes the movement toward a global society inevitable, but such social movements as the spread of mass schooling can greatly accelerate economic change at every level from the family to the nation. With these changes will come demographic change.

The major change of demographic significance – and perhaps the most significant economic and social change – has been that from family production to capitalist production within a labour market external to the family. In the system of family production, high fertility was no disadvantage, whereas low fertility could be destructive. Family production was controlled by family morality, which gave power to the old and usually to the male, and which frequently sharply differentiated production and consumption roles by age and sex. Family morality formed the greater part of the culture (or superstructure) and often had strong religious underpinnings. The advantages that powerful family members obtained from high fertility did not pass quickly as capitalist production grew, partly because the age-old morality ensured them of more than an equal fraction of consumption and partly because family production of domestic goods and services by wives and children has waned slowly even in the most industrialized societies. Thus high fertility may continue in spite of a major decline in non-domestic family production, as long as family morality does not decay – in other words, as long as the wealth flow continues from the younger to the older generation. Family morality could hardly have decayed anywhere if family production had remained the dominant form of production worldwide. But once it began to lose its dominant position, as in the West, the new societal or capitalistic morality could develop and could be exported. It is quite possible that such a morality can be at least partly grafted on to a society with a high level of family production and that it can be an element in a premature (by the precedents of Western history) fertility decline.

There have long been threats to family morality, quite apart from the development of capitalist production. These include any form of religion that is not family-centred (and even ancestral) and any form of law that is external to the family – anything, in fact, that belongs to the Great Tradition rather than the Little Tradition.[16] The least dangerous type of religion is one that enshrines the family as

16 The Great Tradition is comprised of the religious and cultural values found throughout the society and handed down as the common possession of the culture. The Great Tradition is known to the more educated or urbanized and is the tradition found generally in literature. The Little Tradition is confined to populations outside the central tradition—above all the villagers—is concerned with local gods and beliefs, and varies greatly from place to place. Robert Redfield and colleagues of the Chicago anthropology school originally applied the term to Latin America, but it is now widely used in the analysis of Indian society and is even more generally used as an analytical tool for all traditional societies.

a necessary unit, such as Hinduism, and especially one that enshrines the sex and age segmentation of family production and addresses itself chiefly to the patriarch, as in Islam. But even these religions can become more interested in the individual, as did Buddhism in splintering from Hinduism. The greatest danger developed in the West: Judaism addressed itself to the individual as well as the family; Catholicism did not only that but did so from a huge extra-familial, institutionalized base; Protestantism appealed almost solely to the individual (and could hardly have developed if there had not been sufficient capitalist production to have modified family morality). Any type of state organization and authority – certainly the raising of troops – offered potential danger to the uniqueness and unity of the family. This was particularly so with regard to the law, especially in the case of both the Roman law of the Republic and Empire, and English common law.

The school has a very complex relation with these Great Traditions. It is another of the extra-family institutions. But much of its impact on the family lies in the fact that it serves as a medium for these other institutions – for religion, state morality, state legal tradition, and national cultural and historical traditions. In most developing-world villages, the usual way that the first generation of schoolchildren explain the impact of education is that it makes them part of a much larger world – often they just say 'of the world'. Governments have always been in competition with the family for loyalty; governments that were unable to maintain a share of this loyalty ceased to function. This is particularly true in the developing world. The survival of governments depends on competition with families, and, as is clear from our analysis of school textbooks, governments regard schools as their chief instruments for teaching citizenship – for going over the heads of the patriarchs and appealing directly to the children. In doing so, they inevitably emphasize the importance of the new generation and so strike yet another blow at family morality and family economics.

Nevertheless, family morality can prove remarkably resistant to change. The history of the West proves that: fertility did not fall in Britain until it was an advanced industrialized economy with only 17 per cent of its population working in primary production and contributing less than 10 per cent of gross national income, and with 25 per cent of its population living in centres with more than 100,000 inhabitants. However, that pattern is unlikely to repeat itself; the existence of the Western model and its spread – even when inadvertent – by national educational systems will see to that. The only exception may be the Muslim countries, where religion supports family role segmentation and where, in many cases, levels of female education are likely to remain low. The tropical African family system has so far also proved resilient, and wealth flows have continued upward, even in the middle class, because of a strong cultural emphasis on what the young owe to the old (partly perhaps because respect for ancestors is still prevalent).[17] In fact the traditional family expects to remain intact, and so eventually overreaches itself. It has always taken risks and has always attempted to maximize its income and resources. Hence, when an outside labour market develops, children are encouraged to earn income and bring it into the household. They are even sent to school to ensure that they can eventually earn higher incomes. Some traditional families have used their younger people to earn outside incomes for millennia (in the Middle

---

17 Caldwell (1976a, 1976b, and 1977); Caldwell and Caldwell (1978). Of Yoruba women of completed fertility interviewed in Ibadan in 1973 and 1974–75, only 1 4 per cent deliberately had 'small' families of five or fewer live births.

East and the Mediterranean) while retaining control of them and their income and spending relatively little on them. This situation may disappear everywhere within the next half-century; if it does pass as quickly as this, mass schooling rather than mass industrialization will have been responsible.

The family system of morality and production has been little described and has begun to pass without even the circumstances of its passing being noted, precisely because it was so all-embracing. It was not a morality; it was the morality, and hence commonsensical and unremarkable. When it does pass, within a generation or two the old morality is remembered with nostalgia; the respect for the old is remembered as childhood humility, not as the rigid system that it was. The first generation of schoolchildren who emerged from it were usually treated differently from the way earlier generations had been treated. Because of their schooling, many expected the kind of treatment they received without realizing this was an innovation, while their parents and grandparents moved, often awkwardly, to accept and engineer this new status without realizing just how irrevocable the step was. To the researcher and to some of the teachers and other citizens, this transition was visible in the towns of Ghana 20 years ago, when many families were composed of a mixture of children who went to school and those, often somewhat older, who had not been and would never go (Caldwell 1968). Most parents treated school children quite differently from the way they treated their illiterate siblings, and few of the schoolchildren seemed in any way aware of this. In later life, even as social scientists, they will probably be unable to recall the transition.[18]

One can generalize further. Those who have participated in the affairs of state or the church have always been at least partly outside the confines of the system of family production, and they have had to modify its morality. This is also true of soldiers, scholars, migrants, large merchants, and anyone who employs others. Almost by definition, those who have interpreted, written, read, and challenged historical records have long been members of these numerically marginal groups. As family production and its determining morality passes, the very memories of it pass. Later generations, who live outside the system, do not regard those who were involved in family production as having been in the mainstream of history.

This brings us to an important point in the analysis of the change in relative child–adult status (and also wife–husband status) effected by education. The magnitude of the change is so great because it rests not only on what the school teaches, but also on how the educated child sees himself (especially relative to uneducated parents or siblings) and how his other relatives (especially uneducated parents or siblings) see him. These different perspectives are crucial elements in permanently changing relative inter-generational status. They are, for instance, the greatest factors in altering the relationship between an educated daughter-in-law and an uneducated mother-in-law to a point where the former can intervene individually to care for her children and to change the traditional balance of consumption and treatment within the family, with dramatic effects on child mortality (Caldwell 1979).

---

18 Of school-age children in Western Nigeria in 1973, 28 per cent of those who did not go to school were taken to a doctor when sick, compared with 55 per cent of schoolchildren. (Changing African Family Project, Survey 2).

REFERENCES

Caldwell, John C (1968) *Population Growth and Family Change in Africa: The New Urban Elite in Ghana,* Canberra: Australian National University Press.

– (1976a) 'Toward a restatement of demographic transition theory', *Population and Development Review* 2, nos 3/4, pp322–366.

– (1976b) 'Fertility and the household economy in Nigeria', *Journal of Comparative Family Studies* 7, no 2, pp193–253.

– (1977) 'The economic rationality of high fertility: an investigation illustrated with Nigerian survey data', *Population Studies* 31, no 1, pp5–27.

– (1979) 'Education as a factor in mortality decline: An examination of Nigerian data', *Population Studies* 33, no 3, pp395–413.

– (1980) 'The mechanisms of demographic change in historical perspective', *Population Studies* 34, no 3, pp5–27.

– and Pat Caldwell (1978) 'The achieved small family: Early fertility transition in an African city', *Studies in Family Planning* 9, no 1, pp1–18.

– (1980) 'The partially hidden syllabus in infant and primary school textbooks in Ghana, Nigeria and Kenya: the family message' (unpublished paper).

Carnoy, Martin (1974) *Education as Cultural Imperialism,* New York: Longman.

Clignet, Remi (1975) 'The liberalizing and equalizing functions of schools: An overview', *Comparative Education Review* 19 no 1.

Deng, Francis Mading (1972) *The Dinka of the Sudan,* New York: Holt, Rinehart & Winston.

Epstein, Erwin H (1971) 'Education and Peruanidad: 'internal' colonialism in the Peruvian Highlands', *Comparative Education Review* 15, no 2.

Fakhouri, Hani (1972) *Kafr El-Elow: An Egyptian Village in Transition,* New York: Holt, Rinehart & Winston.

Fraser, Thomas M (1966) *Fishermen of South Thailand: The Malay Villagers,* New York: Holt, Rinehart and Winston.

Giraure, Nelson (1975) 'The need for a cultural programme: Personal reflections', in *Education in Melanesia,* ed J Brammal and Ronald J May, Canberra: Research School of Pacific Studies, Australian National University; Port Moresby: University of Papua New Guinea 1975.

Goody, Jack and Ian Watt (1963) 'The consequences of literacy', *Comparative Studies in Society and History* 5, pp336–337.

Greenfield, Patricia Marks and Jerome S Bruner (1966) 'Culture and cognitive growth', *International Journal of Psychology* 1, no 2.

Kirk-Greene, Anthony H M 'Bureaucratic cadres in a traditional milieu', in *Education and Political Development,* ed James S Coleman, Princeton: Princeton University Press.

Lannoy, Richard (1971) *The Speaking Tree: A Study of Indian Culture and Society,* Oxford: Oxford University Press.

Lewis, Oscar (1960) *Tepoztlán: Village in Mexico,* New York: Holt, Rinehart & Winston.

Mandelbaum, David G (1970) *Society in India,* Berkeley: University of California Press.

Masemann, Vandra (1974) 'The 'hidden curriculum of a West African girls' boarding school', *Canadian Journal of African Studies* 8, no 3, pp479–494.

Mbugua, J N (1971) *Mumbi's Brideprice,* Nairobi: Longman Kenya.

Mead, Margaret (1956) *New Lives for Old; Cultural Transformation-Manus, 1928–1953,* New York: William Morrow.

Mensah, Isaac Dankyi (1975) 'Note to the teacher', in *Citizen Education for Schools,* Books 1–6 Accra: Afram Publications.

Musgrove, F (1952) 'A Uganda secondary school as a field of culture change', *Africa* 22, no 3, pp234–249

Nash, Manning (1970) 'Education in a new nation: The village school in Upper Burma', in *From Child to Adult*, ed John Middleton, New York: The Natural History Press (Studies in the Anthropology of Education, American Museum Sourcebooks in Anthropology).

New Link Reader; The New Peak Reading Course (1973) Nairobi: Oxford University Press, East African Branch (9th reprint; first published 1963).

Ogunsheye, Ayo (1965) 'Nigeria', in *Education and Political Development*, ed James S Coleman, Princeton: Princeton University Press.

Olayomi, J A (1970) 'My family', in *Civics and Social Studies for Young Nigerians* London: Collins, 1970.

Omari, T Peter (1960) 'Changing attitudes of students in West African society toward marriage and family relationships', *British Journal of Sociology* 11, no 3.

Read, Margaret (1970) 'Education in Africa: its pattern and role in social change', in *From Child to Adult*, ed John Middleton, New York: The Natural History Press (Studies in the Anthropology of Education, American Museum Sourcebooks in Anthropology).

Redfield, Robert (1970) 'Culture and education in the midwestern highlands of Guatemala', in *From Child to Adult*, ed John Middleton, New York: The Natural History Press (Studies in the Anthropology of Education, American Museum Sourcebooks in Anthropology).

Sutton, Francis X (1965) 'Education and the making of modern nations', in *Education and Political Development*, ed James S Coleman, Princeton: Princeton University Press.

Tilman, Robert O (1967) 'Education and political development in Malaysia', in *Education and Development in Southeast Asia*; L'Institute de Sociologie Symposium, Brussels, April 1966 Brussels: Collection du Centre D'Etude du Sud-East Asiatique, Université Libré de Bruxelles.

Wiser, William H and Charlotte Viall Wiser (1971) *Behind Mud Walls, 1930–1960; with a sequel: The Village in 1970,* Berkeley: University of California Press.

Yates, Barbara A (1971) 'African reactions to education: the Congolese case', *Comparative Education Review* 15, no 2, pp161–167.

Chapter 6

Population Pressures and Development

Albert O Hirschman

Few topics in the theory of economic development have evoked such unanimity as population growth. With increases in per capita income widely accepted as the objective of development or as the best available approximation to it, population is firmly relegated to the denominator of the expression which we want to maximize and any increase in numbers can only be considered a setback on the road to development. Such expressions as the population growth that 'swallows up' increases in output in whole or in part, such images as walking up a downward moving escalator (Singer 1949), and the virtually obligatory quotation from Lewis Carroll: 'Here it takes all the running you can do, to keep in the same place' – all testify to the universal assumption that the exclusive effect of population growth is to frustrate economic development. Some writers are of course aware of the fact that demographic stagnation or declining population growth were high on the list among the explanations for the falling behind of France as a major political and economic power, and were one of the three pillars of the stagnation thesis in the United States. But any disturbing ideas on that account could be quickly discarded by the reassuring, if somewhat shapeless, thought that the problems of developed and underdeveloped countries are entirely distinct.

In the face of such unanimity, we shall present with considerable reluctance some reasons which make us think that population pressures are to be considered forces that may stimulate development. We are fully aware that this is a dangerous thought – dangerous not so much for the world at large as for the reputation of the author; and in order not to expose ourselves too long to the heavy fire which will certainly be opened on us, we shall dispose of what we have to say with the utmost brevity.

Let us start out by invoking Duesenberry's (1949, p84) 'fundamental psychological postulate', which says that people will resist a lowering in their standard of living. If they do this as a result of cyclical depression why should they not also react in some way against their incomes being squeezed by an increase in population? Our first proposition is therefore that *population pressure on living standards will lead to counterpressure, that is, to activity designed to maintain or restore the traditional standard of living of the community.* Leaving the validity of this proposition for later consideration we shall assume for the moment that this counterpressure is partially or wholly successful in restoring per capita incomes. Thus far, then, the psychological postulate yields at best a mechanism of equilibrium – that is, of stagnation rather than development.

But the situation is not really the same after this process, for in its course the community has learned, through wrestling successfully with new tasks. Our second proposition is therefore that *the activity undertaken by the community in resisting a decline in its standard of living causes an increase in its ability to control its environment and to organize itself for development.* As a result, the community will now be able to exploit the opportunities for economic growth that existed previously but were left unutilized.

In short, the learning a community does when it reacts to population pressures increases the total stock of its resources much as investment adds to total productive capacity. To revert to the images mentioned earlier: walking up downward escalators or running in the same place is excellent exercise and practice for people who need to improve their walking or running performance. Anyone who has watched attempts by public and private bodies to cope with the traffic, water supply, electric power, housing, school, and crime problems of a growing city can have little doubt that the qualities of imagination and organization developed in these tasks of *maintaining* standards of living in the face of population pressures are very similar to those that are needed to *increase* per capita incomes. The basic determinant of development which we have called the 'ability to invest' is decisively enhanced in the course of the struggle to accommodate more people.

Returning to our first proposition, we cannot claim that it is more than a variant of an old idea. Many writers, Malthus among them, have remarked on the incentive effects of the need to provide for one's wife and children. Others have examined the stimulating effect of population increases, not on the individual's 'natural indolence', but on society's. In this respect, much that is incisive has been said, in particular by the Belgian sociologist and philosopher Dupréel who has traced the many ways in which an increasing population leads to improved performance of the administrative, political, and cultural processes (Dupréel 1928). But while these direct positive influences and actions of population growth on individual motivations and economic and political developments are of interest, we think it more useful to stress the *reaction* mechanism that is set up when population growth depresses, or is about to depress, living standards, for the recognition of this reaction mechanism permits us to go beyond the following, somewhat unsatisfactory summary of the problem by Schumpeter (1947, p149):

> *Sometimes an increase in population actually has no other effects than that predicted by classical theory - a fall in per capita real income; but at other times it may have an energizing effect that induces new developments with the result that per capita income rises.*

By viewing the 'energizing' effect as potentially induced by the 'classical' effect, we can at least attempt to reduce the complete indeterminateness of this statement.

Our affirmation that a society will attempt to react to the 'dilution' of total income that comes with larger numbers is of interest only if the reaction can be successful - that is, if there is some 'slack' in the economy that can be taken up. This assumption is of course contrary to the basic hypothesis of the neo-Malthusian models - namely, 'all productive forces are fully utilized - ie, there are no unemployed resources - the supply of land and capital is fixed' (Peacock 1952-53, p115). This formulation is not even sufficiently strong if we wish to stipulate that it is impossible to squeeze more output from the available resources without a prior increase in per capita incomes out of which new savings can be extracted. We must then also suppose that production is *optimally* organized, that all existing technological and organizational knowledge that does not require capital outlays is fully applied. Obviously, even in densely populated underdeveloped areas, such a situation will be exceedingly rare.[1]

The panorama changes abruptly if it is granted that a margin of possible improvements exists, and if, more generally, we revert to our diagnosis of underdevelopment as a state where labour, capital, entrepreneurship, etc. are potentially available and can be combined, provided a sufficiently strong 'binding agent' is encountered. Then an increase in incomes is by no means the only way of starting the economy on an upward course. Nevertheless, there is some question whether population pressure can be considered an 'inducement mechanism' in the sense in which we have used this term. How will it cause the possible improvements to be made? How will it call forth the latent resources of the economy?

Among the inducement mechanisms we have studied, from the various complementarity effects on down, population pressure must rank as the least attractive one. In the first place, it works through an initial decline in per capita income rather than through, for example, an uneven expansion in output. Secondly, it is less reliable than the other mechanisms we have considered. In our previous, vaguely similar mechanism – that is, losses in foreign exchange income leading to industrialization, we could point to several solid links in the reaction chain: specific, now unsatisfied, needs; 'forced savings' of a kind; the interest of the heretofore importers or foreign suppliers, etc.[2]

In the case of population pressures, on the other hand, we are provided only with an aspiration to return to the status quo ante, but generally not with specific means or intermediate reaction links for doing so. Nevertheless, in some of the following situations, the passage from aspiration to reality becomes plausible or is more readily visualized than in others:

1. The probability of a strong reaction is greater if the population increase comes as a sudden shock. A community may not feel impelled to 'make a stand' when population increases and declines in living standards are slow, just as workers will sometimes experience greater difficulty in maintaining their real wages in the face of creeping inflation than when prices rise a good 20 per cent a year. For this reason, the dramatic decline in mortality rates and the consequent massive increase in numbers that is taking place today in underdeveloped areas holds greater promise of a vigorous reaction than the far slower increases of previous epochs.
2. A population increase is likely to be more action-stimulating if it is combined with increased urbanization and therefore leads to obvious needs and

---

1 Malthus can be quoted in support of this view: 'There are few large countries, however advanced in improvement, the population of which might not have been doubled or tripled, and there are many which might be ten or even a hundred times as populous, and yet all the inhabitants be as well provided for as they are now, if the institutions of society and the moral habits of the people, had been for some hundred years the most favourable to the increase of capital, and the demand for produce and labour.' (Malthus, 1830, reprinted in Glass, 1953, pp151–2).
2 Note that this mechanism is in turn less reliable than the one utilized in Duesenberry's construction. In the case of a sudden absence of a desired good because of balance-of-payments difficulties, consumers cannot protect their previous standard of living just by saving less as Duesenberry's consumers are wont to do in a depression.

pressures for more overhead facilities, such as housing, schools, and public utilities.

3. Again, the reaction may be facilitated if population growth takes place in underdeveloped countries which as a result of the increase in numbers pass minimum production thresholds in a number of important industries, as compared to more populous countries where these thresholds have long been passed or to much smaller countries where they remain far away.

4. The reaction may be easier to accomplish if the increase affects primarily the upper classes of society, or at least the upper classes along with the lower classes, for the need to provide for one's children is in this case more likely to take the form of increased entrepreneurial activity.

5. Finally, the closer a country actually is to the rigid assumptions of the neo-Malthusian models which we mentioned above, that is, the more fully and perfectly its resources are already utilized, the less room there is for any reactions outside of the most direct ones – namely, birth control and postponement of marriage. Precisely because of the assumption of fixed resources, this reaction to population pressures has virtually monopolized the attention of demographers. From our point of view, the 'preventive checks' are only one of the many forms which the reaction mechanism can take. Under present conditions, in fact, it is in many countries more difficult to visualize population pressures resulting in effective birth control measures than in improvements of agricultural techniques and in stepped-up capital formation in industry and public utilities. In any event, our second proposition applies here also, even though perhaps somewhat indirectly: for a people that is induced to exercise foresight to the point of adopting effective birth control techniques is again learning that one's environment can be controlled and changed and will therefore be better equipped for coping with the tasks of development.

All in all, population pressure still qualifies as an inducement mechanism in the sense that it presents the developmental forces within a society with an opportunity to assert themselves. It supplies 'the motive and the cue for passion' (though admittedly it fails to provide many cues for action). Thus it seems wrong to say that population pressures act as an obstacle to development. There are circumstances under which these pressures are unsuccessful in performing their stimulating role just as relative price increases are at times ineffective in calling forth increases in the supply of the 'signalled' commodities.

The view that has been presented is consistent with the fact that population pressures have demonstrably been an integral part of the development process in all countries that are economically advanced today. It would surely be most unrealistic to look at the population increases in Europe in the 19th century and at those in, say, Brazil and Mexico today as a depressing influence on economic development. But if this is granted, then we must ask the partisans of the classical view to explain why population growth, like some of the lesser Homeric gods who throw their support to the winning side at the height of battle, suddenly becomes a stimulant to economic development after having long played the role of obstacle. In our view, no such switch ever occurs; rather we are able to account by a single hypothesis for a stream of events within which we might distinguish three periods: during the first, per capita incomes do not increase, but countries, in reacting to population pressures, acquire the abilities to launch undertakings that will lead to genuine economic growth; during a second period, per capita incomes begin to rise, with economic growth continuing to draw strength from population growth; and only at a later stage does economic growth wean itself from population growth and becomes self-sustained.[3]

What conclusion can be drawn from the preceding remarks for population policy in underdeveloped countries? Certainly not that they should institute a system of generous family allowances. In the first place, we have already stated our view that population pressures are a clumsy and cruel stimulant to development. Actually, underdeveloped countries are today abundantly supplied with this stimulant, whether they want it or not, as a result of the universal and rapid decline in mortality rates. Secondly, we consider the spread of birth control as one important form which the reaction to population pressure can take, and one that, if it occurs, brings with it basic attitude changes that are favourable to development.

Our policy conclusions, then, are somewhat anticlimactic. Any practical usefulness of our reasoning lies in the fact that it leads to a less alarmist attitude toward the population problem than is displayed by the current literature with its 'traps' and the need for a huge jump to break out of them. This kind of reasoning derives, of course, from the comparisons of population growth with output growth rates. A highly sophisticated version of this approach is given by Leibenstein; he demonstrates that if a country has a population growth rate of, say, 1 per cent per year, it is not sufficient for it to achieve an output growth rate in excess of 1 per cent; for when output and therefore income rise, population may rise even more; so that to overtake population growth for good, the country may have to achieve a rate of output growth that is a multiple of the initial rate of population growth; and it must achieve this rate not gradually but in one jump, for at any intermediate point the country's rate of income growth will be dragged down again to its low level starting point (Leibenstein 1954 and 1957; Nelson 1956).

Our approach leads us to take a far calmer view of the situation. We have shown that if a country is at all able to offset, be it even partially at first, the effect of the population increase, then we may have confidence that, through the learning acquired in this process, it will be able to do progressively better in marshalling its productive forces for development so that eventually output growth will overtake population growth. If a community makes a genuine effort to defend its standard of living in the face of population pressures, it need not be afraid of imaginary traps, for cumulative growth is then already in the making: just as income can rise in advance of consumption, so can economic progress get under way before being registered in per capita income increases.

REFERENCES

Dupréel, E (1928) 'Population et progrès' in Deux essais sur le progrès, Brussels.
Duesenberry, J S (1949) *Income, Saving and the Theory of Consumer Behaviour*, Harvard University Press, Cambridge.
Leibenstein, H (1957) *Economic Backwardness and Economic Growth*, Wiley, New York.
− (1954) *A Theory of Economic-Demographic Development*, Princeton University Press, Princeton.

---

3 With population still growing in all economically progressive countries, we actually have no conclusive empirical evidence about the existence of this stage.

Malthus, T R (1830) *A Summary View of the Principle of Population*; reprinted in D V Glass, ed, *Introduction to Malthus*, Watts, 1953, London.

Nelson, R R (1956) 'A theory of the low-level equilibrium trap', *American Economic Review* 46, pp894–908.

Peacock, Alan T 'Theory of population and modern economic analysis', *Population Studies* 6 (1952–53), p115.

Schumpeter, J 'The creative response in economic history', *Journal of Economic History* 7, November.

Singer, S H (1949) 'Economic progress in underdeveloped countries', *Social Research* 16, March.

Chapter 7

Demography and the Balance of Power

William H McNeill

Balance of power seems inadequate as a full explanation of the two [world] wars. The ferocity with which they were fought, and the far-reaching transformations that the war effort precipitated, made society over. War aims and political ideologies may have misled all concerned; but behind the bitter struggles one can surely discern a demographic factor as ineluctable as the geometry of power rivalries.

This perception offers a second approach to an understanding of the two wars. For, if the democratic and industrial revolutions were, among other things, responses to a population squeeze that impinged on western Europe towards the end of the 18th century, the military convulsions of the 20th century can be interpreted in the same way, as responses to collisions between population growth and limits set by traditional modes of rural life in central and eastern Europe in particular, and across wide areas of Asia in rather more diversified and variegated fashion as well. Assuredly, a basic and fundamental disturbance to all existing social relationships set in whenever and wherever broods of peasant children grew to adulthood in villages where, when it came time for them to marry and assume adult roles, they could not get hold of enough land to live as their forefathers had done from time immemorial. In such circumstances, traditional ways of rural life came under unbearable strain. Family duties and moral imperatives of village custom could not be fulfilled. The only question was what form of revolutionary ideal would attract the frustrated young people.

Ever since the mid-18th century, European and world populations have been out of balance. Lowered death rates allowed more children to grow to adulthood than in earlier centuries; but birth rates did not automatically adjust downward. Quite the contrary, they were likely to rise, since with fewer lethal epidemics, couples more often survived throughout their child-bearing years.[1]

For a century or more in central and eastern Europe, increasing numbers simply meant increasing wealth. More labour improved cultivation, broke new land to the plough, and intensified agricultural production in many different ways. Nevertheless, such responses had a limit; and by the 1880s it seems clear that diminishing returns had set in drastically in nearly all European villages situated between the Rhine and the Don. This was signalized by two changes. First, between 1880 and 1914 emigration assumed extraordinary proportions, carrying millions

---

1 On the concept of a 'vital revolution' see Helleiner (1965), pp79–86; and Thomlinson (1965), pp14 ff.

across the seas to America and projecting other millions eastward into Siberia as well. Second, diverse forms of revolutionary discontent began to affect villagers as well as townspeople in central and eastern Europe during these same decades.

Pressures on village custom and traditional social patterns intensified until 1914, when World War I diverted their expression into new channels and, by killing many millions of people in central and eastern Europe, did something to relieve the problem of rural overpopulation. But it was not until World War II brought much greater slaughter, as well as massive flights and wholesale ethnic transfers, that central and eastern European populations replicated the French response to the revolutionary upheavals at the beginning of the 19th century by regulating births to accord with perceived economic circumstances and expectations. As a result, after 1950 population growth ceased to put serious strain on European society.[2]

Diverse experiences in coping with population growth go far to explain the attitudes and behaviour of the European powers on the eve of World War I. By mid-century, France and Great Britain had each in its own contrasting way gone far to resolve the internal tensions that rapidly rising rural populations had created in those lands between 1780 and 1850.[3] Rising real wages registered this fact during and after the 1850s. Deliberate limitation of births among the French tied population growth to economic experience and expectation. In Great Britain, those who could not find satisfactory work at home went abroad, where careers in lands of European settlement were readily available.[4]

Russia's position was like that of Great Britain in the sense that migration towards a politically accessible and thinly inhabited frontier was available to rural folk who faced unacceptable constriction of traditional patterns of life in their native villages. Between 1880 and 1914 something over six million Russians migrated to Siberia and about four million established themselves in the Caucasus as well. Simultaneously, from the westernmost provinces of Russia an additional flood of about two and a half million emigrated overseas, though most of these were Poles and Jews, not ethnic Russians.[5] These safety valves were supplemented by expanding urban employment, thanks to railroads and the manifold forms of industrial and commercial expansion provoked by cheapened overland transport. Nevertheless, much of rural Russia simmered with discontent in the first decade of the 20th century, as demonstrated by the sudden flare-up of revolutionary violence in 1905–6.

The really difficult demographic problem of the late 19th and early 20th

---

2 For an overview of the population phenomena of the war era see Kulischer (1948).

3 Britain's Irish problem was not exactly solved by the catastrophe of the potato blight and resultant famine of 1845–46; but population growth abruptly gave way to population wastage in Ireland, thanks to accelerated emigration and rigorous postponement of the age of marriage until the newlyweds could inherit land. After 1845 the political tensions of Ireland were therefore no longer fed by rising population but took especial venom from the prolonged sexual frustration which became the normal lot of Irish countrymen waiting to inherit land before they dared to marry. On the psychological and sociological consequences of the remarkable demographic regime that prevailed in Ireland after the famine see Arensburg (1937).

4 Chain migration whereby one successful emigrant saved money to finance his relatives' emigration made it possible for even the very poor to get across the ocean in statistically significant numbers. As a result the emptying out of English villages with the decay of crop farming after 1873 produced no serious political disturbance in Great Britain. It did raise the tide of emigration from the British Isles to an all-time high in the years 1911–13 Cf Ensor (1936), p 500.

5 Reinhard et al (1968), pp401, 470; Treadgold (1957), pp33–35.

centuries came in the regions of Europe between the French and British on the west and the Russians on the east. In Germany, for example, the average annual surplus of births over deaths in the decade 1900–1910 was 866,000, yet Germany's remarkable industrial and commercial expansion provided so many jobs that Polish farm workers had to be imported to cultivate east German estates.[6] Nonetheless, the strains rapid urbanization put upon older patterns of life were very great. Germany's ruling elites were mostly drawn from rural and small-town backgrounds and often felt endangered by the new, thrusting urban elements. Marxist revolutionary rhetoric, popular among industrial workingmen, was particularly frightening. Simultaneously, many Germans felt endangered by impending Slavic inundation from the east. The result was a strong sense of beleaguerment and a more rigid, reckless support of Austria–Hungary in the summer of 1914 than would otherwise have seemed sensible.[7]

It is ironic to reflect on the difference between German and French developments. Had the German old regime been less successful in coping with the population surge in the 19th century, some sort of revolutionary movement might well have come to power in Germany with an attractive, universalist ideology, suited to appeal to other peoples of Europe as the ideals of the French revolutionaries had done in the 18th century. But instead, the German bid for European hegemony was fought out in the name of narrowly exclusive, nationalist, and racist principles, designed rather to repel than attract others. Success in industrializing so rapidly, in other words, may have foreclosed Germany's longer-range chances of winning the wars of the 20th century in the name of some form of revolutionary socialism. Marxist prescriptions for the future thus went astray. Instead, by a twist of fate that would have appalled Karl Marx, after 1917 the Russians made Marxism the ideological instrument of their state power.

Before 1917, however, this remarkable reversal of roles was unimaginable. In the regions of Europe lying east and south of Germany, industrial expansion entirely failed to keep pace with population growth.[8] Consequently, the most acute manifestations of political distress appeared within the borders of the Hapsburg and ex-Ottoman empires. (Russia's Polish provinces belong in this category too.) Overseas emigration, though very great,[9] was insufficient to relieve the problem. Youths who pursued secondary education in hope of qualifying for white-collar employment were strategically situated to communicate revolutionary political ideals to their frustrated contemporaries in the villages. They did so with marked success, beginning as early as the 1870s in Bulgaria and Serbia,[10] and at

---

6 Between 1880 and 1914 nearly half a million German farm workers left the east. According to Hagen (1980), the total was 482,062.

7 Analysis of how the 'archaic' character of German political leadership on the eve of the war helped to precipitate the catastrophe has become standard among German historians since Fritz Fischer pioneered this approach with his famous books, *Griff nach der Weltmacht* (1961) and *Krieg der Illusionen* (1969).

8 Paralleling similar failures within the British Isles in such parts as the Scottish Highlands and southern Ireland.

9 About 4 million persons left Hapsburg lands for overseas destinations between 1900 and 1914. Emigration from Russia's western provinces was about 2.5 million, and from Italy was so massive as to depopulate some southern villages. Reinhard et al (1968, pp400–1), gives a table of European emigration showing relevant statistics for the pre-World War I decades.

10 In Serbia, the Radical party, founded in 1879, set up a rural party machine and agitational network that changed the basis of politics in that country within a decade or so. Cf Dragnich (1974), pp17–22 For Bulgaria, see Black (1943), pp39 ff.

somewhat later dates in other parts of eastern Europe. The Balkans, accordingly, became the powder keg of Europe. It was appropriate indeed that the spark that triggered World War I was struck by Gavrilo Princip, a youth whose efforts at pursuing a secondary school education had entirely failed to provide him with satisfactory access to adult life but had imbued him with an intense, revolutionary form of nationalism.[11]

World War I did something to relieve rural overcrowding in central and eastern Europe, Millions of peasant sons were mobilized into the rival armies and something like 10.5 million died.[12] In the aftermath, nationalist revolutions in the Hapsburg Empire (1918–19) and socialist revolutions in Russia (1917) did little to relieve peasant overcrowding. Except in Hungary, both forms of revolution did succeed in depriving prewar possessing classes of most of their landed property. But land redistribution among an already impoverished peasantry did little to improve productivity. Indeed it usually worked in an opposite way, since the new owners lacked both capital and know-how with which to farm efficiently. The postwar settlement therefore quite failed to relieve the difficulty of too many people trying to pursue a traditional peasant style of life. The Russians responded between 1928 and 1932 with a state programme of industrial investment supported by forcible collectivization of agriculture. In the rest of eastern Europe, when depression came in the 1930s, rural distress commonly found anti-Semitic expression, since Jewish middlemen were numerous enough to be vulnerable to the charge that they prospered by buying cheap and selling dear at the peasantry's expense.

Hence it was not until World War II provoked a far more massive die-off in eastern Europe, totaling perhaps as much as 47 million,[13] that a more brutal but enduring solution to the problem of too many people trying to live on too little land emerged. For it was during and after World War II that the inhabitants of eastern Europe began to limit births. Birth rates swiftly sank towards a much lower level than before; so low, indeed, that in some countries population replacement ceased to be assured without alien immigration.[14]

As births came into systematic relation with economic expectations all across the face of Europe,[15] the crisis period through which central and eastern Europe had passed between 1880 and 1950 came to an end. Family patterns and sex habits changed; customs and mores of peasant life altered; and the demographic regime that had fomented World Wars I and II ceased to prevail.

---

11 Nationalism appealed more than socialism to east European peasants and former peasants because it could be interpreted as meaning the dispossession of ethnically alien landlords and urban property owners without infringing peasant property in the slightest. The Serbian Radical party, accordingly, shed its founders' socialism as it succeeded in gaining peasant support. On socialist beginnings of the Radicals see McClellan (1964).

12 This figure is the remainder when French and British war losses are subtracted from the global figure of 13 million for World War I casualties offered by Reinhard et al (1968), p 488. Estimates are very loose at best, for record keeping broke down in all defeated countries, and epidemics of typhus and influenza killed many civilians as well as soldiers. Such deaths are sometimes classed as war related, sometimes excluded.

13 Ibid, p 573. Margin for error is even greater in World War II than in World War I calculations, if only because more than half the casualties were civilian.

14 Cf Coale et al (1979); Heer (1968), pp193–240; Reinhard et al (1968), p610.

15 With the exception of Albania and Albanian populations inside Yugoslavia, among whom a Moslem heritage and mountainous habitat combined to preserve traditional sexual and family patterns. Cf Salt and Clout (1976), p 13. Political manifestations of the resulting population pressure became troublesome in Yugoslavia in 1981.

Elsewhere in the world, of course, the demographic surge followed different rhythms. In China, for example, collision between mounting rural population and available land became acute as early as 1850 and found expression in the massive and destructive Taiping Rebellion, (1850–64).[16] Asian peasantries did not again respond to revolutionary ideals on a massive scale until after World War I. Suffice it here to refer to the career of Mohandas Gandhi (1869–1948), whose first successful efforts to appeal to the rural classes of India dated from the early 1920s and to that of Mao Tse-tung (1893–1976), whose mobilization of Chinese peasant support for his version of Marxism dated from 1927. The linkages that prevailed in Europe between overcrowding on the land and revolutionary politicization of rural populations were duplicated in much of Asia during ensuing decades,[17] and in some regions of Africa as well. But conditions varied greatly from region to region, and in many tropical climates disease regimes that kept human numbers efficiently in check continued to prevail until after World War II.

Japan's 20th-century imperial aggression coincided with a surge in that nation's population growth that crested only after World War II, although maximal rate of increase came earlier.[18] But World War II brought decisive metamorphosis to Japanese rural life, and, after the war, birth rates started down at almost the same time as in central and eastern Europe. To all appearances, therefore, Japan also passed through its version of the modern demographic crisis during World War II, just as most of Europe did.[19]

Obviously, revolutionary expressions of rural frustration when insufficient land is available to allow young people to live as their parents had done have not vanished from the earth. Outbreaks in Latin America, parts of Africa, and in southeast Asia continue to occur. But for World Wars I and II, Japan's population surge, and the chronologically parallel crisis in eastern and central Europe was what mainly mattered. Having changed their demographic pattern, these lands are unlikely to become again the seat of comparable military-political unrest.

---

16 About 40 million died in that rebellion; and an additional 8 million Chinese emigrated to borderlands and overseas in ensuing decades. The country's population of about 430 million in 1850 was cut back to only 400 million in 1870 according to Reinhard et al (1968), p476.
17 For China, cf Fei (1953).
18 Japan's population rose as follows:

	Total	Increment	Percent
1880	36.4 million	–	–
1890	40.5	4.1	11
1900	44.8	4.3	11
1910	50.9	6.1	14
1920	55.9	5.0	10
1930	64.4	8.5	15
1940	73.1	8.7	13.5
1950	83.2	10.1	14

Source: Reinhard et al (1968), pp479, 566, 640.

19 For Japanese rural population growth and political protest see Yoshihashi (1963); Fukutake (1967); Dore (1959); Black et al (1975), pp179–85, 281; and Mosk (1977), pp655–74.

REFERENCES

Arensburg, Conrad (1937) *The Irish Countryman*, London: Macmillan.

Black, Cyril (1943) *The Establishment of Constitutional Government in Bulgaria*, Princeton: Princeton University Press.

Black, Cyril E, et al (1975) *The Modernization of Japan and Russia*, New York: Free Press.

Coale, Ansley J, et al (1970) *Human Fertility in Russia since the 19th century*, Princeton: Princeton University Press.

Dore, Ronald P (1959) *Land Reform in Japan*, New York: Schocken Books.

Dragnich, Alex N (1974) *Serbia, Nikola Pašić and Yugoslavia*, New Brunswick, NJ

Ensor, R C K (1936) *England, 1870–1914*, Oxford: Clarendon Press.

Fei, Hsiao-t'ung (1953) *China's Gentry: Essays in Rural-Urban Relations*, Chicago: University of Chicago Press.

Fischer, Fritz (1961) *Griff nach der Weltmacht*. Düsseldorf; translated as *Germany's Aims in the First World War*, London: Chatto & Windus, 1967.

Fischer, Fritz (1969) *Krieg der Illusionen*. Düsseldorf; translated as *War of Illusions: German Policies from 1911 to 1914*, London: Chatto & Windus, 1975.

Fukutake, Tadashi (1967) *Japanese Rural Society*, Tokyo: Oxford University Press.

Hagen, William W (1980) *Germans, Poles, and Jews: The Nationality Conflict in the Prussian East, 1772–1914*, Chicago: University of Chicago Press.

Heer, David M (1968) 'The Demographic Transition in the Russian Empire and the Soviet Union', *Journal of Social History* 1, pp193–240.

Helleiner, K F (1965) 'The vital revolution reconsidered', in *Population in History*, ed D V Glass and D E C Eversley. London: Arnold.

Kulischer, Eugene M. (1948) *Europe on the Move: War and Population Changes, 1917–1947*. New York: Columbia University Press.

McClellan, Woodford D (1964) *Svetozar Marković and the Origins of Balkan Socialism*, Princeton.

Mosk, Carl (1977) 'Demographic transition in Japan', *Journal of Economic History* 37, pp655–74.

Reinhard, Marcel, André Armengaud, and Jacques Dupâquier (1968) *Historie générale de la population mondiale*, 3rd ed Paris: Montchrestien.

Salt, John and Hugh Clout (1976) *Migration in Post-war Europe: Geographical Essays*, Oxford: Oxford University Press.

Thomlinson, Ralph (1965) *Population Dynamics: Causes and Consequences of World Demographic Change*, New York: Random House.

Treadgold, Donald W (1957) *The Great Siberian Migration*. Princeton: Princeton University Press.

Yoshihashi, Takehiko (1963) *Conspiracy at Mukden: The Rise of the Japanese Military*, New Haven: Yale University Press.

Part II

Individuals and Families

Demographic change is largely a consequence of individual decisions, typically made within a family setting. This is evident enough for decisions on marriage, family size and the timing of births, and migration – though recognizing that in some societies and for some groups the range of choice may be constrained by poverty, social pressure or political dictate, and in the extreme case outcomes may be wholly involuntary. Individual decisions are significant also, if to a lesser degree, in determining mortality: they may affect exposure to risk of injury or disease and responses to ill-health. A first step in explaining demographic change is therefore to understand how these decisions are made – that is, the nature of the so-called behavioural calculus that applies at the individual or family level – and to identify the immediate factors that influence decision outcomes. (For a *sufficient* explanation we must do much more than this. The selections in Part III are concerned with the effects of broader social and political arrangements on demographic outcomes. A different literature, not sampled in the present collection but an emerging source of insight, draws on evolutionary biology to argue for the demographic significance of innate behavioural predispositions – see, for example, Betzig et al. 1988, Hill et al. 1995, Kaplan 1996.)

A ready-made behavioural calculus exists in the form of micro-economic theory, the apparatus designed to model the decisions of firms and consumers. Many economists argue that the family can be modelled in an analogous way. They would maintain, in Gary S. Becker's formulation, that 'all human behaviour can be viewed as involving participants who maximize their utility from a stable set of preferences and accumulate an optimal amount of information and other inputs in a variety of markets' (Becker 1976). *Demographic* behaviour, in particular fertility, was one of the first cases to be elaborated. Such behaviour can be viewed as being determined jointly with decisions on household savings, labour market participation, (private) investment in education, and other matters affecting individual or family wellbeing. The now large body of work describing this approach represents a major advance in understanding the relationships between population change and development. Becker's pioneering series of studies on fertility and family are brought together in his *Treatise on the Family* (1991). Other discussions of the new household economics, as the approach is known, are to be found in Theodore W. Schultz (1974) and T. Paul Schultz (1981), and, at a less technical level, in Tommasi and Ierulli (1995).

Fundamental to much of this work is the 'household production function', conceptually analogous to the familiar production function for a firm. The inputs to household production are its members' purchases of goods and services, the environmental amenities it can draw on, and, not least, the time of its members. These are combined to form, as outputs, the health, sensual pleasure, prestige, and so on, that are the immediate constituents of wellbeing ('commodities' in Becker's usage). Both the number and the 'quality' of children contribute to a household's (or family's – the distinction is often blurred) wellbeing, so childbearing and childrearing choices can be treated alongside other production decisions in the household's welfare maximization.

The analogy of family with firm extends to the problem of linking micro-economic analysis to macro-economic conditions. The family, like the firm though to a lesser degree, is influenced by – and, in the aggregate, influences – those conditions. The link is explored in Becker's paper included in this section. (See also Theodore W. Schultz in Part I and, for an array of analytical exercises investigating family decisions in a general-equilibrium economic setting, Nerlove et al. 1987.)

It might be supposed that there would be no difficulty estimating these behavioural models from household survey data. This has not proved to be the case. Estimation requires drastic simplification of model specification to derive testable predictions, and extensive recourse to proxies in place of unobserved variables – the most common instance being the use of female wage rates to signify the value of time. Moreover, the large volume of survey data accumulated since the 1970s (particularly through two elabourate international projects, the World Fertility Survey and the Demographic and Health Surveys) sheds comparatively little light on the economics of family life. These surveys have mostly been concerned with monitoring parental (mainly women's) family planning intentions and practice, based on the premise that fertility change is determined more by knowledge and use of contraception than by demand for children. (See Pritchett 1994 and Potts 1997 for the poles of this long-running debate, and Bongaarts 1993 for the middle ground. Easterlin and Crimmins 1985 present a modelling approach that gives strong weight to the costs of birth control.)

The new household economics is open to various criticisms. Some sociologists were dismissive from the start, in no doubt of the answer to Judith Blake's caustic query: Are babies consumer durables? (Blake 1968). Also critical but more appreciative are Berk and Berk (1983). For criticism from economists, for neglect of historical or institutional factors or for inattention to feminist perspectives, see Pollak and Wachter (1975), Arthur (1982), and Folbre (1994). Yoram Ben-Porath (in this Part) suggests a judicious paring down of the Beckerian ambition: the micro-economic approach to fertility 'is not an attempt to put everything that matters into a straight-jacket – it is just a framework that can accommodate many things.'

There are other frameworks for understanding fertility, less formal – some would say less rigorous – than Becker's, highlighting different aspects of the family and demographic change. Blake (in this Part) identifies the salient utilities and costs of children to their parents and explores how they are governed by the institutional structure of society. This is the basis for a plausible heuristic account of demographic transition (a roughly comparable, more formalized, account is given by Leibenstein 1957, 1975). For other writers, including Amartya Sen and Nancy Folbre (both in this Part), families are miniature societies, not atomistic decision-making entities. Conflicts of interest and imbalances of power within them – between generations (Caldwell 1982) or, as in these examples, between sexes – warrant explicit attention as influences on behavioural and welfare outcomes. Caldwell and, more insistently, Cleland and Wilson (1987) also stress the significance for demographic behaviour of 'ideational' change – shifts in beliefs and value systems that may be concomitants of but, it is claimed, may also be independent of, economic change.

A more formal, organizational analysis of family structure and fertility determination, applying the concept of transaction costs, has been sketched out by Ben-Porath (1980) and Pollak (1985): if Becker's household is illuminated by the standard theory of the firm, Ben-Porath's is by the parallel theories of R.H. Coase and Oliver E. Williamson (see Williamson and Winter 1991). More generally, the unbundling of the family reveals a major part of what can be called the political economy of fertility (pursued further in the article by Susan Greenhalgh in Part III).

This discussion and the selections that follow refer chiefly to fertility. A different strand of individual- and family-level theorizing is concerned with migration, both rural–urban and international. Micro-economic approaches to rural–urban migration have found wide acceptance. A familiar modelling premise is that individuals maximize their expected gains (to themselves or to their families) from relocating to a higher-wage but less secure labour market, a process formalized in the Harris–Todaro model (see Khan 1987). Oded Stark (1991) explores various elabourations on this and related behavioural assumptions. A comprehensive review of theoretical approaches to migration, structural as well as economic, is given by Massey et al. (1993).

REFERENCES

Arthur, W. Brian (1982) review of Gary S. Becker, *A Treatise on the Family; Population and Development Review* 8: pp393–397.

Becker, Gary S. (1976) *The Economic Approach to Human Behaviour*, University of Chicago Press, Chicago.

Becker, Gary S. (1991) *A Treatise on the Family*. Enlarged edition, Harvard University Press, Cambridge, Massachusetts.

Ben-Porath, Yoram (1980) 'The F-connection: Families, friends, and firms and the organization of exchange', *Population and Development Review* 6: pp1–30.

Berk, Richard A. and Sarah F. Berk (1983) 'Supply-side sociology of the family: The challenge of the New Home Economics', *Annual Review of Sociology* 9: pp375–395.

Betzig, Laura, Paul W. Turke, and M. Borgerhoff Mulder (eds.) (1988) *Human Reproductive Behaviour: A Darwinian Perspective*, Cambridge University Press, Cambridge.

Blake, Judith (1968) 'Are babies consumer durables? A critique of the economic theory of reproductive motivation', *Population Studies* 22: pp5–25.

Bongaarts, John (1993) 'The supply-demand framework for the determinants of fertility: an alternative implementation', *Population Studies* 47: pp437–456.

Caldwell, John C. (1982) *Theory of Fertility Decline*, Academic Press, London.

Cleland, John and Christopher Wilson (1987) 'Demand theories of the fertility transition: An iconoclastic view', *Population Studies* 41: pp5–30.

Easterlin, Richard A. and Eileen M Crimmins (1985) *The Fertility Revolution: A Supply-Demand Analysis*, University of Chicago Press, Chicago.

Folbre, Nancy (1994) *Who Pays for the Kids? Gender and the Structures of Constraint*, Routledge, London.

Hill, Kim, H.M. Hurtado, and A.M. Hurtado (1995) *Ache Life History: The Ecology and Demography of a Foraging People*, Aldine de Gruyter, New York.

Kaplan, Hillard (1996) 'A theory of fertility and parental investment in traditional and modern human societies', *Yearbook of Physical Anthropology* 39: pp91–135.

Khan, M. Ali (1987) 'Harris-Todaro model', in John Eatwell et al (eds.) *The New Palgrave: A Dictionary of Economics*, Macmillan, London.

Leibenstein, Harvey (1957) *Economic Backwardness and Economic Growth*, Wiley, New York.

Leibenstein, Harvey (1975) 'The economic theory of fertility decline', *Quarterly Journal of Economics* 89: pp1–31.

Massey, Douglas S., et al. (1993) 'Theories of international migration: A review and appraisal', *Population and Development Review* 19: pp431–466.

Nerlove, Marc, Assaf Razin, and Efraim Sadka (1987) *Household and Economy: Welfare Economics of Endogenous Fertility*, Academic Press, Orlando, Florida.

Pritchett, Lant (1994) 'Desired fertility and the impact of population policies', *Population and Development Review* 20: pp1–55.

Pollak, Robert A. (1985) 'A transaction cost approach to families and households', *Journal of Economic Literature* 23: pp581–608.

Pollak, Robert A. and Michael L. Wachter (1975) 'The relevance of the household production function and its implications for the allocation of time', *Journal of Political Economy* 83: pp255–277.

Potts, Malcolm (1997) 'Sex and the birth rate: human biology, demographic change, and access to fertility-regulation methods', *Population and Development Review* 23: pp1–39.

Schultz, Theodore W. (ed.) (1974) *Economics of the Family: Marriage, Children, and Human Capital*, University of Chicago Press for the National Bureau of Economic Research, Chicago.

Schultz, T. Paul (1981) *Economics of Population*, Addison-Wesley, Reading, Massachusetts.

Stark, Oded (1991) *The Migration of Labour*, Blackwell, Oxford.

Tommasi, Mariano and Kathryn Ierulli (eds.) (1995) *The New Economics of Human Behaviour*, Cambridge University Press, Cambridge.

Williamson, Oliver E. and Sidney G. Winter (eds.) (1991) *The Nature of the Firm: Origins, Evolution, and Development*, Oxford University Press, Oxford.

Chapter 8

The Micro-economics of Fertility

Yoram Ben-Porath

In recent years there has been a revival of work by economists on demography, particularly fertility. Here are some comments on the nature of the micro-economic work on fertility, a subjective view of the methodology, the promise and limitations of this work.[1] This is not a survey article; I shall assume that the reader is familiar with the research considered here and shall discuss the issues I have picked out of a fairly heterogeneous body of work without going into details of who said what and to whom. The current work on the economics of fertility has been influenced by Becker (1960 1965), Richard Easterlin (1968, 1969, 1973), and Harvey Leibenstein (1951, 1973).[2] There is considerable methodological and substantive variety, but the common thread running through the work is the desire to study and understand fertility behaviour by means of some kind of economic reasoning. This should be distinguished from two other types of work in economic demography: the study of the economic implications of population growth, and the policy-serving literature.

Some may argue that the business of economists is to study the relationship between fertility and so-called economic variables, particularly income. An alternative view is, however, that what economics can bring to demography is not 'variables' but a framework and an approach. Standard micro-economic analysis has approached the study of behaviour through the notion that people behave as if they were trying, given their preferences, to make the best choice possible with their limited resources. Preferences for commodities, activities or states that in some way affect the welfare of the consumer are expressed through a 'utility function'. When this is applied to the analysis of fertility children appear in the utility function as well as ordinary commodities. Often only the number of children appears, but the children can be distinguished by birth order and expression can be given to the concern of parents with their children's traits, acquired or innate, their happiness or their future success.

The direct consequences of having children for the happiness of their parents

---

1 Some of the issues have been ably discussed in Namboodiri (1972). For a different view, see Blake (1968).
2 A useful bibliography is to be found in the supplement to the March/April 1973 issue of the *Journal of Political Economy*. In his 1973 article, Richard Easterlin has provided an overview of the field, together with his own contribution; some of the work has been surveyed by Schultz (1973). My debt to them and others will be felt throughout this paper.

obviously extend over long periods (and according to the testimony of some parents of teenage children, may not have the same significance throughout the life-cycle). Having a child implies a commitment of resources over long periods as well, so the proper framework is a life-cycle model, where both preferences and resources over the life-cycle are considered. Still, for some purposes one can shrink the model into a one-period model without much loss. The relevant resources constraint would in any case not be the family's current income but a broader concept that extends over longer periods and that encompasses the non-market resources of the family. Obviously, the limited resources and the methods available to convert them into children and other commodities determine the costs, in a broad sense, at which children can be acquired and raised. The household production model (Becker 1965) has been regarded by many as a useful framework to take account of the role of the time of the members of the family, their productivity in raising children and in other activities and of other questions related to the activity within the household.[3] Again, for many purposes, this part of the model can be folded up.

This model of choice, the theory of investment with the distinction between long-run and short with the emphasis on speed of adjustment, the distinction between flows and stocks, the models that treat behaviour under uncertainty, and various other tools in standard economic analysis, have proved to be adaptable to questions of family size and thus provide a framework (and a language) where the connection between family size and other exogenous factors and aspects of behaviour can be logically traced under various assumptions. This helps the intuition and can provide ways of checking the consistency of seemingly independent guesses about cause and effect. The adaptability of the economic framework to population problems is probably the major reason for the resurrection of economic demography. More complex issues arise once the theory is being used as a source of testable hypotheses or as means of understanding a specific reality. Only some of these issues will be discussed here.

IRRATIONALITY

The most common objection to the micro-economic theory of fertility is the belief that behaviour with respect to fertility is irrational and thus cannot be understood or captured via a mechanism based on rational decision-making. What kind of rationality is assumed in the theory? The theory of household choice does not claim that each individual goes through an explicit calculus of pleasure and pain as a guide to behaviour, and this is certainly true when it is applied to fertility. It is recognized that the process each individual goes through is very complicated and varies among individuals. The assumption is that one possible way of capturing and making sense out of the common elements of behaviour is to derive propositions as if people were acting according to a specific rule – maximizing a utility function subject to a resource constraint. There is no guarantee, of course, that this is a good strategy.

One source of difficulty lies in the values that preclude control of family size

---

3 See Willis et al (1973) in the March/April 1973 supplement of the *Journal of Political Economy*. For a critical view of the household production model, see Pollak and Wachter (1974).

or dictate some norms of family size and inability to control efficiently for family size. This is, of course, an old problem; what economists would like to be able to say is that if certain types of behaviour with respect to marriage or fertility turn out to be optimal for many people for a long period of time, they will be institutionalized and become social rules of behaviour, giving the individual signals that substitute for individual explicit decision-making. When society is divisible into several well-defined classes, and when basic conditions remain stable over time, social institutions and procedures can assume a prominent role as carriers of signals for individual behaviour. In such cases, it does not make sense to regard the social institutions as outside intruders to the rational scheme but as part of the game. However, when things change rapidly, social institutions may lag behind and act independently, interfering with rather than facilitating rational individual behaviour. The methodology of economics may be deficient in not giving any criteria by which we can identify *a priori* the various cases. One might have a feeling about how successful a model based on rational decision-making will be in any specific situation (see Tobin 1973). It may well be that in some empirical contexts nothing can be learned from a model based on the rational paradigm, but there is no reason to think that any intuitive assessment of the 'rationality' of a group of people would be a good predictor of success or failure.

These considerations do not necessarily eliminate the heuristic value of the theoretical exercises, but they may have serious implications for the empirical work. Obviously, if differences in fertility between couples at any point of time are dominated by differences in the speed at which people perceive and adjust to a new level of optimum family size rather than by differences in the optimum size, then differential fertility (in a cross section) cannot be the testing ground for hypotheses that 'explain' differences in the optimum (desired) family size, even if the latter were relevant for the long term development of average fertility. Conversely, the theory that would be required to explain differential fertility is, in such a case, more dynamic than what we have at present.

Another prong of the irrationality argument has to do with contraception. It is often argued that where the use of contraceptives is limited, one can assume irrationality with respect to family planning. It is also claimed that demographic transition is partly a consequence of the spread of modern contraceptives. The demand for contraceptives is probably determined together with the demand for children. At any point in time, people are not going to invest in acquiring the knowledge and the habits of modern contraception if they anyhow want many children; likewise, there is no reason to believe that new contraceptives would be developed if there were no demand for them. This is not to deny that there have been autonomous factors permitting the development of new contraceptives. The decline in the cost of birth prevention could encourage family limitation (see below). Still, the spread and development of modern contraceptives is a corollary rather than a cause of demographic transition (a similar view has been presented by Easterlin 1969).

DESIRED VERSUS ACTUAL

This leads to the general question of the desired versus the actual number of children. The preceding discussion suggests that one cannot be very happy with the distinction between wanted and unwanted children. An appropriate model is

one where people choose not a number of children but a strategy of family formation which includes choice of a method of contraception out of several alternatives,
each implying a different degree of certainty. Obviously, it does not make sense to
argue that each individual has exactly the number of children that he would have
liked under conditions of perfect and costless, control (see Michael and Willis 1973).

This problem should be distinguished from another aspect of the desired
versus actual dichotomy. Conditions change over the life-cycle and this may alter
the desired number of children so that couples may find themselves at any point
of time with more or fewer children than they actually want. This possibility is of
course known to parents in advance and may well affect the way they go about
forming the family. The fact that children are to some extent an irreversible
commitment (their presence is irreversible, but families finding themselves with
'too many' children may have the option of cutting expenditure on them) or that
the decision not to have more children becomes irreversible, do not mean that
economic analysis is impossible, but that it become more complicated. (Attempts
to consider the dynamic elements and the uncertainty involved are contained in
Gregory 1973, and Heckman and Willis 1973.)

BUT...

But, of course, there is a lot of unhappiness about the straight borrowing of the
bare utility function. This has two aspects: it is argued that more has to be specified about the nature of 'tastes' if non-trivial results are to be derived (see, for
example, Leibenstein 1973). This has to do with the desires or needs that lie
behind the 'utility' of children and with more general aspects of tastes and the
nature and costs of substitutes. (In his treatment of demand, Lancaster (1966)
makes the distinction between the ultimate needs and the actual activities and
goods that provide them.)

In applying the standard economic model, we like to assume no systematic
taste differences and to put the burden of explanation on changes (or differences)
in fertility on 'prices' and 'income', both interpreted in a very broad sense. In the
empirical work, we take care of possible important taste differences by 'holding
constant' certain demographic variables. Richard Easterlin has suggested that the
standard of living experienced in the parents' home may affect the taste for
children of the next generation, and has used this idea to explain the swings in
fertility in the United States (see Easterlin 1968).

Very difficult is the sequential problem concerning taste formation within the
same generation. It seems plausible to argue that people do not have well defined
preferences concerning children before they have them and that preferences
crystallize while the experience of having children is going on, and as their traits
are observed. Little work has been done on the sequential aspect of the decision
concerning children (see Ben-Porath and Welch 1972) and practically nothing
concerning the sequential aspects of taste formation. There is renewed interest in
endogenous taste in economics, particularly in radical economics. Not unrelated
is the issue of dependence in tastes across individuals.

A fundamental unsolved problem is that in economics the 'consumer' or the
decision-maker speaks with one voice in the theory, but the household, the couple,
the family, where decisions are being made on education, food and shelter has
more than one voice. Husband and wife may want different things and have differ-

ent ideas about the way things should look in the family. The final decisions bestow a certain distribution of benefits upon the members of the family, reflecting the power structure and the balance between altruism and egoism in the family. Obviously, tastes with respect to children may differ between any man and any woman randomly picked. Those that have selected themselves into married couples are more alike in terms of their tastes concerning children but complete unanimity is probably not the rule. Thus, the behaviour of families can change as the weight in decision-making shifts towards or away from the wife. The children may have an increasing say as they grow up and approach independence, and the preferences and the interests of parents and children may diverge – these are further complications. We cannot say whether the omission of such considerations from the theory is a serious limitation or not; this will be established only when a serious attempt to go in this direction has taken place.

SHIFTS IN SUPPLY

The micro-theory of fertility is mostly a theory about the demand for children; while supply considerations are important to the extent that they come out of market prices or the shadow prices of scarce own resources, the biological and health considerations which shift the 'supply curve' of children and which are paramount in traditional demography have been often neglected by economists. In considering contraception one is already considering some elements of supply, those which have to do with the determination of the costs, monetary or psychic, of limiting the number of births. Easterlin (1969, 1973) has stressed the need to integrate demand and supply considerations. In extreme cases only one set of factors dominates. In a healthy population with widespread birth control and a small desired number of children, the forces that shift supply may be relevant only through the effect on contraception. At the other extreme, it is trivially clear that if people want more children than they can get, fertility is dominated by supply-shift considerations. This case merits the, again trivial, reminder that when people have as many children as they can, it does not mean that they did not want as many. That is to say, uncontrolled fertility is by itself no proof of 'irrationality'. (It is, indeed, not inconceivable to think of cases where, from the 'pure' economic point of view, the optimum number of children exceeds the biologically possible number.) More interesting are those cases where supply and demand considerations offer alternative explanations of certain phenomena. Thus, for example, in analysing the relationship between fertility and child mortality, it has been found that women who have lost more children have tended to have more births. This can be understood as a supply reaction, because the narrowing of the interval between conceptions raises the expected number of possible births. It is also possible to interpret this phenomenon as if it were generated by the demand side; the demand explanation would be that people do indeed want a certain number of survived children, an additional child death detracts from this number, and it may also contribute to a revision of the desired number. When some demographers speak of 'replacement' of deceased children, they already imply a 'demand view'. The extent of replacement suggests something about the nature of the demand for children (Ben-Porath 1973; O'Hara 1972; Schultz 1973a). In order to distinguish between the two hypotheses, one can focus on diverse population groups where one or another consideration can be reasonably expected to be absent; also, one can examine the parameters involved and see whether they are consistent with a pure supply model.

What economists often find is a tendency in demographic literature sometimes to neglect obvious behavioural interpretations in favour of biological explanations. What experienced demographers criticize, often justly, in the invaders is a tendency to ignore the biological side altogether.

AN ILLUSTRATION

In order to illustrate some of these points, let me discuss very briefly three hypotheses that are motivated by the central empirical generalization of the decline in fertility that accompanied economic growth over time, and the inverse association between family size and socio-economic status in cross-section data. In considering the following examples one should distinguish between the possible 'stages' or functions in the development of the theory; (a) fitting the problem into a framework providing a possible rationale for certain types of behaviour – that is, the formulation of hypotheses; (b) testing the conformity of the hypothesis with the facts; and (c) choosing among competing hypotheses.

Family Size and the Cost of Contraception

Think of the cost of contraception as being proportional to the number of avoided births. The total cost of having an additional child is the cost of raising a child minus the cost of avoiding a birth. Obviously, the lower the latter, the higher is the marginal cost of a born child. On the other hand, a lower cost of avoiding births, other things constant, means a higher real income. Thus, if we compare two families equal in all respects except that one is faced with a lower cost of contraception, the latter may be pushed to have more of all normal goods, possibly also children because of the higher real income, but it will tend to have fewer children because of the higher marginal cost of an additional child. If we want to say that this second effect is more important than the positive effect, we must rely on our knowledge (or assumption) that if there is a positive effect of income on desired family size, it is very small.

If we are willing to hypothesize that people with more schooling have better information and access to cheaper or more efficient methods of birth control, we have one possible explanation for the relationship between education and fertility. This argument depends on the assumption that education is associated with better information and lower prices (or greater efficiency) in contraception relative to other goods or activities, something that is not easy to check.

The Cost-of-time Hypothesis

A hypothesis that has occupied much of the recent literature is that raising children and the resulting utility from children entails the use of various inputs purchased outside the household (from nappies to the educational services provided by schools), and own inputs – the parents' time, primarily the mother's. If children are more intensive in the value of the wife's time than other commodities, then we may expect the (marginal) cost of children to rise with the value of the wife's time. For women who work in the market, this value is determined in the market. For women who do no market work, it is determined within the household by the value at the margin of the wife's time once it has been optimally allocated. There is of course plenty of evidence suggesting that women with more schooling earn higher wages in the labour market.

Child Quality

The fact that couples with higher income (or of higher socio-economic status) tend to have fewer children and spend on them more than couples down the ladder, can easily lead to the argument that richer families have fewer children because they are faced with a higher price for children. Gary Becker in his early paper (Becker 1960) has argued that the expenditure on children is not a price imposed on the family from the outside but rather an expression of the family's free choice: parents derive utility from having children who are better fed, clad, and bred ('quality') and therefore, at any given prices of inputs (food, clothes, education), people with higher income desire to spend more on their children. Becker has used this argument in order to reject the idea that the expenditure on children determines the number of children.

Sociologists (for example Blake 1968) and other economists (Duesenberry 1960) have resisted the presumed independence of the expenditures on and the number of children. The basis for the sociological counter-argument was that there are social pressures forcing the rich to send their children to college, feed them, etc., thus indeed imposing a higher price for children on the rich. Most economists would accept the possibility that some individuals are pressured to conform to a group norm, but would reject the idea that an average group behaviour (that is, the prevalence of high expenditure on the children of the rich) has been created by everybody pressuring everybody else to do something they basically do not want to do (see above). It is however possible to argue, as Robert Willis (1973) has done, that parents' preferences may link the standard of living of their children to their own. A suggestion concerning the link between the number of children and expenditure on them which still preserves the idea that the expenditure is voluntary comes from Becker and Lewis (1973). They point out that adding a unit of 'quality' (achieved, for example, by a $1 expenditure) implies spending $2 on 'quality' if the couple desires at the same time to have two children, and implies the spending of $6 if the couple desires to have six children. At the same time, the cost of an extra child would be $1500 per year for a couple that regards this as the optimum expenditure per child while the cost of an extra child for a family that regards $3000 as the optimum would be $3000. In other words, the (shadow) prices determined internally for each of the goods (children and quality of children) are strongly related, the quantity of each good affecting the price of the other. Thus, if there is a tendency of families to raise expenditure on children as their income rises, this by itself causes the price of children to rise and should reduce the number of children.

We have three hypotheses, and we could of course list more, which are linked to some aspects of the inverse association between fertility and income level or socio-economic status (Simon 1969). They are all grounded in broad (and trite) empirical generalizations, so that conformity to these generalizations is neither a surprise, nor an achievement. None of them are entirely new. Their usefulness depends first of all on any heuristic value they may have – each is couched in terms that can do something to clarify the structure of the problem and link the phenomena with other aspects of behaviour. The next stage, the empirical useful-ness of the hypothesis, of course depends on the ability to say something about 'facts' that goes beyond the original empirical generalization that lay behind it, either by adding details or by accounting for related behaviour. The richness of an hypothesis, how much it adds to our ability to understand several aspects of behaviour in a unified framework, is a major criterion for judging the approach.

In the empirical work it is futile to ask for clean tests in which everything else is 'held constant'. Relevance depends on some degree of robustness, on the ability of a specific explanation or a theory to stand out in the data even when some things are free to vary. It is not, in my view, very constructive to ask whether a hypothesis is 'valid'. Every idea is the beginning of a line of research in which there is a dialogue between theory and fact. It may end in a conclusion or a judge-ment that something is not important, rather than not valid, and still what goes on along the way may be useful. Once the criterion is importance and not accep-tance or rejection in the statistical sense, the question arises: which is the dominant explanation in any specific situation? With the very limited number of variables that we usually have and considering that each measured variable is a proxy for several 'true' variables, this is certainly a difficult question.

Space does not allow a detailed exposition, but the value-of-time hypothesis can illustrate some of the problems that I leave unmentioned. It was Mincer (1963) who suggested that as income changes there is not only an income effect, but other things which tend to generate substitution effects against children, change as well. This basic distinction between income effects and substitution effects is common to most of the literature. The question is what are the important real-life causes of substitution effects? Mincer has shown that the wage of women is behind the inverse cross-section association of fertility and income, and he thereby directed attention to the value of the wife's time as the origin of the substitution effect. Inspection of the relationship between fertility and education has shown that the association with education tends to be more systematically negative for women or mothers than for husbands. This is consistent with Mincer's hypothesis, provided that we regard education as a reasonable proxy for the value of the wife's time. Further inspection has indicated that the inverse association is not linear, that it tends to be steeper at the lowest levels of schooling. Also, there is a tendency for this relationship to be steeper in earlier periods, among older people in more backward populations. Robert Willis (1973) has refined the hypothesis by pointing out that the value of time of women who do not work at all rises with the income of their husbands and not with their own opportunity cost in the labour market. At higher income levels of husbands, more women are unaffected by the labour market margin and therefore as income rises there should indeed be a flattening of the fertility-education relationship. In the process, a greater sophistication has been obtained concerning the measurement of the cost of time (see Gronau 1973). Others have tried to examine in some detail how the allocation of time to children varies with the mother's education, integrating more explicitly the various aspects of women's time allocation, the demand for children, and the demand for quality in children (Hill and Stafford 1972; Leibowitz 1972). Once we assume that education of women is associated not only with the cost of time but with greater demand for quality in children or with higher efficiency in producing quality, things become more complicated. The renewed interest in the quality–quantity nexus reflects a realization that an explanation of fertility requires integration of several aspects of behaviour. Human capital theory approached the decision on education and health of children using investment theory. The utility of parents for the education of their children and the possible relationship between this and the number of children have to be further developed.

It is also possible in any specific context to come to the conclusion that a static model does not give a satisfactory interpretation of the facts. The specifics of the education–fertility association in Israel had led me to believe that a diffusion process may be the important element in shaping the data, particularly the convergence to almost undifferentiated fertility in the more developed part of the population (Ben-Porath 1973). Again, education is likely to be a carrier of the diffusion process as well. Accordingly, I become sceptical about the importance of the cost-of-time hypothesis in this particular context.

These comments all refer to empirical work on cross-section data, but probably the most important stage in the empirical work is the ability to go with the hypothesis from the cross-section differentials to the understanding of time series, particularly where there are turning points or differences between subgroups in the population. Most of the work in the economics of population has not yet reached that stage. (Richard Easterlin is one of the few who tried his ideas on time series.)

POLICY ADVICE

Population research is now very much motivated (and financed) by concern with the population explosion and the desire to devise policies that will affect population growth. The type of research discussed here is oriented to the understanding of behaviour. Obviously, the better the understanding of behaviour, the easier it is to forecast future developments and to assess intelligently the possible consequences of various policy measures. The current state of research is, in my view, such that there is not much that policy-makers can already get from empirical research by way of concrete parameters or numbers. This is so both because of the tentative nature of a lot of the work, and because there is no simple translation from the variables used in research to so-called policy instruments. There is a danger that pressure to get policy advice – an excess demand for such advice – would lead to its deterioration.

What the micro-economic treatment of fertility could already contribute to people concerned with policy are the benefits of a more or less unified but flexible framework. At the moment, the basic idea common to the whole approach rather than some specific findings may prove most useful. One obvious point should be stressed: the research strategy that tries to explain behaviour as if it were generated by an attempt by individuals to optimize given external conditions does not assert that such behaviour is optimum from the social point of view. The maximization of individual utility is not a guarantee of achievement of the social good, nor is it a guarantee of achieving the social 'bad'. When a divergence occurs, social policy may force people to change their behaviour or it may affect the conditions according to which individuals make decisions, while leaving them free to pursue private optimization under socially optimal conditions.

The conceptual distinction between the effect on behaviour of becoming better off and the effect of the changing relative prices of different commodities (the distinction between income and substitution effects) may be very relevant for various policy measures. This is not an attempt to put everything that matters into a strait-jacket – it is just a framework that can accommodate many things. It is a common error to forget some of them when a specific policy measure is considered. A child allowance generates income effects, depending on the way that it is financed and on how permanent it is expected to be; it also generates a substitution effect which lowers the price of children relative to everything else. Subsidized education is again associated with income effects, depending on the way it is financed; it lowers the price of quality of children versus the quantity of children and other goods, but it may encourage or depress fertility, depending on the degree to which quality is more of a substitute for the number of children relative to other goods. While current research may not be able to give an answer to this last question, the framework can at least save the policy-maker from some hasty conclusions.

REFERENCES

Becker, Gary S (1960) 'An economic analysis of fertility' in *Demographic and Economic Change in Developed Countries*, pp209-31, Princeton: Princeton University Press, New Jersey, (Universities – National Bureau Conference Series, No 11).

– (1965) 'A theory of the allocation of time' *Economic Journal* 75, pp493-517.

Becker, Gary S and H Gregg Lewis (1973) 'On the interaction between the quantity and quality of children' *Journal of Political Economy* 81, no 2, Part II, ppS279-S288.

– (1973b) *On Child Traits and the Choice of Family Size*, Jerusalem: Falk Institute (Discussion Paper, no 731).

– (1973c) *Fertility in Israel: A Mini-Survey and Some New Findings*, Jerusalem: Falk Institute (Discussion Paper, no 736).

Ben-Porath, Yoram and Finis Welch, (1972) *Chance, Child Traits and Choice of Family Size*, Santa Monica, California: Rand Corporation (R–1117–NIH/RF).

Blake, Judith (1968) 'Are babies consumer durables?' *Population Studies* 22, pp5-25.

Duesenberry, James (1960) 'Comment on Gary S Becker', An Economic Analysis of Fertility' in *Demographic and Economic Change in Developed Countries*, Princeton: Princeton University Press (Universities-National Bureau Conference Series, no 11).

Easterlin, Richard A (1968) *Population, Labour Force, and Long Swings in Economic Growth – The American Experience*, New York: Columbia University Press (National Bureau of Economic Research: General Series, no 86).

– (1969) 'Towards a socio-economic theory of fertility: a survey of recent research on economic factors in American fertility', In S J Behrman, Leslie Corsa Jr and Ronald Freedman (eds), *Fertility and Family Planning: A World View*, Ann Arbor, Michigan: University of Michigan Press.

– (1973) *The Economics and Sociology of Fertility: A Synthesis*, Department of Economics, University of Pennsylvania, July (2nd draft).

Gregory, Paul R (1973) *A Stock Adjustment Model of Fertility: The White and Nonwhite U S Populations (1964-1970)*, (Preliminary draft).

Gronau, Reuben (1973) 'The effect of children on the housewife's value of time', *Journal of Political Economy* 81, no 2, Part II, ppS168-S199.

Heckman, James J and Robert J Willis, (1973) *Estimation of a Stochastic Model of Reproduction: An Econometric Approach* (Preliminary draft for the Conference on Research in Income and Wealth, 30 November-1 December, 1973) New York: National Bureau of Economic Research.

Hill, C Russell, and Frank P Stafford, (1972) *Allocation of Time to Preschool Children and Educational Opportunity*, Ann Arbor: University of Michigan, Institute of Public Policy Studies (discussion paper).

Lancaster, Kelvin J (1966) 'A new approach to consumer theory', *Journal of Political Economy* 74: pp132–57.

Leibenstein, Harvey (1957) *Economic Backwardness and Economic Growth*, New York: John Wiley.

– (1973) *The Economic Theory of Fertility Decline*, Harvard University, Cambridge, Massachusetts (Harvard Institute of Economic Research, Discussion Paper no 292).

Leibowitz, Arleen S (1972) *Education and the Allocation of Women's Time*, New York: National Bureau of Economic Research (mimeo).

Michael, Robert T and Robert J Willis, (1973) *Contraception and Fertility: Household Production Under Uncertainty* (preliminary draft for the Conference on Research in Income and Wealth, 30 November–1 December, 1973) New York: National Bureau of Economic Research.

Namboodiri, N Krisknan (1972) 'Some observations on the economic framework for fertility analysis', *Population Studies* 26, no 2, pp185–206.

O'Hara, Donald J (1972) *Changes in Mortality Levels and Family Decisions Regarding Children*, Santa Monica, California: Rand Corporation (R-914-RF).

Pollak, Robert A and Michael L Wachter, (1973) *The Relevance of the Household Production Function and Its Implications for the Allocation of Time*, Philadelphia: University of Pennsylvania, September 1973 (revised February 1974) (The Wharton School of Finance and Commerce, Department of Economics Discussion Paper, no 262).

Schultz, T Paul (1973a) 'Explanation of birth rate changes over space and time: a study of Taiwan', *Journal of Political Economy* 81, no 2, Part II, ppS238–S274.

– (1973b 'A preliminary survey of economic analyses of fertility', *American Economic Review: Papers and Proceedings* 63, no 2, pp71–8.

Simon, Julian (1969) 'The effect of income on fertility', *Population Studies* 23; pp327–41.

Tobin, James (1973) 'Comment on T Paul Schultz, Explanation of birth rate changes over space and time: a study of Taiwan', *Journal of Political Economy* 81, no 2, Part II, pp S275–S278.

Willis, Robert J (1973) 'A new approach to the economic theory of fertility behaviour', *Journal of Political Economy* 81, no 2, Part II, pp S14-S64.

Chapter 9

Family Economics and Macro Behaviour

Gary S Becker

Modern economists neglected the behaviour of families until the 1950s. Since then, economic analysis has been used to explain who marries whom and when (if ever) they divorce, the number of children and investments in each child's human capital, the extent and timing of labour-force participation by married women, when elderly parents rely on children for support, and many other family choices. A fair conclusion, I believe (need I remind you of my biases?), is that the economic approach contributes important insights toward explaining the large decline in birth rates during the past 100 years, the rapid expansion in the labour-force participation of married women after the 1950s, the explosive advance in divorce rates during the past two decades, and other major changes in the family. Family economics is now a respectable and growing field.

Yet perhaps because family economics is a new field, only a small literature considers the implications for other parts of economics. The family is such an important institution that progress in understanding how it behaves is justification enough for any discipline. But most economists are not particularly concerned about family behaviour. Your interest must be stimulated through a demonstration that its study helps in the analysis of other problems.

In this address I try to maintain your interest by exploring the contribution to macro-economics from the progress in family economics. This is a challenge not only because macro behaviour is a central part of economics, but also because its link to the family may seem remote and unimportant. By macro-economics I mean the analysis of economywide behaviour. Much of the time is spent on long-term economic growth, although I also discuss short and long cycles in economic activity, and the interaction between overlapping generations through Social Security, transmission of inequality, and in other ways.

Of course, one paper even by a macro expert cannot do justice to these topics, and I do not pretend to be such an expert. My purpose is to help you recognize that many conclusions in these and presumably other macro areas change radically when family choices get the attention they deserve. I apologize for the technical nature of some of the discussion that may seem out of place in a presidential address.

I. THE MALTHUSIAN AND NEOCLASSICAL MODELS

In considering the relation between economic growth and the family, it is natural to begin with Thomas Malthus's great contribution. Although usually called the Malthusian theory of population growth, a more appropriate name is the Malthusian theory of wages and average income. His first monograph, subtitled 'With Remarks on the Speculations of Mr. Godwin, M. Condorcet, and Other Writers', begins with an objection to the conclusion of these writers that the economic position of mankind will continue to improve over time. In the process of rebutting their arguments, Malthus develops his famous theory of population growth and reaches much more pessimistic conclusions about the long-term economic prospects of the average family.

You will recall that the Malthusian model assumes diminishing returns to increases in the level of population – that is, to increases in employment – when land and other capital are fixed. The analytical heart of his model (I am not concerned with the details of what he actually said) is consistent with constant returns to the scale of labour and capital, as long as the capital stock, including usable land, does not respond to changes in wages and interest rates.

The response of fertility and mortality to changes in income determine the Malthusian supply of population. Population grows more slowly when wages are low because the average person marries later and thereby has fewer children (the preventive check on population), and also because deaths increase when families are poorer (the positive check). Historical studies indicate that the effect of the economy on age at marriage was considerably greater, at least in Europe, than was its effect on death rates (see Ronald D Lee 1987b, pp450–51). Therefore, I will ignore the positive effect and consider only the preventive check through changes in the number of children.

The long-run equilibrium wage rate is found at the point on the positively inclined population supply curve where the average family has two children. The economy's production function then determines the stationary level of population that is consistent with this long-run wage rate. There is no presumption that this equilibrium wage is at the subsistence level, especially if the positive check through death rates is not important. In this model, tastes for marriage and children, not vague notions of subsistence, determine long-run wages.

The long-run wage is stable in the Malthusian model when shocks push the system out of equilibrium. For example, if an infectious disease destroys much of the population, as the Black Death destroyed perhaps 25 per cent of certain European populations during the 14th century, the decline in population raises the marginal productivity of labour. The resulting rise in wages encourages families to marry earlier and have more children. Population begins to grow and its increase over time lowers wage rates back toward equilibrium. Ultimately, this dynamic process restores both the wage rate and the level of population to their long-run levels.

If the amount of usable land increases, wages rise and that stimulates higher birth rates. Again, the growth in population continues to lower wage rates until eventually the long-run wage is restored. However, population is permanently higher because the amount of land is greater.

This example brings out that the equilibrium wage is more immune to shocks in the Malthusian system than is the level of population. Indeed, if tastes are stable over time – the Malthusian model, along with George Stigler and myself (1977), assumes *de gustibus non est disputandum* – and if technology does not continue to improve, the equilibrium wage rate remains fixed by the point on the stable supply curve where the typical couple has two surviving children. The Malthusian model does help some in explaining very long-term changes in European wage rates prior to the 19th century (Lee 1987b, gives a good analysis of the evidence). People evidently married earlier when wages were above the equilibrium level and married later when they were below.

It is ironic that Malthus's first essay on population was published in 1798 at the close of the 18th century. Although his system was accepted by many leading economists of the 19th century (see John Stuart Mill, 1848, Book I, Ch X), events after publication were not kind to the theory. Fertility eventually fell sharply rather than rose as wage rates and per capita incomes continued to advance during much of the 19th and 20th centuries in the United States, Western Europe, and Japan.

The contradiction between the theory and events explains why most economists during the first half of this century showed little interest in explaining long-term trends in income and population. But the subject is too important to remain neglected, and Robert Solow, David Cass, and others developed the neoclassical growth model in the 1950s and early 1960s. This model incorporates two major advances over the Malthusian model. Each person maximizes utility that depends on present and future consumption. More important is the recognition that changes in the capital stock respond to rates of return on investments. Unfortunately, the neoclassical model also takes a sizeable step backward from Malthus by assuming that fertility and other dimensions of population growth are independent of wages, incomes, and prices.

I trust that the basic properties of a simple neoclassical model are familiar. What may not be generally appreciated is that despite the different assumptions, the analytic structures of the neoclassical and Malthusian models are quite close and many of their implications are similar. If technology and preferences do not change over time, both models have stable steady-state levels of per capita income. The neoclassical equilibrating mechanism works through changes in the rate of investment, while the Malthusian mechanism works through changes in the rate of population growth. To illustrate, if the capital-labour ratio exceeds its steady-state level, the rate of return on capital is below and the wage rate is above their steady-state levels. In the neoclassical model this discourages investment, which lowers the capital–labour ratio over time (with exogenous population growth). In the Malthusian model this encourages population growth, which also lowers the capital-labour ratio over time (with exogenous investment in capital). We have seen that a shock to population in the Malthusian model has no effect on the level of population or per capita income in the long run. Similarly, in the neoclassical model a shock to the capital stock (perhaps wartime destruction of capital) has no long-run effect on the aggregate capital stock or per capita income.

The persistent growth in per capita incomes during the past two centuries is no easier to explain within the neoclassical framework than within the Malthusian. Of course, the neoclassical model postulates exogenous technological progress to 'explain' continuing growth in per capita incomes, but the need to rely on 'exogenous' progress is a confession of failure to explain growth with the model. Moreover, the Malthusian model can equally well postulate exogenous progress to 'explain' persistent growth.

II. THE FAMILY AND ECONOMIC GROWTH

After a short while, the economics profession became disenchanted with the neoclassical model, presumably because it, too, did not help in understanding progress. The excitement reflected in hundreds of papers that extended and elabourated this model in the 1950s and 1960s gave way during the past 15 years to a lack of interest in the analytics of growth that is a little reminiscent of the situation during the first half of the century.

Fortunately, a more relevant growth model is available through combining the best features of the neoclassical and Malthusian models and by adding a focus on investment in knowledge and skills. The neoclassicists are right to emphasize endogenous capital accumulation and utility maximization. Malthusians are right to stress the response of fertility and other components of population growth to changes in the economy, and that these responses can greatly influence economic change.

I will sketch out a modified neoclassical model where parents choose both the number of children and the capital (human or physical) bequeathed to each child. Parental altruism or 'love' toward children provides a powerful framework for the analysis of both the quantity and so-called quality of children. Altruism means that the utility of parents depends on the utility of each child. The assumption of altruism is realistic for the vast majority of families, although parent-child inter- actions are determined also by other motives. Presumably, the altruism per child is negatively related to the number of children, so that an additional child lowers the utility per child to parents in the same way as (please excuse the analogy) an additional car lowers the utility per car.

Such altruism is easily grafted on to the neoclassical utility function by letting parents' utility depend on their own life-cycle consumption and separately on their degree of altruism per child, the number of children, and the utility of each child. This formulation has the important implication that preference for parents', relative to children's, consumption (so-called time preference) is not exogenous but rises as the number of children increases.

The resources available to parents from the capital they inherit and labour earnings are spent either on own consumption, on the costs of rearing children, or on transfers to children of human and other capital. Since child rearing is time intensive, the cost of rearing children is positively related to the value of parents' time. Income per capita would rise between the parents' and the child's genera- tions if the total capital bequeathed to each child exceeds the capital inherited by each parent.

Parents choose optimal values of their own consumption, the number of children, and capital transferred to each child, while taking into account the cost of rearing children and the dependence of their utility on the utility of children. This analysis has many implications for the behaviour of fertility that Robert Barro and I explore elsewhere (see 1987 and 1988). Here I concentrate on a few that alter implications of the neoclassical model about capital accumulation and growth.

If the number of children demanded by the typical family is positively related to the income of parents (the Malthusian assumptions), or at least if it is not strongly negatively related, then this model also has stable steady-state levels of the capital–labour ratio and per capita income. But these steady states depend on variables that change the demand for children.

One example is the consequences of an extended but temporary decline in income and productivity – perhaps due to the disorganization induced by a lengthy depression. In the neoclassical model, this has no long-run effect on either per capita or aggregate income. In our modified model, an extended decline in productivity can permanently lower aggregate income because birth rates may fall when productivity, wages, and interest rates fall. Recall the sharp decline in birth rates during the Great Depression.

Just over a decade ago, Barro (1974) showed that a dose of family economics radically alters traditional conclusions about the effects of budget deficits on private savings. For example, deficits to finance Social Security payments tax future generations to support the elderly. Altruistic parents who leave bequests to their children do not seek an intergeneration redistribution of incomes, so they would increase their bequests to offset the effect on children of future taxes. If these families are common, Social Security payments and other public expenditures financed by taxes on future generations would not have much effect on private savings. This is the so-called Ricardian equivalence theorem.

A larger dose of family economics gives more radical implications in some respects but also has more conventional implications for the relation between Social Security and savings. Various comments on Ricardian equivalence emphasize that some families do not leave bequests; I will discuss these families in Section IV. Development economists have long recognized that parents value children who provide support during old age. A Social Security system that replaces child support of parents with public support raises the net cost of children to parents (not to society) since they are no longer as useful to elderly parents. As a result, a Social Security system tends to reduce the demand for children. Social Security also reduces the demand for children by parents who do not receive support but provide bequests. The net cost of children to these parents also increases when they raise bequests to offset the effect of Social Security taxes on children.

For reasons given earlier, a lower demand for children raises the capital bequeathed to each child. Therefore, Social Security and other public transfers between generations would raise private savings per child, and, as a result, raise wage rates and the capital–labour ratio in the next generation. Yet total private savings of the present generations would fall, as in a conventional life-cycle analysis with no bequests, if the decline in fertility exceeds the greater saving for each child.

Consider next an example from tax incidence. A tax on income from capital initially lowers after-tax returns and discourages investment. In the neoclassical model, capital then falls over time until the after-tax rate of return again equals the given rate of time preference. In public finance jargon, a tax on capital would be fully shifted in the long run.

A difficulty with this conclusion is the neoclassical assumption that fertility is fixed, which is especially inappropriate for very long-term changes in incidence. Fertility would fall as capital fell in response to the tax if fertility is positively related to per capita income. A fall in fertility lowers preference for present consumption and raises the demand for investment in each child through the interaction between the quality and quantity of children. Then the equilibrium after-tax rate of return must also fall, and the tax on capital is only partially shifted even in the long run.

The conclusion is more radical if fertility is negatively related to per capita income (for reasons discussed next). Fertility then increases when the stock of capital falls. Since the increase in fertility lowers investment per child, the equilibrium after-tax rate of return would have to increase. That is, we have the paradox that a tax on capital is eventually shifted by more than 100 per cent! Let me assure the theorists that this strange result does not violate the second-order conditions.

Does a negative relation between fertility and per capita income imply that children are an 'inferior' good (to use the economist's infelicitous language)? The answer is no, because the cost of rearing children increases when the capital-labour ratio and per capita income rise since wage rates and the value of parents' time spent on children rise along with the capital-labour ratio. Fertility would fall if the positive effect on fertility of an increase in income is weaker than the negative effect due to the rise in cost. The substitution effect often dominates the income effect in rich countries, for child care in these countries requires considerable time and energy of parents.

If fertility is negatively related to per capita income, an increase in the capital-labour ratio above its steady-state level would reduce fertility and thereby encourage more investment per child. The capital-labour ratio would continue to increase over time if this positive effect on investment dominates the negative effect of a lower rate of return. Consequently, a negative relation between fertility and per capita income can destabilize what is otherwise a stable steady state (see the formal analysis in Robert Tamura 1986).

Demographers have long been aware that fertility eventually declines as a country develops. Less well appreciated (although see the earlier literature by R R Nelson 1956; Robert M Solow 1956, pp90-1; S C Tsiang 1964, and others on low-level 'traps') is that a negative relation between a country's fertility and its income can destabilize a steady-state equilibrium and cause a protracted period of rising per capita incomes. However, although a decline in fertility is an important stimulus in early stages of development, it alone cannot explain sustained growth over a century or longer. In the absence of other forces, a growing economy with neoclassical production functions but without continuing technological progress eventually moves to a stable steady state with low fertility and high per capita incomes.

A promising approach to sustained growth that complements the role of fertility builds on the special properties of education and other learning. The important property for this purpose is that investments in education and other human capital are more productive when past investments are larger. That is to say, accumulation of knowledge and skills in the past eases the acquisition of additional knowledge. The mastery learning concept in education pedagogy uses this property to organize the teaching of mathematics and other subjects to children (see Benjamin S. Bloom 1976). Such a production technology implies that rates of return on investments in human capital may not fall and may even rise as the stock of human capital grows.

Perhaps it was reasonable in Malthus's time to neglect investments in human capital, but there is little excuse for the neglect in neoclassical growth theory. Modern economies spend enormous amounts on education and other training of children, and parents' investments in children are a far more important source of an economy's capital stock than are bequests or the life-cycle accumulation of physical capital. Dale Jorgenson and Barbara Fraumeni (1987) estimate that human capital comprises over 70 per cent of the total capital stock in the United States. This estimate may be too low because it does not include the contribution of human capital to output in the household sector (the authors do try to estimate household output). Seventy per cent may be higher than the true fraction because it makes no allowance for the contribution of 'raw labour' to output. I would guess that the true ratio of human capital to the total capital stock may be as high as 90 per cent or as low as 50 per cent. Of course, even this lower percentage signifies a large contribution. The neglect of human capital in wealth and income accounts greatly distorts comparisons of savings propensities and the accumulation of wealth.

Only recently have growth models begun to appreciate the potential of the learning-by-having property of human capital for generating sustained growth in per capita incomes (see Paul Romer 1986; Robert E Lucas, Jr 1988; and Robert G King and Sergio Rebelo 1986; pioneering earlier work includes Kenneth J Arrow 1962; Yoram Ben-Porath 1967; Hirofumi Uzawa 1965; and Sherwin Rosen 1976). Kevin M Murphy and I are developing an analysis that combines such a human capital technology with unskilled labour, physical capital, and endogenous fertility that results from altruism. (See Gary S Becker 1971, pp204, 207–208, for an earlier effort to combine human capital, unskilled labour, and physical capital.) Our model has a 'Malthusian' equilibrium where per capita income is constant and low and fertility is high. However, if this equilibrium receives big enough technology and other shocks – good luck may be required – the economy takes off toward a perpetual growth equilibrium with a decline in fertility and increased investment per child. Knowledge continues to grow through its embodiment in additional human capital.

Family economics is critical to the analysis since choices about number of children and investments in each child's human capital helps determine whether the economy ends up at a 'good' (i.e., growth) equilibrium or at a 'bad' (i.e., Malthusian) equilibrium. Obviously, we do not have the full answer to economic growth – public policies, conglomeration effects, and other considerations are surely important – but I do believe that our story contributes a sizeable part of the answer.

III. SHORT AND LONG CYCLES

Let me now turn briefly to the relation between family behaviour and cycles in aggregate output and other variables. For centuries marriages, births, and other family behaviour have been known to respond to fluctuations in aggregate output and prices. In an early use of regression analysis in the social sciences, G Udny Yule (1906) demonstrated that English marriages and births in the 19th century moved together with the business cycle. Subsequent studies showed that higher order as well as first births, divorce rates, and possibly the labour-force participation of secondary workers, all fluctuated procyclically in many countries (see, for example, Becker 1960, and Morris Silver 1965). Birth rates in the United States apparently became countercyclical after many married women entered the labour force. Children are cheaper during recessions because the value of time spent on children by working mothers is low then (see William P Butz and Michael P Ward 1979). Investments in education and other human capital are much less procyclical than investments in physical capital also because the foregone value of time spent in school is cheaper during bad times (Linda N Edwards 1975).

Of course, none of the competing macro models of business cycles – be they Keynesian, monetarist, neoclassical, or real – rely on family behaviour to cause business cycles. However, declining population growth was a major cause of the secular stagnation feared by Alvin H. Hansen (1939) in his presidential address to our Association almost 50 years ago. Family behaviour may play more than a negligible role even in generating ordinary business cycles. For example, an increase in the labour supply of married women or young people when household work or school becomes less attractive can induce cyclical responses in aggregate output and other variables. Cycles started by shifts in labour supply induce a negative relation between wage rates and aggregate output over business cycles. This would help explain why cyclical fluctuations in real wages appear to be less positively related to cyclical fluctuations in aggregate output than is implied by business cycles models that emphasize the demand side.

Although family behaviour presumably has only a small part in the generation of ordinary business cycles, it is likely to be crucial to long cycles in economic activity. Malthus claimed that family choices cause long-term fluctuations in the economy through the lagged effects first of marriages on births and then of births on the size of the labour force (see Maw Lin Lee and David Loschky 1987). Modern demographic analysis generates long cycles in population growth rates through the relation between aggregate fertility and the age distribution, and perhaps also between fertility and the size of a cohort (see, for example, James C Frauenthal and Kenneth E Swick 1983, and Ronald Lee 1987a). In our modified Malthus–neoclassical model, family choices cause long cycles not only in population growth, but also in capital, output, and other variables if the elasticity of the degree of altruism per child with respect to the number of children declines as families get larger, a reasonable assumption. Fertility and per capita income then fluctuate in generation-long cycles whenever the economy is disturbed away from the steady state (for a proof, see Jess Benhabib and Kazuo Nishimura 1986).

In the 1920s, the Russian economist Nicholas D. Kondratieff claimed that capitalist economies exhibit long-term fluctuations of about 50 years' duration in output and prices (see Kondratieff 1935). Simon Kuznets (1958) later argued that long-term fluctuations only last about 20 years. If long cycles of the Kondratieff or Kuznets type exist – we will need another 200 years of data to determine whether they do exist or are just a statistical figment of an overactive imagination – they almost certainly will depend on fertility and other family decisions that biologically require a long time to implement.

IV. OVERLAPPING GENERATIONS

The intrinsic risks faced by the elderly, sick, and unemployed are surely no greater in rich countries like Germany and the United States than in poor countries like China and India, nor do these risks rise as a country develops. Yet the first large-scale Social Security programme was introduced by Germany a mere 100 years ago. China, India, and numerous other countries still have only modest programmes that exclude many of their old people. We take publicly financed schools for granted, but they were unimportant until the latter half of the 19th century. Public and private programmes that protect against the consequences of illness and unemployment are even newer and less common than Social Security and public schools.

Throughout history the risks faced by the elderly, young, sick, and unemployed have been met primarily by the family, not by state transfers, private charity, or private insurance. Children usually cared for elderly or infirm parents, the unemployed looked to their families for temporary support, and parents have spent much time, money, and energy to rear and train their children. Despite the rapid growth of Social Security payments in the past few decades, almost 20 per cent of women aged 65 and over in the United States still live with their children.

The altruism and love of parents, children, spouses, and other relatives have helped protect family members against the hazards of childhood, old age, and other risks. When altruism is insufficient – unfortunately, it often is – what sociologists call social norms frequently emerge that pressure children, parents, spouses, and other relatives into helping out family members in need. In addition, family members use their frequent interaction with one another to raise the level of guilt experienced by a member when he or she does not help out.

The formal analysis of the interaction among overlapping generations began with Paul A. Samuelson's brilliant paper in 1958. This spawned an enormous literature that continues up to the present. Although Samuelson had relevant *obiter dicta* about social compacts, altruism, and family obligations, his model and that of most of the subsequent literature assumes that each person enters the analysis as a young adult without personal connections to older cohorts. A long review of overlapping generation models in the recent *New Palgrave Dictionary* (see John Geanakoplos 1987) has no discussion whatsoever of familial relations between members of overlapping generations. I claim that the neglect of childhood and of the intimate relations among parents, children, husbands–wives, and other family members misled these studies sometimes into focusing on minor problems and diverted attention away from some important consequences of the overlapping of generations (the discussion in the next few paragraphs draws partly on Becker and Murphy 1988).

One example of the emphasis on unimportant problems is the concern with the plight of older people when there are few durable assets that can finance consumption at old age. In an influential literature on the demand for money, the social role of money is even attributed to a durability that enables older people to finance consumption by selling to the next generation money accumulated when young (see, for example, Thomas Sargent 1987, Ch 7, and Neil Wallace 1980). Yet when anthropologists study simple societies that do not have money or other durable assets, they find that old people finance their consumption mainly by relying for support on children and other kin. Indeed, children have been an important resource and money balances an unimportant resource of the elderly in practically all societies, whether simple or complicated.

General equilibrium theorists are concerned about the continuum of equilibria, inefficiency, and other problems that arise in models where overlapping-generations persist indefinitely into the future (see, for example, Geanakoplos 1987, or Timothy J Kehoe 1987). Although these problems would not completely disappear, I conjecture that they would be much less important if overlapping-generations models incorporated the informal trades and assistance available to parents, children, and other members of the same family.

Ever since Plato's Republic, philosophers have worried about whether parents invest sufficiently in the health, skills, and morals of their children. Overlapping-generations models usually neglect childhood and concentrate on savings by young adults and their trades with old adults. The treatment of children by parents not only is so important in its own right, but it also greatly influences the relations between older and younger adults (Allan Drazen 1978, is one of the few earlier studies that recognizes the importance of investments in children for overlapping-generations models.)

I cannot do more on this occasion than present the bare bones of an analysis of how families respond to the demands of both old age and childhood. The analysis is straight-forward when altruistic parents leave bequests to their children. The combination of altruism and bequests eliminates any difficulties in financing the wealth-maximizing investment in children's health, training, and other human capital. For if the marginal rate of return on additional human capital exceeds the rate on assets, both parents and children would be better off with additional capital. Parents can save less to offset the negative effect on their consumption of greater spending on their children's human capital, and they can reduce bequests to offset the effect of lower savings on consumption at old age.

Bequests also partly insulate parents from many risks of old age. The opportunity to draw on bequests provides an annuity-like protection against an usually long life and other risks of old age. For example, parents who live longer than expected reduce bequests to help finance consumption in the additional years. If bequests are not a large part of children's assets, bequests can give elderly parents excellent protection against various hazards, and yet changes in bequests do not have much influence on children's welfare. In effect, children help support their parents in old age, although their support is not fully voluntary.

The analysis is less simple when parents do not leave bequests, perhaps because they are not very altruistic or because they expect their children to be better off than they are. These families tend to underinvest in children and underprotect parents against the hazards of old age because bequests are not available to finance investments and old-age support.

Social norms, feelings of guilt, and similar mechanisms may greatly moderate the degree of underinvestments and underprotection. They can induce even selfish parents to invest in children and selfish children to care for sick or poor parents. Economists neglect concepts like norms and guilt because no one really knows how they evolve. Moreover, sociologists (perhaps I should say 'we' sociologists since I am now officially also a sociologist) are too prone to use norms as a *deus ex machina* to explain behaviour that is difficult to explain in other ways. Nevertheless, there can be little doubt that norms and other intangible mechanisms do greatly affect the relations between family members in many societies, although presumably, they do not work as well as bequests in linking generations together.

Parents in richer countries have more resources to spend on children and to protect against the hazards of old age. Why then have public expenditures on both the young and old grown rapidly during the past 100 years in western countries as they have become richer? One reason is that social norms are weaker in the anonymous urban communities of industrial countries where elderly parents often live far from adult children. A more analytically tractable reason is the high rates of return in modern industrial societies on investments in the health and training of children. Recall my discussion of the role of human capital in economic development. Parents are eager to finance profitable investments in children called for by economic development, as long as they can draw on gifts and bequests that they would give to children. But gifts and bequests would become nil in many families that invest a lot in their children. These families would underinvest in children, particularly when pressure from norms is weak. The growth in public support of schooling and other investments in children as countries develop would then appear to be mainly a response to the positive effect of economic development on the benefits from human capital.

Since families that do not leave bequests are vulnerable to the hazards of old age, it is not difficult to understand why public expenditures on Social Security and medical care for the elderly have also grown rapidly in industrial countries. However, you may be surprised to find out that public expenditures on the old have not been at the expense of the young. Since 1940 in the United States, the ratio of expenditures per child under age 22 to expenditures per adult age 65 or over has hardly changed. Our analysis that combines investments in human capital with old-age support does explain why expenditures on the old and young grew in tandem. By contrast, the popular view of generation fighting – that public expenditures on the elderly grew rapidly because the old became politically power-ful as they became more numerous – cannot explain why expenditures on children grew just as rapidly.

The overlapping-generation framework is also a natural one to consider inequality and the transmission of wealth and poverty across generations. Families help perpetuate inequality because children inherit abilities and other 'endowments' from parents. Moreover, parents are the major source of the assets and human capital of children. This enormous influence of the family led my esteemed teacher, Frank H Knight, to claim that 'where the family is the social unit, the inheritance of wealth, culture, educational advantages, and economic opportunities tend toward the progressive increase of inequality...' (1935, p50).

Abilities and other endowments regress downward from parents to children in successful families where parents earn a lot, and they regress upward in unsuc-cessful families where parents earn little. The poor underinvest in each child also because they have larger families and less stable marriages. Therefore, children from poorer families tend to earn more than their parents but below the average of their generation, and children from richer families tend to earn less than their parents but above their generation's average.

Earnings depend not only on endowments but also on investments in human capital. Our earlier analysis implies that richer families do not tend to underin-vest in their children's human capital because these families leave gifts and bequests. Poorer families do tend to underinvest in children because they are not likely to leave gifts and bequests. The poor underinvest in each child also because they have large families and less stable marriages. Therefore, the relation between the earning of fathers and sons in richer families would depend mainly on the relation between endowments, while the relation between earnings of fathers and sons in poorer families would depend also on the degree of underinvestment in children. Put differently, without offsetting government subsidies to investments in the human capital of poorer children, low earnings would be more persistent across generations than high earnings – the so-called 'culture of poverty' across generations would exceed the 'culture of privilege'.

In every country with data that I have seen – this includes the United States and several European countries (see Table 1 in Becker and Nigel Tomes 1986), a few Asian countries, and some Latin American countries (James J Heckman and Joseph V Hotz 1986, consider the evidence for Panama) – earnings strongly regress to the mean between fathers and sons. Probably much less than 40 per cent of the earnings advantages or disadvantages of fathers pass to sons, and few earnings advantages or disadvantages survive three generations. Evidently, abili-ties and other endowments that generate earnings are only weakly transmitted from parents to children. This tendency to go from 'shirtsleeves to shirtsleeves' in three generations began long before industrialization and government support of education and other human capital. The 14th-century Arab historian and philoso-pher, Ibn Khaldûn said (I owe this reference to my wife, Guity Nashat), 'Prestige is an accident that affects human beings. It comes into being and decays inevitably... It reaches its end in a single family within four successive generations.' (1958, p279)... 'As a rule, no dynasty lasts beyond the [span] of three generations' (p343).

In all these countries, low earnings as well as high earnings are not strongly transmitted from fathers to sons, and Knight's claim about family life causing growing inequality is inconsistent with the evidence. Still, data for both the United States and England do appear to confirm the implication of our theory that low earnings persist more than high earnings across generations (see W Stanley Siebert 1987). Of course, *incomes* of the rich regress down more slowly between generations than do their *earnings* because rich children receive gifts and bequests from parents (see Becker and Tomes 1986, Table 2).

V. CONCLUDING REMARKS

I was attracted to the family by its obvious importance in all countries, no matter what the economic system or stage of development. People spend much of their time in a dependency relation – toward parents when children and toward grown children in old age – marriage is a crucial step for most people, children absorb time, energy, and money from their parents, divorce often causes economic hardship and mental depression, and so forth. Economic studies of the family are growing at a steady pace and they are influencing the way other social scientists look at this fundamental institution.

The economic analysis of family behaviour stimulated the development of techniques and perspectives that already has affected many parts of microeconomics, especially agricultural and labour economics, but also the study of industrial organization and preference theory. For example, the treatment of marriage as a sorting of men and women into small 'partnerships' through a reasonably efficient marriage market influenced the analysis of how workers and managers are allocated to different firms. Viewing divorce as a joint decision by husbands and wives based largely on information gathered from living together encouraged some studies of employment separations to blur the analytical distinction between quits and layoffs and to emphasize the information about working conditions and productivity gathered from on-the-job experience.

The message of this address, however, is not the importance of the family *per se*, even though family welfare is the principal goal of a well-run economic system. Nor that analytical techniques developed to understand family choices are valuable in other parts of economics. The message is that family behaviour is active, not passive, and endogenous, not exogenous. Families have large effects on the economy, and evolution of the economy greatly changes the structure and decisions of families. I illustrated how families and the economy interact through a discussion of economic growth and other issues in macroeconomics. A heightened awareness of the interaction between economic change and family choices will hasten the incorporation of family life into the mainstream of economics.

REFERENCES

Arrow, Kenneth (1962) 'The economic implications of learning by doing', *Review of Economic Studies* 29, June, pp155–73.

Barro, Robert J (1974) 'Are government bonds net wealth?', *Journal of Political Economy* 82, November/December, pp1095–117.

– and Gary S Becker (1987) 'Fertility choice in a model of economic growth', unpublished paper, Harvard University.

Becker, Gary S (1960) 'An economic analysis of fertility', in *Demographic and Economic Change in Developed Countries*, Princeton: Princeton University Press for the National Bureau of Economic Research.

– (1971) *Economic Theory*, New York: A Knopf.

– (1981) *A Treatise on the Family*, Cambridge: Harvard University Press.

– and Robert J Barro (1988) 'A reformulation of the economic theory of fertility', *Quarterly Journal of Economics* 103, February, pp1–25.

– and Kevin M Murphy (1988) 'The family and the state', *Journal of Law and Economics* 31, April, pp1–18.

– and Nigel Tomes (1986) 'Human capital and the rise and fall of families', *Journal of Labor Economics* 4, July, ppS1–S39.

Ben-Porath, Yoram (1967) 'The production of human capital and the life cycle of earnings', *Journal of Political Economy* 4, August, pp352–65.

Benhabib, Jess and Kazuo Nishimura (1986) 'Endogenous fluctuations in the Barro-Becker theory of fertility', New York University.

Bloom, Benjamin S (1976) *Human Characteristics and School Learning*, New York: McGraw-Hill.

Butz, William P and Michael P Ward (1979) 'The emergence of countercyclical US fertility', *American Economic Review* 69, June, pp318–28.

Cass, David (1965) 'Optimal growth in an aggregative model of capital accumulation', *Review of Economic Studies* 32, July, pp233–40.

Drazen, Allan (1978) 'Government debt, human capital, and bequests in a life-cycle model', *Journal of Political Economy* 86, June, pp505–16.

Edwards, Linda N (1975) 'The economics of schooling decisions: teenage enrollment rates', *Journal of Human Resources* 10, Spring, pp155–73.

Frauenthal, James C and Kenneth E Swick (1983) 'Unit cycle oscillations of the human population', *Demography* 20, August, pp385–98.

Geanakopolos, John (1987) 'Overlapping generations model of general equilibrium', *The New Palgrave Dictionary of Economics*, vol 3, London: Macmillan.

Hansen, Alvin H (1939) 'Economic progress and declining population growth', *American Economic Review* 29, March, pp1–15.

Heckman, James J and Joseph V Hotz (1986) 'The sources of inequality for males in Panama's labor market', *Journal of Human Resources* 21, Fall, pp507–42.

Jorgenson, Dale W and Barbara M Fraumeni (1987) 'The accumulation of human and non-human capital, 1948–84', Cambridge: Harvard University.

Kehoe, Timothy J (1987) 'Intertemporal general equilibrium models', Economic Theory Workshop, University of Chicago, January.

Khaldûn, Ibn (1958) *The Muqaddimah*, vol 1, trans Franz Rosenthal New York: Basic Books.

King, Robert G and Sergio Rebelo (1986) 'Business cycles with endogeneous growth', unpublished paper, University of Rochester.

Knight, Frank H (1935) 'The ethics of competition', in *The Ethics of Competition and Other Essays*, Chicago: Allen and Unwin.

Kontratieff, Nicholas D (1935) 'The long waves in economic life', *Review of Economics and Statistics* 17, May, pp105–15.

Kuznets, Simon (1958) 'Long swings in the growth of population and in related economic variables', *Proceedings of the American Philosophical Society* 102, pp25–52.

Lee, Maw Lin and David Loschky (1987) 'Malthusian population oscillations', *Economic Journal* 97, September, pp737–39.

Lee, Ronald D, (1987a) 'Population cycles', in *The New Palgrave Dictionary of Economics*, vol 3, London: Macmillan.

— (1987b) 'Population dynamics of humans and other animals', *Demography* 24, November, pp443–67.

Lucas, Robert E, Jr (1988) 'On the mechanics of economic development', *Journal of Monetary Economics* 22, July, pp3–42.

Malthus, Thomas Robert (1933) *An Essay on Population*, London: J M Dent.

Mill, John Stuart (1848) *Principles of Economics*, London.

Nelson, Richard R (1956) 'A theory of the low–level equilibrium trap', *American Economic Review* 46, December, pp894–908.

Romer, Paul (1986) 'Increasing returns and long-run growth', *Journal of Political Economy* 94, February, pp1000–37.

Rosen, Sherwin (1976) 'A theory of life earnings', *Journal of Political Economy* 84, August, ppS45–S68.

Samuelson, Paul A (1958) 'An exact consumption-loan model of interest with or without the social contrivance of money', *Journal of Political Economy* 66, December, pp467–82.

Sargent, Thomas (1987) *Dynamic Macroeconomic Theory* Cambridge: Harvard University Press.

Siebert, W Stanley (1987) 'Inequality of opportunity: an analysis based on the microeconomics of the family', in *Microeconomic Issues in Labor Economics: New Approaches*, ed R Drago and R Perlman, Brighton, UK: Wheatsheaf Books.

Silver, Morris (1965) 'Births, marriages, and business cycles in the United States', *Journal of Political Economy* 73, June, pp237–55.

Solow, Robert M (1956) 'A contribution to the theory of economic growth', *Quarterly Journal of Economics* 70, February, pp65–94.

Stigler, George J and Gary S Becker (1977) 'De gustibus non est disputandum', *American Economic Review* 67, March, pp76–90.

Tamura, Robert (1986) 'The existence of multiple steady states in one sector growth models with intergenerational altruism', unpublished paper, University of Chicago.

Tsiang, S C (1964) 'A model of economic growth in Rostovian stages', *Econometrica* 32, October, pp619–48.

Uzawa, Hirofumi (1965) 'Optimal technical change in an aggregative model of economic growth', *International Economic Review* 6, January, pp18–31.

Wallace, Neil (1980) 'The overlapping–generations model of fiat money', in *Models of Monetary Economics*, ed J H Kareken and N Wallace, Minneapolis: Federal Reserve Bank of Minneapolis.

Yule, G Udny (1906) 'On the changes in the marriage- and birth-rates in England and Wales during the past half century: with an inquiry as to their probable causes', *Journal of the Royal Statistical Society* 69, March, pp88–132.

Chapter 10

Co-operation, Inequality, and the Family

Amartya Sen

Social relations between different persons typically involve both conflict and congruence of interest. Economic analysis of social problems cannot go very far without coming to grips with both the combative and the co-operative aspects of interpersonal and intergroup relations. It is, however, possible to emphasize one of these two aspects more than the other, and indeed it is easy to see that various economists have chosen a rather different balance of what to stress and what to neglect.

Adam Smith's focus on the congruent aspects of interests of different people is, of course, well known, with his pointer to the advantages that each gains from the other's pursuit of self-interest.[1] On the other hand, Marx's analysis of class conflicts and exploitation focused particularly on combative aspects of intergroup relations.[2] Of course, Marx too devoted much attention to exploring the congruent elements in social relations (for example, the widely shared benefits that capitalist development may bring to a feudal society). Indeed, both elements figure in the writings of all the major economists, and the differences lie in the emphasis placed on congruence versus conflict. Walras's investigation of the mutual benefits from the general equilibrium of production and trade, and Keynes's study of how the effective demand of one may create employment for another, primarily focus on elements of congruence. In contrast, Ricardo's analysis of the adverse effects of profitable machinery on workers' employment, and Pigou's investigation of negative externalities imposed by polluting factories on the community, point the finger at conflict. Even though the emphasis varies, in any rich investigation the elements of congruence and conflict both tend to be firmly present.

Social institutions can be seen as dealing with elements of congruence and conflict in particular ways. For example, the market mechanism provides an opportunity for different parties to benefit from each other's complementary activities through exchange, and, at the same time, the relative prices serve as means

---

1 'It is not from the benevolence of the butcher, the brewer, or the baker, that we expect our dinner, but from their regard to their own interest' (Adam Smith, 1976 [1776], pp26–7). While Smith chose to focus on this aspect of interpersonal relations as far as economic exchanges are concerned, he did not, in the least, ignore conflicts of interest that people have to face in a society and the need to go beyond the pursuit of self-interest to achieve a harmonious and good society. In fact, moving away from the particular issue of economic exchanges, in a more general context Smith argued that while prudence is 'of all virtues that which is most helpful to the individual,' 'humanity, justice, generosity, and public spirit, are the qualities most useful to others' (Adam Smith, 1975 [1790], p189).
2 See particularly Karl Marx, 1883.

of dealing with interest conflict, yielding particular distributions of mutual benefits, rejecting others. While both buyer and seller may gain something from the transaction (non-transaction will hurt the interests of both), a higher price can favour the seller and hurt the buyer (different terms of trade yield different distributions of benefits). When exchanges and prices are determined by the market mechanism (for example, bringing demand and supply into balance), definitive use is made of co-operative opportunities arising from congruent interests, and at the same time some distribution of benefits is selected while others are rejected, thus addressing the issue of conflict.

Family relations, similarly, involve a combination of congruence and conflict. Obvious benefits accrue to all parties as a result of family arrangements, but the nature of the division of work and goods determines specific distribution of advantages and particular patterns of inequality. It is important not to lose sight of either of these functions that families fill, since a model of pure conflict (for example, a 'zero sum' game being played by the man and the woman) or a model of pure congruence (for example, every member of the family having shared goals and identical interests) would undoubtedly miss something of substance in family relations. It is fair to say that in the standard economic literature, there have not been many models of pure conflict (even though journalistic discussions of conflicts between the sexes may give the impression of unalloyed conflict), whereas models of pure congruence are indeed common.

While Gary Becker has explored the possibility of seeing family relations *as if* they were market relations, dealing with congruence and conflicts in a special – and in this context rather implausible – way, much of his 'treatise on the family' turns on the assumption of induced congruence: 'In my approach the 'optimal reallocation' results from altruism and voluntary contributions, and the 'group preference function' is identical to that of the altruistic head, even when he does not have sovereign power' (Becker 1981, p192). The so-called household production models often have this character, as do models of 'equivalence scales', even though it is not necessary to develop these models in this particular form.[3] The conflicts are effectively 'eliminated' by agreed preferences and goals. The pursuit of efficiency then becomes, in this reduced framework, the central problem, with problems of inequality and injustice getting little recognition or attention.

In analysing the role of 'institutional mediation' in influencing social and economic development and demographic change, it is important to avoid the limitations of frameworks that would emphasize pure congruence (even in an induced form), or pure conflict (even between particular groups, such as men and women). This essay is devoted to exploring the requirements of a more adequate framework and seeking insights that we may get from such a framework in reading the experiences of India's rural economy and society.

ISOLATION AND CO-OPERATION

The combination of congruent and conflicting elements in social relations can take many forms. A special class of games has attracted a good deal of attention

---

3 For an illuminating account of the various components in these different approaches to family behaviour, see A Deacon and J Muellbauer (1980). The underlying issues are clarified further in John Muellbauer's comments on my Tanner Lectures, included in A Sen (1987a).

in the form of the so-called Prisoner's Dilemma.[4] In this two-person game, the pursuit of each party's own goals leads to substantial frustration for both, since each inflicts more harm on the other through this pursuit than the gain that each receives from selfishness.

This type of conflict can be extended and analysed in terms of the Isolation Paradox[5] This is an n-person version of the conflict of which the Prisoner's Dilemma is a special case when $n = 2$, and it has the feature of permitting a *plurality* of 'collusive solutions' that happen to be superior to the atomistic outcome for both parties.[6] In general, this plurality of collusive solutions introduces an aspect of the problem that is neglected in the classic case of the two-person Prisoner's Dilemma. Indeed, in terms of the analysis presented in the preceding section, it should be obvious that a fuller understanding of the combination of congruent and conflicting interest requires us to consider a richer class of problems than the Prisoner's Dilemma would allow, even though the basic conflict – between individual and collective pursuits of goals – captured by the Prisoner's Dilemma remains and has to be incorporated and integrated in this social analysis.

The Isolation Paradox has an important application in the study of population, in capturing the jointly self-defeating nature of strategies based on the pursuit of individual advantages. It is often believed – not without reason – that a larger number of children may enhance a family's own security, and especially the security of the older members of the family. The private costs of raising additional children may not be very great, and with a larger number of children born, the probability of receiving support from one's children in old age is indeed, ceteris paribus, enhanced. There are also other possible private benefits from larger families – for example, providing employment support even when the parents are not retired and old, and providing greater protection against land usurping and crop robbery.[7] While an expansion of family size may well suit the interests of the respective families or of their heads *taken in isolation*, it is quite possible that the total population expansion as a result of having larger families may exert a downward pull on the living standard of all families involved. The overall impact may be a worsening of the position of all families, even though each family benefits from its size given the size of other families.[8] Similar examples of the Isolation Paradox can be found in other inter-family relations – for example, overutilization of land through excessive grazing and the consequent deterioration of land quality and communal assets.[9] Still other examples can be found in problems of taxation, savings, work effort and incentives; and the general problem indeed has very wide relevance.

Problems of 'isolation' provide an argument for 'interventionism', as has often been stated. All parties may benefit from the restraint imposed on each against the pursuit of its individual goals, and the state may try to bring about such an improvement through its controlling powers. There are, of course, important

---

4 See particularly R D Luce and H Raiffa (1957).
5 See my 'Isolation, assurance and the social rate of discount', (1967).
6 A K Sen (1984) *Resources, Values and Development*, pp136–138.
7 Some of these issues were taken up in the paper presented by Christopher Bliss at the Eighth World Congress of the International Economic Association in December 1986 and in the discussions that followed its presentation.
8 These issues were discussed and assessed in the *World Development Report 1984*, produced under the leadership of Nancy Birdsall.
9 On this, see M H Glantz (1976) and G Dahl and A Hjort (1976). See also my *Poverty and Famines: An Essay on Entitlement and Deprivation* (1981), pp104–105.

problems in determining the nature of control and intervention needed for producing a collusive solution, and also the nature of effective enforcement. But there is a prior and more basic problem – namely, that of selection of one particular collusive solution among many that may be better for everyone than the atomistic outcome. While rules-of-thumb may be of some use, there are many different rules-of-thumb, and there is a problem of choice involved here too. Of course, it is possible to impose a simple formula as the basis for finding a 'salient' solution – for example, insisting on 'no more than two children' in practical population policy (rules of this kind have been tried particularly in China). But there is a substantive issue of fairness and distributional judgement that has to be tackled in taking even the first step toward responding to the Isolation Paradox through public action.

On the other hand, it has been widely noticed that in many real-life situations in which the goals of different members take the form needed for the Isolation Paradox (and the Prisoner's Dilemma) to hold, actual behaviour may deviate from pure self-interest and may be more directed toward mutual advantage. Codes of conduct aimed at joint benefits seem to influence individual behaviour, even in the absence of formal contracts and enforcement.

Even in experimental games, such departure from allegedly 'rational' behaviour has been systematically observed.[10] It may take the form of acting according to *as if* goals for the sake of mutual benefit, treating joint actions as the relevant instrument of execution, and adopting a less 'individualistic' view of the choice of action. There are obvious problems in squaring such conduct with the normal tenets of 'rational' behaviour. Often this has been done by considering repetition of games over time, with people behaving implicitly co-operatively in search of *future* co-operation from others. There is, however, an argument that this cannot work when the game is repeated a finite number of times.[11] The problem has usually been dealt with in the game-theoretic and related literature through assuming some kind of a 'defect' in people's knowledge, understanding, or memory.[12]

This way of solving the problem is rather ad hoc, aside from being quite peculiar for a theory of rationality that insists on informed goal-maximizing logic for other results. If success of achievement depends on failure of knowledge or memory, greater success in knowing or recollecting may bring about failure in results. There is an internal tension in all this *within* the standard model of rationality, aside from doubts as to whether this is why people actually behave the way they do in situations of the Isolation Paradox.[13]

---

10 See, for example, L B Lave (1962) and A Rapoport and A M Chammah (1965).

11 The argument is simple enough. Any interest that a person has in behaving 'well' must (within the tenets of standard rationality models) arise from the effect that such good behaviour may have on the future behaviour of others. Obviously such an argument cannot give a reason for behaving 'well' in the final round, since there is then no point in trying to influence the conduct of others (there being no further rounds). But if people are not going to be influenced in their behaviour in the last round, there obviously is no argument for behaving 'well' in the last-but-one round for the sake of influencing future behaviour of others. Thus in the last-but-one round also, no one has any reason to behave well, within the tenets of standard rationality. This argument can be extended backwards all the way to the first round, and no one ends up having any incentive – in this reasoning – for behaving 'well' in any round whatsoever.

12 It is sometimes assumed that people do not know how many times the game will be played. Another possible assumption is that each player thinks that the other player may, in fact, enjoy co-operating (even though he or she really does not). Another assumption takes the form of a limited memory of each player in recalling what happened. See, for example, R Axelrod (1984); D Kreps et al (1982); R Aumann and S Sorin (1986) and Kaushik Basu (1987).

13 On this general issue, see A K Sen (1987b), Lecture 3.

It can be argued that a better approach to understanding social solutions to problems of isolation can be found by making a more radical departure in the characterization of individual behaviour and action. I have tried to discuss the nature of the departure elsewhere,[14] but I shall present the main features of the alternative approach briefly. It is helpful to think of the alternative approach as based on three different – but interrelated – leads coming from three thinkers belonging to altogether different traditions – namely, Kant, Smith, and Marx.

Kant's analysis of the categorical imperative is, of course, mainly ethical. The need to 'universalize' the basis of individual action is, primarily, a moral demand. The relevance of this moral concept in the present context lies in the fact that a person's action may well be influenced by ethical considerations in addition to prudential ones. The notion of what we 'ought' to do is not, of course, the same as what we 'will' actually do, but it would be remarkable if the former had no impact on the latter. The problem of isolation and the social failures resulting from it had engaged the attention of classical writers – including Hobbes and Rousseau – a great deal, and Kant's analysis of ethics and the behaviour norms derivable from it does address this question.[15]

The second lead comes from Adam Smith's discussion of the role that 'rules of conduct' play in saving society from what Smith called 'misrepresentation of self-love.'[16] Smith argued that by 'habitual reflection' we come to accept certain rules of behaviour, and do not depart from them even when we can see some immediate advantage from that departure. The approach here is only partly ethical, and the pragmatic issue of the important instrumental role that rules can play is the main point of focus.

The third lead relates to Marx's analysis of the nature of self-interest and perception. In this analysis, our own perception of self-interest is in fact a 'socially determined' perception.[17] What we see as 'our own interest' already includes certain identities with others, and our consciousness of what makes us better off and what we want to achieve incorporates distinctly social elements.

In understanding the empirical observation that problems of 'isolation' often get implicitly resolved in actual behaviour in many situations, use can be made of Kantian, Smithian, and Marxian departures from the models of 'individual rationality', in terms of which much of the discussion of modern economics is conducted. The Prisoner's Dilemma and related problems are just one class of social situations for which these departures are quite crucial. There may be nothing particularly difficult in explaining the committed behaviour of individuals in some situations of the Prisoner's Dilemma type, if the determinants of individuals' behaviour are modified in the ways suggested by Kant, Smith, and Marx. Crucial to this broader view of human behaviour is the importance of norms, rules, and perceptions.

Before completing this section, I ought to make two clarificatory statements. First, I do not claim that every situation of the Prisoner's Dilemma type will be implicitly resolved in this 'co-operative' way, yielding the right collusive solution, because of the hold of norms, rules, and social perceptions on our behaviour. Indeed, that would altogether 'over-explain' the nature of the reality under discus-

---

14 Ibid.
15 Immanuel Kant (1785).
16 Smith (1970 [1790]), p160.
17 See particularly K Marx and F Engels (1945 [1845–46]).

sion. Many conflict situations of the Prisoner's Dilemma type *do not* get resolved. The role of norms, rules, and perceptions can be important, but there is no guarantee that they will yield the collusive solution in every case. The point, rather, is to note the possibility of the dilemma being resolved in some situations if appropriate norms of behaviour, based on rules of conduct or social perceptions, happen to emerge and happen to act powerfully enough. The impasse identified by narrow models of 'individual rationality' is disestablished, but there is no guarantee that the difficulty will invariably disappear. Problems of 'isolation' can be very deep indeed, and the fact that social values and perceptions try to respond to these challenges does not mean that the problems will, in fact, invariably be solved. For my present purpose, the social responses involved are as important as the nature of the solutions that emerge.

Second, as was discussed earlier, the Prisoner's Dilemma is a very limited type of game, in which there is a unique collusive solution that is superior to the atomistic outcome based on self-interested behaviour. Even the *n*-person extension of this game in the form of the 'Isolation Paradox' does not entail that feature of uniqueness of the collusive solution. Given the multiplicity of collusive solutions that exist, an important issue is the relation between alternative norms, rules, and perceptions and alternative co-operative solutions that may exist – some more favourable to one and others more favourable to another.

The coexistence of congruent and conflicting elements applies even to the choice between different co-operative solutions. That fact is indeed quite central to the analysis of inequality sustained by value systems, including intrafamily inequalities and sex bias. The value system that leads to implicitly co-operative behaviour within a group may well be directed toward a particularly unequal solution in the choice between different co-operative outcomes. Even though the unequal solution may be superior for all parties to the result of fully atomistic and individualistic behaviours, nevertheless one group may systematically receive a lower share of the benefits of co-operation than another. Once the attention is shifted from the resolution of the Prisoner's Dilemma (with a unique co-operative outcome) to the general problems of 'isolation' (with multiple collusive possibilities), the question of inequality becomes central.

The general issues raised in this section are pursued in the analysis that follows on the institution of the family and its role in rural development, with particular reference to Indian rural society.

CO-OPERATIVE CONFLICT AND THE FAMILY

The coexistence of congruence and conflict of interest in family relations makes it tempting to consider the nature of family allocation in terms of the so-called bargaining problem formalized by J F Nash (1950). In the classic formulation of this problem, there are two persons with well-defined and clearly perceived interests in the form of two cardinal utility functions. If the two individuals fail to co-operate, the outcome (sometimes called 'the status quo position' or 'the breakdown position') is one that can be improved for both parties through co-operation. Many co-operative solutions are superior to the breakdown position, but they are not, of course, equally good for both parties. Concentrating only on the 'efficient' solutions, if solution A is superior to solution B for person 1, then for person 2, B is superior to A. Even though both parties seek – explicitly or implicitly – a collusive outcome (this is the element of congruence in the relationship), they have strictly divergent interests in the choice among the collusive solutions (this is the element of conflict). Nash proposed a particular solution of the 'bargaining problem' as the likely outcome, and other contributors have proposed other solutions.

There have been several attempts at using the framework of the 'bargaining problem' to understand the institution of the family.[18] This format has the advantage of tracing the problem of conflict of interest within the family, rather than assuming it away as do models of 'household production' and related theories developed by Becker and others. The 'bargaining problem' format also has the advantage of combining the conflicting elements with the co-operative ones in a single framework, so that the issues of male – female conflict and related matters do not have to be faced in isolation from the co-operative aspects of family life.

The main difficulty of the 'bargaining problem' format as applied to male–female divisions arises from the fact that it gives no role to problems of perception of interest and legitimacy, which can be seen as central to social situations of this type (as discussed in the preceding section). If the notion of self-interest of the individual in a social context is itself 'socially determined', that fact has to be incorporated in the formulation of the co-operative conflict itself. With notions of obligation and legitimacy affecting the ethics of behaviour (without necessarily taking a fully Kantian form) and influencing actual choices, the perceptions underlying these ideas must be given some room in the formulation of the problem.

It is, in fact, possible to distinguish between some *objective* aspects of a person's interest and his or her *perception* of self-interest. The latter may incorporate not merely sympathy for others, but also certain senses of 'identity' with other members of the group. In so far as that identity plays an important logistic part in family behaviour, it has a status of its own, but perceptions of self-interest based on such an identity may not pay adequate attention to the particular person's own well-being, including such elementary matters as work and leisure, health and morbidity, undernourishment and adequacy of diet.

It is, in fact, reasonable to see a person's well-being in terms of that person's capability of achieving valuable 'functionings'.[19] A person's 'functionings' are his or her 'doings' and 'being', for example, eating, sleeping, resting, being entertained, having fun, being happy. The relevant functionings include, inter alia, the most elementary ones, such as being well nourished and avoiding escapable morbidity, but also more sophisticated forms of fulfilment, including psychological and cultural functionings. The *valuation* of these functionings is a matter for reflection and cannot be simply inferred from the prevailing perceptions that pre-reflectively dominate day-to-day actions of individuals. This is, of course, precisely the context in which Marx invoked the notion of 'false consciousness' and pointed to an important dichotomy.

It is possible to characterize 'co-operative conflict' taking note of this dichotomy. The interpersonal division of 'benefits' in the form of functional achievements and the capability to achieve may be influenced by–among other things – the nature of perceptions that prevail in the community about self-interest and legitimacy of behaviour. The prevailing atmosphere of cohesive and

---

18 See, among others, M Manser and M Brown (1980); M B McElroy and M J Horney (1981); and A K Sen (1985a).
19 See A K Sen (1985b, 1985c and 1987).

well-integrated family perspectives – without any perceived combats – may go hand-in-hand, with great inequalities emerging from perception biases. The choice among co-operative solutions may be distinctly unfavourable to a group–women, for example – in terms of objective criteria of functional achievements, without there being any *perceived* sense of 'exploitation', given the nature of perceptions of self-interest and conceptions of what is legitimate and what is not.

This is not the occasion to discuss the details of this formal structure of 'co-operative conflicts' in a social setting, which I have done elsewhere,[20] but two of the points of departure of this structure from the standard model of the 'bargaining problem' may be briefly mentioned here.

Perceived interest response given other things, if one person's perception of self-interest attaches less value to his or her own well-being, then the collusive solution will be less favourable to that person, in terms of well-being.

Perceived contribution response given other things, if in the accounting of the respective outcomes, a person is perceived as making a larger contribution to the overall well-being of the group, then the chosen collusive solution will become more favourable to that person.

The inferior position of women in traditional societies may have much to do with perception problems associated with these two elements in the selection among collusive solutions. Consider the issue of self-interest in the particular context of sex inequality in India. The existence of widespread inequality between men and women, and between male and female children, has been observed in terms of various criteria of differential mortality, morbidity, and so on. One of the more stark reflections of that inequality is the simple ratio of females to males (the sex ratio) in the Indian population, which is only 0.93 – that is, there are only 93 women per 100 men.[21] It has, however, been pointed out that these inequalities are not seen as real inequalities in Indian society, especially in rural Indian society.

Some authors have, in fact, disputed the viability of the notion of 'personal welfare' in societies with value systems of the kind that prevail in rural India.[22] It has even been argued that if a typical Indian rural woman were asked about her personal welfare, she would find the question unintelligible, and if she were able to reply, she might answer the question in terms of her understanding of the welfare of the family as a whole. The idea of personal welfare, it has been argued, may itself be unreal in such a context.

This lack of a sense of inequality and of exploitation is undoubtedly an important part of the reality of Indian rural society. On the other hand, it is not at all clear that the right conclusion to draw from this is the non-viability or non-reality of the notion of personal welfare. In fact, this perception bias is a part of the 'co-operative' outlook that helps achieve collusive solutions that operate in the family system – collusive solutions that often happen to be characterized by inequality. Objectively, inequalities often survive by making allies out of the deprived.

This process of 'false consciousness' is particularly important in those cases of conflict where the different parties happen to live together, as in the family. The

---

20 See A K Sen (1985a) and Irene Tinker (1990).
21 See A K Sen (1985a), Appendix B. Among the many other pertinent investigations of women's status are Barbara Miller (1981); Pranab Bardhan (1984); J Kynch and A K Sen (1983); and Devaki Jain and Nirmala Banerjee (1985).
22 For a particularly illuminating presentation and defense of this point of view see Veena Das and Ralph Nicholas (1981).

role that non-individualistic, self-denying perceptions play in the exploitation of Indian women has to be more fully understood in order to appreciate the survival and strength of intrafamily inequalities in rural India. The perception problems are not, of course, immutable. With politicization and educational change, and also better understanding of the objective inequalities between the sexes in India, substantial shifts in perceptions can be expected to come about. To some extent this has been happening already.[23]

In addition to the problem of perception of self-interest, there is also that of perception of individual contributions to family well-being. In the division of labour in which women are often confined to working within the household, while men earn an income from outside, the male productive role may well be perceived as very much stronger than the female contribution. This is, of course, an extremely complex problem, and notions of who is 'contributing' how much have many causal antecedents that call for closer scrutiny. However, the 'deal' that women get vis-à-vis men is clearly not independent of these perception problems regarding contribution.

In her pioneering analysis of women's role in development, Ester Boserup noted that women appear to fare relatively better in those societies in which they play the major part in acquiring food from outside – for example, in some African regions with shifting cultivation (Boserup 1970). Outside earning may also play an important role in the contrast within India between the North and the South. It has been noted that in India in the regions where women have little outside earning or 'gainful' employment (for example, Punjab and Haryana – sex dispari-ties are on the whole sharper than in the southern states, where women have a much greater role in outside activities and earnings. Indeed, even the crude indicator of sex ratio (females per 100 males) is as low as 87 and 88 in Haryana and Punjab respectively, in contrast with the southern Indian states (96 in Karnataka, 98 in Andhra Pradesh and Tamil Nadu, and 103 in Kerala). There are many factors in the North – South contrast, but outside earnings and activities seem to be an important part of the story.[24]

It can, of course, be argued that activities within the household are in no sense less productive than activities elsewhere, since the latter are–in an important way – parasitic on the former. It is only because some people cook and rear children that others can work in the fields or the factories and earn income from outside. Division between 'gainful' and other activities is quite arbitrary; there is no way of describing one category of these activities as 'unproductive' and the other as 'productive', when the latter would be impossible without the former. But the issue is not whether activities within the household are *really* less productive, but whether they are *perceived* as such. And in so far as they are so perceived, that fact itself will have its own influence on the division of benefits within the family.

---

23 One simple example of this relates to the issue of health perceptions of men and women. In a health survey taken in Singur, near Calcutta, in 1944 – the year after the Bengal famine – the All-India Institute of Hygiene and Public Health reported certain remarkable differences in the perceptions of ill health by men and women – for example, widows having much lower perceptions of being ill than widowers. This can, of course, be a reporting hesitation, but that issue itself relates to a certain view of the legitimacy of particular perceptions. The situation, however, has changed over the years. The latest surveys in Singur do not repeat the same biases. Indeed, in neighboring Calcutta, women's self-perception of greater ill health is systematically reported. On these questions see my *Commodities and Capabilities*, (1985c), Appendix B.
24 On this question see Pranab Bardhan (1984, 1987).

Various empirical studies at the micro level have indicated that women's status and well-being within the family tend to increase quite sharply when, as a result of economic change, women start having a greater role in outside activities and have outside sources of income.[25]

The importance of outside earnings in incomes in the calculation of 'returns' from rearing male and female children has been emphasized in other empirical studies.[26] This consideration of 'returns' docs rclatc statistically to differences in child care, especially to the neglect of female children in rural North India.[27] The rewards that elderly members of the family may obtain from surviving children may be particularly influenced by the ability to earn outside income; and the male superiority in that respect, given the market traditions and biases, may thus be influential. Further, social arrangements whereby daughters move away after marriage, and are thus less able to support their own parents, may also be an important factor.

However, the model of 'cool, calculating decisions' by parents to neglect female children on the grounds of lower rates of 'returns' in rearing them has appeared to be unconvincing to many scholars.[28] There is a big issue here concerning the social origins of family behaviour. The same statistical observations can also be given other causal explanations, involving social perception of women's contributions and accepted ideas of legitimate behaviour. More involvement of men vis-à-vis women in 'gainful' activities can affect social perception of what is 'due' to men (vis-à-vis women) and to boys (vis-à-vis girls).[29]

Outside earnings can influence intrafamily divisions both directly, by influencing returns to childrearing, and indirectly, through their effects on perceptions of contributions and legitimacy of division of benefits among members of the family. The broad cultural features of different societies reflect traditions of work division and related perceptions. One of the factors that may be relevant in understanding the contrast between Africa and India in the relative survival of women vis-à-vis men is the extent of female participation in so-called gainful activities. India has a much lower sex ratio than Africa – to wit, 93 versus 102. Many factors can be introduced in explaining this difference, including the fact that the reduction of mortality and the expansion of longevity in India have been differentially beneficial to males and females.[30] But the greater role of women in outside economic activities in Africa (especially in sub-Saharan Africa) may also be important in the contrast between Africa and India (and South Asia in general).

There are, however, variations within Africa, and in drawing this contrast between Africa and Asia, regions of Asia other than South Asia would also have to

---

25 See for example, Zarina Bhatty (1980). See also other empirical works referred to in my 'Gender and co-operative conflicts', (1990).

26 See, particularly, Mark R Rosenzweig and T Paul Schultz (1982); J Behrman (1988).

27 See Barbara Miller (1981) and Monica Das Gupta (1987). The discrimination against female children is particularly strong for second and later daughters, Das Gupta shows.

28 See N Krishnaji (1987) and Alaka Basu (1988).

29 On this question see A K Sen (1990); see also Bina Agarwal (1991).

30 Views differ as to whether or not this is the standard pattern. A contrary view has been presented by Samuel H Preston (1976, p121): 'It is clear that the frequency of systematically higher female mortality declines monotonically as mortality levels improve'. Tim Dyson (1987) differentiates between a phase of mortality reduction and longevity expansion in which males benefit relatively more, and an equalizing process from which both sexes gain. Certainly, the sex ratio in India has systematically fallen since the beginning of this century, reducing the number of females per 100 males from a reported 97 in 1901 to 93 in 1971. The sex ratio now seems to be slowly rising.

be considered. There are grounds for dividing Africa into Northern and non-Northern regions, and similarly dividing Asia into Southern Asia (including India), Western Asia, and Eastern and South-eastern Asia.[31] In the fivefold division of Asia and Africa,[32] the ranking of life expectancy of females vis-à-vis that of males turns out to be (in descending order): non-Northern Africa, Eastern and Southeastern Asia, Western Asia, Northern Africa, Southern Asia. The ranking of the ratios of outside activity rates of females vis-à-vis males is much the same: non-Northern Africa, Eastern and South-eastern Asia, Western Asia, Southern Asia, Northern Africa. Only the last pair is reversed in position. The figures for life expectancy ratios, sex ratios and activity rate ratios are given in Table 1.

Table 1 *Gender differences in life expectancy and female earning activities: Africa and Asia*

Region	Life expectancy ratios (female/male) 1980–85		Activity rate ratios (female/male) 1980	
	Value	Rank	Value	Rank
Non-Northern Africa	1.071	1	0.645	1
Eastern and South-eastern Asia	1.066	2	0.610	2
Western Asia	1.052	3	0.373	3
Northern Africa	1.050	4	0.158	5
Southern Asia	0.989	5	0.336	4

Source: Calculated from United Nations tapes on 'Estimates and projections of population' (1985) and from the ILO's *Yearbook* (1986) of statistics, and presented in A Sen (1986).

It would be a mistake to draw a very clear lesson from this broad interregional contrast of Asia and Africa. However, the importance of female outside activity in the empirical findings is not inconsistent with expectations on the grounds of the theoretical analysis of co-operative conflicts involved in family divisions, especially as mediated through perceptions of contributions and interests.

CONCLUDING REMARKS

This has been a largely theoretical essay, discussing the problem of co-operative conflicts in the evolution and working of social institutions, and concentrating particularly on the family as an institution. The coexistence of congruence and conflict of interest makes the problem of institutional mediation a particularly complex one in the process of economic development. Benefits to all parties can accrue from the emergence and use of particular institutions, but the division of these benefits calls for systematic investigation. The process of development has to be judged not only in terms of average improvement, but also in terms of

31 The motivation underlying the divisions is discussed in my paper 'Africa and India: What do we have to learn from each other?' (1986).
32 China, however, is excluded from these categories. The Chinese experience has many special features, on which see Jean Drèze and Amártya Sen (1989, Chapter 11).

inequalities and disparities, and their causal antecedents.

I have argued that institutional models that eschew the problem of conflict within the family (as in some models by Gary Becker and others working in similar traditions) miss something quite central to an understanding of the family as an institution. The absence of *overt* recognition by family members of conflict within the family is, of course, an important fact, but its importance lies in the way this overt sense of 'harmony' influences the real *nature* of co-operative conflicts. It is particularly an issue of perception and of perceived legitimacy. Indeed perception bias is itself one of the important parameters in the determination of intrafamily divisions and inequalities.

Models fashioned in the tradition of the 'bargaining problem' (pioneered by J F Nash) have advantages over the unified objective function approach, making room for congruent as well as conflicting elements in interpersonal relationships. However, they too do not incorporate *perceptions* of well-being and of contribution as explicit variables in the analysis. The approach defended here starts off from the 'bargaining problem', but enriches it by bringing in notions of legitimacy related to perceptions of contributions and perceptions of well-being as determining variables.[33] These perceptions and the related norms and rules of conduct are instruments of resolution of action conflicts and are also mechanisms for legitimizing and sustaining unequal resolutions of interest conflicts.

The approach outlined here is a very general one and is particularly concerned with identifying important (and often neglected) variables, rather than specifying particular quantitative hypotheses. I have tried to argue that variables such as perceptions of contributions and legitimacy can have a profound impact on the co-operative conflicts that influence intrafamily divisions and the well-being of family members. The subjective perceptions are among the objective determinants of family behaviour and its far-reaching consequences.

REFERENCES

Agarwal, Bina (1991) 'Social Security and the family' in E Ahmad et al (eds), *Social Security in Developing Countries* Oxford: Clarendon Press.

Aumann, R and S Sorin (1986) 'Cooperation and bounded rationality', mimeo.

Axelrod, R (1984) *Evolution of Cooperation* New York: Academic Press.

Bardhan, Pranab (1984) *Land, Labour and Rural Poverty: Essays in Development Economics* New York: Columbia University Press.

— (1987) 'On the economic geography of sex disparity in child survival in India: a note', mimeo, University of California, Berkeley.

---

33 For a less hurried description of this alternative approach, see my 'Gender and co-operative conflicts', and Drèze and Sen (1989). The influences of variables other than outside activity (such as literacy and female education) on co-operative conflicts are also discussed there. One of the interesting cases is the state of Kerala in India, which has a female-male ratio higher than 1.03 and strong female advantage in life expectancy, similar to that in Europe and North America. Kerala is distinguished from the rest of India in having a long tradition of high literacy (including high female literacy), an active public health service, and a matrilineal inheritance system for some of the communities in the state. The big push toward high literacy and female education was initiated in parts of what is now Kerala by Rani Gouri Parvathi Bai, the ruling queen of Travancore (a 'native state', formally outside British India), as early as 1817. These and related matters are discussed in Drèze and Sen (1989), Chapters 4, 11, and 13.

Basu, Alaka (1988) *Culture, the Status of Women and Demographic Behaviour*, New Delhi: National Council of Applied Economic Research.

Basu, Kaushik (1987) *On Ethics and Economics*, Oxford: Blackwell.

Becker, Gary S (1981) *A Treatise on the Family*, Cambridge, Massachusetts: Harvard University Press.

Behrman, J (1988) 'Intrahousehold allocation of nutrients in rural India: Are boys Favoured? Do parents exhibit inequality aversion?', *Oxford Economic Papers* 40.

Bhatty, Zarina (1980) 'Economic role and status of women: a case study of women in beedi industry in Allahabad', ILO Working Paper.

Boserup, Ester (1970) *Woman's Role in Economic Development*, London: Allen & Unwin.

Dahl, G and A Hjort (1976) *Having Herds: Pastoral Herd Growth and Household Economy*, Stockhom: University of Stockholm.

Das, Veena and Ralph Nicholas (1981) '"Welfare" and "well-being" in South Asian societies', American Council of Learned Societies/Social Science Research Council Joint Committee on South Asia, SSRC, New York.

Das Gupta, Monica (1987) 'Selective discrimination against female children in rural Punjab, India' *Population and Development Review* 13.

Deacon, A and J Muellbauer (1980) *Economics and Consumer Behaviour*, Cambridge: Cambridge University Press.

Drèze, Jean and A K Sen (1989) *Hunger and Public Action*, Oxford: Clarendon Press.

Dyon, Tim (1987) 'Excess female mortality in India: uncertain evidence on a narrowing differential' mimeo, London School of Economics.

Glantz, M H (1976) *The Politics of Natural Disaster: The Case of the Sahel Drought*, New York: Praeger.

Jain, Devaki and Nirmala Banerjee (1985) *Tyranny of the Household: Investigative Essays on Women's Work*, New Delhi: Vikas.

Johansson, S Ryan (1983) 'Deferred infanticide: excess female mortality during child-hood', mimeo, University of California, Graduate Group in Democraphy, Berkeley.

Kant, Immanuel (1907 [1785]) *Fundamental Principles of Metaphysics of Ethics,* trans. T K Abbot. London: Longman.

Kreps, D; P Milgrom; J Roberts and R Wilson (1982) 'Rational cooperation in finitely repeated Prisoner's Dilemma', *Journal of Economics Theory* 27.

Krishnaji, N (1987) 'Poverty and sex ration: some data and speculations', *Economic and Political Weekly* 22.

Kynch, J and A K Sen (1983) 'Indian women: well-being and survival', *Cambridge Journal of Economics* 7.

Lave, L B (1962) 'An empirical approach to the Prisoner's Dilemma game', *Quarterly Journal of Economics* 76.

Loutfi, M F (1980) *The Rural Women: Unequal Partners in Development*, Geneva: ILO.

Luce, R D and H Raiffa (1957) *Decisions*, New York: Wiley.

Manser, M and M Brown (1980) 'Marriage and household decision-making: a bargaining analysis', *International Economic Review* 21.

Marx, Karl (1887 [1883]) *Capital: A Critical Analysis of Capitalist Production; 3rd ed*, London: Sonnenschein.

Marx, K and F Engels (1947 [1845–46]) *The German Ideology*, New York: International Publishers.

McElroy, M B and M J Horney (1981) 'Nash bargained household decisions: toward a generalization of the theory of demand', *International Economic Review* 22.

Mies, Maria (1982) *The Lace Makers of Narsapur*, London: Zed Press.

Miller, Barbara (1981) *The Endangered Sex: Neglect of Female Children in Rural North India*, Ithaca, New York: Cornell University Press.

Nash, J F (1950) 'The bargaining problem', *Econometrica* 18.

Preston, Samuel H (1976) *Mortality Patterns in National Populations*, New York: Academic Press.

Rapoport, A and A M Chammah (1965) *Prisoner's Dilemma: A Study in Conflict and Cooperation*, Ann Arbor: University of Michigan Press.

Rosenzweig, Mark R and T Paul Schultz (1982) 'Market opportunities, genetic endowment and intrafamily resource distribution: child survival in rural India', *American Economic Review* 72.

Sen, A K (1990) 'Gender and cooperative conflicts', in Irene Tinker (1990).

Sen, A K (1967) 'Isolation, assurance and the social rate of discount', *Quarterly Journal of Economic* 81; reprinted in A K Sen, *Resources, Values and Development*, Oxford: Blackwell and Cambridge, Massachussetts: Harvard University Press.

— (1981) *Poverty and Famines: An Essay on Entitlement and Deprivation*, Oxford: Clarendon Press.

— (1985a) 'Women, technology and sexual divisions', *Trade and Development*, (UNCTAD) 6.

— (1985b) 'Well-being, agency and freedom: The Dewey Lectures 1984', *Journal of Philosophy* 82.

— (1985c) *Commodities and Capabilities*, Amsterdam: North-Holland.

— (1986) 'Africa and India: What do we have to learn from each other?' C N Vakil Memorial Lecture at the Eight World Congress of te International Economic Association, december; published in Kenneth J Arrow, ed. *The Balance Between Industry and Agriculture in Economic Development*, vol 1: *Basic Issues*, London: Macmillan.

— (1987a) *The Standard of Living*, ed Geoffrey Hawthorn, Cambridge: Cambridge University Press.

— (1987b) *On Ethics and Economics*, Oxford: Blackwell.

Smith, Adam (1976 [1776]) *An Inquiry into the Nature and Causes of the Wealth of Nations*, Oxford: Clarendon Press.

— (1975 [1790]) *The Theory of Moral Sentiments*, Oxford: Clarendon Press.

Tinker, Irene (ed) (1990) *Persistent Inequalities: Women and World Development*, New York: Oxford University Press.

Chapter 11

Fertility Control and the Problem of Voluntarism

Judith Blake

The problem of voluntarism is emerging as a central issue in debates about policy to control fertility. Since most of the world's people are having, and want to have, families larger than will ensure low or zero growth rates in the near future, policy makers must ultimately face the need to reduce family-size desires. Indeed, it is already true that spokesmen for 'instituting' coercion and 'maintaining' voluntarism have taken polarized positions. On the side of coercion are those who argue for penalties to be imposed on parents after a given number of children, and similar measures.[1] On the side of voluntarism are those who claim that the most a policy should do is to provide the means of family planning and thus preserve 'the right to choose.'[2]

However, both the coercion approach and the laissez-faire approach ('the right to choose') suffer from a serious empirical flaw. They each assume that free choice and voluntarism now exist, and that they are marred only by incomplete distribution of contraceptives. One approach says that voluntarism must be curtailed, the other claims that it must be preserved at all cost. Neither recognizes that it does not exist right now. Neither takes into account that at present, reproductive behaviour is under stringent institutional control, and that this control constitutes, in most societies, a coercive pro-natalist policy. Hence, an effective anti-natalist policy will not necessarily involve an increase in coercion or a reduction in the 'voluntary' element in reproduction, because individuals are under pro-natalist constraints right now. People make their 'voluntary' reproductive choices in an institutional context that severely constrains them not to choose non-marriage, not to choose childlessness, not to choose only one child, and even not to limit themselves solely to two children. If we can gain insight into the coercions and restraints under which we currently operate, it may become more obvious that an anti-natalist policy can be one that is more voluntary – allows a wider spectrum of individual choice – than is presently the case. Let us first examine why individuals may be said to be under constraint and suffer coercion, in any society, regarding reproduction.

To understand how societies exercise control over the number of children individuals want to have, we need some schematic model of the determinants of

---

1 See, for example, Garrett Hardin (1968); Paul R Ehrlich and Anne H Ehrlich (1970), and Kenneth Boulding (1964).
2 Frank W Notestein (1970), p448.

family size preferences. In presenting this model, I shall start with three assumptions. First of all, we are dealing here with preferences that discount variability in mortality. So, we are speaking of preferences for a number of living children. Obviously, any given set of preferences concerning living children will require more births when mortality is high and fewer when it is low. People's calculations, the subjective probabilities under which they operate, will introduce some lag in the number of births desired in periods of shifting (typically declining) mortality. However, for reasons that I hope will soon become clear, I believe it is naïve to assume that, with nothing else changing, people will adjust their fertility to below their prior preferences in response to declining mortality. The most one can hope is that fertility will adjust to match the declining mortality. A second assumption is that we are dealing with the family size they would prefer if they could control both fecundity and undesired pregnancy. In other words, this is a family-size preference distribution that may not be empirically expressed in a real society because, in a real society, a share of people know they are sterile, or subfecund, and they may answer questions about preferences in terms of actualities. The same holds true for lack of control over unwanted pregnancy. So, we are attempting, for the moment, to rule out purely conditional factors influencing people to adjust their preferences up and down. Third, the framework assumes that whether the preferred family-size goals are large or small, they are goals and, hence, can be analysed in terms of a means-end framework. The model explicitly rules out the notion that in one type of society reproductive behaviour is simply a resultant (something that just happens), or something about which structured expectations are lacking. Thus, I am saying that, given the constraints and coercions concerning reproduction in any society, pursuit of those reproductive goals is as 'rational' or 'calculated' in one society as in another. The same framework holds for all societies. I shall discuss this point in more detail after the framework is presented. Finally, I should perhaps remind the reader that family-size preferences are not the only influences on fertility, whether measured by period birth rates or the family size of cohorts. For example, fertility levels and family size may be greatly influenced by involuntary factors such as infecundity.[3]

In a very general sense, the institutional structure of every society defines and controls what it is that individual couples 'get out of' having children – the rewards or utilities for having a family – and how much couples must sacrifice to have them – the costs. Thus, it is fair to say that all of the specific variables that are said to 'affect' family-size preferences – urbanization, educational level, possession of modern consumer goods, female labour force participation, or whatever, actually may be said to affect the utility of children and their costs. Thus, urbanization or modernization can be cited as influential on family-size preferences because there are things about these very broad complexes that make children less useful and more costly. What kinds of utilities and costs are involved? It is convenient to set out the model as follows:

---

3 Kingsley Davis and Judith Blake (1956). This article presents a framework for analysing both voluntary and involuntary influences on fertility generally. The present framework is concerned with factors leading individuals to want larger or smaller families and, hence, to attempt action to make families large or small.

A. The Utilities of Children

1. Economic utilities
    Examples:
    > a. child labour;
    > b. help in old age.
2. Non-economic utilities
    Examples:
    > a. conferral of kinship statuses. (One can, for example, only attain the status of 'parent' by having children);
    > b. creation of a customized personal group that is larger and more varied than a dyad. Family size preferences may be greatly affected by how long individuals want to preserve this family-type of group in their lives;
    > c. long term extension of oneself, one's family, one's group – the immortality syndrome;
    > d. performance of religious rituals after one's death that are believed necessary for salvation, future incarnations, etc;
    > e. 'psychic income' of various origins – children as household pets, children as objects of affection, children as givers of affection, etc.

B. The Costs of Children

I. Direct Costs
    1. Economic
    Example:
    > prices of children of various qualities; such prices include not only present standards of consumption, but standards of preparation (like education).
    2. Non-economic
    Example:
    > non-cash parental inputs – socializing jobs of a personal nature.

II. Indirect Costs
    1. Economic
    Examples:
    > a. quality, as expressed in price, of one's own desired style of life, over and above that shared as overhead with children. The things one forgoes at the consumption level in order to be able to afford children – recreation, clothing, travel, club memberships;
    > b. earnings of the wife that may be sacrificed.
    2. Non-economic
    Example:
    > alternative uses of time and energy over and above the normal working day (that is, alternative uses of 'leisure' time) – recreation, do-gooding, being 'creative', being 'cultured.'

The difference between a high and low fertility society is not that, in one, people calculate regarding reproduction and in the other they do not. They calculate in both. Rather, it is that the utilities and costs in terms of which the calculations are made differ. And, in any given society, the way in which these utilities and costs are structured, the model in terms of which individuals have to operate is largely beyond their control. To a very great extent, they are handed the schedule of utilities and costs and they then make their family-size 'decisions' within this predetermined framework. It is, unfortunately, not now possible to assign many quantitative values to either the utility or costs elements in the framework. However, this situation is beginning to improve. At least two young economists, for example, are doing excellent estimates of the direct economic costs of children in the United States.[4] When such work is more widely extended, I believe the model will be found to have predictive powers. As I hope to show by the use of concrete examples below, it is certainly a reasonable framework within which to place comparative and historical variations in family-size preferences.

A word is necessary before proceeding further concerning the saliency of repro-ductive goals. It is often said that the mass of the people in developing countries seem not even to have thought about wanting a specific number of children. Developing peoples do not, sometimes, appear to think of more or fewer children as an issue, as something about which one formulates definite expectations. In a superficial sense, this may be true. The questions we ask concerning family-size preferences on surveys, doubtless force answers that are not part of the usual thought processes of the respondents. However, I think it is an error to assume that vagueness, or difficulty in formulating a response to such a question, or a direct claim by the respondent that he has not thought about the issue, can be taken to imply a vacuum. Even more in error is the assumption that this appar-ently unstructured situation can be readily manipulated by propaganda and 'education'. Rather, we need to remember that the existence of a goal can be ascer-tained by a variety of responses, not simply the ability to offer a direct verbal one. This is particularly true if the goal is one of the 'givens' in a society. The person does not have a firmed up, highly articulate response because the need for such a response has never been presented. But, if he is challenged by someone taking action that assumes his goals do not exist, or that they are different from what they may in fact be, then such goals can become more salient. One may get a response that is covertly or overtly hostile – systematic apathy or expressed outrage. In this sense, one might cite the relative ineffectiveness of family-planning efforts in rural India as a sort of public test of the family-size goal (see Lewis 1975). Family planners assumed that Indians had small-to-moderate size families as a goal. The programmes have thus represented a challenge. The response has been apathy and foot-dragging. If the programmes were to be pushed very hard, the response could be widespread open hostility. A goal is there and, contrary to what was thought, it is not consonant with early and systematic use of contraceptives.

Now, in order to make the discussion of coercion and constraint regarding family-size preferences more concrete, it is instructive to contrast the situations of traditional, agricultural societies and modern, industrial ones.

Characteristically, demographers are fond of pointing out that the fertility of traditional, peasant societies has had to be high, to counterbalance the high and

---

4 Thomas Espenshade has worked on this problem for two years at International Population and Urban Research, University of California, Berkeley. See his monograph, *The Cost of Children in Urban United States* (Espenshade 1973). Boone Turchi, an economist at the University of North Carolina, is presently finishing a dissertation on the same subject.

fluctuating mortality. Those societies that were not able to produce the requisite fertility simply did not stay around. Unfortunately, some people have tended to regard this long-term evolutionary statement as a perfectly adequate explanation of the motivation of individuals. Individuals are said to be primarily motivated in their family-size preferences by the mortality situation. They want large families because of high mortality. Reduce the mortality and, presto, everyone 'adjusts'. This view of the situation leaves out of account entirely that the way in which societies have adjusted to high mortality is through their institutional structure, not through the unlikely chance that some would, for inexplicable reasons, contain a majority of individuals dedicated to maintaining a demographic balance, whereas others would be wiped out for lack of such altruists. Those societies that have survived, motivated individuals not merely to compensate for the average mortality situation, but to over-compensate for it, and thus offset the disastrous effects of mortality peaks. The institutional structure that has provided this motivation has, however, had a positive rather than a preventive focus. To be sure, the family and kinship in traditional peasant societies has functioned in such a way as to overcompensate for mortality. But the family-size desires of individuals have been geared, independent of mortality, to a utility-cost schedule that has the family and the kinship structure as its focus. The weights in this schedule have been such as to make people want to do what the society needed – produce large families. People have been hooked into a system in which kinship and the family are ends in themselves, and are also instrumental in bringing about other ultimate goals. This fact must be understood in order to comprehend why, when the mortality conditions change, the fertility response is often extremely sluggish. Indeed, as Tabbarah (1971) has pointed out, it may be that in some peasant societies people are very far from achieving the number of living children they desire, and hence a decline in mortality simply aids them in achieving their family-size goal.[6]

Let us consider first the utilities of children in traditional, agricultural societies. These comprise not only the well-understood economic advantages, some of which Laila El-Hamamsy (1972) has outlined so well in her paper on belief systems and family planning in Moslem societies particularly, but the non-economic utilities as well. Individuals not only use children for labour and depend on them for care and assistance later in life, they also gain the only rewarded statuses in the kinship system through having children and, thereby, becoming parents. And, the kinship system is either the pre-eminent one, or among the most pre-eminent in the society. Other sectors, non-kinship sectors, are typically linked with kinship in some intrinsic fashion. For example, a priestly role will simultaneously be a familial role rather than belonging to a celibate, or one will depend for salvation on rituals performed by others after one's death, rather than on one's own conduct and efforts. Because structures alternative to kinship and the family may well be suppressed, the individual is highly dependent on the family for protection, influence and support, and social status. The more the society is oriented around kinship, and the more other roles depend on the basic kinship roles, the more, by definition, non-economic, as well as economic utility the individual enjoys by creating and maintaining a family. It is important also to bear in mind that this type of social structure deals very heavily in intangible rewards that are pursued through labour intensive, poorly capitalized activities such as prayers, ritual, ceremony, gestures of respect and deference, visiting, etc. The utilities that are socially supported for the ordinary person are salvation through the fulfilment of familial obligations, the performing of kinship roles so as to receive approval and avoid sanctions, the achievement of some honoured status in the religious structure, etc. In these circumstances, and with no alternative utilities on the horizon, rational behaviour consists in going after those that exist.

What about the costs of children? In subsistence economies, the direct economic costs of children tend to be camouflaged by a lack of the enforced accounting that a monetary system introduces. More important, the range of quality in children is likely to be held down by the overall societal limitations. When, for example, excellent medical and dental care are unavailable and educational facilities are marginal, children of privilege and children of poverty are more similar than in modern societies. The direct non-economic costs of offspring are also minimized by the availability of a wider kinship network to help with child-rearing, and by the fact that the authoritarian position of parents allows them to place older children *in loco parentis* with respect to younger ones. In general, the expectation is not that the parents put out enormous amounts of effort, but that they receive from children.

At the level of indirect economic costs, it is obvious that given the limited opportunities for social and geographic mobility, little competes with children. Parents do not have an enormous and nagging sense of things forgone, things on which they could have spent their money or resources, had they not had so many children. Wives do not see earnings going a glimmering. By the same token, indirect non-economic costs are restricted. The range of activities on which one could spend one's energies, one's leisure time, is circumscribed. Moreover, children do not typically compete with these as they would in a society in which such activities are often most enjoyably pursued without children around. In sum, therefore, when one looks at utilities and costs, economic or non-economic, direct or indirect, one finds a situation that maximizes what the individual is likely to regard as his gain by having children in relation to other possible gains, and minimizes the costs to him. But we have to realize that, with respect to both utilities and costs, these are pro-natalist, and are kept pro-natalist, by means of intense social control over such elements as the roles and activities of women and youth, as well as over social and geographical mobility. An individual's family-size desires are thus 'voluntary', only in the very limited sense that, given this highly controlled situation, and the implicit and explicit coercions in maintaining the utilities and costs as they are, he 'chooses' to have a large family.

I believe that instructive contrasts with presently developing societies emerge from a consideration of why Western Europeans wanted to reduce their family size. It is quite clear that factors other than declining mortality were influential. For example, in England and Wales completed family size began to decline among the cohort of women who married in 1871.[5] With the cohort marrying around the turn of the century most of the decline that was ever to occur had already done so. By contrast, the largest drops in mortality occurred after 1900. Basing his conclusions on 250 international life tables (mostly for Western countries), Stolnitz (1955–56) emphasizes the remarkable acceleration in mortality declines beginning around the turn of the century, whereas the gains in life expectancy in the middle decades of the 19th century were relatively slight. With life expectancies at birth

---

5 See, for example, E A Wrigley (1969), pp196–9.

of well under 50 years, Western Europeans and the British were already reducing their family size.

It is also important to bear in mind that fertility declines were not in response to worsening levels of living, but to greatly improved ones. Moreover, they occurred soonest and most drastically among the classes that were becoming prosperous most rapidly – the new professional and business classes. Among the professional classes in Great Britain who married in the last decade of the 19th century, completed family size was already down to an average of 2.8 children.[6]

It thus appears that Western Europeans were reacting not simply to increased reproductive efficiency (lessened mortality among the young), nor to economic deprivation, but to a major change in the utilities and costs of children, including, it must be remembered, non-economic utilities and non-economic costs. This major change in the utilities and cost schedule resulted from the modernization process, but not merely from the technological and economic changes that occurred. Equally influential were the changes in the entire system of social stratification – the bases of social honour, prestige, and life chances – and the way in which the family related to this emerging social system. If we refer to the utilities-costs framework, I think it is easy to see that the social revolution that accompanied the industrial revolution operated to make children less rewarding and more costly than they had been in the past. Moreover, the decreased utility and enhanced cost were most likely to impinge first on the prosperous urban classes.

With regard to utilities, the movement of economic activity away from the home and family shifted the economic burden almost entirely on to the husband and father. Children were no longer an economic utility. What was left was their non-economic utility. This continued to be of great importance, but could be achieved by small-to-moderate size families. Moreover, the non-economic utility of children is vulnerable to changes in social support for the family and for familial roles in the society. For example, alternative means whereby women can achieve social status other than motherhood reduce the average non-economic utility of child-bearing.

With regard to costs, urbanization and modernization meant that the direct economic costs of children increased, whether for housing in dense urban areas, food that increasingly had to be purchased, or compulsory education. Perhaps more important, however, was the enormous expansion of indirect costs of both an economic and a non-economic nature. This has been documented brilliantly by Banks in his book *Prosperity and Parenthood* (Banks 1954). Banks' research shows an accelerating rise in standards, as well as levels, of consumption – what economists would call a major change in 'tastes'. During the early and middle 19th century in Britain, there was a major increase in the uses of money, time, and effort in ways that competed with children. Banks documents the emergence of 'high-style' living standards among the burgeoning professional classes – gourmet tastes in wines and foods, the institution of the vacation, discriminating furnishings for the home, elegant clothing, servants as a sign of middle-class respectability, and so on.

What Banks does not discuss is why such a change in consumption standards occurred. What led the English middle and upper classes to become so involved in this immense effort to consume in ever more discriminating and expensive ways?

---

6 Wrigley (1969), p 186

Here it is clear that such a change cannot be explained within an economic framework. One has to recognize the sociological function of such consumption in the changing stratificational picture of the 19th century. This was a time when the power of a hereditary aristocracy was finally being shaken. The dynamism of industrialization and modernization was making possible a rapid rise of new classes – meritocracies of professionals and businessmen. The society was experiencing unprecedented social and geographical mobility. These new classes deeply desired to consolidate their economic positions by also appearing to be 'cultured' and knowledgeable consumers. In fact, since the social honour accorded the life-style of the aristocracy long outlasted its political power, the rising middle class had a major problem of 'measuring up' with which to contend. Moreover, since the increased social mobility rendered many people strangers in new settings, their life-styles were of great importance symbolically as indicators of how they should be treated by others. With traditional status indicators gone, the rising classes became enmeshed in a compulsive system of using consumption as a means of indicating achievement and commanding deference. Additionally, since the overall increase in mobility was a threat, as well as an opportunity to all concerned, the new classes were eager to throw up exclusionary barriers against those below them in the social scale.

Finally, it is important to remember that once a status system based heavily on ascription (on the status of one's family rather than one's accomplishments) is overthrown (through the loss of castes or a functioning aristocracy), individuals do not have a choice concerning whether they will participate in the new system. They must make an effort to achieve and maintain a respectable social status, or they run the risk of becoming virtual nonentities in the society. Under these modern circumstances, it is not deprivation that causes the immense efforts and sacrifices made by the well-to-do, but relative deprivation. The more affluent everyone gets, the more relatively deprived each individual may feel – the more he finds that his resources are never quite enough to counter real and imagined threats to his position in life, the prestige he has, the amount of social honour he can command.

Banks also documents the intense anxiety experienced by parents concerning the future of their children in such a rapidly changing society. In such circumstances, the direct economic costs of education for children rose disproportionately as parents attempted to engage in what might be called educational overkill as a means of assuring their children's futures. As the servant class declined in numbers and the nuclear family became more isolated from other kinsmen, the direct non-economic costs of children rose. Parenthood became a definite occupation rather than a part of one's usual daily activities. Time and effort had to be assigned to it – or at least could not be simultaneously assigned to something else. At the level of indirect non-economic costs, the rising level of consumption meant that there were many things alternative to children on which individuals could spend their hours and their effort – a genuine world of recreation opened up for the non-aristocrats.

The anti-natalist effect of a modern system of social stratification has been best documented for England. The fact that, in some countries, voluntary fertility declined without an industrial revolution comparable to England's may seem anomalous. Indeed, France is usually cited as the principal anomaly in this regard. Without going into details, I believe that the seemingly deviant cases will fall into line, if one refrains from tying the voluntary fertility decline to the industrial revolution in such a literal fashion. In the classic English case, the industrial revolution functioned to reduce the utilities of children and increase their costs. But, it is not the only process that can reduce such utilities and increase costs. Obviously, the utilities-costs framework can be affected primarily by political, rather than economic and social, influence. Eastern Europe and Russia bear this out.

In sum, although one may prefer one kind of political regime to another, it is by no means clear that an intended anti-natalist effect on the utilities-costs schedule is, by definition, more coercive than an economic and social situation that leaves individuals few genuine options concerning family size, whether large or small. The historical record does not allow us to equate economic and social influence with 'voluntarism', and government policy with 'coercion'. At present, we appear to be in what might be called a pre-Keynesian era with regard to population policy. This is particularly serious for the developing countries. I fail to see how such countries can resolve their fertility-control problems if they are encouraged to think that the utilities-costs framework must be left intact until it is changed by an industrial revolution. History may not repeat itself so conveniently.

REFERENCES

Banks, J A (1954) *Prosperity and Parenthood*, London: Routledge and Kegan Paul.

Boulding, Kenneth (1964) *The Meaning of the 20th Century*, New York: Harper & Row.

Davis, Kingsley and Judith Blake (1956) 'Social structure and fertility: an analytical framework', *Economic Development and Cultural Change* 4, pp221–35. April.

Ehrlich, Paul R and Anne H Ehrlich (1970) *Population, Resources and Environment*, San Francisco: W H Freeman & Co.

El-Hamamsy, Laila Shukry (1972) 'Belief systems and family planning in peasant societies' in *Are Our Descendants Doomed?*, ed. Harrison Brown and Edward Hutchings, J R. New York: Viking.

Espenshade, Thomas (1973) *The Cost of Children in Urban United States*. Institute of International Studies, University of California, Berkeley. Reprinted by Greenwood Press, Westport, Conn, 1976.

Hardin, Garrett (1968) 'The tragedy of the commons', *Science* 162, pp1243–48.

Lewis, John P (1972) 'Population control in India' in *Are Our Descendants Doomed?*, ed. Harrison Brown and Edward Hutchings, Jr. New York: Viking.

Notestein, Frank W (1970) 'Zero population growth', *Population Index* 36, October–December.

Stolnitz, George J (1955–56) 'A century of international mortality trends: I', *Population Studies* 9, pp24–55.

Tabbarah, Riad B (1971) 'Toward a theory of demographic development', *Economic Development and Cultural Change* 19, pp257–75.

Wrigley, E A (1969) *Population and History*, New York: McGraw-Hill.

Chapter 12

Patriarchy and Fertility Decisions

Nancy Folbre

At the very core of feminist theory, in virtually all its incarnations, lies a central insight about the nature of motherhood. However distinctive women's biological capacities may be, it is the social and historical context of child-bearing and child-rearing that largely determines their structure and meaning. To many feminists, this social and historical context inextricably links motherhood to the larger pattern of patriarchy. The social relations which govern human reproduction often reinforce the domination of women and the exploitation of women's labour.

Feminist scholars have made a great deal of progress in exploring this issue since Friederich Engels first formally broached it in *The Family, Private Property, and the State*. Yet despite an overriding concern with the social aspects of mother-hood, feminists have had remarkably little to say about a long-run secular trend that has transformed family life – the demographic transition to lower fertility rates. Over the last 200 years, women in the United States and France, as well as many other countries, have gradually but consciously limited their fertility, and radically diminished the proportion of their adult years devoted to the care of young infants. A similar process of fertility decline has long been under way in many areas of the developing world.

If feminist theory does in fact offer a unique insight into women's position in society, it must also offer some distinctive contribution to the explanation of fertility decline. Similarly if forms of social control over women's reproductive capacity do represent an important component of patriarchal inequality, an analysis of changes in the utilization of that reproductive capacity must help reveal some of the laws of motion of patriarchy. Both of these ambitious claims are to be explored here in some detail.

The starting point of this explanation is a brief review of existing theories of fertility decline. Many social scientists have emphasized the role that modernization plays in changing traditional attitudes toward family size. Particularly when developed to include consideration of the patriarchal elements of both traditional and modern culture, this approach offers important insights into the process of demographic change. Unfortunately, it offers no explanation of why or how attitudinal change occurs. Economic approaches aspire to provide such an explanation, stressing the economic factors that increase the economic costs of children and provide a material incentive for fertility decline. But conventional economic approaches narrowly assume that the costs of children are primarily determined by technological changes that affect the productivity of children's labour and the 'opportunity cost' of a mother's time – what a mother could have produced or earned had she devoted time to purposes other than child-rearing.

Missing from both conventional economic and non-economic explanations of fertility decline is any explicit consideration of economic inequalities between the sexes and between the generations. Yet such inequalities provide both a means of enforcing patriarchal attitudes and a means of forcing women and/or children to bear most of the costs of child-rearing. Analysis of these inequalities clarifies the necessity for a major revision of the economic approach to fertility decisions that can accommodate the role of such social and political factors. The claim that families respond to changes in the costs and benefits of children makes sense if and only if it is stated in non-economic terms. These costs and benefits hinge upon differences in economic power between women, men, and children, *and* upon the ways in which these differences find expression in political struggle and cultural change.

In this article, I argue that the transition to capitalism modifies some traditional patriarchal inequalities, increasing the cost of children to parents, and to men in particular. In developing this argument, I do not assume that family decisions can be reduced to a consideration of material costs and benefits, merely that they are affected, in the long run, by economic constraints. I devote most of my attention to changes in the structure of economic power, but emphasize, from the outset, that such changes merely create opportunities for political struggle whose realization depends upon a particular historical and cultural context. The political economy of fertility decisions which I outline is extremely schematic. Although many sources of historical evidence and contemporary data are mobilized to support and defend this theoretical framework, its primary value lies in the development of hypotheses that can serve as a useful guide to future research.

The first section of this article is devoted to a review of the demographic literature which centres on a critique of neoclassical economic theories of fertility decline. The second section presents the first part of my argument that patriarchal inequalities affect the costs of children. Reviewing a large and diverse body of literature describing societies in which elder males own or control access to the means of production, I defend two distinct, but interrelated hypothesis. First, patriarchal control over adult children enhances parents' ability to enjoy positive economic benefits and/or to substantially defray the costs of children; second, patriarchal control over women enhances men's ability to shift a significant portion of the cost of children to individual mothers, by increasing the length of their workday and lowering the opportunity cost of their time. In the third section, changes in these particular forms of patriarchal control are linked to the growth of market production and wage labour. Although the transition to capitalism leads to the genesis of new motives and mechanisms for control over women's labour power, it diminishes patriarchal authority over adult children and therefore reduces the economic benefits of large families. As a result it contributes to a decline in desired family size which weakens resistance to women's demands for control over their own reproduction and modifies the traditional sexual division of labour. Both these changes, in turn, contribute to the continuing process of fertility decline. Some of the more significant political implications of this transformation of family life are outlined in the final section.

THEORIES OF FERTILITY DECLINE: A THEORETICAL OVERVIEW

When the theory of the demographic transition was first articulated, decline in fertility rates was often pictured as an automatic response to the decline in mortality rates that seemed to precede it. By increasing the probability of an individual child's survival, improvements in public health make it possible for parents to raise the same number of children to maturity even if they give birth to a smaller number. But while parents probably do notice and respond to changes in mortality, most demographers agree that their 'compensation' for improvements in life expectancy cannot account for the scope and magnitude of fertility decline. In most advanced capitalist countries reductions in births have begun to override and overtake reductions in death rates, so much so, in fact, that many countries face the prospect of negative population growth in the near future. Furthermore, some historical studies have revealed situations in which fertility decline *preceded* mortality decline or persisted despite actual increases in mortality (Temkin-Greener and Swedlund 1978; Shin 1977).

Some social scientists have argued that technical innovations in modern contraceptive technology (first the condom, sponge, and diaphragm, later oral contraceptives and intrauterine devices) are a major determinant of fertility decline. But they have been forced to substantially qualify their argument. In the first place, historical records from both the United States and France clearly show that the origins of fertility decline lie much deeper in historical time than even the simplest of modern contraceptives (Temkin-Greener and Swedlund 1978; Ostcrud and Fulton 1976; van de Walle 1974). In the second place, surveys of many areas of the developing world show that the supply of contraceptive technology does not affect fertility levels unless there is a latent demand for birth control. Family planning services tend to have only a marginal impact in areas where levels of *desired* family size remain high (Mauldin and Berelson 1978; Kenya 1979). Birth control technology may be a contributing factor, but it is neither a necessary nor a sufficient condition for fertility decline.

Emphasizing changes in desired family size, many historians and sociologists have placed the weight of their explanation of fertility decline upon attitudinal changes that are associated with the process of modernization. Many proponents of this general approach, such as Edward Shorter, Lawrence Stone, and Carl Degler, provide fascinating documentation of historical changes in the manifestations of patriarchal control within families in Europe and the United States (Shorter 1975; Foucault 1980; Stone 1979; Degler 1980). Similarly, many anthropologists and sociologists convincingly describe a wide variety of patriarchal traditions giving way before the process of modernization in some Third World countries (Smelser 1967; Lerner 1963; Inkeles and Smith 1974). However insightful these contributions, they raise at least as many questions as they answer. Why do women begin to 'assert their individuality'? Why do parents begin to view children differently? Even those modernization theorists who acknowledge the role of economic change sidestep any exploration of the specific links in the larger chain of casualty.

Economists, on the other hand, tend to focus on changes in family income or exogenously given changes in the price or cost of children. Revising Thomas Malthus's assumption that families would not resort to fertility control, some economists have formulated a neo-Malthusian view that fertility decline is primarily a response to economic stress brought about by population growth. The view has been particularly influential in American historical demography, where Kenneth Lockridge, Phillip Greven, and Richard Easterlin, among others, have argued that the press of population against ever-more scarce land was a major impetus to social change (Perlman 1980; Easterlin 1976; Greven 1970). Many economists, however, have questioned the view that population increase inevitably leads to economic stress, and some U.S. historians have taken the land scarcity argument to task for ignoring the growth of commercialization (Simon 1977; Serron 1980; Main 1965). Some populations may live in an economic world in which all other factors of production are fixed, and technological change does not occur. But this situation is clearly not relevant to the more general case in which fertility decline accompanies an increase in wealth, incomes, and wages. Both over time and across families in most populations, it is prosperity, not poverty, that is associated with lower levels of fertility (Simon 1977).

The seemingly paradoxical effect of income on fertility has prompted many economists to shift their attention to changes in the cost of children. As income goes up, parental expenditures on children tend to increase more than proportionately. Part of the explanation for this lies in the fact that children's contributions to family income, contributions which effectively defray their cost, tend to be lower in economics at higher levels of economic development.

A spate of relatively recent studies show fairly conclusively that children constitute an important economic asset for families in many areas of the developing world (Nag 1972; Nag et al 1978; Rosenzweig 1978; Tunda 1979). Although most of these studies have focused on the work of young children, or children residing within the household, increasing attention is being devoted to the remittances that older children send home to their parents. Similarly, contemporary research in social history reveals the importance of adult children's economic contributions in 18th- and 19th-century Europe and the United States (Berkner 1973; Braun 1978; Tilly and Scott 1978).

Efforts to explain this pattern have led to the hypothesis that the process of industrialization leads to technological changes that increase the cost of children. This hypothesis dwells on changes in the potential benefits of young children's labour, as well as increases in the costs that they impose. Industrialization curtails opportunities for the types of work that young children can effectively perform, and the demand for skilled labour dictates increases in levels of education. The costs of schooling become increasingly significant. Modern production methods lead to a growing separation between home and work, and draw women into the wage labour force, where they find it difficult to combine child care with income-earning activities. Opportunities for women to earn a higher market wage raise the opportunity cost of children – the income and/or product forgone in order to provide child care.

This hypothetical scenario has motivated many multivariate statistical analyses of the relationship between levels of industrialization and cross-national or cross-regional fertility differentials (Beaver 1974; Hicks 1974; Bizien 1979). Such statistical approaches seldom make explicit their assumptions regarding the way in which families respond to increases in the cost of children. This theoretical gap has been filled by neoclassical economists who have followed Gary Becker's lead in developing an elegant and internally consistent model of household decision-making (Becker 1960). In its original formulation, the neoclassical approach treated children as consumption goods. More recent applications by Mark Rosenweig and Robert Evenson incorporate the possibility that children contribute to household income (Rozenweig and Evenson 1977; Rozenweig 1977; Rozenweig and Schultz 1982; Willis 1980).

The neoclassical economic theory represents the antithesis of the modernization theory. Rather than attributing central importance to changes in attitudes, it assumes that attitudes remain constant over time, in the form of a joint utility function embodying the family's tastes and preferences. This formal assumption sets the stage for the hypothesis that families respond to changes in prices and incomes in an economically rational manner, always seeking to maximize their utility. This hypothesis generates a number of empirically testable hypotheses and has stimulated a great deal of empirical research. The results are somewhat inaccessible to those who lack familiarity with the mathematics of constrained optimization. They are, however, remarkably consistent with predictions.

Simply stated, neoclassical theory provides a micro-economic foundation for the claim that an increase in the price or cost of children will lead to a decrease in the number of children demanded, all else equal. This claim may be perfectly correct. But it implies that the cost of children is exogenously given, determined in advance just like the price of a good produced for sale in a competitive market. 'All else equal' is an economistic assumption that overlooks the fact the parents can directly affect the cost of children, by choosing how much money to spend on them, and that children can directly affect their own price, by choosing how much they will contribute to parental income.

The proviso 'all else equal' is not empirically testable, and it cannot be convincingly applied to an explanation of demographic change. The family is not a static, unchanging institution, a decision-making black box. It is a group of individuals who make collective, but not necessarily consensual decisions. It is prone to conflict and compromise, to domination and resistance.

A number of neoclassical economists grant that household decisions may reflect differences in bargaining power between family members (McElroy and Horney 1978; Manser and Brown 1978). But the possibility that changes in bargaining power might affect fertility decisions has never been conceded. Such a concession would undermine the entire neoclassical economic approach because it invites consideration of the role of non-market forces, such as political struggle, in economic change.

The failure to incorporate any consideration of changing power relations within the family constitutes what many feminists might consider a fatal error of omission. But the failure to explore the way in which such changing power relations affect the costs and benefits of children renders the neoclassical approach incomplete even on its own terms.

Changes in the nature of work and the extent of education may make it difficult for *young* children to make a pecuniary contribution to family income, but they increase the potential contribution of *mature* children. It is *adult* children, not young children, on whom parents rely in old age.[1] Adult children with educational levels higher than their parents, and with access to more lucrative, modern forms of employment, could constitute a much more valuable economic asset than children in a rural, agricultural setting. But potential contributions to family income are distinct from actual contributions. Adult children, unlike minors, exercise considerable discretion over their economic transfers to parents.[2]

---

1 Since many women are not capable of child-bearing after the age of 40, their youngest child is likely to be at least 20 years old by the time they reach 60.
2 For an empirical treatment of this issue, see Nancy Folbre (1984).

Similarly, the opportunity cost of women's time is determined not only by 'technical' factors such as their potential market wage, or potential productivity in household production, but also by the actual number of hours of productive labour which women sacrifice to child care. Mothers who give up leisure time, rather than work time, to care for children are imposing costs primarily on themselves rather than on the family as a whole. The extension of their workday effectively lowers the cost of children to all other family members.

There is a great deal of evidence suggesting that economic inequality between family members affects the way in which family decisions are made. This evidence, reviewed in the next section, supports the claim that patriarchy affects the costs and benefits of children. It also serves as the basis for the larger argument that changes in desired family size cannot be explained either as the result of an ideological process of modernization or a technological process of industrialization, but must be seen as part of a larger, more complex social process – the transition to capitalism.

PATRIARCHY AND THE FAMILY

In its common usage, patriarchy connotes male domination. Its etymological meaning, however, is 'rule of the fathers'. To Engels and many others, the father's desire to ensure the legitimacy of his offspring, his 'genetic immortality', was a primary motive for control over women's sexuality (Engels 1968 [1884]. Marxist feminists, on the other hand, have emphasized the ruling class's desire to ensure the existence of a large inexpensive labour force (Quick 1977). Both of these explanations may be plausible, but they overlook a far more direct connection between production and reproduction characteristic of societies in which elder males control a means of production. A growing body of research on the social history of the family in Europe and the United States suggests that individual fathers were able to materially benefit from their adult children's labour partly because they wielded a great deal of power over them. Such material benefits provide an economic motive for male control over women's reproductive capacity.

William Goode offers a broad overview of economic relations between the generations.

> *Until industrialization parents in the West could control their children's choice of spouse largely through control over inheritance, for land was almost the only potential source of income. The farm youth could not marry without his father's permission, because by his own effort he could not gain enough money with which to buy land. Throughout most of the West, a dowry system was followed, so that the girl's chances of marrying were negligible unless her family was willing to present her with a sufficient marriage gift (Goode 1979).*

Lawrence Stone (1979) and Alan McFarlane (1978) note some of the more specific features of patriarchal control over children within the English landowning class. Phillip Grevin (1970) and Robert Gross (1976), among others, offer accounts of relations between fathers and sons in colonial Massachusetts which suggest a conflict over control of land. Lutz Berkner (1973) argues that adult sons in Austria often grew impatient waiting to come into their inheritance. Their dependence on their fathers as a source of wealth reinforced their willingness to devote labour or income to the care of their elderly parents. Louise A. Tilly and Joan Scott, describing France in the 18th century, write that 'in some cases parents formalized a working daughter's responsibility to the family wage economy by arranging to receive her wages from her employer' (Tilly and Scott 1978).

In many developing countries, elder males have successfully parlayed their control over means of production into control over the labour power of children. 'Familial modes of production', writes John Caldwell, 'are characterized by relations of production between kin that give the more powerful of the decision makers material advantage'. He notes that the household decision makers are likely to be the old and the male (Caldwell 1978). Describing mainland China, S. Cheung claims that 'until only a few decades ago, parents in China held property rights in children'.[3] Janet Salaff's recent monograph on working daughters in Hong Kong shows that filial loyalty may lead to patriarchal exploitation, even where daughters have entered the wage labour force (Salaff 1981).

A number of African case studies concur. In a volume of essays on the persistence of high fertility, G W Jones points out, 'in a patriarchal social structure (e.g., much of West Africa and the Moslem World) the father can (and often does) keep sons unmarried until quite a mature age, and even after they have married and perhaps taken up residence separately, the fruits of the sons' labour continue to flow to the father in the sense that he maintains control over the land they work (Jones 1977, p20). Per Kongstad and Mette Monsted (1980) describe a division of labour between subsistence and cash production which allows fathers to appropriate a significant portion of the products of both children's and women's labour.

None of these studies imply that children would not contribute to patriarchal or parental income in the absence of pecuniary rewards or coercive practices. Filial responsibilities are strongly defined by cultural norms that may persist long after the material basis for them has begun to disintegrate. Furthermore, families often represent a relative community of interest in which personal gain is not always a primary consideration. But the very existence of inequality within the family suggests that it is cemented together by far more than love or charity. Purely voluntary contributions to parental income are likely to be less predictable, less reliable, and smaller in magnitude than contributions that are either involuntary or based on the expectation of significant future rewards.

If children have no independent access either to land, capital, or another source of income, such as wages, their potential economic gains from conformity to parental demands are quite significant. An increase in children's ability to garner income independently of parents diminishes such gains (see Tilly 1978, p41). Whether parental ability to benefit from control over their adult children's labour operates on the level of the individual household or reflects a larger set of attitudes that have or once had material economic basis in the society as a whole, it enhances the economic benefits of children and therefore increases the economic incentives to high fertility. But although the benefits of children's labour may be enjoyed by both parents, the costs of providing that labour are not necessarily shared equally. Even if mothers receive the same share of total family income that fathers do, they may work longer and harder for it. And even though women almost always have some bargaining power within the household, their ability to influence the allocation of resources within the family is often quite limited.

If high fertility rates were simply a manifestation of the potential economic

---

3 See S Cheung (1972). He writes: 'Provided that a child obeys his parent, he is a relatively secure asset holding' (p641).

gains from children, one might assume that women would freely choose to bear large numbers of children. In fact, women's freedom of reproductive choice is often constrained by forms of patriarchal oppression which are coercively pro-natal.[4] Marriage laws in the United States and Europe traditionally guaranteed a husband's legal right to intercourse with his wife with or without her consent, and similar laws are operative in many areas of the developing world (O'Faolain and Martines 1973). Abortion rights are a relatively recent (and not necessarily permanent) gain for women in the United States, and are limited largely to low fertility countries such as Japan, France, and the Soviet Union. Modern contraceptives, significant because they offer women the historically unprecedented opportunity to prevent conception without the full and conscious co-operation of their sexual partners, are illegal in many countries, inaccessible in many others.[5] Extremely punitive sanctions are applied worldwide to sexual practices unlikely to culminate in pregnancy, particularly when indulged in by members of the same sex.

Coercive pro-natalism can also take the form of economic inequalities that impose severe penalties on women who choose not to marry or to dissolve a marriage through separation or divorce. Like inequality between parents and children, inequality between women and men appeared in pre-capitalist Western Europe in the form of unequal ownership and control of wealth. In both pre-industrial England, France, and the United States, the wife and the mother of the family unit exercised no legal or formal control over land (Newland 1980, p3). Unmarried women who inherited property often received a guaranteed income from property held in trust or received a small sum of money in place of land. Women who lived in countries with legal systems derived from Roman law remained under the guardianship of a male all their lives. It was not until the mid-19th century that some of the Roman law countries (led by Scandinavia) made adult, single women legally independent (op cit).

Similarly clear-cut inequalities typify many areas of the developing world. There is tremendous variation in legal institutions regarding female property rights, but the only area of the world with a significant history of female land ownership is Africa (Pala 1976). Even within Africa, many cultures have a long tradition of vesting control of land in male hands (Mblyni 1971, 1972, n.d.). Under Islamic law, women's rights to inherit property are automatically limited to shares less than those male relatives receive. Kathleen Staudt (Staudt 1980) notes that daughters in Nepal are denied the right to inherit leaseholds granted to deceased fathers, although sons can inherit (op cit).

No systematic comparisons of cross-national patterns of female wealth ownership have been conducted, but International Labour Office (ILO) data show that women are far more under-represented among employers and the self-employed ('own account workers') than in the labour-force as a whole. Women outnumber men only in the 'unpaid family worker' category (International Labour Office 1978). However important their contribution outside the market economy, it is not a contribution that offers potential for economic independence.

Even among the propertyless, patriarchal inequalities can reduce women's ability to garner an independent income and make them far more economically

---

4 For a discussion of the concept of coercive pro-natalism, see Judith Blake (1974) and Leta Hollingsworth (1974).
5 Legal restrictions on contraception exist in the following countries (in which abortion is also illegal, barring risk of mother's life): Ireland, Malta, Brazil, Saudi Arabia, Chad, Gabon, Libya, Malawi.

dependent on marriage than men. Strong sanctions are often imposed on female participation in economic activities. The most extreme example is the Moslem practice of purdah, which makes it difficult for women to work at all outside the home (see Mernissi 1975; Saadawi 1980; Cain et al 1979). In at least two countries, Senegal and the Philippines, husbands have a legal right to prevent their wives from working outside the home (Boye 1980; Cortes 1980). Employers in Japan commonly forced women to resign from their jobs upon marriage until this practice was ruled unconstitutional in 1965 (Cole 1971; Lebra et al 1976). Even sanctions which take the relatively benign form of disapproval or protective legislation tend to reinforce women's specialization in certain sex-segregated tasks (Jelin 1983). These tasks are almost always less remunerative than men's (International Labour Office 1978).

Such significant differences in women's and men's access to wealth and income reduce the economic bargaining power of individual women within the family, thus making it possible for husbands to impose their own family size decisions on wives. These differences may also make it possible for fathers to shift much of the cost of children on to mothers. Although there have been few efforts to explore such disparities, some studies reveal that food is distributed quite unequally between the sexes, and several cross-national empirical surveys show that women work much longer hours overall than men (Szalai 1975; Horowitz 1981; see also Evenson et al 1979; Hartmann 1981). Differences in the length of the total workday for women and men may partially reflect differences in the intensity of work, but they indicate that leisure time is often distributed quite unequally between the sexes. They also indicate that women may bear a disproportionate share of the cost of children. Theresa Ho's analysis of household survey data from the Philippines demonstrates that additional child care responsibilities have a much more significant effect on the length of the workday than on hours of market work (Ho 1979).

Patriarchal inequality bestows some direct material benefits upon individual men. But some of the benefits that men enjoy are indirect in nature. They are embodied in future benefits from children's labour which may be largely paid for by women's efforts. Changes in the net cost of children both affect and are affected by changes in women's economic roles. A decline in children's economic contributions to the household can reduce the indirect benefits to men of forms of inequality which increase the birth rate. As a result, women may gain more freedom to make reproductive decisions. An increase in women's bargaining power can lead women to reduce the labour that they contribute to the household. As a result, a larger part of the cost of children may be shifted to men.

This interrelationship between patriarchal inequality and the costs of children clarifies the potential relationship between changes in patriarchy and changes in desired family size. There is good reason to believe that the transition to capitalism helps set these potential interactions into actual motion.

PATRIARCHY AND THE TRANSITION TO CAPITALISM

Marx and Engels argued long ago that the growth of capitalism would undermine the basis of the patriarchal family. The proletariat were being dispossessed of the private property which was, in their view, one of the primary causes of sexual inequality. Working-class women were being forced to enter the labour-force, and would therefore lose their economic dependence upon men and assume a new role in the struggle for socialism that would eliminate the last vestiges of sexual inequality even as it superseded capitalist exploitation.[6]

Widespread recognition of the persistence of patriarchal inequalities within capitalism (as well as within socialist countries) has completely discredited this sweeping generalization. Engels clearly neglected the possibility that patriarchal interests might be reflected in policies set by employers, trade unions, and the state which would define the terms of women's participation in the labour-force (Hartmann 1979). He also ignored the possibility that wage labour would not replace household production and child rearing, but would simply increase the length of women's workday. But Engels and Marx were both correct in noting that patriarchal control over children would be weakened by the growth of wage labour, a process that manifested itself in England through the parliamentary debates over the child labour laws.[7]

In the course of capitalist development, families owning their own means of production become increasingly less common. The per centage of the population that is 'self-employed' becomes quite small, and self-employment increasingly takes the form of professional employments that do not effectively utilize family labour. Although the process of proletarianization is well under way in most areas of the developing world, ILO data show that 'unpaid family workers' tend to comprise a large portion of the labour-force in countries with relatively low levels of per capita income and high levels of fertility (International Labour Office 1978).

Proletarianization does not eliminate the economic importance of the family, which continues to serve as an income-pooling unit long after its members begin to receive their income from sources outside the family (Tilly and Scott 1978). But the potential influence of the family upon individual members' welfare is somewhat diminished. As opportunities for employment outside the home become available, children come to rely less and less upon inheritance of their father's assets, particularly if those assets are too small to afford a better source of income than wage employment. As parents join the wage labour-force, the relative value of the tangible property which they can convey to their children is reduced. Because ownership and control of 'family' assets is commonly vested in the elder male head of household, decrease in the importance of these assets effectively reduces the economic basis for patriarchal authority over children.

Intergenerational transfer of wealth continues to play an important role in determining individuals' economic destinies. But for most families, transfer of physical assets becomes far less important than transfer of 'human capital' in the form of 'investments' in children's education. The prolongation of school attendance imposes new costs on parents. In addition to the direct expenditures

---

6 Engels (1968 [1884]). See also Karl Marx (1967 [1867]): 'However terrible and disgusting the dissolution, under the capitalist system, of the old family ties may appear, nevertheless modern industry, by assigning as it does an important part in the process of production, outside the domestic sphere, to women, to children of both sexes, creates a new economic foundation for a higher form of the family and/or relations between sexes' (p489).
7 Marx (1967 [1867], p489). Discussing the English Parliament he writes, 'The force of facts (however) compelled it at last to acknowledge that modern industry, in overturning the economic foundation on which was based the traditional family, and the family labour corresponding to it had also unloosened all traditional family ties. The rights of the children had to be proclaimed.' See also *The Communist Manifesto*: 'Do you charge us with wanting to stop the exploitation of children by their parents? To this crime, we plead guilty' (Tucker 1972, p349).

required to keep a child in school, school attendance reduces children's participation in market work and/or home production. Education confers important benefits in the form of enhanced productivity and increased earnings, but it also increases children's economic independence from their parents.

The 'gift' of education, unlike a bequest, cannot be made contingent upon conformity to certain expectations. Once given, it can hardly be revoked. Parents are hard put to deny such a gift, partly because of their concern for their children's future welfare, partly because compulsory education and child labour laws limit their legal ability to put children to work.[8]

Parents are not necessarily caught by surprise. Anticipating the effect of changes in relations between the generations, they may take measures to preserve their relative bargaining power. By consciously limiting family size, families owning property can increase the size of the share of their assets that children will inherit. By investing a great deal in the education of a smaller number of children, they may increase their children's future earnings more than enough to offset potential losses in their share of those earnings.

But the expansion of market production definitely weakens traditional forms of patriarchal control over children and can lead, in the long run, to a reduction in children's propensity to contribute to parental income. The International Value of Children Survey conducted by the East-West Population Institute, for instance, revealed that many respondents felt that children are now less willing to support their parents in old age and are less willing to give part of their wages to their parents when they start working. In Hawaii, 41 per cent of respondents felt this way; in Thailand, 63 per cent, in Japan, 64 per cent (*Value of Children* 1977–8). In all cases, a majority of respondents disapproved of these changes.

Children do not abruptly abandon their responsibilities to parents, but they play an increasingly important role in defining the extent of those responsibilities. They may seek to legitimate their new independence by transferring a part of their traditional responsibility to the state. In his recent history of poverty in the United States, James T Patterson writes that:

> the allure of old age insurance to the middle classes was not the benefits they would ultimately receive themselves, which few Americans calculated carefully. Rather, it was the assurance that they would not have to take care of their parents in the here and now (Patterson 1981).

Charles Hohm has shown that government-implemented social security programmes are associated with lower levels of fertility (Hohm 1975). Hohm and others tend to treat the advent of such programmes as incidental to the process of economic development. Yet social security programmes may represent a response to the decline in intergenerational transfers as well as a rationale for a continued decline.

The transformation of economic relationships between parents and children is so closely intertwined with the transformation of economic relationships between women and men that neither can be understood in isolation. Women's employment outside the home does not have an immediate or a dramatic effect on their bargain-

---

8 For an account of working-class resistance to mass public education, see Michael B Katz (1968). On the 'morality' governing relations between parents and children and how it is affected by education, see John Caldwell (1980).

ing power, because patterns of market employment are shaped by patriarchal forms of inequality. Women often receive lower levels of education and often gain less labour-market experience than men precisely because of the demands of household production and child care. The fact that men may initially bring more formal skills and more reliable work commitment to the employer provides one of the rationales for a sexual wage differential. Ironically, the sexual wage differential, once established, creates a new economic imperative for women to continue to assume primary responsibility for child care simply because they cannot replace the earnings that would be lost if fathers took time off from wage work.

The circular reinforcement of the traditional division of labour is strengthened by the emergence of new motives for the reproduction of sexual inequality. Employers perceive certain advantages to forms of discrimination which segment the labour force (Gordon 1972). Male-dominated trade unions seek to improve their bargaining position by restricting women's access to the skilled trades (Foner 1979; see also Jameson 1977; Jacoby 1977). New mechanisms of enforcing sexual inequality also appear. In many areas of the Third World the introduction of capitalist relations of production actually worsens women's position as they are excluded form the modern sector of the economy (Boserup 1970; Chaney and Schmink 1976).

But the direct effects of capitalism on women must be distinguished from its indirect effects upon the family economy. Although the sexual wage differential seems to persist in the course of economic development, other forces come into play to modify the traditional sexual division of labour. Primary among these are the changes in desired family size brought about as the economic benefits of children are reduced. When women invest a great deal of time in child-bearing, part of the productivity of their work lies in expected returns from their adult children's labour. As these returns diminish, a sexual division of labour that channels women into child-bearing and child rearing becomes more costly to individual families. Fertility decline and the expansion of public education reduce the amount of time mothers devote directly to child care, and the expansion of commodity production increasingly provides cheap substitutes for home-produced goods and services. As a result, women begin to have difficulty finding non market activities that contribute significantly to the family's standard of living.[9]

Although men tend to resist changes that reduce their bargaining power in the home, they recognize and respond to a decline in the economic value of women's household labour. Thus, they may encourage their wives to seek wage employment to increase the family's ability to purchase market goods. Women's entrance into the wage labour-force is not simply the result of modernization or technological change. It is the result of competition for the labour of children, and competition in the production of goods and services. In this competition, capitalism slowly emerges as the victor.

Here again, a circular, cumulative casualty comes into play. As women with fewer children begin to spend relatively more time in the market and less time in the home, they gain labour-force experience that delegitimates the argument that their commitment to wage labour is not as great as men's. Women begin to demand, and sometimes to obtain, better employment opportunities. Men may be threatened by women's new economic assertiveness, but as the economic benefits

---

9 An interesting aspect of this transition in the United States is the increase in the late 19th century of 'market' production performed at home. See, for instance Joan M. Jensen (1980).

of children diminish further, and as women's potential contribution to the family's total earnings increases, men become increasingly aware of the economic benefits of family planning. Thus, legal gains in rights to contraception and abortion are more often the consequence, rather than the cause, of declines in desired family size, and while feminists often initiate the struggle for such reforms, men often see good reason to support them (see, for instance, Banks and Banks 1964).

Women's improved capacity to plan births can enhance their bargaining position in the family and strengthen demands that men participate more fully in housework and child care. But such progress is by no means automatic. Many employers' hiring and promotion practices discourage men from more active participation in parenthood. Many state policies allow increased freedom of exit from marriage to result in increased freedom of exit from parenthood – for men. In the United States, for example, shockingly low levels of compliance with court-mandated child support payments have resulted in a situation in which many women bear complete financial responsibility for their children and a disproportionate number of female-headed families are driven below the poverty-level (Pearce 1979). In the long run, the increased risk of such poverty may have the effect of lowering fertility rates even further.

Changes in the attitudes of women, men, and children, as well as technological changes, clearly play an important role in fertility decline. But the effects of such changes upon the family cannot be adequately conceptualized unless they are incorporated in a larger theoretical framework that clarifies the motives and the mechanisms of patriarchal inequality. The theoretical perspective outlined above hearkens back to Marx's and Engel's conviction that the growth of capitalism would weaken the patriarchal family. But rather than asserting that the expansion of wage labour and the concentration of private property eliminate the basis for inequality between women and men, the perspective suggests that such changes diminish the economic benefits of children without providing any new forms of economic support for child-rearing.

This theoretical framework points quite specifically to the importance of two empirical issues that demographers have almost wholly neglected, the percentage of lifetime income that children contribute to parents and the distribution of the costs of children between women and men in the family (see Folbre 1984). Both of these manifestations of the relative bargaining power of parents and children, women and men, within the family may partially reflect differences in their control over and access to means of production. But they are also linked to a larger process of political struggle.

POLITICAL IMPLICATIONS

The history of the feminist movement is a history of shifting patterns of support for and opposition to feminist demands. Individual men may be strongly in favour of reducing family size, so long as this does not directly affect the division of labour or the balance of power in the household. Employers may be optimistic about increases in female labour-force participation until it becomes apparent that such increases may escalate demands for sexual equality in the workplace and diminish the size of the next generation of workers. In both instances there is a contradiction between short-run effects and long-run consequences. Changes that initially seem desirable for men as well as women are carried 'too far' when

133

they begin to weaken aspects of patriarchal inequality that continue to serve important material interests. When feminists propose political innovations that help families 'catch up' with the effects of social change, to adapt to such trends as fertility decline, they enjoy a certain popularity. But when feminists press beyond 'adaptive' prescriptions to suggest ways in which women might actively speed up the transformation of family life, they meet with substantial resistance. The recent defeat of the Equal Rights Amendment is a case in point.

The backlash against feminism in the United States has been led by partisans of the traditional patriarchal family, but it has found adherents among many who simply fear for the survival of the family itself. Ironically, the family inspires a new loyalty in part because its traditional patriarchal aspects have been weakened. Inequalities between women and men persist, but they do not persist unabated. The economic and demographic changes described above have not led to any visible lessening of the sexual wage differential, but they have improved women's position within the family. At the same time, they have undermined the economic stability of family life.

Child-rearing in the United States today stands out as a activity that is conducted despite, rather than because of, economic self-interest. The decision to raise a child imposes truly phenomenal economic costs upon parents and provides virtually no economic benefits. The fact that these costs continued to be incurred bears testimony to some of the intrinsic rewards of parenthood. These rewards may be misperceived or misunderstood, and women may pay more than an equal share of the price for them. But parenting constitutes one of the few truly craftlike activities of modern life, where process is as important as productivity and where the happiness of individuals involved overrides most other concerns. Like many other craft activities, parenthood cannot persist as anything more than a luxury unless it can sustain some economic viability.

In some European countries the state has at least partially acknowledged this problem, providing income transfers specifically designed to defray the cost of additional children as well as state-subsidized child care (Cook 1978; Teich and Winston 1980; Kammerman 1980). But even these programmes, generous by comparison with the modest tax deductions offered in the United States, provide relatively little support. They have not effectively slowed the decline in population growth which has aroused concern in many European countries.

The great fear that women may reject their traditional child-rearing responsibilities embodies more than a desire to preserve the patriarchal status quo. It grows, at least in part, out of the recognition that no other persons and no other institutions are apparently willing to assume these responsibilities. Feminists must continue their exploration of the relationship between patriarchy and motherhood. But we must also move beyond this critical analysis to a much more explicit consideration of the ways in which parenthood could and should be organized. Such considerations lead far beyond the division of labour within the family to an economic issue which is of overarching importance for society as a whole. Who should pay the costs of rearing the next generation?

REFERENCES

Banks, J A and Olive Banks (1964) *Feminism and Family Planning in England*, New York: Schocken Books.

Beaver, Stephen E (1974) *Demographic Transition Theory Reinterpreted*, Lexington, Massachussetts: D C Heath.

Becker, Gary (1960) 'An economic analysis of fertility' in *Demographic and Economic Change in the Developed Countries*, Princeton: Princeton University Press.

Berkner, Lutz (1973) 'The stem family and the developmental cycle of the peasant household: an eighteenth-century Austrian example', in *The American Family in Social-Historical Perspective*, ed. Michael Gordon, New York: St Martin's Press.

Bizien, Yves (1979) *Population and Economic Development*, New York: Praeger.

Blake, Judith (1974) 'Coercive pronatalism and American population policy', in *Pronatalism: The Myth of Mom and Apple Pie*, ed. Ellen Peck and Judith Senderowitz, New York: Thomas Crowell.

Boserup, Ester (1970) *Women in Economic Development*, New York: St Martin's Press.

Boye, Mame Madiare (1980) 'Women who submit and are silent', *People* 7, pp 16–17.

Braun, Rudolph (1978) 'Proto-industrialization and demographic change in the canton of Zurich', in *Historical Studies of Changing Fertility*, ed Charles Tilly, Princeton: Princeton University Press.

Cain, Mead; S R A Kahnam and Shamour Nahar (1970) 'Class, patriarchy, and the structure of women's work in rural Bangladesh', *Population and Development Review* 5 (September), pp405–38.

Caldwell, John C (1960) *African Rural–Urban Migration*, New York: Columbia University Press.

— (1978) 'A theory of fertility: from high plateau to stabilization', *Population and Development Review* 4 (December), pp553–78.

— (1980) Mass education as a determinant of the time of fertility decline', *Population and Development Review* 6 (June), pp225–56.

Chaney, Elsa M and Marianne Schmink (1976) 'Women and modernization: access to tools', in *Sex and Class in Latin America*, ed. June Nash and Helen Icken Safa, New York: Praeger Publishers.

Cheung, S (1972) 'The enforcement of property rights in children and the marriage contract', *Economic Journal* 82 (June), pp641–57.

Cole, Robert E (1971) *Japanese Blue Collar: The Changing Tradition*, Berkeley: University of California Press.

Cook, Alice H (1978) *The Working Mother: A Survey of Problems and Programs in Nine Countles*, Ithaca: New York State School of Industrial and Labor Relations, Cornell University.

Cortes, Irene (1980) 'Fighting for real equality', *People* 7, pp23–4.

Degler, Carl (1980) *At Odds: Women and the Family in America from the Revolution to the Present*, New York: Oxford University Press.

Easterlin, Richard A (1976) 'Population change and farm settlement in the northern United States', *Journal of Economic History* 36 (March), pp45–75.

El Saadawi, Nawal (1980) *The Hidden Face of Eve: Women in the Arab World*, London: Zed Books.

Engels, Friederich (1968 [1884]) *The Origin of the Family, Private Property and the State*, Moscow: Progress Publishers.

Evenson, Robert E; Barry Popkin and Elizabeth King-Quison (1979) 'Nutrition, work, and demographic behaviour in rural Philippine households', Economic Growth Center, Paper no. 308, Yale University.

Folbre, Nancy (1984) 'Household production in the Philippines: a non-neoclassical approach', *Economic Development and Cultural Change* 32 (January), pp. 303–30.

Foner, Philip S (1979) *Women and the American Labor Movement: From World War I to the Present*, New York: Pantheon Books.

Foucault, Michael (1980) *The History of Sexuality, vol. 1, An Introduction*, transl. Robert Hurley, New York: Pantheon Books.

Goode, William (1970) *World Revolution and Family Patterns*, New York: Free Press.

Gordon, David M (1972) Theories of Poverty and Underemployment. Lexington, Massachussetts: D.C Heath.

Greven, Philip (1970) *Four Generations: Population, Land, and Family in Colonial Andover, Massachusetts*, New York: Cornell University Press.

Gross, Robert (1976) *The Minutemen and Their World*, New York: Hill & Wang.

Hartmann, Heidi (1979) 'Capitalism, patriarchy, and job segregation by sex', in *Capitalist Patriarchy and the Case for Socialist Feminism*, ed. Zillah R. Eisenstein. New York: Monthly Review Press.

– (1981) 'The family as the focus of gender, class, and political struggle: the example of housework', *Signs* 6, pp366–94.

Hicks, Whitney (1974) 'Economic development and fertility change in Mexico, 1950–1970', *Demography* 11 (August), pp407–21.

Ho, Teresa (1979) 'Time costs of child rearing in the rural Philippines', *Population and Development Review* 5 (December), pp643–62.

Hohm, Charles (1975) 'Security and fertility: an international perspective', *Demography* 12 (November), pp629–44.

Hollingsworth, Leta (1974) 'Social devices for impelling women to bear and rear children', in *Pronatalism: The Myth of Mom and Apple Pie*, ed. Ellen Peck and Judith Senderowitz, New York: Thomas Crowell.

Horowitz, Grace (1981) 'Intra-family distribution of food and other resources', Report to the Nutrition Economic Group, U.S. Department of Agriculture.

Inkeles, Alex and David H Smith (1974) *Becoming Modern: Individual Change in Six Developing Countries*, Cambridge: Harvard University Press.

International Labour Office (1978) *Yearbook of Labour Statistics*, Geneva.

Jacoby, Robin Miller (1977) 'The Women's Trade Union League and American feminism', *Class, Sex, and the Woman Worker*, ed. Milton Canto and Bruce Laurie, Westport, Connecticut: Greenwood Press.

Jameson, Elizabeth (1977) 'Imperfect unions: class and gender in Cripple Creek, 1894–1904', in *Class, Sex, and the Woman Worker*, ed. Milton Canto and Bruce Laurie, Westport, Connecticut: Greenwood Press.

Jeline, Elizabeth (1983) 'Women and the urban labour market', Working Paper no. 77, World Employment Programme, International Labour Office, Geneva.

Jensen, Joan M (1980) 'Cloth, butter, and boarders: women's household production for the market', *Review of Radical Political Economics* 12 (summer), pp14–24.

Johnson, G E and W E Whitelaw (1974) 'Urban rural income transfers in Kenya: an estimated remittances function', *Economic Development and Cultural Change* 22 (April), pp473–79.

Jones, G W (1977) 'Economic and social supports for high fertility: a conceptual framework', in *The Economic and Social Supports for High Fertility*, ed. Lado T Ruzicka. Canberra: Department of Demography and Development Studies Centre, Australian National University.

Kammerman, Shiela (1980) 'Child care and family benefits in six industrialized countries', *Monthly Labor Review* 103 (November), pp23–8.

Katz, Michael B (1968) *The Irony of Early School Reform: Educational Innovation in Mid Nineteenth-Century Massachusetts*, Boston: Beacon Press.

Kenya, Central Bureau of Statistics, Ministry of Economic Planning and Development (1979) 'Major highlights of the Kenya Fertility Survey', *Social Perspectives* 4, (December), pp1–12.

Kongstad, Per and Mette Monsted (1980) *Family Labour and Trade in Western Kenya*, Copenhagen: Scandinavian Institute of African Studies, Centre for Development Research.

Lebra, Joyce; Joy Paulson and Elizabeth Powers (eds) (1976) *Women in Changing Japan*, Stanford, California: Stanford University Press.

Lerner, David (1963) *The Passing of Traditional Society: Modernizing the Middle East*, Glencoe, Illinois: Free Press.

Lockridge, Kenneth (1970) *A New England Town: The First Hundred Years*, New York: W. W. Norton.

Main, Jackson T (1965) *The Social Structure of Revolutionary America*, Princeton: Princeton University Press.

Manser, Marilyn and Murray Brown (1978) 'Marriage and household decision-making: a bargaining analysis', Discussion Paper no. 376, State University of New York at Buffalo.

Marx, Karl (1867) *Capital*, vol. 1: *A Critical Analysis of Capitalist Production*, New York: International Publishers.

Mauldin, W Parker and Bernard Berelson (1978) 'Conditions of fertility decline in developing countries, 1965-75', *Studies in Family Planning* 9, pp89-146.

Mblyni, Marjorie M (1971) 'Participation of women in African economies', Research Paper no. 71, Economics Research Bureau, University of Dar es Salaam.

— (1972) 'The status of women in Tanzania', *Canadian Journal of African Studies* 6, pp371-77.

— (nd) 'Women: producers and reproducers in peasant production',Occasional Paper no. 77, Economic Research Bureau, University of Dar es Salaam.

McElroy, Marjorie B and Mary Jean Horner (1978) 'Nash-bargained household decisions: toward a generaliation of the theory demand', unpublished paper, Duke University.

McFarlane, Alan (1978) *The Origins of English Individualism*, New York: Cambridge University Press.

Menissi, Fatima (1975) *Beyond the Veil: Male-Female Dynamics in a Modern Muslim Society*, New York: John Wiley.

Nag, M (1972) 'Economic value of children in agricultural societies: evaluation of existing knowledge and an anthropological approach', in *The Satisfaction and Cost of Children: Theories, Concepts, Methods*, ed. J. T. Fawcett, Honolulu: East-West Center.

Nag, M; B White and R C Peet (1978) 'An anthropological approach to the study of the economic value of children in Java and Nepal', *Current Anthropology* 19 (June), pp293-306.

Newland, Kathleen (1980) 'Righting ancient wrongs', *People* 7, p3.

O'Faolain, Julia and Lauro Martines (eds) (1973) *Not in God's Image: Women in History from the Greeks to the Victorians*, New York: Harper & Row.

Osterud, Nancy and John Fulton (1976) 'Family limitation and the age at marriage: fertility decline in Sturbridge, Massachusetts, 1750-1850', *Population Studies* 30 (November), pp481-94.

Pala, Achala A (1976) *African Women in Rural Development: Research Trends and Priorities*, Overseas Liaison Committee Report no. 12 Washington DC: American Council on Education.

Patterson, James T (1981) *America's Struggle Against Poverty, 1900-1980*, Cambridge: Harvard University Press.

Pearce, Diana (1979) 'Women, work, and welfare: the feminization of poverty', in *Working Women and Families*, ed. Karen Feinstein, Beverly Hills: Sage Publications.

Perlman, Mark (1980) 'Population and economic change in developing countries: a review article', *Journal of Economic Literature* 19 (March) pp74-82.

Quick, Paddy (1977) 'The class basis of women's oppression', *Review of Radical Political Economies* 9 (autumn), pp42–53.

Rempel, Henry and Richard A Lobdell (1978) 'The role of urban-to-rural remittences in rural development', *Journal of Development Studies* 14 (April), pp324–31.

Rosenzweig, Mark (1977) 'The demand for children in farm households', *Journal of Political Economy* 85 (February), pp123–46.

— (1978) 'The value of children's time, family size, and non-household child activities in a developing country: evidence from household data', *Research in Population Economics* 1, pp331–47.

Rosenzweig, Mark and Robert Evenson (1977) 'Fertility, schooling, and the economic contribution of children in rural India: an econometric analysis', *Econometrica* 5 (July), pp1065–79.

Rosenzweig, Mark and T Paul Schultz (1982) 'Market opportunities, genetic endowments, and the intrafamily resource: distribution', *American Economic Review* 72 (September), pp803–15.

Salaff, Janet W (1981) *Working Daughters of Hong Kong: Female Piety or Power in the Family*, New York: Cambridge University Press.

Serron, Louis A (1980) *Scarcity, Exploitation and Poverty: Malthus and Marx in Mexico*, Norman, Oklahoma: University of Oklahoma Press.

Shin, E H (1977) 'Socioeconomic development, infant mortality, and fertility: a cross sectional and longitudinal analysis of sixty-three selected countries', *Journal of Development Studies* 13 (July), pp348–412.

Shorter, Edward (1975) *The Making of the Modern Family*, New York: Basic Books.

Simon, Julian (1977) *The Economics of Population Growth*, Princeton: Princeton University Press.

Smelser, Neil (1967) 'Toward a theory of modernization', in *Tribal and Peasant Economics*, ed. George Dalton, Garden City, New York: Natural History Press.

Staudt, Kathleen (1980) 'The landless majority', *People* 7, p. 8.

Stone, Lawrence (1979) *The Family, Sex and Marriage in England, 1500–1800*, New York: Harper & Row.

Szalai, Alexander (1975) 'Women's time: women in the light of contemporary time-budget research', *Futures* 7 (October).

Teich Adams, Carolyn and Kathryn Teich Winston (1980) *Mothers at Work: Public Policies in the United States, Sweden and China*, New York: Longman.

Temkin-Greener, Helena and Alan C Swedlund (1978) 'Fertility transition in the Connecticut valley, 1740–1859', *Population Studies* 32, pp27–41.

Tienda, Marta (1979) 'Economic activity of children in Peru', *Rural Sociology* 44 (summer), pp370–91.

Tilly, Charles (1978) 'The historical study of vital processes', in *Historical Studies of Changing Fertility*, ed. Charles Tilly, Princeton: Princeton University Press.

Tilly, Louise A and Joan W Scott (1978) *Women, Work and Family*, New York: Holt, Rinehart & Winston.

Tinker, Irene (1981) 'Energy for essential household activities', Occasional Paper C-2 (June), Centre for International Development and Technology.

Tucker, Robert C (ed) (1972) *The Marx-Engels Reader*, New York: W. W. Norton.

The Value of Children: A Cross National Study (1977–78) vol. 3: *Hawaii*, by F. Arnold and J. T. Fawcett; vol. 4: *Thailand*, by C. Buripakdi; vol. 5: *Taiwan*, by Wu Ts'ung-hsien; vol. 6: *Japan*, by T. Iritani, Honolulu: East–West Population Institute.

van de Walle, Etienne (1974) *The Female Population of France in the Nineteenth Century: A Reconstruction of Eighty-Two Departments*, Princeton: Princeton University Press.

Willis, R J (1980) 'The old age security hypothesis and population growth', in *Demographic Behaviour: Interdisciplinary Perspectives on Decision-Making*, ed. Thomas K. Burch, Boulder, Colorado: Westview Press.

Part III

Societies and States

We can tell a story of sorts about population change and development by focusing on individual and family demographic decisions. The micro-economics of household behaviour, covered in the first two selections in Part II, provides such an account. Much is missing from it, however. It omits nearly all that distinguishes one society from another. Moreover, it contributes little to an understanding of how demographic decisions may make sense for individuals or families while at the same time in the aggregate producing highly unfavourable outcomes for the society. The existence of such negative spillover effects or externalities associated with demographic behaviour is plausibly a substantial part of the 'population problem' in the contemporary developing countries – and a principal rationale for public policy directed at modifying that behaviour. To correct this imbalance of attention calls for a wider-angled view: one that extends beyond the family to encompass the larger features of social structure and dynamics that can influence demographic outcomes and, to some degree, can be influenced by them. We need to take a more institutionally-informed and society-specific approach – where, as Norman Ryder (1983) puts it, 'the unit of analysis is not the individual act but the normative instruction.'

The supra-family elements that call for consideration here include patterns of social organization (based on kin, community, or other kinds of affiliation), economic institutions like labour and capital markets and property rights, local government administration and other manifestations of state authority, and cultural patterns and beliefs. With longstanding economic and cultural contact among nations and increasing globalization in numerous domains of human activity, the international system may also be a significant factor in population and development (see Demeny, in this Part).

In a pre-industrial society, high mortality necessitated high fertility (or high recruitment by migration) if the society was to survive. At the same time, a perceived demographic threat of societal impoverishment through dilution of resources may have given support to practices that limited population expansion. Maintenance of demographic balance was thus likely to have been a perennial problem, and behaviours and beliefs that made for that balance would have tended to become institutionalized in the society; we may speak of a 'demographic regime'. The forces sustaining such a regime might include social pressures and sanctions affecting marriage and women's roles, limitations on migration and settlement, and expectations of conformity to social class norms. These are not immutable but neither are they easily evaded or altered at will by individual action. (For discussion and illustrations, see Cain et al 1979, Davis and Blake 1956, and Davis, in this Part.)

While it had certain homeostatic characteristics, pre-industrial demographic change as revealed in recent studies belies any picture of smooth sailing under technological and institutional constancy. But the transformation of material and social conditions that came with economic development was of a different order. This transformation was treated in several of the selections in Part I. Technological advances and new ideas (about economic and social organization, authority, nature and the supernatural, and much else) work through existing institutional structures in a society to influence its demographic behaviour – and, not incidentally, to modify those structures themselves. These complex relations yield the diversity of observed experience of demographic transition. A large research literature records and seeks to explain this experience. A number of contributions to it were cited in the introduction to Part I above; other general and regional treatments include Gillis et al. (1992), Guzmán et al. (1996), Hawthorn (1978), Kleinman (1980), Leete and Alam (1993), Lesthaeghe (1989), Nag (1975), and Watkins (1991), and the selections by Ryder and McNicoll in this Part. The important case of changing relations between the sexes is treated by Folbre and Sen, in Part II, and by Boserup, in this Part.

We need to be clear about the sense in which the term *institution* is used here. An institution is a cluster of behavioural rules or regularities governing human actions and relationships in recurrent situations. It is not something tangible, to be contrasted with 'intangible' cultural or ideational factors. Rules of kinship and social stratification, labour market structures, and the system of land tenure and property rights are among the institutions that have particular salience for demographic outcomes – not least by constraining social mobility and gender roles (Potter 1983; Cain and McNicoll, in this Part). More abstract processes linked to development, such as individualization and secularization, are manifested in particular institutional trends (see Lesthaeghe and Surkyn 1988).

Institutions are always in flux, adapting to changing circumstances, though neither quickly in most cases nor necessarily in a way that might seem best to an outside observer. Institutions, as Paul David (1993) writes, are carriers of history; they are path-dependent. We should therefore be suspicious of functionalist descriptions of institutions and institutional change: such descriptions tend to impose more coherence on a situation than really exists, in effect becoming 'just-so' stories. But we should be cautious too of the exaggerated mutability that is sometimes assumed in order to avoid the charge of timeless analytical conservatism. In social theory a familiar opposition is drawn between structure and agency; we need to pay attention to both (see Greenhalgh 1995, Hammel 1990, Kreager 1986).

The complexity of social organization and cultural practice properly defeats single-factor explanations of demographic change – indeed, it can make for a rich explanatory stew within which competing interpretations readily co-exist. This should not be surprising, since we are in effect dealing with the determinants of social change, a perennially contentious topic in the social sciences. Acknowledging that in any search for explanation not everything can be simultaneously in play, the excerpts below each contain an implicit judgment of relative institutional salience that justifies the narrowing of focus to a particular set of relationships.

We commonly take for granted that the analytical units of main demographic import are national states. National governments are part of a country's societal structure but also seek to regulate that structure and to determine development outcomes. The state, the national government as a political and administrative entity, can thus be contrasted with the 'society', now referring to the array of non-state institutional forms within the country (see Migdal 1988). For population, the state is the potential locus of explicit policy measures intended to direct demographic change; inevitably, it is also a source of incidental influence on that change – of what is sometimes termed implicit population policy (Johansson 1991). Untangling and making sense of these interwoven intended and unintended effects in a given institutional context is the task of a political economy of demographic change (see Greenhalgh, in this Part).

Whether states in fact can exercise much purchase over demographic outcomes is a matter perennially in dispute. For migration, the effects, through simple regulation, can clearly be substantial; for mortality, the direct effects of health expenditures are likely to be swamped by indirect effects working through education and economic growth and distribution. For fertility, with the rare exception of strong-armed government action, the relevant decisions are highly decentralized. They lie within what is usually a private domain, protected by notions of freedom of reproductive choice. Supporters of family planning programmes believe that the potential government influence on fertility outcomes, working through such programmes, is nevertheless substantial. Many critics are more sceptical, seeing the programme role as peripheral to a demographic course that is set by the currents of economic and cultural change. A public policy role would remain, in that those currents are to some degree directed by the state, but possible demographic effects would rarely be a primary consideration. (See Demeny, 1986 and in this Part; Jones 1988; and Bull, in Part V.)

REFERENCES

Cain, Mead, Syeda Rokeya Khanem, and Shamsun Nahar (1979) 'Class, patriarchy, and women's work in Bangladesh', *Population and Development Review* 5: pp405–438.

David, Paul A. (1993) 'Historical economics in the long run: some implications of path-dependence', in G.D. Snooks (ed.) *Historical Analysis in Economics*, Routledge, London.

Davis, Kingsley and Judith Blake (1956) 'Social structure and fertility: an analytic framework', *Economic Development and Cultural Change* 4: pp211–235.

Demeny, Paul (1986) 'Population and the invisible hand', *Demography* 23: pp473–487.

Gillis, John R., Louise A. Tilly, and David Levine (eds.) *The European Experience of Declining Fertility: A Quiet Revolution. 1850–1970*, Blackwell, Cambridge, Massachusetts.

Greenhalgh, Susan (ed.) (1995) *Situating Fertility: Anthropology and Demographic Inquiry*, Cambridge University Press, Cambridge.

Guzmán, José Miguel, et al (eds.) (1996) *The Fertility Transition in Latin America*, Clarendon Press, Oxford.

Hammel, E.A. (1990) 'A theory of culture for demography', *Population and Development Review* 16: pp455–485.

Hawthorn, Geoffrey (ed.) (1978) *Population and Development: High and Low Fertility in Poorer Countries*, Cass, London.

Johansson, S. Ryan (1991) 'Implicit policy and fertility during development', *Population and Development Review* 17: pp377–414.

Jones, E.L. (1988) *Growth Recurring: Economic Change in World History*, Oxford University Press, Oxford.

Kleinman, David S. (1980) *Human Adaptation and Population Growth: A Non-Malthusian Perspective*, Universe Books, New York.

Kreager, Philip (1986) 'Demographic regimes as cultural systems', in David Coleman and Roger Schofield (eds.) *The State of Population Theory: Forward from Malthus*, Blackwell, Oxford.

Leete, Richard and Iqbal Alam (eds.) (1993) *The Revolution in Asian Fertility: Dimensions, Causes, and Implications*, Clarendon Press, Oxford.

Lesthaeghe, Ron (ed.) (1989) *Reproduction and Social Organization in Sub-Saharan Africa*, University of California Press, Berkeley.

Lesthaeghe, Ron and Johan Surkyn (1988) 'Cultural dynamics and economic theories of fertility change', *Population and Development Review* 14: pp1–45.

Migdal, Joel S. (1988) *Strong Societies and Weak States: State-Society Relations and State Capabilities in the Third World*, Princeton University Press, Princeton.

Nag, Moni (1975) *Population and Social Organization*, Mouton, The Hague.

Potter, Joseph E. (1983) 'Effects of societal and community institutions on fertility', in R.A. Bulatao and Ronald D. Lee (eds.) *Determinants of Fertility in Developing Countries*, Academic Press, New York.

Ryder, N.B. (1983) 'Fertility and family structure', *Population Bulletin of the United Nations* 15: pp15–34.

Watkins, Susan Cotts (1991) *From Provinces into Nations: Demographic Integration in Western Europe, 1870–1960*, Princeton University Press, Princeton.

Chapter 13

Institutional Patterns Favouring High Fertility

Kingsley Davis

In analysing the institutional factors responsible for fertility, one finds the main key in the family, for human society accomplishes the function of bearing, nourishing, and socializing children primarily through the universal instrumentality of the nuclear family.[1] It is through the relations of the nuclear family to the rest of society, then, that we can expect to find the social factors controlling the level of fertility.

EFFECT OF THE COMPOSITE FAMILY AND JOINT HOUSEHOLD

In primitive and agrarian societies, as is well known, the nuclear family is less independent of the wider kinship structure than it is in industrial societies. Its formation through marriage, its economic position, and the conduct of its members are all governed by elder relatives to a greater degree. In sociological terms, the nuclear family of procreation tends in agrarian societies to be controlled by other kinship groups, notably by the two families of orientation.

One common arrangement in terms of which such control is facilitated is the joint household, which arises when the newly married couple are required to live with the parents of one or the other partner. Such an arrangement is quite prevalent in underdeveloped areas,[2] but even where it is absent the nuclear family tends to dwell close to and be under the surveillance of the in-laws. Furthermore, it is not simply a matter of dwelling arrangements and social control, but also a matter of economic solidarity. The joint household and the composite family often function as an economic unit.

Given this subordination and incorporation of the nuclear family by wider kinship groups, several consequences tend to follow which are conducive to abundant reproduction.

---

1 The term 'nuclear family' is used by G P Murdock (1949, Ch 1) to describe the unit consisting of mother, father, and children. This unit has also been variously characterized as the 'primary' or 'immediate' family, as in the works of Lloyd Warner.

2 For the 159 societies for which he secured adequate information on residence and inheritance rules, Murdock found 149 to require residence with extended relatives (op cit, p38). The majority of these societies, 98 in all, required patrilocal residence. It is hard, however, to reconcile his table on p38 with that on p32 where the proportion of 'independent' families is higher.

1. The economic cost of rearing children does not impinge directly on the parents to the same extent that it does where the nuclear family is a more independent unit. With a common household and a joint economy, with three or more generations present, one's own child draws out of the general exchequer, not out of his parents' income alone.
2. The inconvenience and effort of child care do not fall so heavily on the parents alone. With grandparents, aunts, uncles, and older cousins in the household, the care of the young children may be so distributed among the entire ménage that no particular strain is put upon the parents. In fact, as has often been pointed out, the joint household is an excellent arrangement whereby young mothers, in the prime of life and thus capable of maximum productivity, are freed during working hours for work in the fields or in handicraft, while older women and older children, less productive economically, look after the infants and younger children. Thus, the mother's maternal function does not have to compete with her economic function as in an industrial society.
3. The age at marriage can be quite young, because, under joint household conditions, there is no necessary implication that the husband must be 'able to support a wife and family' before he gets married. In this respect, there seems to have been a difference between West European society, even prior to industrialism, and that of most other parts of the pre-industrial world. The historian, Russell, has pointed out that in the Middle Ages there was a tradition linking the nuclear family with a piece of land adequate to maintain the family.

> *In each village there were usually a certain number of holdings of similar character which required the efforts of a mature male, physically and mentally; about thirty acres of land together with a quota of animals upon the manor... Obviously only the full holdings could be expected to care for a family satisfactorily in the eyes of the lay population. Thus naturally marriage would be restricted to those who had holdings... The principle of no holding, no marriage, operated as a fairly effective check upon population increase. The conditions of mortality tended to make the average age of marriage for the young man vary between twenty-two and twenty-five years. It also meant that the weak in mind or body were not permitted to marry... (Russell 1949, p104).*

Thus, West European society tended to set the nuclear family apart a long time ago – a fact which is borne out by Western legal history, kinship terminology, and courtship custom. As Western peoples became more commercial and more urban, the rule that land is necessary to form a marriage became extended to mean that a job is necessary. In this way, as commercial and industrial positions came to require apprenticeship and training, and as land became scarce, the way was paved for the postponement of marriage to fairly advanced ages.[3] The more one looks into the matter, the more it appears that the structure of the family in Western industrial societies is not wholly a product of urban-industrialization but is in part a product of cultural peculiarities extending back at least into Medieval times. In fact, it can be argued that the West European family

---

3 Such postponement, especially noticeable in the latter half of the 19th and early 20th century, was carried to an extreme in Ireland and the Scandinavian countries See Glass (1953), pp25–54; Arensberg and Kimball (1940); and Hajnal (1953).

structure was one factor in the origin of the industrial revolution in North-western Europe.

Family organization in non-European agrarian societies, however, is different from that of pre-industrial Europe. Especially in Asia, it often embodies the principles of joint residence and joint economic responsibility. Furthermore, the parents in many of these societies are morally obligated to find mates for their children and to marry them at an early age. In the patrilocal joint household the bride simply joins her husband's family and the groom continues to live there. The bride can contribute to the joint economy even though young, and the groom is not required to be financially independent. In India, in 1891, nearly a fifth of the girls below 15 years of age, and 89 per cent of those aged 15–19, had been married. The marriage age in India is rising, but as late as 1951 nearly 10 per cent of Indian girls under 15 and three-fourths of those 15–19 had been married.[4] In such countries as India, Korea, Formosa, and Turkey, practically no women 20–24 are single. It is obvious that, other things equal, the younger the age at marriage, the higher the ultimate fertility, especially since a woman's reproductive capacity is apparently greatest in her late teens and early twenties.

4. With an emphasis on kin solidarity the compulsion to marry is often quite strong. Especially with patrilocal residence arrangements, the daughter may be viewed as a potential liability to her family of orientation, to be satisfactorily married at all costs. From the standpoint of the groom's family, a marriage represents not only an alliance with another strong family line but also an essential means of expanding one's own agnatic line. The necessity of getting one's children married may indeed by viewed as a religious and moral obligation. As a consequence, fewer persons go through life without marrying than in the case of the industrial nations. In fact, in India in 1981, a higher proportion of women aged 20–24 had been married (97.3 per cent) then were ever married by any age in Western countries. In Denmark in 1787, for example, only 91 per cent of the women aged 45–49 had ever been married; and in France in 1881 only 87 per cent of the women of this age had ever been wed.

5. The young wife is motivated to have offspring as early as possible and in considerable number. Given the joint family and the prevailing rule of patrilocal residence, the bride is a stranger among her husband's relatives. Because of her newness and because of her youth, she is often assigned a low position in the restricted hierarchy of women. She has little she can call her own until a child is born. The birth of a son proves her contribution to her husband's line and thus begins her rise to a higher position within the domestic circle. Offspring also give her something to lavish her affection on, something on the basis of which she can stand up for herself. In cultures where the father's bond with the child is a strong one, the birth of offspring gives the wife extra standing in his eyes; and in cultures where divorce is easily possible for the male, as in most Muslim countries, the wife views offspring as a means of holding her husband. Under such circumstances it is not strange that a young married woman has little incentive to avoid childbirth.

---

4 See K Davis (1954), pp85–86.

6. The man is strongly motivated to demand offspring. The structure of the joint family ordinarily rewards not only the mother's but also the father's reproduction. Often the children are viewed as belonging to him and his family, and the sons as perpetuating his family line. More tangibly, numerous children help to strengthen the patrilineally organized composite family by the sheer weight of numbers. In so far as this family remains a viable economic and social unit, it gains economic and political strength by having an abundance of youthful members. Young adults can thus provide security for their old age even when few other means are available, and they are encouraged to do so by their elders.

     The male's motivation is seen further in what may be called 'sociological cures' for sterility. A barren wife not only suffers stigma, but she may be divorced to make room for a new and presumably more fertile wife. A women who bears only daughters may suffer the same fate. In addition, in some agrarian cultures at least, the wife's barrenness may be a just cause for the acquisition of a concubine or a second wife or for the adoption of children of her husband's relatives.

THE SEGREGATION OF MALE AND FEMALE ROLES

So far we have traced some of the effects of subordinating the nuclear family to wider kinship groups. An additional influence on fertility is the tendency of stable agrarian societies to segregate sharply the roles of men and women. This tendency is often connected with the dependent status of the nuclear family in the joint household, because when several related men and several women dwell together, strong avoidance rules are required to reduce the possibility of prohibited sexual contact and sexual rivalry. But the segregation of male and female roles is found in agrarian societies with or without joint household arrangements, and thus may be viewed as a somewhat independent factor in high fertility.

The institutional restriction of the feminine sphere may reach an extreme degree – as in the practice of purdah in Muslim and to some extent in Hindu culture, and in the seclusion of females in agrarian Latin cultures. The effect of such limitation is to confine women largely to the household and to identify them with reproduction, so that their lives revolve around home and children. Female education is regarded as unnecessary if not actually immoral. Women, therefore, have little knowledge, sophistication, or independence. They cannot conceive of a glamour role or a career role which would compete with the child-bearing role. They cannot complain that children prevent their getting outside the home, because outside activities are excluded anyway.

With the segregation of roles, the gulf between the man's and the woman's world becomes so wide that communication between husband and wife is reduced to a minimum – particularly with reference to sexual topics, for the woman is supposed to have no knowledge or initiative in such matters. Curiously, husband and wife in many cases may never discuss the one thing that presumably represents their special bond, sex and reproduction. Toward this aspect of life the woman has mainly a non-rational approach – religious, superstitious, and incurious. The husband views reproduction as his prerogative, something taken for granted and involving simple compliance on the wife's part.[5]

A further consequence of feminine seclusion is that, when economic development first begins, women do not proportionately enter the industrial and commercial labour market. As a result the cities in many underdeveloped areas (notably in Asia) are heavily masculine.[6] The occupations that Westerners now regard as chiefly feminine – nursing, teaching, stenography, domestic service, retail selling – are generally staffed by men. Entry into such occupations would take women out of the home and give them a sense of conflict between pregnancy and economic gain. Also it would take them to towns and cities, where rearing children is more difficult. The exclusion of women from the labour market therefore continues for them the conditions favourable to high fertility even after considerable economic development has occurred.

AGRARIAN SOCIETY AND THE FAMILY

The features of family organization barely sketched above are well adapted to a peasant mode of existence. In traditional agriculture the main instrument of production, apart from land, is human labour. To learn any skill involved does not require formal education but merely observation and practice. Children can thus start producing at an early age. Women can work in the fields and in the household handicrafts without much hindrance from constant child-bearing. Furthermore, the type of agriculture in which most of the product is consumed at home rather than sold, in which hand labour substitutes for capital, and in which the level of living is consequently extremely low – this is the type in which the means of transportation and communication are scant, and in which consequently the rural village is extremely isolated. The state, in such circumstances, tends to be a distant mechanism scarcely less rapacious and unpredictable than the marauding thieves from which it supposedly protects the village. The village must therefore protect itself as best it can. Its means of social control must be strong, and thus family controls and the authority of the elders can be easily enforced. Without much geographical or social mobility, kinship can serve as a principle basis of social position. The division of labour can be simple, resting heavily on the ascription of status on the basis of kinship, caste, age, and sex. With mortality high from disease, occasional famine, disaster, and war, the constant struggle is to maintain the population. Children strengthen and continue both the family and the village, and the institutional mechanisms favouring their appearance are strongly rooted.

The whole economic and family context represents an intricate and tightly integrated complex which can survive an amazing length of time. Favourable conditions are responded to by an irrepressible expansion of numbers; unfavourable conditions are met by a remarkable power of survival and recuperation. As a consequence the stable agrarian mode of life has achieved a wide distribution over the world and still includes over half of humanity. It has in recent times encountered a force strong enough to liquidate it – the impact of urban–industrial civilization. But the corrosive power of this impact is not always

---

5 J M Stycos and Reuben Hill (1953, pp140–2) have particularly emphasized the lack of communication between husband and wife as a factor in high fertility See also Stycos (1954), p61.
6 See Cooper (1951), pp125–126; and K Davis (1951), pp139–141. The cities of 500,000 or more in India in 1931 had 175 males for every 100 females.

manifest. Sometimes it affects the stable agrarian society, not as an unfavourable condition, but as a favourable one. If the underdeveloped area continues to remain agricultural, its participation in the world economy being that of a supplier of raw materials; if security is guaranteed by a colonial government or by world peace; and if mortality is reduced by the impact of modern medical science and public health – if these things happen, as they often have, the effect is to maintain those parts of the social structure most favourable to a high birth rate. The agrarian society therefore expands; it may even send millions of people overseas while its home population is growing rapidly. Eventually, however, the expansion runs into problems of congestion. Conditions either must become worse and the expansion cease, or industrialism must destroy the agrarian institutional complex and thus substitute a new economic and social order which no longer responds to economic growth by an automatic, reflex increase of population.

RELIGIOUS AND ETHICAL VALUES

Little has been said thus far about the role of religious values in maintaining a high birth rate. The omission is deliberate, for it seems more reliable to reason in terms of social organization than in terms of avowed values. Motivation is always motivation within a situation. Without an awareness of the circumstances in which people are placed, we can say little or nothing about their values. The latter at best tend to be vague and protean, furnishing the observer with a skimpy basis for predicting behaviour.

However, it is worth noting that the religious paraphernalia of agrarian societies is generally in consonance with the institutions producing a high fertility. The desire for sons in patrilineal societies – whether the religion be Muslim, Hindu, or Buddhist – is reinforced by supernatural beliefs and ritualistic practices. The authority of the elders is strengthened by the tendency to regard them as somewhat sacred, as being near the other world. The segregated role of the woman is ritualistically defined, so that its violation becomes a religious as well as a moral offence; and the wife's subordination to the husband may be expressed by worship of him and his lineal ancestors. All told, despite the diversity found in different cultures, the value system seemingly serves to bolster the institutional arrangements already described.

BALANCING FACTORS

Our intention has not been to imply that every feature of agrarian social structures favours fertility. On the contrary, any social order has functions other than reproduction which its members must perform, and some of these are both partly antithetical to reproduction and equally as important for societal survival. It follows that no society is so organized as to get from its women anything near the maximum child-bearing of which they are biologically capable. Some of the mechanisms that dampen fertility are the prejudice against widow remarriage (Hindu), the taboo on intercourse after childbirth (many cultures), easy divorce (Muslim), monogamy, an insistence on legitimacy, restraints on medical knowledge and practice with reference to pregnancy and parturition, and the prejudice against procreation after grandchildren have already appeared.

However, our purpose here has been merely to consider some of the widespread institutional patterns favouring reproduction, particularly in the massive agrarian societies that are archaic rather than strictly primitive.

REFERENCES

Arensberg, Conrad M and Kimball, Solon T (1940) *Family and Community in Ireland*, Cambridge: Harvard University Press.

Cooper, Eunice (1951) 'Urbanization in Malaysia', *Population Studies* 5 (November).

Davis, K (1951) *Population of India and Pakistan*, Princeton: Princeton University Press.

− (1954) 'Fertility control and the demographic transition in India', *The Interrelations of Demographic, Economic, and Social Problems in Selected Underdeveloped Areas*, New York: Milbank Memorial Fund.

Glass, David V, ed (1953) *Introduction to Malthus*, London: Watts.

Hajnal, John (1953) 'The marriage boom', *Population Index* 19 (April), pp80–101.

Murdock, George P (1949) *Social Structure*, New York: Macmillan.

Russell, Josiah C (1949) 'Demographic values in the Middle Ages', in ed George P Moir *Studies in Population*, Princeton: Princeton University Press.

Stycos, J M (1954) 'Cultural checks on birth control use in Puerto Rico', in *The Interrelations of Demographic, Economic and Social Problems in Selected Underdeveloped Areas*, New York: Milbank Memorial Fund.

Stycos, J M and Reuben Hill (1953) 'Prospects and birth control in Puerto Rico', *Annals of the American Academy of Political and Social Science* 285 (January), pp140–2.

Chapter 14

Population Growth and Agrarian Outcomes

Mead Cain and Geoffrey McNicoll

The effects of population growth on agricultural development are typically portrayed along lines of Malthusian pessimism or Boserupian optimism, with occasional syntheses that bravely straddle this gulf. We argue in the chapter that such models, attempting to isolate a simple demographic-economic system in which population-induced changes in technology and institutions can be traced out, misstate the effects of population growth in most circumstances of interest in the contemporary Third World and ignore the major determinants of agrarian outcomes. The undoubted importance of population growth in such historical transitions as the establishment of permanent field cultivation or the decline of the manorial system does not imply the existence of large routine demographic effects on the structure and thence the performance of the agricultural economy. Agrarian outcomes defined in terms of the rate of growth of per capita product are to a considerable degree tied to forms of institutional arrangements in two areas neglected in most discussions of population and agrarian change: the family system and local-level community and administrative organization. These institutional forms are often relatively immune to population growth, and indeed they may have extraordinary persistence in the face of economic and demographic change. Their origins in most cases far predate the modern era of population growth, deriving from fundamental needs for societal continuity and security. Under certain configurations of such institutions, population growth induces productivity improvements that accommodate or feed back effects that tend to restrain that growth. Under other configurations, perhaps once equally 'satisfactory' in meeting societal needs, no such responses are generated; instead, the system rachets itself to higher and higher levels of population density without commensurate product growth in an all-too-familiar process of immiserization.

This is not to argue that agrarian outcomes are fully determined, because labour, investment and technology in the agricultural economy are in part governed by factors exogenous to it, and institutional change bearing on this economy can come about in a wide variety of ways (including by deliberate or fortuitous policy measures) to offer escape from such an economic and demographic impasse. Nor do we claim that, within a given institutional configuration, population growth effects on the distribution of wealth or income are minor (although that may in fact typically be so). But the case set out here does suggest a need to rethink the role of population in agrarian change. Plausibly the most significant effect of rapid population growth is not any simple contribution to or detraction from productivity but rather that of altering the social and political costs of purposive institutional change, sometimes perhaps easing a necessary transition but more commonly raising those costs, even to virtually prohibitive levels.

MECHANISMS OF POPULATION-INDUCED AGRARIAN CHANGE

Malthus has frequently been castigated for failing to recognize the first stirrings of technological change that was to transform the agrarian economies of his time. Yet his predictive failure, such as it was, derived not from any inability to imagine positive responses to the potential threats to livelihood of unrestrained population growth, but rather from a dim view of the likelihood that most people would as a general rule avail themselves of those responses. (J S Mill, with the same theoretical bent as Malthus but a rosier view of his fellow man, saw a future of steady economic progress.) It takes little complicating of the Malthusian system, however, and no greater faith in mankind, to make population growth itself an all but irresistible force of economic change.

Historical research and contemporary observation leave little doubt of the determinative role of population growth in the adoption of sedentary cultivation. With increasing population density the ecological stability of swidden (slash-and-burn) agriculture is lost, as fallow periods become insufficient to permit regeneration of forest cover. Natural soil fertility is progressively exhausted, the land subject to erosion and laterization and to the invasion of savannah grasses. The swidden cycle cannot continue, and sedentary cultivation (the techniques of which may have long been known) is adopted. Gourou (1965) and Bartlett (1955-61) document numerous instances of this transition. In some societies a complex body of customary law developed to assign and keep track of the slowly solidifying rights of cultivators to permanent occupancy of former swidden land.

On evidence such as this, Boserup (1965) drew her broad conclusions about density-induced productivity improvements in agriculture. In essentials, sustained population growth produces a situation of labour abundance and land scarcity with consequent effects on relative factor prices, and induces efforts to establish contractual arrangements that permit more exclusive use of land. Some form of enclosure takes place; incentives for investment rise sharply; and land yields increase.

The same argument can be applied to another major agrarian transition: from the European manorial system of lord and villein to landlord and tenant or to freeholding peasant proprietors. This is done in a well-known study by North and Thomas (1971, 1973). Closure of the land frontier in Western Europe occurred in the late Middle Ages. Continued population growth thereafter, North and Thomas argue, led to a restriction in common property use of land and enabled the manorial lord to demand greater labour time or payment in kind for his protective and judiciary services. Property rights in labour were attenuated, property rights in land strengthened. Such changes, of course, were slowed by the inertia of custom.

> *We would not expect a once-and-for-all jump from common property to fee-simple private property: in terms of political and military strife the costs of abrogating the conflicting customs of the manor would have been prohibitive. Rather we would expect successive steps to reduce freedom of entry and to increase the degree of exclusiveness in land use. (North and Thomas 1973, p23).*

(A host of second-order considerations that disguise these gross effects and intro-duce regional variations need not concern us here.)

The classic manor in the North and Thomas model is seen as a contractual arrangement suited to a situation where factor and product markets barely exist and where enforcement costs (dealing especially with problems of shirking accurate determination of output) militate against sharecropping, fixed wage payments in kind, or fixed rents in kind (North and Thomas 1973, pp31–2). The gradual development of product markets and financial intermediaries from the 13th century onwards spread a generalized knowledge of prices and offered substantial market-scale economies to be reaped, lowering the cost of market-based transactions. Market development in turn can be traced at least in part to the effect of population growth 'accenting the differences in factor endow-ments between regions' and hence enlarging the gains from trade (*ibid.*, pp50–7).

As these two examples might suggest, large shifts in agrarian production relations and in their associated forms of contract are rare events. For the most part, declines in wage-rent ratios result in familiar shifts along production possi-bility frontiers, with substitution of labour for capital, and perhaps in capital-saving innovation. (Distortions in factor prices and the 'compulsive sequences' that in part govern technological change (see Rosenberg (1976, p111) may, of course, interfere with such responses.) However, there are also effects of population growth with more routine potential impact on agrarian institutions. Tracing out these effects is becoming a popular topic of research (see, for example, Binswanger and McIntire 1984, Hayami and Kikuchi 1982). Practitioners follow North and Thomas in focusing on demographic influences on transaction costs in factor and product markets; unlike North and Thomas, however, they are concerned to explain the minutiae of institutional adjustment rather than the transformation of whole systems.

Hayami and Kikuchi's treatment of population growth in high-density wet-rice agrarian systems in Asia illustrates the genre. The initial condition here is one of pervasive share-cropping, seen as representing 'a saddlepoint between the tenant's strong risk aversion and the landlord's calculation of transaction cost' (1982, p34). Despite improvements in technology and infrastructure, labour demand often cannot keep abreast of labour supply as rapid population growth continues, resulting in declining returns to labour per unit of land and increasing returns to land. This process promotes further concentration of land, leading toward an agrarian system of large commercial farmers and a landless proletariat. Acting against this polarization, however, are the high transaction costs of wage-labour contracts in comparison with either family labour or traditional patron-client ties where contracts are informal and embedded in continuing multi-faceted relationships. One outcome observed by Hayami and Kikuchi (1982, p53n) in several South-east Asian settings is the institutional adjustments within patron-client systems that tend to produce allocative outcomes that mirror neoclassical marginal returns while preserving traditional forms. Whether the resulting arrangements are robust enough to resist pressures of polarization remains very much in question.

Binswanger and McIntire (1984) adopt a more stylized approach, focusing not on particular historical cases but rather on the logical consequences of popula-tion growth for production relations in agriculture, given certain behavioural postulates and the existence of risk and information costs. The 'base case' they consider is that of a semi-arid or arid economy with simple technology where land is virtually a free good. The implications of population growth for the evolution of factor and output markets are then traced out. For example, with increasing population density, land eventually acquires scarcity value and, thus, value as collateral. This emergence of a superior collateral asset dramatically increases the supply of credit; the development of credit markets, in turn, has additional consequences, including the creation of money-lenders and a class of landless people.

While differing in ambition, these various attempts to model the influence of population growth on agrarian institutional change clearly share many features. They interpret institutional arrangements as locally efficient ways of coping with risk and transaction costs under given production conditions. Population growth alters those conditions through a variety of means (changed factor proportions, scale effects, savings behaviour, induced technical change, and so on), in turn yielding a different array of risks and transaction costs, and making an alternative institutional configuration a more efficient arrangement. It does not follow that the system will abruptly shift to the new configuration, because the change itself is likely to entail political or economic costs; but the long-run likelihood is that that shift will occur.

In actual current or recent instances of agrarian change, disentangling population-induced effects from other changes in the system usually involves a large measure of speculation. Typically, the situation is one where new agricultural techniques are being introduced and there is growing use of modern inputs – in both cases, not strictly demand-generated phenomena. Government extension programmes expand over an ever-greater range of activities. Education is spreading; knowledge of the world penetrates even remote areas through radio and television. Each of these changes may have economic effects. Moreover, the concept of population in agriculture, as defined simply by occupation or industry division, loses the limited value it once had as rural families increasingly come to resemble miniature highly diversified conglomerates, many of them with a foothold in the urban sector. Within this welter of social change, there are necessarily massive ceteris paribus assumptions in seeking to identify and explain intrinsic system responses to population growth.

INSTITUTIONAL DETERMINANTS OF AGRARIAN OUTCOMES

There is, however, a more fundamental limitation to the kinds of studies we have been describing, if they are seen as more than *ad hoc* explanations of observed patterns of change in particular situations. While an interest in agrarian outcomes naturally requires a focus on agrarian institutions, to restrict the field of vision simply to those institutions is to omit elements of the institutional structure that may critically influence those outcomes. In particular, we shall argue, both the family system and the forms of local-level community and administrative organization are major determinants of agrarian success or failure. Certain forms of such institutions go far to guarantee positive results – that is, the long-run expansion of per capita product and population growth brought down to moderate or low levels. Other configurations all but ensure the opposite outcome: stagnant or falling productivity and continued rapid population growth. In the discussion following, we refine and defend this hypothesis. If correct, most of the distinctions that 'new institutional economists' such as Hayami and Kikuchi try to explain (in the details of the tenure system and labour contracts, in the timing of emergence of financial intermediaries, and so on) are second-order issues. They concern the fine structure of agrarian systems whose gross productivity performance is in large measure determined elsewhere.

Of course, family and community systems, and to some extent local administrative structures, are societal inheritances, and they usually and properly are seen as fixtures rather than as matters for policy deliberation. To recommend a correct choice in such domains is like medical advice that recommends careful choice of one's grandparents. Abstracting from such difficulties does not remove them, however, and in the present case there are some policy avenues available, which are mentioned briefly at the end of this chapter.

Family Systems

For the purposes of this argument, there are three broad kinds of distinction to be made among family systems: how they deal with intergenerational property transfer; their control over establishment of new households; and their marital fertility responsiveness to the changing economics of children.

First, family systems can be distinguished by the success or failure with which they preserve the integrity of agricultural holdings from one generation to the next, through rules of property devolution, in the face of varying rates of population growth. Systems of primogeniture, such as prevailed in much of pre-industrial North-west Europe and Japan, are relatively successful in this respect, in contrast to the practice of partible inheritance which is typical of South Asia – and is becoming typical of Africa with the emergence or strengthening of individual land ownership rights.

Family systems can be further distinguished according to whether and by what means they provide mechanisms for adjustment of population growth in response to varying economic conditions. In pre-industrial North-west Europe, the rules of family formation permitted adjustment through the timing of marriage. According to these rules, marriage marked the establishment of an independent household, for which a prior accumulation of capital was necessary. Many young people acquired this capital through employment in domestic service (Kussmaul 1981). Times of economic hardship saw the period of service extended and marriage delayed. Similar (probably more stringent) controls of new household formation existed in pre-industrial Japan, associated with the high value accorded to preservation of the family land-holding and descent line, and perhaps also with collective village responsibility for land tax. In this way, Japan experienced near constancy of rural population over generations. (See Fukutake 1972, Hanley and Yamamura 1972, T C Smith 1977.) No comparable mechanism of response and adjustment exists for the joint family formation systems once prevalent elsewhere in Europe, and still so in most of contemporary Asia and the Middle East. There, the timing of marriage is not responsive to variations in economic conditions, because marriage is not coincident with the formation of an independent household: a newly married couple typically is sheltered for a period as a member of an elder's household (Hajnal 1982). Nor are there economic constraints on early marriage or household establishment in traditional, lineage-dominant family systems of Africa – nor appreciable signs of such constraints appearing as these systems are increasingly stressed.

The family systems of pre-industrial North-west Europe and Japan, however, were never exposed to the kind of rapid population growth that has been experienced by less developed countries since the 1950s, and it is certain that, if they had been exposed, the 'marriage valve' would not have provided an adequate adjustment. In the face of modern-era rates of population growth, adjustment must entail some reduction in marital fertility. This brings us to a third criterion for distinguishing family systems: their implications for the economic value of children to parents and, thence, for the extent to which secular mortality decline alone will produce a private incentive for reductions in marital fertility. The discussion here is necessarily somewhat speculative.

Particular family systems appear to have distinct structures of incentive with potential bearing on marital fertility. This is most evident with respect to the security and welfare of elderly parents. In societies of North-west Europe, from a very early period in history, there seems to have been little connection between the number of surviving children and the welfare of parents in old age (Gaunt 1983, Hajnal 1982, R M Smith 1984). For those with property, an explicit retirement contract was the typical means of securing food and other necessities in old age until death. The existence of such contracts suggests the limits of unenforced filial obligation; it also points to the fact that the contracted partners of the elderly need not have been children (although children may have been preferred) or even kin. For those without property, the prospect of ageing appears to have been predictably, grim. The evidence for England, for example, suggests that for those without property a pattern of life-cycle poverty produced a regular disparity in economic status between an elderly parent and his or her children (R M Smith 1984). For this class, the fate of the elderly rested with publicly provided relief for the poor. Under these circumstances, one may conjecture that concerns about economic security in later life did not figure prominently in reproductive decisions or behaviour. In the event of secular mortality decline, it is similarly unlikely that security concerns would affect the prospect of a compensating adjustment in marital fertility.

In the joint family system, however, there is a strong connection between children and the economic well-being of aged parents. In fact, co-resident children are the system's solution to the dependency problems of the elderly for both propertied and propertyless alike. A secular mortality decline would be experienced rather differently under the joint system. Depending on how security needs are defined, the proliferation of surviving children following the mortality decline may well be perceived as a windfall gain: security in old age, which before the decline was as uncertain as child survival, seems reasonably assured after the decline. With respect to adjustment in marital fertility, therefore, the path to demographic equilibrium may well be blocked as long as the family remains the dominant welfare institution or until financial markets develop to an extent that annuities become widely available (or a public agency intervenes) (Cain 1983).

Among societies that have a joint family system, one further distinction must be made relating to how security needs are defined. In many such societies, it is not children, undifferentiated by sex, who are looked to by parents for security in old age but rather sons. In other societies, children of either sex may satisfy security requirements. For any given mortality decline (and other things being equal), one can expect a larger adjustment in fertility in societies of the latter type than in societies where the preference for sons is strong. This follows from the simple observation that fertility will be higher if parents set a goal of two sons (for example) than if their goal is two children of either sex.

Marital fertility is also seemingly insulated from economic change in African family systems. In the dominant patriarchal variants of such systems, children become members of the husband's lineage, but their subsistence is largely the responsibility of their mother. The mother, however, as in the joint family case, later may expect to have to rely on her children for support in her widowhood and old age. Whether the decay of lineage influence will lead to a family-level incentive structure that promotes a marital fertility response to the effects of population growth is a critical question for Africa's future.

Under conditions of land scarcity, the joint family system thus appears to be less conducive to successful agrarian outcomes than were the systems that evolved in pre-industrial north-west Europe and Japan, particularly in the face of rapid population growth. Partible inheritance promotes a splintering of agricultural holdings; the system lacks a mechanism comparable to the European marriage valve or its Japanese equivalent; and the family as the locus of welfare functions creates a structure of incentives that inhibits the responsiveness of marital fertility to secular mortality decline. *Mutatis mutandis*, much the same can be said about African family systems.

Community and Local Administration

The second component of a society's institutional structure that we would argue can have a strong effect on agrarian outcomes is the local-level social organization above the family – in particular, the characteristics of its community and administrative structure. The stereotype of traditional rural society posits solidary hamlets or 'natural villages' as the next important social unit after the family. Though the *gram raj* or village republic is no longer taken seriously as a depiction of historical reality, in most rural societies local supra-family groupings did exert considerable influence over their members' behaviour in certain domains of life, including matters bearing on the family economy and fertility. That influence has weakened, and its domains have narrowed, but in many societies an appreciable residue remains. Similarly, most rural societies in the past and present have local outposts of government administration, whether concerned minimally with civil order (and, often, surplus extraction) or more fully with the broad and expanding range of activities that governments promiscuously take on. The positive roles for local government lie in creating a conducive setting for economic enterprise and, perhaps coincidentally (through ensuing changes in the economics of children), for fertility decline. In addition, although potentially in conflict with these facilitative roles, local government is sometimes directly involved in programmatic efforts to raise output, alleviate poverty, and reduce fertility.

The important distinguishing characteristics of community systems for present purposes are their degree of corporateness and territoriality. The former quality governs the capacity of the group (or of an élite within it) to influence the behaviour of members to suit group interests, however those may be defined. The latter affects the likelihood that demographic behaviour will be included in the kinds of behaviour subjected to group pressure. Territoriality also facilitates orderly governance: land stays where it is.

Kinship is the chief competitor to territory in defining community systems in traditional rural societies. Natural villages may have kin ties linking many of their members, but their principal identification is as a territorial unit with more or less fixed boundaries. There are cases, however, where kinship takes precedence over territory, where clans or other kinds of corporate kin-groups dominate the local-level social landscape. Bangladesh is often cited as an instance of this situation (see Bertocci 1970); sub-Saharan Africa could provide many others. In some societies, there are several distinct bases of affiliation, no one of them dominant, each generating a system of local groupings with a particular domain of influence (see, for example, Geertz 1959 on Bali). And there may be extreme cases – exemplified apparently by the Ik of Uganda (Turnbull 1973) – where there is no significant affiliative principle.

Pre-industrial Japan and Switzerland can be taken as illustrations of strong corporate-territorial community systems. Villages in both countries could and did exact a high degree of conformity from members and tightly controlled new household formation, and they could presumably cope readily with free-rider problems. Modern examples, different from one another in many respects but not in these ways, are villages in China and South Korea – mobilized in support of government policies and programmes but still far from being mere instruments of government authority. (See the account by Parish and Whyte (1978) of the largely successful resistance by the leadership of village communities in China – the production brigades – to co-optation as local government agents.) These cases contrast strikingly with, say, villages in contemporary Nepal, which appear to be nearly helpless to enforce sound agricultural and forestry practices under rapid population growth, let alone to regulate that growth itself, or in Bangladesh, where the prominent local-level organizational roles are played by kin-groups and factions rather than territorial communities. In Africa, similarly, village organization has traditionally been quite weak in comparison to tribe and lineage. There seems little indication that the gradual conversion of tribal land systems into private smallholdings is being accompanied by the strengthening of village roles.

Corporateness and territoriality are community characteristics that appear to facilitate demographic restraint even under an adverse family system. Whether they also help to promote vigorous economic performance is more questionable: indeed, a strong case can probably be made that they as often as not impede it. (The incompatibility between village-level institutional arrangements deemed necessary to meet demographic objectives and those seen as best designed to promote rapid economic growth is a problem currently bedevilling agrarian policy in China.)

The local-level organizational structures relevant to agrarian outcomes also include the lower reaches of the government administrative apparatus. The territorial basis of this apparatus can be taken for granted. An important consideration in its effectiveness, however, is the societal level down to which it operates. It is arguably impossible for government to make natural villages effective administrative units, since the face-to-face contact that characterizes them generates local pressures and loyalties strong enough to capture any officialdom at this level. On the other hand, there are problems in having the lowest level administrative unit too far above the village. Historical evidence suggests that the administrative vacuum set up by such a gap will be quickly filled by informal political entrepreneurs, ready to act as brokers in relationships between government and governed and in the process forging a new, extra-administrative organizational system designed to maximize brokerage. Such systems grew up in the colonial period in South Asia as an outcome of the attempts by the colonial authorities to extract revenues with minimal effort. The beneficiaries of the system compose a powerful coalition that can block change. This administrative legacy has been a major impediment to rural development and achievement of lower fertility in both Bangladesh (see Arthur and McNicoll 1978) and parts of northern India.

Family-community Configurations

The combination of family system and local community and administrative organization defines a rural institutional environment that can variously promote or impede agrarian development. Historically, the European family system was very often associated with a corporate-territorial community structure. While the resulting pattern of economic growth and demographic regulation owed something to the organizational design at each of these levels, under the prevailing low-to-moderate rate of population growth, the family was the main locus of control. If family controls on marriage were overwhelmed – supposing, say, that Europe had been faced with the pace of demographic change of the present-day developing countries – then the option of a strong community role existed. (Rapid population growth need not, of course, threaten rural welfare if there is an open land frontier, as there was in pre-industrial America, or if a substantial fraction of the rural population's natural increase is being drawn into the cities.)

In the case of the other two kinds of family systems considered – joint and African – community (and administrative) organization is altogether more significant. These family systems lack the in-built demographic regulation that the European system provided; higher-level feed-backs or government interventions are likely to be needed to curtail rapid population growth or to counter its economic ill-effects. In much of East and South-east Asia, the institutional forms existed on which community roles in agrarian development could be based, although their potentials were somewhat obscured prior to the land reforms of the 1950s. Governments of otherwise quite divergent political orientations recognized and made use of these structures in the development effort. An effective and, at least in the economic sphere, relatively non-intrusive administrative system was another important element of success. In contrast, South Asian and sub-Saharan African patterns of community organization seem to offer little similar scope for mobilization, even if a supportive local government system existed. Some individual families can and do prosper, nevertheless, in such an environment, but, without a vigorous and labour-absorbing non-agricultural economy, the institutional obstacles confronting broad-based rural development are severe.

No serious typological intent underlies this discussion. Even the brief account of rural institutional forms in the present chapter introduces further distinctions that should enter any minimally adequate attempt at classification of family-community configurations. That such classifications are feasible and would be potentially enlightening contributions to debate on population growth and agricultural development we have little doubt.

THE PERSISTENCE OF INSTITUTIONAL FORMS

The family is sometimes portrayed as an institution that is relatively malleable in the face of economic or demographic change. Until quite recently, for example, a common perception held that the household in Western Europe experienced a radical transformation in the course of agricultural and industrial development, evolving from an extended to a nuclear structure during this period. While in function the family unquestionably did undergo fundamental change – as the workplace increasingly became separated from the household, for example, and as formal education came to replace some of the socialization functions of the family – in many respects the common perception was incorrect: the North-western European household appears never to have been extended in structure (or at least not for a millennium). The emerging image of the family through the centuries is one of remarkable continuity and persistence in form (Laslett and Wall 1972).

In the developing countries, a similar perception of malleability in family structure is evident in the scholarly work of the 1960s and 1970s that focused on the relationship between household structure and fertility within particular societies (Burch 1983). This research was informed largely by an anticipation that modernization in the post-war period would lead to a shift from 'traditional' extended family forms to 'modern' nuclear families. Now, of course, it is understood that the joint family system produces life-cycle periods of both nuclear and joint household residence. It is further understood that the period of joint residence is generally greater for wealthier families than it is for the poor. There is very little evidence, in fact, that post-war economic, social or demographic change has had an appreciable impact on the prevailing systems of household formation and structure in most developing countries. Certainly, the extent of change anticipated by the research just mentioned was unwarranted.

The major features of the North-western European system of household formation – late age at marriage for both sexes, the independence of a couple after marriage, and the circulation of young unmarried people among households as servants – can be observed as early as the 12th century and before. Analogous rules of household formation in joint systems – early marriage for men and even earlier marriage for women, residence of the newly married couple for a period in the parents' or another elder's household, and the subsequent splitting of households with several married couples – also seem impervious to change through time. Although the historical statistical record is much thinner for the joint household system, the distinctive and quite invariant distributions of household composition that the joint system produces have been shown for societies as disparate as rural India in 1950, Nepal in 1976, rural China in 1930, and 15th-century Tuscany (Hajnal 1982). Evidence on African family systems is scarcer still. That these also show considerable resilience, however, is suggested by the observation that Caribbean family arrangements retain discernible African characteristics that survived the trauma of slavery.

What accounts for the persistence of household formation systems? First, as noted earlier in the case of intergenerational property transfers and welfare institutions, particular family systems are associated with distinctive solutions to a variety of problems common to all societies. This functional integrity generates considerable inertial force. Second, one can discern patterns of advantage and interest associated with particular family systems that also serve as a source of resistance to change. In the joint system, the older generation might be viewed as a blocking coalition that, in order to achieve security for itself, is prepared to transfer the associated costs to younger generations. Men as a group can, in situations of male dominance, represent a similar conservative force, as can local élites. A third factor contributing to the persistence of family and kinship institutions is family morality (notions of right or wrong applied to the behavioural options governing family formation, dissolution, property devolution, and so on) and its reification in religious doctrine, ritual, and socialization practice. (Formal religion may also have a determining role in the evolution of particular family systems; Goody (1983) presents a persuasive argument to this effect in the case of Europe.)

We do not of course argue that joint or lineage-based family systems are immutable up to extremes of economic deprivation. Feed-back effects from economic and demographic behaviours bring pressures to bear on family arrangements and make realities increasingly depart from culturally specified ideals. That these feed-backs by and large have not been determinative under historical rates of population growth and technological change does not mean that they will be similarly ineffectual under the conditions obtaining today. As a case in point, we noted earlier that lineage roles in African family systems appear to be diminishing. While there is no consensus on the scope and significance of resulting changes in the family, possible outcomes include an emerging dominance of female-headed households (like those prevalent in the Caribbean) and a shift toward the nuclear family.

Like the family, community structures also tend to be stable arrangements although subject to erosion under rapid social and economic change. Family reconstitution studies, notably in England and Japan, have traced village demographic histories over centuries: individual family lines disappear, but the community is preserved. A very different illustration of stability is given by Wertheim (1964) in a description of pioneer settlement in Sumatra, Indonesia, outside the government resettlement programme. The settlers, drawn from densely populated rural Java, were confronted by vast areas of potentially cultivable forest. Far from shifting to extensive agriculture to accord with their new factor proportions, they instead constructed precise replicas of Javanese villages, resembling 'the ways of colonies of ants who by instinct know how to construct new communities, but ignore the outward factors which may endanger the existence of the community' (p205).

Several factors making for this stability of community structure can be cited. In an insecure environment, especially one with high rates of mortality and debility, the family unit is too small to offer a reliable means of risk-spreading. Cultivation of the needed social ties for this purpose over a larger group becomes an essential part of an individual's survival strategy. Because this is the case for all, the reciprocal exchange relationships that are generated acquire cultural validity, forming what is sometimes called a moral economy. Opting out of such a system, aside from physically departing, becomes very costly to the individual. For a few people early in the development process, and for many eventually, the economic gains to be made by severing such obligations outweigh those costs. There are also exogenous changes that tend to erode community values as contacts with urban life expand and as local labour and product markets are absorbed into the larger economy. These processes of attenuation ultimately suburbanize rural society, supplanting community institutions by others more specialized and less tied to locality.

Local administrative organization, although at first sight something changeable at will or whim by government, is another institutional characteristic that tends to persist. Successive governments may differ greatly in political orientation but be quite alike in their interests at the grass-roots level (in civil order, revenue-raising, and mobilization for economic growth). Administrative designs tend to gravitate to those that have worked before. Non-territorial affiliative ties (based, for example, on kin, clan, or tribe) can also be highly resilient, and in some cases they can undermine efforts to introduce 'rational' bureaucratic structures in local government or economic enterprise. Observations of this problem in Sub-Saharan African societies underlie Hyden's pessimistic views (1983) of early establishment of sound institutional bases for development in that region.

As we argued was the case with family systems, an important contributor to stability of social organizational forms is simple self-interest on the part of those who see themselves benefiting from the status quo. Part of those benefits can readily be applied to system maintenance. Powerful blocking coalitions to oppose institutional change are familiar in any development process. Where the benefits to such groups are large, as in the political brokerage arrangement mentioned above, the blocking efforts are likely to be similarly strenuous. In more developed economies the outcome may be the kind of economic sclerosis vividly described by Olson (1982). Short of radical institutional shake-ups through war or revolution or hyperinflation, the main hope of escape is that eventually the prospective benefits of new arrangements become great enough to permit the buying out of opposition.

Finally, a factor that promotes stability of organizational forms at supra-village levels is the spatial logic of markets and administration. In the former case, this logic dictates an economic structure of marketing areas, typified by the elegant hexagons of Christaller-Lösch central-place theory (see Whyte 1982). Local administrative systems, not surprisingly, often make such areas into administrative units, adding selected government functions to the economic functions of market towns, and thus transferring the stability of the one to the other. The commune in China was an administrative division roughly superimposed on the marketing area (Skinner 1965).

AGRARIAN IMPASSES AND RESOLUTIONS

In this chapter, we have argued that prevailing patterns of family and community organization in most contemporary developing countries pose difficulties for successful agrarian outcomes that did not have to be faced in many historical cases. Very broad distinctions in institutional forms have been used in order to simplify exposition, but a finer grained treatment would probably not change the essentials of the argument.

Agrarian development in the contemporary world confronts the added difficulty of having to take place under conditions of rapid population growth. Where a vigorous, labour-absorbing industrial sector exists, this growth may be of little consequence: ultimately most of the rural population will be drawn into the modern economy. For the majority of the developing countries today, any such prospect is at best distant. We have seen how some common institutional configurations can protect population growth from negative feed-back effects. In turn, population growth militates against certain kinds of institutional change that could help establish such feed-back. Under these circumstances, the broadly defined agrarian system (encompassing family and other local institutions as variables rather than parameters) is in an impasse. Endogenous mechanisms of population-induced technical and institutional change are no match for its resilience.

What are the possible kinds of change that might resolve such an impasse and set the system on a new development path? A simple fourfold classification can cover the field. First, there is the possibility that sheer informational activity, spreading knowledge of alternative systems and behaviours and of the potential gains they have to offer, can itself effect the escape. Both demographic behaviour and the roles assigned to local government and community could be candidates for reconsideration. The case can be stated in terms of reducing the transaction costs associated with changing (as opposed to operating) an institution. Such costs include those of 'reaching agreement to make a change or, if agreement cannot be reached by negotiation, the cost of using force or other means to obtain acquiescence' (Cheung 1982, p38). In an argument concerning prospects for broad-scale emergence of private enterprise in China, Cheung maintains that the high cost of obtaining reliable information about alternative economic arrangements has been a major obstacle to this direction of institutional change. Analogous arguments might be made in the case of interest to us here.

Less ethereal than this is the prospect of escape through technological change. In a loose variant of once-popular equilibrium-trap models, a sudden surge in agricultural production associated with new technology creates a situation in which the relative costs of institutional change are quite low. This is apparently what has happened in the Indian Punjab and in other areas where the Green Revolution package of technology has most successfully taken hold. The modestly labour-using properties of this technology, combined with the dramatic productivity gains that it has engendered, have elevated many indigenous Punjabis to a *rentier* status, while drawing migrant labour from the neighbouring, less developed areas of Uttar Pradesh and Bihar. The availability of such migrant labour reduces the potential for polarization and friction within the indigenous population (as does the absence of caste among the dominant Sikh community). The broad base of development and welfare gains in this region (real wages have improved also) can generate a slack in which the economic rationales for particular institutional forms (including perhaps such fundamental characteristics as parent-child relationships) recede and there is scope for new configurations to emerge. New advances in agricultural technology since the Green Revolution show some promise of yielding opportunities of this sort in many other regions.

A third class of policy comprises what can be called minor structural change – interventions that may themselves have relatively low political costs but that may set up repercussions with larger consequences. Examples would be devolutionary shifts in systems of local finance, reallocation of government functions among centre and locality, and privatizing (or easing government monopoly) of certain kinds of service activities. Changes in the direction of tightening local controls or organizing formerly inchoate interest groups could also fall in this category.

Finally, the agrarian impasse can be resolved through radical structural change in periods in which the high social and political costs are discounted. The erratic agrarian history of modern China gives little confidence that a system created through such a process will necessarily be efficient; more promising East Asian examples are perhaps the Japanese colonial agrarian reforms in pre-war Korea and Taiwan, and the post-war land reforms in these countries.

Our purpose in this chapter is not to derive policy, and the preceding paragraphs are no more than a token gesture in that direction. Rather, our concern is with expanding the domain of interest of research on agrarian change to encompass fundamental societal institutions that play a large part in determining long-run outcomes. That these institutions are singularly intractable in the face of the usual array of levers of government policy is a poor reason for neglect.

REFERENCES

Arthur, W B, and G McNicoll (1978) 'An analytical survey of population and development in Bangladesh', *Population and Development Review* 4, pp23–80.

Bartlett, H H (1955–61) *Fire in Relation to Primitive Agriculture*, Ann Arbor: University of Michigan Department of Botany.

Bertocci, P J (1970) 'Elusive villages: social structure and community organization in rural East Pakistan', Ph D dissertation, Michigan State University.

Binswanger, H P, and J McIntire (1984) 'Behavioural and material determinants of production relations in land-abundant tropical agriculture', Discussion Paper no ARU 17, Agricultural and Rural Development Research Unit, World Bank.

Boserup, E (1965) *The Conditions of Agricultural Growth*, Chicago: Aldine.

Burch, T K (1983) 'The impact of forms of families and sexual unions and dissolution of unions on fertility', in *Determinants of Fertility in Developing Countries*, ed R A Bulatao and R D Lee, vol 2 New York: Academic Press.

Cain, M (1983) 'Fertility as an adjustment to risk', *Population and Development Review* 9, pp688–702.

Cheung, S N S (1982) *Will China Go 'Capitalist'? An Economic Analysis of Property Rights and Institutional Change* London: Institute of Economic Affairs.

Fukutake, T (1972) *Japanese Rural Society*, Ithaca, New York: Cornell University Press.

Gaunt, D (1983) 'The property and kin relationships of retired farmers in northern and central Europe', in *Family Forms in Historic Europe*, ed R Wall, J Robin, and P Laslett, Cambridge: Cambridge University Press.

Geertz, C (1959) 'Form and variation in Balinese village structure', *American Anthropologist* 61, pp991–1021.

Goody, J (1983) *The Development of the Family and Marriage in Europe*, Cambridge: Cambridge University Press.

Gourou, P (1965) *The Tropical World: Its Social and Economic Conditions and its Future Status* (4th ed), London.

Hajnal, J (1982) 'Two kinds of preindustrial household formation system', *Population and Development Review* 8, pp449–94.

Hanley, S B, and K Yamamura (1972) 'Population trends and economic growth in preindustrial Japan', in *Population and Social Change*, ed D Glass and R Revelle, London: Arnold.

Hayami, Y, and M Kikuchi (1982) *Asian Village Economy at the Crossroads*, Tokyo: University of Tokyo Press.

Hyden, G (1983) *No Shortcuts to Progress: African Development Management in Perspective*, Berkeley: University of California Press.

Kussmaul, A S (1981) *Servants in Husbandry in Early England*, Cambridge: Cambridge University Press.

Laslett, P, and R Wall, eds (1972) *Household and Family in Past Time*, Cambridge: Cambridge University Press.

North, D C, and R P Thomas (1971) 'The rise and fall of the manorial system: a theoretical model', *The Journal of Economic History* 3, pp777–803.

— (1973) *The Rise of the Western World: A New Economic History*, Cambridge: Cambridge University Press.

Olson, M (1982) *The Rise and Decline of Nations: Economic Growth, Stagflation and Social Rigidities*, New Haven, Conn : Yale University Press.

Parish, W L, and M K Whyte (1978) *Village and Family in Contemporary China*, Chicago: University of Chicago Press.

Rosenberg, N (1976) *Perspectives on Technology,* Cambridge: Cambridge University Press.

Skinner, G W (1965) 'Marketing and social structure in rural China, Part 3', *Journal of Asian Studies* 24, pp363–99.

Smith, R M (1984) 'Some issues concerning families and their property in rural England 1250–1800', in *Land, Kinship and Life Cycle,* ed R M Smith, Cambridge: Cambridge University Press.

Smith, T C (1977) *Nakahara: Family Farming and Population in a Japanese Village, 1717–1830,* Palo Alto, California: Stanford University Press.

Turnbull, C (1973) *The Mountain People,* London: Cape.

Wertheim, W F (1964) 'Inter-island migration in Indonesia', in his *East-West Parallels,* The Hague: van Hoeve.

Whyte, R O (1982) *The Spatial Geography of Rural Economies,* New Delhi: Oxford University Press.

Chapter 15

Institutional Analysis of Fertility Transition

Geoffrey McNicoll

The historical declines of mortality and fertility in Western countries are broadly linked to economic growth and accompanying social change. These links are the subject of the theory of demographic transition. As a strand of now disavowed modernization theory, demographic transition theory seemed to many to have unjustly survived the demise of its progenitor. But rejection did eventually come. The theory was overdetermined, it neglected the subtleties and variability of the transition process, and it abstracted from historical specifics (Greenhalgh, 1990, p92). Yet seen from sufficiently afar, it presented a fair, first-order account of demographic change and its covariates in the large. In its full-blown form (see, for example, Notestein, 1983 [1964]), the theory was at least institutionally rich. Some later variants have sought to strip away the encrustations in an effort to reveal an essential relationship – a risky endeavour, in that there may be no single such relationship at the core.

Historical fertility transition exemplifies this picture, showing similarity across societies at a distance but diversity at close-up. Adding contemporary cases of fertility decline greatly increases the diversity. Yet undeniably there are strong forces making for convergent outcomes as well. Urban industrial life-styles and consumption patterns create similar pressures for low fertility wherever they are found. Ambitions for and anticipations of those futures may have behavioural import much earlier. The degree of institutional convergence to be expected, however, remains controversial.

Take the case of the family. A familiar line of argument associated particularly with Talcott Parsons holds that families increasingly become nuclear in urban industrial societies. Caldwell's transition theory incorporates an assumption of this sort: convergence to the conjugal 'Western' family (Caldwell 1976). Convergence is a plausible expectation for joint families, which after all are nuclear for some part of their life-cycle, but may be less so for African systems. The weak conjugality characterizing those systems may as plausibly persist, with the decay of lineage then leading to a Caribbean-type family pattern of visiting unions and largely female-headed households. (See Frank and McNicoll 1987.) Low fertility may be similarly attainable under either family system (the Caribbean region's total fertility rate is now below 3), but the economic and social policies that would best promote it may differ greatly.

Caldwell's theory, of course, is to do with parent–child rather than conjugal relations. The turning point in fertility transition is posited to be the stage of 'wealth flow reversal', when children, from being an economic asset to the family, become instead an economic burden. To the extent children are still wanted, it is for non-economic reasons. That change in the family Caldwell associates with a shift in cultural orientations toward acceptance of nuclear-family models and behaviours purveyed in the media and often in formal education. A more materialist stand is taken by Seccombe (1991), who attributes the reversal to development of a formal labour market which undermines parental authority exercised through control of property. In either case, the effective change, in so far as parental behaviour is concerned, comes when parental expectations about their children are affected. Under the theory's predictions, path-dependent constraints that may formerly have preserved the two kinds of family structures as distinct equilibria are overcome.

An analogous situation may exist at the community level. I remarked earlier that kin-group or factional membership can be seen as an alternative basis to simple residence in defining local-level social organization. The two affiliative principles create alternative equilibrium community structures. For demographic outcomes, the distinction lies in the fluidity of membership in the non-territorial groupings, with the consequent likelihood that no upper limit on size of group would be enforced. Rising population density might eventually bring about the 'peasantization' of such a system, giving significance to village-type communities; or the system's stability may be preserved, its demographic dysfunctionality notwithstanding. Entrenched local power holders would tend to support the latter outcome: their ability to capture the reins of program reform is seen in innumerable failed co-operative movements, community development schemes, and land reforms.

For many other kinds of social institutions, the equilibrium structure, if any can be detected, is much more complex and possibilities for change more varied. There is very plausibly an institutional analogue of 'punctuated equilibrium', with comparatively sudden – but not necessarily policy-driven – shifts in the comparative salience of different structures (see Hodgson, 1993). For example, legal systems in some societies are a complex overlay of uncodified traditional law, religious law (perhaps more than one system), and civil law, typically with overlapping jurisdictions in the major fertility-related areas of family and property. Over time, the civil code is likely to emerge gradually as the dominant system; along the way, however, in any particular behavioural domain a switch in the applicable system can happen much faster: the alternative is already in place. Less formalized systems of cultural authority are also arenas in the contest for social control, whether in a simple behavioural sense or, more profoundly, in influencing language, categories of thought, and moral values. Benedict Anderson (1991) gives a classic account of how this cultural weaponry has been deployed in the colonial and subsequent nation-building enterprises, using as one example the census-taker's struggle with the concept of ethnic identity. Closer to the fertility domain, one might instance the rapid loss of authority befalling Catholic teaching on birth control in Western countries, in competition with less rigorous situation ethics.

In developing countries, a change that has had large implications for fertility transition has been the expansion of state power at the expense of other social institutions. In communist systems the takeover was virtually complete, as a matter of principle. Even in more pluralist societies, development strategies, influenced by statist philosophies, greatly weakened the independent roles of countervailing institutions of social control. (Other social and economic changes, notably the increased mobility of labour, helped to bring about the same outcome.) The state thereby gained more power to influence fertility, at the expense of society being able to wield less power. (Migdal 1988, describes this opposition in a more general context.) However, since fertility was hardly a priority item on a crowded development agenda, that power was seldom used.

Recognition of the scope and variety of institutional change is a necessary corrective to the ill-informed notion of institutions as timeless structures. It also greatly complicates the analytical task. Like other kinds of evolutionary change, institutional change is in some degree constrained by the past. Over the long term, its outcomes may be largely unpredictable, although possibilities may be narrowed by existence of equilibrium patterns and by convergent forces in the society. Among the latter are adjustments to behaviour and expectations – institutionalization is a never-ending social process. In the case of fertility these complications arise with respect to a raft of institutional arrangements that bear (sometimes quite incidentally) on reproductive behaviour. On a broad canvas, fertility transition can be linked to the institutional changes that accompany economic development; however, to understand fertility patterns and the course of fertility change in the detail needed to inform population policy design requires close investigation of those institutional arrangements in the particular society concerned.

INSTITUTIONAL ASPECTS OF FERTILITY POLICY

Fertility policies can operate by altering prices (and endeavouring to alter preferences) attaching to various behaviours within a given institutional system, or they can seek to modify the system itself. The latter policies are chiefly of interest here. Moreover, policies of either kind rapidly become institutionalized themselves: they can be studied in the same way that other institutions are.

Families are necessarily influenced by a wide variety of government actions, few of which have any such intent. Where that intent does exist, the effectiveness of the action is often unclear. Billboards displaying a beaming couple with two or three well-dressed children have long been part of the publicity component of family-planning programmes; television soap operas conveying the contrasting effects on well-being of small and large families are a more recent popular variant. Quite possibly, these have some residual effect, although construction of a new image of the family is inevitably a much more complex and drawn-out process than establishing a particular consumer-good preference. Family change is also the objective of some legislative efforts: setting minimum ages for marriage; making schooling compulsory and child labour illegal; forbidding a requirement for dowry and enforcing property and inheritance rights for women; and so on. Few states have not enacted these kinds of provisions; they are the stuff of many international instruments and declarations; yet the will or capacity to give effect to them is lacking in many poor, high-fertility countries. Without either an elaborate administrative structure reaching down to the household or a similarly elaborate fiscal system, governments have little purchase on the family economy – or on the demographic behaviour that is influenced by it.

A different route of engagement with the family is the attempt to alter inherent power relations within it. Changes in generational power – of children vis à vis their parents – is at the centre of Caldwell's view of the influence of mass education on fertility (Caldwell 1980). 'Empowerment' of women is the aim of numerous educational and extension programmes in place or planned by international development agencies. In many societies, it is argued, women desire fewer children than their husbands; giving their preferences more weight would lower fertility. Family planning extension workers, typically dealing with female clients only, may perhaps have such an empowerment effect: that indeed has been claimed in one report on a well-known experiment on service delivery being conducted in Matlab, Bangladesh (Simmons *et al.* 1988).

Less potentially sensitive for government than interventions at the family level are policies that seek to gain purchase on fertility behaviour through communities or local government. Both China and Indonesia found ways to draw on community pressures in the early stages of their respective economic development strategies. In both countries, this level of social control was also drawn on in achieving their early successes (those of the 1970s) in fertility decline.

Sustained economic growth and the processes of political development make the opportunity for this policy route short-lived. A major ingredient of that growth would often have been grass-roots economic freedom, setting up the dynamics of capitalist development. (Recall Stephen Cheung's argument on the irreversibility of change following from land privatization in China after the first Dengist reforms [Cheung 1982].) Expansion of the labour market reduces the significance of community boundaries. Authoritarian rule at the local level is undermined, but so too are the local institutional bases of community solidarity. A more private and autonomous domestic sphere takes on a new inviolacy and the scope for fertility policy is radically reduced. Fortunately, that same economic growth is also likely to have lessened any need for such policy.

For many societies, of course, the policy route vanished before it could be tried, a casualty of labour mobility and the seeming imperative for centralization of government authority. Efforts to extend government programmes into localities are still made in those circumstances, but are successful only to the extent that there is a demand for the programme's services at the price offered. (How much demand there is for fertility regulation services and the shape of the demand curve are both highly contentious issues – a remarkable situation after 25 years or more of programme activity.) For some other societies a comparable route could still be constructed: not mimicking the earlier examples but making innovative use of each society's own institutional inheritance.

Fertility policy that is designed with close reference to the institutional setting in which it is to operate should be able to marshal collateral support and lessen the social costs it imposes, or their equivalent political costs. But if the policy set from which the choice is made is itself truncated, any selection may be far from optimal in that respect. A strong case can be made that such a truncation has occurred. In the earlier discussion of institutional change, path dependency entered in understanding the variation of fertility regimes and the constraints on their directions of change. Path dependency is also relevant in explaining how fertility policy has evolved.

It is a striking, though seldom-noted, fact that the strategy for fertility reduction that Western countries promote for the third world is unlike anything that could be drawn from their own experience. That experience included, for Europe and Japan, an initial rural setting characterized by firm community-based regulation of marriage and of establishment of a household. There and in the United States, fertility transition, when it came, was associated with social and economic changes that strongly pushed up the perceived costs of children to parents: mass education – but typically in good measure locally financed; less child labour and more access by women to the formal labour market; fewer kin over which to share child-raising costs in a more mobile and urbanizing society; new consumption opportunities; and so on. Accompanying these were cultural changes such as the romanticization of childhood and new-found moral obligations of parenthood. (Governments, to the extent they took any interest in fertility, sought to preserve familistic values against the flood, ultimately in vain.) Yet what these countries recommended to others were government extension schemes to provide subsidized contraceptive supplies and services – schemes at odds with the increasingly anti-statist views now found in other areas of development policy.

A partial explanation as to why this happened, in the spirit of the earlier discussion, would be accidents of history. For its 19th and early 20th century advocates, such as Marie Stopes and Margaret Sanger, contraception was a means of emancipating and empowering women. Sanger in particular was also alarmed over the problems of global population growth – evident in her successful efforts to mobilize scholars that led to the formation in the 1920s of the International Union for the Scientific Study of Population and the Population Association of America. To her, the natural answer to rapid population growth was the neo-Malthusian one: a worldwide acceptance of contraception. The policy content of classical demographic transition theory was minimal – reducible, in a later formulation, to the slogan that development is the best contraceptive. But when, in the 1950s and 1960s, a practical intervention to restrain fertility was sought, instead of thinking harder about the micro-institutional basis of past transitions, the family planning model was at hand. Development theory at the time emphasized government direction, so the public sector was granted a virtual monopoly. The medicalization required by some modern methods of birth control gave programme authority to a strong professional group, the doctors. Foreign aid and international agencies became powerful advocates of family-planning programmes, with research funds directed accordingly. (For the United States, the story from transition theory to family-planning programme in the context of foreign policy and the Cold War is told compellingly by Simon Szreter 1993; on inward-looking funding priorities, see Demeny 1988.)

At a finer-grained level, the choice of the technology of birth control has also shown signs of path-dependent development. The case of the persistence of 'traditional' and quite ineffective contraceptive methods in modern-day Japan, backed up by abortion, is attributed by Samuel Coleman (1983) to a powerful medical lobby protecting its turf (medical abortion) against threat (oral contraception, sterilization), to a private family planning association that gains its income from sales of condoms, and to entrenched sex-segregated conjugal roles within the Japanese family. Greenhalgh (1990, p98) remarks of the case:

> *In Japan, and probably elsewhere as well, contraceptive practice is embedded in relationships of power and economic advantage at every level of the family planning system, from national bureaucracy, to local family planning organization, to individual couple.*

In India, one can surmise, the fact that sterilization is the most prevalent contraceptive method is not a consequence of some cultural quirk or of economic exigency, but is a similar case of technological, administrative, and political lock-in.

Institutional dominance creates and then is reinforced by dominance of ideas. That a country seeking to lower its fertility should establish a family-planning programme now has the status of a truism. China, where fertility policy was in many respects an entirely different process, is added to the collection of success stories – typified as a strong and effective family-planning programme, albeit with an unfortunate coercive tinge. Indonesia, also with some amount of muscle applied in the early years, is seen as entirely mainstream. But this lumping together has the unfortunate result of obscuring such distinctions, creating the impression – and often the reality – that a family-planning programme is something that can be taken off the shelf. A more illuminating classification of anti-natalist policies would be in terms of the governance and local organizational structure of society, with the means of contraception and ways of delivery secondary issues.

VARIETIES OF FERTILITY TRANSITION

The perspective on fertility I have set out in this essay can be illustrated by a discussion of recent world experience of fertility trends. I am not concerned with comprehensive description, but with a brief, selective presentation of differences in structure and outcome. My starting point is a fourfold typology of broad patterns of fertility transition, roughly identified with world regions. These might be telegraphically referred to as 'traditional capitalist' (Latin America), 'soft state' (South Asia), 'radical devolution' (China) and 'growth with equity' (East and South-east Asia, apart from China). A fifth pattern, as yet showing only slight signs of fertility decline, could be termed 'lineage dominance' (sub-Saharan Africa). I borrow these titles and parts of the following descriptions from an unpublished paper by Paul Demeny and myself. The demographic data are from United Nations (1991).

'Traditional capitalist'. The modern variant of the kind of fertility transition experienced by Europe and North America is probably best represented by the large countries of Latin America outside the so-called southern cone (where fertility has been moderately low for decades), notably Brazil and Mexico. Here, total fertility has fallen by half, from 6 to 3, since the early 1960s.

These trends seem tied to socio-economic changes of the kind that enter classic statements of demographic transition theory. Mortality had declined substantially by the end of the 1960s in each of these three countries, and the 1970s saw rapid urbanization and falling shares of the labour-force in agriculture. By 1980, two-thirds of the population was urban. Per capita incomes were high by Asian or African standards, but the averages obscured large inequalities – and falls as well as rises over time. For both rich and poor, however, high fertility became increasingly incompatible with urban industrial life.

Urbanization, and the fall in private demand for children that accompanies it – in *favela* as much as in suburb – is clearly a substantial part of this story. It is also an uninteresting part: low urban fertility is neither a surprise nor a puzzle. The (smaller) rural decline may owe something to the conventional demand-effects of income and educational advances, but possibly more to the agrarian institutional structure. In the Brazilian case, consolidation of land into larger holdings led to the mass conversion of tenant farmers into wage labourers – a process of proletarianization – with likely dampening effect on fertility. (The same process led to massive rural-urban migration.) In Mexico, the labour absorption capacities of the rural sector, particularly through the *ejido* system, had plausibly delayed a fertility decline until the system became demographically saturated.

Government concern and involvement with family-size decisions and promotion of contraception were quite strong, although late in coming, in Mexico. In Brazil, they were largely absent: indeed, earlier energetic public efforts to introduce modern contraception could very likely have hastened the pace of decline, lessening the high social costs of the route actually followed.

'Soft state'. A somewhat different model of fertility transition is epitomized by much of the Indian subcontinent. Along a broad northern swathe of this region, encompassing Pakistan, Uttar Pradesh, Madhya Pradesh, Bihar and Bangladesh, fertility decline has been slow and, for the most part, fairly slight. In many other Indian states and in Sri Lanka, fertility has dropped significantly. Overall, India's fertility has fallen from about 6 to about 4 over four decades. United Nations projections, even though they assume rapid fertility decline to replacement level in South Asia, point to a 70 per cent population increase over the next 30 years in that region, in contrast to 28 per cent for East Asia. India is expected to overtake China in population by about 2030.

In the terms of the earlier discussion of institutional endowments, South Asian social structure appears to have few homeostatic qualities – showing instead a picture of caste- and class-riven villages and the lower reaches of government captured by local élites. (Establishment of more accountable local administration – accountable both to higher administrative tiers and to the citizenry – appears to have been a major factor in the successes in social development seen in Kerala and some other Indian states.) Families, however, may well have experienced a Caldwell-style shift toward nuclearized autonomy and with it a more exposed fertility calculus. At the same time, an array of cultural and economic changes have probably reduced parental expectations of old-age support from their children.

The role of the state in the development process, influenced by the administrative inheritance from colonial times and the emphasis on central planning that was then popular in development theorizing, has been ambiguous: strong, often meddling, but in important respects undemanding. The epithet of 'soft state', bestowed on countries of South Asia by Gunnar Myrdal, referred specifically to government inability or reluctance to impose obligations on people – not a bad thing in many respects, unless (as often was the case) this simply left the way clear for extra-governmental exploitation or *sub rosa* bureaucratic rent-seeking.

Family planning conforms to this picture. A family-planning programme was begun in India in the early 1950s and under Health Ministry auspices took on the heavily bureaucratized features of other Indian government activities. Programme targets and performance statistics had to be conveyed through a multi-layered hierarchy able to diffuse accountability and inclined to exaggerate results. Large interstate differences in programme effectiveness emerged, reflecting distinctive administrative cultures and local socio-economic conditions. While monetary incentives to clients have played a longstanding role in the programme, aside from a short period during the emergency of 1975–76 force and administrative pressure have been generally absent. Pakistan and Bangladesh have similarly well-established family-planning programmes with either negligible (Pakistan) or modest (Bangladesh) success records.

There is much in the South Asian fertility record that resembles the 'traditional capitalist' model. Moreover, a principal difference from that model as it applies to the broader economy – namely, an interfering government and large public sector – is now being narrowed as deregulatory policies take effect. Although governments of the region, especially India's, have East Asian patterns in mind as they chart new development paths, the outcome at least for fertility may be more like Brazil, with the impetus for fertility decline being the changing private demand for children in an institutionally 'thin' environment.

'Radical devolution'. The most distinctive model of fertility transition in world experience is the case of China, where the total fertility rate plummeted from 6 children per woman in the 1960s to below 2.5 by the end of the 1970s. Although having no resemblance to the capitalist path, this transformation was similarly achieved at high social cost.

The conditions that made possible this dramatic change were set up in the massive agrarian reforms of the 1950s – not the short-lived, abortive efforts late in the decade to establish communes as the basic unit of rural society, but the earlier land reform and lower-level collectivization that built on and mobilized pre-existing neighbourhood and village solidarities, while destroying the landlord and lineage interests that had overlain them. Local territorial solidarity was reinforced by collective agricultural taxes and the obligations imposed on villages to fund many of their own social services. The boundaries of local units were further accentuated by government restraints on migration and economic diversification. Under these circumstances, it would be reasonable to expect that high fertility incentives within these units would rapidly erode.

Complementing this radical devolution of economic and social accounting was the strong political and administrative structure established by Party and government that could convey programme directives from the centre and apply rewards and sanctions for performance. This structure proved highly effective for delivery of health services, with life expectancy reaching 65 years by the late 1970s, well above the levels that experience elsewhere would predict to correspond with China's economic status at that time. When state policy shifted to anti-natalism in the 1970s, it was equally effective with family planning services. The decline was speeded by political pressures, backed by sanctions, applied by local cadres, transmitting provincial and national dictates. But it is unlikely that the government could have prevailed to the degree it did had there been intense public resistance to smaller families.

The system that yielded considerable success in meeting government health and family-planning objectives was much less effective in generating dynamic economic performance. The Dengist reforms after 1979, effectively restoring private incentives (and obligations: the 1980 marriage law made support of elderly parents primarily a family responsibility), released the family-level economic dynamism that had been blocked by the former collective arrangements and by political and bureaucratic dead weight. Maintenance of stringent control over fertility, even extending to the attempted limitation to one child per family, has proved increasingly difficult as the economy burgeons under 'market Leninism' and as a large floating population grows up beyond official surveillance. However, China's status as a low-fertility country, with family size choices for the great majority of couples securely contained in the range of one to three children, is not likely to be affected.

'Growth with equity'. The outstanding success of the East Asian hyper-growth economies, led by Japan, that has made that region such a large contributor to world manufacturing trade, and Taiwan and South Korea exemplars for development policy, has its counterpart on the demographic side. Fertility in Taiwan started to fall in the early 1950s, South Korea a decade later; both are now at levels below replacement. The so-called 'second-tier' countries of South-east Asia, especially Thailand, Malaysia and Indonesia, have also shown strong economic progress and substantial fertility declines. (The Philippines, its political development in some respects closer to Latin American experience, lags on both scores.)

The standard description of the Korea–Taiwan model is 'growth with equity', contrasting with the former orthodoxy of development theory that saw redistribution as in conflict with growth. Fairly radical land reforms in the 1950s laid the basis for small-scale peasant production, supported by effective government extension and financial services. Education and health similarly received high government priority, and, gradually from the 1960s, so did family planning. Impressively, the shift to an industrial economy was accomplished without the price distortions, large urban-rural wage differentials, and growing income inequality that typically attend these processes.

In contrast to the 'traditional capitalist' model, government roles in this case extended well beyond the vigorous promotion of state and private economic enterprise to cover also the enlightened provision or support of a variety of social services. And, in contrast to the 'soft state' case, in place of a fairly rough-and-ready, class-riven rule of law, there was stringent, even meticulous, administrative and political control. Family-planning programmes, as these developed, however, were and remained defined for the most part as a social service rather than an aspect of government development administration. This was in sharp distinction to China: these governments were authoritarian where they chose to be, but conceded a wider domain of individual privacy surrounding family life.

Fertility began to drop in Taiwan and South Korea before family-planning programmes took hold. Most observers would agree that the programmes facilitated and, to some degree and among some groups, speeded the change. But the underlying course of demographic transition probably had more to do with the style and pace of economic and cultural change than with the details of programme design and operation.

Family-planning programmes are plausibly accorded a greater role in the fertility declines of the second-tier countries, notably Thailand and Indonesia. These two countries, together perhaps with Mexico and Colombia, are exhibited as the chief examples of family-planning programme success. As with Mexico and Colombia, however, it is the timing rather than the fact of fertility decline that has probably been influenced. In Thailand, a growing demand for contraceptive services, stimulated by a fast-growing consumer economy, would likely have elicited development of a private-sector supply system: there were no apparent cultural obstacles in the way of demand increase. In Indonesia, the programme's initial successes owed much to the coincident creation of a much strengthened local government administrative system through which policy objectives could be transmitted and local officials held accountable for results. Service demand subsequently caught up with this top-down program as families confronted the realities of how best to assure their children access to secondary education and modern sector employment. Moves toward a user-pays programme are now in train.

'*Lineage dominance*'. For the most part, the course of fertility in other regions of the world resembles or seems likely to resemble one or other of these four models. The principal possible exception is sub-Saharan Africa. Over coming years this region may fall into line – say, into a kind of South Asian variant: that is the more or less explicit expectation of the major international agencies. The UN estimates sub-Saharan Africa's total fertility to have been virtually unchanged, at a level of around 6.6, from 1950 to 1990 (more recent survey data from a few countries, notably Kenya, show fertility starting to fall in the 1980s); the medium-variant projections then indicate fertility dropping to 5 by 2010 and 3 by 2025. But, as the earlier discussion of this situation implied, it is at least as plausible that Africa will trace a demographic path of its own, one reflecting its distinctive family systems and its kin-based rather than territorial pattern of social organization and governance.

Rapid population growth has meant that increasing parts of Africa are shifting from conditions of labour scarcity to land scarcity. The resulting economic pressures toward privatization of land and lessened demand for rural labour should be expected to have anti-natalist effects. The residue of lineage influence – over land and over family behaviour, particularly marriage – remains powerful in parts of the region, tending to counter those effects, but the trend towards a falling demand for children will no doubt soon dominate if it has not already begun to do so. A more uncertain factor with a large potential to influence the region's fertility future is the AIDS epidemic, both in its immediate demographic impact and through its deeper consequences on economy and culture.

Condensed description and speculation are no substitute for detailed analysis, although the summaries I have just given certainly draw on much fuller accounts. But they can point to features of social setting and policy that are salient for demographic outcomes. In this case, one might observe the manner in which successful policies mobilize and work through the existing local social organization; the consequent need for attention to timing and sequencing of interventions, as the development process alters those local structures; the limited scope for but potentially crucial effect of 'getting institutions right' – the often neglected analogue of the World Bank dictum of 'getting prices right'; and the variant social costs imposed by different policies, or, amounting to the same thing, the variant political capital expended.

REFERENCES

Anderson, Benedict (1991) *Imagined Communities: Reflections on the Origin and Spread of Nationalism* (rev ed), London: Verso.

Caldwell, John C (1976) 'Toward a restatement of demographic transition theory', *Population and Development Review* 2, pp321–366.

Caldwell, John C (1980) 'Mass education as a determinant of the timing of fertility decline', *Population and Development Review* 6, pp225–255.

Cheung, S N S (1982) *Will China Go 'Capitalist'? An Economic Analysis of Property Rights and Institutional Change*, London: Institute of Economic Affairs.

Coleman, Samuel (1983) *Family Planning in Japanese Society: Traditional Birth Control in a Modern Urban Culture*, Princeton: Princeton University Press.

Demeny, Paul (1988) 'Social science and population policy', *Population and Development*

Review 14, pp451–479.

Frank, Odile and Geoffrey McNicoll (1987) 'An interpretation of fertility and population policy in Kenya', *Population and Development Review* 13, pp209–243.

Greenhalgh, Susan (1990) 'Toward a political economy of fertility: anthropological contributions', *Population and Development Review* 16, pp85–106.

Hodgson, Geoffrey (1993) *Economics and Evolution: Bringing Life Back into Economics*, Oxford: Polity Press.

Migdal, Joel S (1988) *Strong Societies and Weak States: State-Society Relations and State Capabilities in the Third World*, Princeton: Princeton University Press.

Notestein, Frank (1983 [1964]) 'Population growth and economic development', *Population and Development Review* 9, pp345–360.

Seccombe, Wally (1992) *A Millennium of Family Change: Feudalism to Capitalism in Northwestern Europe*, London: Verso.

Simmons, Ruth, Laila Baqee, Michael A Koenig, and James F Phillips (1988) 'Beyond supply: the importance of female family planning workers in rural Bangladesh', *Studies in Family Planning* 19, pp29–38.

Szreter, Simon (1993) 'The idea of demographic transition and the study of fertility change: a critical intellectual history', *Population and Development Review* 19, pp659–701.

United Nations (1991) *World Population Prospects 1990*, New York.

Chapter 16

Sociology of Fertility Reduction in High-fertility Countries

Norman B Ryder

The purpose of this essay is to propose some pathways to fertility reduction in developing countries, from the perspective of a sociologist. The account purposely excludes discussion of possible contributions to the same goal through the provision of family planning services, or through manipulation of the economic context of decision-making, by way of governmental taxation or subsidization of particular reproductive categories. Analyses of such activities are well represented in the literature; they are conceptually separable from the kinds of consideration to be introduced here; and, in my judgement, they play an essentially auxiliary and supportive role in the solution to the fundamental problem. (The absence of references in what follows should be construed not as a sign of scholarly ingratitude, but rather as a way of emphasizing the informal tentativeness of the views expressed.)

The euphemism that a country should be termed 'developing' signifies simultaneously that it is now poor and that it need not remain. Behind the title of this paper lies an implicit argument that the achievement of a higher level of living will be more likely if there is a lower interim rate of population growth, and that fertility reduction is a better way to attain that lower rate than either emigration or increased mortality. It is the process of modernization, in the various senses of that term, which produces a higher level of living, and lower fertility is a necessary but not sufficient part of that process. Among the many components of the modernization strategy, proposals for fertility reduction must compete with others for the limited resources of money, talent and organization. It is the consensus of most demographers that the preferable policy is one that leads to earlier rather than later fertility reduction, a point worth making because it is generally agreed also that the achievement of a higher level of living is likely to be accompanied or followed by a lower level of fertility.

Intrinsic to the sociological viewpoint is the prejudice that the important variables affecting behaviour are systemic in character. Changes in such variables are accordingly expected to have wide ramifications throughout many aspects of social life. The comprehensive institutional reformation which I believe to be the most effective pathway to fertility reduction can also be argued to be essential to the modernization of the economy and the society in other respects. Indeed, it may be that the suggestions advanced below with a view to lowering the birth rate have less chance of acceptance for that reason than because they are perceived as contributions to non-demographic goals. In short, a sociological approach impels one to consider demographic change as embedded within the general rubric of societal transformation.

Every society has standardized solutions to its important and pervasive problems, in the form of injunctions and prohibitions, constraints and pressures, concerning individual behavioural decisions. Norms and sanctions channel individual behaviour into directions which, however the individual might regard them in the abstract, are considered desirable from the standpoint of the groups of which the individual is a member and a representative. The process of socialization is designed to eliminate the apparent conflict between individual and group interests by internalizing norms; the pervasive existence and employment of sanctions is testament to the insufficiency of the socialization process.

One such important societal problem is reproduction. High fertility is not the consequence of inherited biological propensities, nor of ignorance of where babies come from and how they might be prevented, but rather of systematic institutionalized prescriptions and proscriptions, instilled by incessant socialization and more or less maintained by vigilant social control. The peculiar responsibility of the sociologist as a behavioural scientist is to assess the ways in which behaviour is influenced by the institutional structure – that is, by the complexes of norms that provide blueprints for role relationships in activities that have consequences beyond the individual. Traditional and modern societies are not infrequently contrasted by the implication that, in the latter, an individual exercises freedom of choice, whereas, in the former, those choices are culturally prescribed – they have already been made by the groups of which the individual is a member. Although members of modern societies may be more inclined than those of traditional societies to proffer reasons for their decisions, those reasons are learned from, and are subject to the test of acceptability to, the larger society. In every culture, individuals exercise volition within a context of constraints; in every culture, decisions are made with reference to the legitimate interests of those who are affected by the decisions and are in a position to influence them.

In my view, the level of fertility in a traditional society and in a modern society alike is an intelligible outcome of the individual decision process. That level tends to be high in the former and low in the latter, not only because of differing material conditions, but also because of the differing normative context. The observed level of fertility in a society is ordinarily a reasonable approximation of the level of fertility intended by the responsible parties, given the 'rules of the game' within the particular economic context. The approach to fertility reduction through the provision of family planning services is oriented to narrowing whatever gap there may be between observed and intended fertility, because of lags in response to change; the approach to fertility reduction through the manipulation of economic variables is oriented to modifying the price and income constraints to be considered in the decision situation; and the sociological approach is focused on modifying the normative context itself.

THE INTERGENERATIONAL CONTRACT

Explicit and implicit understandings exist concerning the future rights and responsibilities of all parties having an interest in a prospective child. In every society, the birth of a child signals the activation of specific and diffuse obligations on the part of various persons with respect to the resources that child will consume, and of rights with respect to the resources that child will produce. Such obligations and rights are patterned to the life-cycle of the child and of the relevant others, with disjunctures occurring typically at the time the child becomes a parent and then the parent becomes a dependent. I call this contract intergenerational because I think the relationship between parent and child (using the latter term in its generational rather than age connotation) is the most important aspect of the family as an institutionalized structure; it obviously extends also to relationships with other members of the families of orientation of parent and child, and of their families of procreation, and, in most developing societies, further into the kinship network. In other, particularly modern, cultures, the non-kin collectivity may be the party with the most significant rights and responsibilities concerning the newborn.

High-fertility norms are sensible responses, on the part of the groups which instil and enforce them, to conditions of high mortality in a peasant agricultural economy. Not only is high fertility requisite to societal survival in a demographic sense, but also it provides the principal source of new energy for the practical solution of the problems of the kinship group. Children are that group's almost sole form of investment to provide a labour supply, defence against external enemies, and the foundation for a primitive social security system. The strength of the kinship group in these respects varies directly with its size; maintenance or enlargement of that size other than by way of fertility is uncommon, probably because of the many problems that incorporation of adults into the group would involve. Marriage is arranged when the individuals to be married are young. The couple, once married, are incorporated inside a larger kinship group (in the sense of having rights and responsibilities, if not in the physical sense) and are enjoined to produce children for the greater good of that group. Children are raised frugally and put to work early. Should numbers of children become too large for the particular couple's resources, the kinship unit provides flexible adoption possibilities or supplementary help. The individual is submerged within the kinship system; the important role relationships are family relationships.

The two fundamental dimensions of the family as a structure are generation and gender. The basic argument of the present section is that economic development is assisted by, and encourages, a gradual shift of power outward from the family in two directions, first toward the larger society and second toward the individual. That shift of power implies a reformation of the normative bargain between the generations (what parents expect from children and what children expect from parents), and such a reformation promotes reduction in fertility, other things being equal.

It is convenient to cast the discussion in the framework of investment, including particularly within that category the investment in human resources. To say it simply, the modern society is more productive than the traditional society. Productivity is a function of the capital that can be created by deferral of consumption. The life-cycle of the human species implies a characteristic timetable of borrowing and lending, as the individual proceeds through successive phases of net consumption, net production, and net consumption. From one perspective, the family can be considered as an institutionalized solution to this intrinsic species problem: it is a system for transferring resources through time – that is, across generations. The terms of this transfer, in both directions, between older and younger generations, are what we here call intergenerational norms.

In the traditional society, fertility is high in part because families are faced with short-run considerations that tend to overwhelm or prohibit attention to long-run considerations. Human resources must be expended in the present rather than saved for the future, lest there be no future. The predominant direction of intergenerational rights and responsibilities in the traditional society is what the child owes the parent, whereas in the modern society, the predominant direction is what the parent owes the child. It is tempting to hypothesize that the turning point of fertility reduction is closely associated with reversal of the direction of temporal obligation. In a sense, society intervenes between parent and child in the interests of the child (and of the society at large), and thereby makes parenthood a much less rewarding venture. There is a large and difficult ethical question in the allocation of society's resources through time, which could be thought of as a maximization problem across cohorts – that is, to what extent should resources be expended to the advantage of present cohorts and to what extent should they be invested to the advantage of future cohorts? (A similar question arises in connection with the depletion of non-renewable resources.) Thus there is an issue of intergenerational equity: what do parents deserve from children, and vice versa? Such an ethical question can scarcely be resolved by resort to notions of democratic representation in a framework of freedom of individual choice, since the children of today and tomorrow have no votes. (They certainly have no voice in the reproductive decision that gives rise to them.)

The fundamental changes in the organization of human society that characterize the shift from traditional to modern consist of a differentiation of kinship structures from other social structures and the functional specialization of family roles. Industrialization and urbanization, with their accompaniments of mobility and specialization, foster secularism over religion (the present and future over the past), the growth of individualism, and the shift of primary individual allegiance from the family and the kinship group towards the larger society. Modernization breaks down ascriptive criteria, emphasizing what one can do rather than who one is (who one's parents are), by minimizing familism and localism. The shift of the focus of work from the rural family to the urban society decreases what children can contribute to family resources and increases what they need to claim from family resources. Their opportunity cost from the standpoint of the non-familial roles of parents also increases, as those roles take on enhanced importance. In an economic sense, a child becomes an inferior good.

This is a propitious context for fertility decline: erosion of the primacy of kinship to the point where parental aspirations can be fulfilled only in ways for which high fertility is either irrelevant or burdensome. Meanwhile, fertility decline increases productivity by reducing the price of capital: the supply of capital increases because of the decrease in child dependency; the demand for capital decreases because of the subsequent decrease in the rate of growth of the labour force. Productivity and reproductivity are mutually antagonistic.

THE INTERESTS OF THE WIFE

Most discussion of fertility reduction concerns ways of inducing couples to set as a reproductive target a lower final parity than comparable couples in the past have had. The burden of the previous argument is that there are many interested and powerful parties in the decision concerning the number of children to be borne. Despite the almost exclusive focus in fertility surveys on desired family size as expressed by the prospective mother, it is apparent in the traditional society that unsurveyed others, such as the husband, his family of orientation (in the typical patrilineal case), the larger kinship group, and the community, care a lot about the outcome because it affects their welfare; accordingly, their preferences carry considerable normative freight and they have diffuse and extensive possibilities of implementing sanctions, should the socialization process be inadequate. The stage for fertility reduction is set by a quite different specification of the appropriate relative influences of these diverse interests, and of the principles to be followed in judging the rightness of a positive or negative decision. The change of specification discussed above was that the question of how a birth will affect the welfare of the parents and the kinship group becomes transmuted into the question of how it will affect the child.

The other important change of specification is the much larger attention given to the interests of the prospective mother. An essential component of the kinship system as an institutionalized arrangement for securing societal survival is that women be coerced into abundant reproduction. Traditional societies promote high fertility by maintaining sharp sex-role segregation. Often the only way for a woman to earn esteem is to contribute to the survival of the group by bearing healthy sons. The burden of bearing and of rearing children has always fallen more directly and heavily on women than on men. Adequate reproduction can be achieved only through considerable social pressure because of the ambivalence many women have toward childbirth and motherhood. Conversely, the liberation of the woman from her typical status as a family chattel is correlated as well as any other single variable with the level of modernization. Fertility reduction would appear to depend substantially on the right of a woman to determine the extent of her commitment to the maternal role, and on the availability of opportunities for her to fill non-familial roles and earn prestige from them. Equality of gender is the final and most difficult step in modernization, including reproductive modernization, and it is a long way from accomplishment in any society, perhaps because its achievement would prejudice the survival of the family institution itself. There seems to be little doubt that a shift towards equality of males and females – that is, the abandonment of ascription of roles on the basis of gender, would exert downward pressure on fertility. The interesting question is whether the reproductivity of the new order would be adequate to replace the population.

INTERNAL POPULATION PRESSURE

High fertility is an institutionalized response to a condition of high mortality. When that condition no longer prevails, normative arrangements that are part of that institutionalized response, such as extended family households, become inappropriate and burdensome; over-population at the household and family level seems likely to promote the abandonment of such arrangements. Residential arrangements that are propounded as cultural ideals can be maintained so long as in actuality conditions prevent their full realization. Aggressive effort to reduce the mortality of children and adults, a desirable goal on many grounds, has the further virtue of bringing immediate pressure on those physical and social designs that were developed for a context in which high mortality made such designs feasible.

Maintenance of internal population pressure would also be promoted by institutionalized constraints on easy adoption, the traditional safety valve for excess offspring, perhaps by formalizing the responsibilities of the new parents to their adopted children. Likewise, restrictions on migration would localize the consequences of high fertility for population growth at the village level, rather than permit the growth to be siphoned off in the direction of urban slums. The institutionalized self-sufficiency of the rural commune within modern Chinese society may be an important element in China's apparently successful strategy for controlling population growth

As a further example of one direction in which to maintain internal population pressure, it may be noted that the aged will tend to expect support from their children to the extent that they, in their younger days, were obliged to support their parents. A crucial part of the impetus to fertility reduction may be played by that particular generation of parents who find themselves in a position of role conflict, in the sense that they feel obligated, because of their traditional upbringing, to provide support for their aged parents, and feel obligated, because of the modern context, to provide support for their children. To the extent that this reasoning is plausible, it would be a tactical blunder to denigrate the responsibilities of parents to their parents, or to provide social security for the aged from general societal funds.

The argument for maintaining internal population pressure as a spur to fertility reduction is incomplete. It may be that family limitation is practised less to secure a future gain than to prevent the loss of what has been achieved. Perhaps sensitivity to the disadvantages of a larger family size is most acute in those who have experienced the social and economic benefits of rising real income, and perceive that further child-bearing would jeopardize those benefits. It would then follow that a sufficient condition for the efficacy of internal population pressure as a spur to fertility reduction would be the prior achievement of some rise in economic well-being. In the history of the demographic transition in Western societies, economic growth preceded fertility decline. The long delay in that fertility decline (and the consequent multifold enlargement of population size) may be explained by the slight pressure on resources, continually eased by migration, without serious jeopardy to a somewhat higher and rising income. In the European experience, mortality decline and urban economic development applied pressure to several points of strain within the family. Mortality decline created a labour-force too large for the family farm. The longer life of the parents postponed the time when the property would pass into the control of their children. More siblings survived, reducing the share of each in their delayed patrimony. Urban economic development offered alternatives to the young and created both spatial and social distance between the family of orientation and the family of procreation.

THE ROLE OF CHANCE

A society with high and variable mortality will press for children early in marriage, before one or both parents die, and for extra children to safeguard against the loss of the necessary minimum number of survivors. Should the result be excessive in relation to the resource base, solutions are available through adopting out. There is substantial uncertainty and anxiety not only about the survival of children, but also about the ability to bear a child or another child. The unpredictability of the future family size is matched by the unpredictability of the relevant other socio-economic circumstances. In such a situation, rationality is a challenging prescription for the individual; perhaps the larger the role of chance, the greater is the tendency to rely on customary and traditional guidance, as distillations of wisdom from past experience. The point is that fatalism is not merely another face of ignorance or superstition, but an intelligible response to high uncertainty. Future aspirations in general hinge on the perception of the reward to be expected for effort. Such effort is unlikely to be forthcoming if the return is fraught with substantial doubt. Moreover, at the level of the larger kinship group and the community, the more likely the occurrence of catastrophe (to the individual), the more advantageous is the attachment of the individual to a population of larger size, on elementary insurance principles.

The inference from this line of thinking is that substantial increase in the exercise of reproductive rationality may await a substantial decrease in perceived uncertainty. Perhaps fertility decline requires a reduction not only in the mean level of mortality, but also in its variance. Certainly an extension of the time horizon for planning in general, as a foundation for investment, is favoured by the lengthening of life or, more precisely, by the perception that life is more certain. One clear policy recommendation, accordingly, is a strong public effort to reduce mortality and, perverse though it may sound, to search for ways to remove limitations on fecundity.

THE INITIATION OF REPRODUCTION

Reproductive decisions have a temporal as well as a quantitative component. Although fertility analyses focus almost exclusively on completed parity, births by and large occur one at a time, at no less than annual intervals, and thus sequentially and incrementally. The actual reproductive decision faced by the couple is whether or not to attempt to prevent each potential ovulation in turn from resulting in conception, except, of course, in the limiting case in which the mode of fertility regulation is either abortion or sterilization. That decision includes consideration of the time elapsed since last pregnancy, the associated age difference between the last child and the one contemplated, the proportion of the parents' lives monopolized by the parental role, and also the differences in age between parents and existing children.

The temporal distribution of fertility is relevant to the discussion of the reduction of the birth rate because the tempo of cohort fertility, in both a static and a dynamic sense, has quantitative implications when translated into period fertility. On the one hand, the later a birth occurs in a woman's life, the smaller is its discounted contribution to annual growth. (The intrinsic rate of natural increase varies inversely with the length of a generation.) On the other hand, a shift from an earlier to a later pattern of reproduction distorts period fertility downward, whereas a shift from a later to an earlier pattern of reproduction distorts period fertility upwards. (The proportional change in the mean age at child-bearing is converted into a like, but inverse, proportional change in ultimate population size.) Accordingly, quantitative objectives such as the reduction of (period) fertility can be achieved in part by modifications of the time pattern of fertility.

It would seem plausible, moreover, that an admonition to delay a birth would be more palatable to the recipient than an injunction to terminate fertility. The adverse consequences of short interbirth intervals are widely recognized, and institutionalized mechanisms for their avoidance, such as extended lactation and ritualized abstinence, are commonly found. The targets for a campaign to delay fertility are younger than those for a campaign to terminate fertility, and perhaps are therefore more receptive to innovation. Indeed, termination at a lower parity, unaccompanied by a delay in the initiation of reproduction, is less effective demographically than it would appear on the surface because termination at a lower parity implies termination at an earlier age, reducing the length of generation and distorting period fertility upward.

Beyond such purely demographic arguments, the force of the case for delay is sociologically strong, particularly with respect to the initial steps in the reproductive sequence. The time of entry into marriage is a crucial point of structural strain in the traditional domination of one's family of procreation by one's family of orientation. Such domination is incompatible with sustained economic advance, whether it be that of the individual or of the social system as a whole. Early arranged marriage is a symptom of and mode of preservation of familism. The early imposition of family obligations traps the man, and especially the woman, within the traditional social structure. Temporary freedom from procreation is necessary to provide the young woman with the opportunity to enlarge her personal horizon and acquire sources of satisfaction alternative to motherhood. The future of developing societies may be much more bound up with the future of their young women than with that of their young men.

Later marriage gives the young person a few adult years in which to become committed to personal or societal rather than familial goals. The later the marriage, the more likely will the couple form their own household, rather than sharing that of the family of orientation. The obligation to support the children is more likely under such circumstances to fall directly on the shoulders of the couple rather than be shared and absorbed by surrounding kinfolk. Basic to the growth of individualism and to the growth of the economy is the principle that one must not marry until a living is assured. Delayed gratification and prudential restraint are essential to the achievement of a higher scale of living; they permit personal capital formation. In particular, the assumption of family responsibilities almost prohibits the continuation of formal education and technical training for personal advance and, collectively, for social modernization. Education is society's agent in the release of the individual from kinship bondage. Education raises social aspirations, increases the anxiety for new goods, and makes children more costly in their own right and in relation to alternative opportunities which must be forgone by the parents. Education can provide a societal alternative to the family as a source of normative orientations, and an enhancement of vision beyond the limited boundaries of the local community – which has always been the ally of the kinship system in the maintenance of ascriptive criteria for placement.

Marriage delay permits the postponement of cohort commitment to the existing system and thereby encourages or at least facilitates social change. Every society is a functioning collectivity with inputs of birth and outputs of death, which persists independently of the lives of its ever-changing membership. To reproduce itself, society must implant its precepts in the minds of each new cohort. Yet this continual threat to stability is also a continual opportunity for society to exploit the new cohorts as the vehicles for initiating change.

The direct demographic consequence of marriage delay is the inferential delay in the initiation of parenthood. Contraception has provided a way to experience copulation without conception. The over-arching purpose of the family planning movement, and of fertility control schemes generally, is to reduce the cost of an act of intercourse. Prudery has inhibited the discussion of copulation in relation to contraception and reproduction, aside from euphemistic allusions to the aesthetic properties of particular types of contraceptive. Furthermore, of all the various ways in which the sexual urge can be gratified, only heterosexual copulation leads to conception. Taboos on alternatives probably are rooted in early cultural concern with maximizing procreation. But the larger issue is that the efforts by society to control non-marital sex are part of the same system of domination of the individual by the family which is at the root of institutionalized high fertility. In that cause, which we have characterized as a bulwark of the traditional society, the young have been permitted two alternatives: either chastity or that regrettable form of venereal disease known as unwanted fertility. The technology that can divorce sex from procreation is an essential ally of modernization and should not be withheld from the unmarried adult.

It is the convention of most fertility surveys to ask individuals not whether they want to be parents, but rather how many children they want to have. In other words, childlessness by choice is literally considered to be out of the question. The logical extension of the argument on the virtues of delaying parenthood is that some proportion of the population considers having permanently infertile unions or separate individual lives. The modern world offers ample opportunity for lives that can fulfil individual aspirations completely without parenthood. This is not a recommendation that individuals pursue selfish ends, so much as a proposal that they be encouraged to dedicate themselves to the building of the new society. One should not underestimate the capacities in the young for such social commitment.

DEMOGRAPHY AS POLITICAL ARITHMETIC

The preceding argument implies that modernization and fertility reduction as an indispensable component of it, require comprehensive institutional reconstitution. To end kinship dominance and create the kind of citizenry needed in a productive society, with rational development and allocation of human resources and systematically higher priority to the future than to the present, society must intervene between the individual and his or her family of orientation. Yet replacement of the kinship system by the national government as the dominant political force is insufficient. The laws and policies of most nations today, respecting marriage and the family, are explicitly or implicitly pro-natalist, and support the family in its position vis-à-vis the individual. An obvious example is the host of legal restrictions on the production, advertisement, display, distribution, and sale of most modes of fertility regulation.

One source of such fertility-supporting policies is the ambivalence most government leaders have about population size and the rate of population growth. Those rulers of nations who are obsessed with the strength of the collectivity, even to the disregard of individual welfare, are generally implacably opposed to fertility reduction. There is a basic conflict between the wealth of a nation, viewed in the aggregate sense from above, and the well-being of the average subject. Individuals profit little by shifting their allegiance from father to fatherland.

Although the case for numbers as a source of political security is probably now more emotional than rational, there prevails a primitive pride in size and in growth, as an extension of the intuition that more is better – particularly more in relation to nearby nations. The organization of the world into nation-states forces the discussion of population problems into the morass of political arithmetic. The counterpart of international conflict prevails within nations as well, wherever there is more than one subpopulation – that is, more than one group having boundary-maintaining mechanisms – and recruitment of membership is essentially through fertility. Fertility reduction is a contentious policy to advocate to the extent that it implies change in the relative sizes of nations and of subcultures within nations.

CONSERVATISM AND FERTILITY

In my judgement, both modernization and fertility reduction are gravely impeded by conservatism. 'Conservatism' is used in two senses. The first is exemplified by those who have vested interests in the status quo, who either support population growth because they profit from it, or support the social structure that ensures it. Their ranks would include the militarists, the owners of property, the employers of labour and the priesthood. The second sense is implicit in the theory of the mainsprings of human behaviour that is disposed to focus on the individual as the primary source of his or her own difficulties, to support research into the characteristics of individuals rather than groups or communities or organizations, and to prescribe cures which may modify individual behaviour but leave the encompassing social structure unchanged. The thesis that prolificacy stems from lust and ignorance is akin to the other essentially conservative notions that unemployment is a reflection of laziness, and that the cure for crime is punishment.

The ideology of the family-planning movement is essentially conservative. Four professional roles are prominent in its ranks, and all four are oriented to the solution of social problems by the manipulation of individual behaviour within an intact unquestioned social structure. First are the doctors who dispense contraceptive cures to patients in clinics. Second are the social workers, the latter-day charity profession, applying Band-Aids to the sores on the body politic. Third are the men with a Madison Avenue mentality, whose surveys reveal a market for the contraceptive product and who view the solution to the problem as essentially a matter of packaging and advertising. Finally there are the philanthropists who support these endeavors, the successful embodiments of a conservative system of free enterprise.

If the above diagnosis of the sources of high fertility is close to correct, then the realistic solution would appear to amount to a social revolution. The conservative ideology of the family-planning movement is a philosophical impediment to that solution because its purpose is essentially counter-revolutionary. The cost of a better way of life in the future, for the developing countries, is a profound change in social values and social institutions. To insist that policy proposals should meet the tests of political feasibility and ethical acceptability is to remove from the universe of discourse what I perceive to be the essential elements of the solution, as well as to ignore the ethical claims of the cohorts yet unborn. Should we misjudge the magnitude of this challenge, mankind may lose its last best chance to escape from the past.

185

Chapter 17

Population and the Status of Women in Rural Development

Ester Boserup

Major increases in population modify the man–land ratio, facilitate specialization and communication, and provide other economies of scale. Whether the impact of these changes on rural development is positive or negative, and the likely feedback effects on demographic trends, depend in the first instance on macro-economic factors, notably including government policy. But, micro-economic factors enter the picture as well. This essay deals with one of those micro-economic factors, namely the subordinate status of rural women as compared with men of the same age and social group. I consider how women's status varies under three types of family organization and land tenure arrangements prevalent in rural areas, and argue that the response of rural populations to economic and demographic change is more or less flexible, depending on the type of family organization.

The status of women varies between rural communities and sometimes between families in the same village. The roles of women are also strikingly different. Christine Oppong distinguishes between seven roles that compete for women's time and energy, but here I shall focus only on those that are most relevant to my subject.

Of course, it is impossible to discuss the multitude of local patterns in a brief review. Nevertheless, family organization and the status of women are related to the agricultural system, which in turn is related to population density and technological levels. Therefore, it is possible to simplify the analysis by distinguishing a few major patterns of interrelationships between population, status of women, and rural development that together describe most rural communities in the Third World.

THE CONFLICT BETWEEN MOTHERHOOD AND WORK

Rural communities at low levels of economic development usually have high levels of fertility. Young children can substitute for adults in many forms of agricultural and domestic work, including child care, animal husbandry, and gathering and transport of food and fuel wood. Therefore, children are likely to contribute more to family production of goods and services than they consume, at least if they are not sent to school.

Moreover, child mortality continues to be high in rural areas of most Third World countries, in spite of the spread of modern medicine and improvements in sanitation. In the recent past, mortality was often so high that many families had few surviving children in spite of high fertility, and many women died before the end of their child-bearing years. In regions with low levels of economic development, a sufficient reproduction of the population was a condition of survival, both of the parents and of the community. The young generation had to support their elders, and in communities where the maintenance of law and order was left largely to members of the family or the village, adult sons had to defend family and village against enemies.

Until recent times, the need for defence against enemies motivated not only parents, but also governments, local and national, to be pro-natalist. The social pressure on parents to maximize family size was bolstered by granting a high status to fathers and mothers of large families, and a low status to the unmarried and infertile, especially women. Under these circumstances, family organization was based on the institution of early and universal marriage for girls, with men tending to divorce or abandon infertile and subfecund women.

Families were organized as autocratic age-sex hierarchies. Younger family members owed obedience to older persons, and the oldest man in the family was the decision-maker. In daily life, men and women could dispose of the labour power of younger members of their own sex according to the customary distribution of labour, but when a change in the distribution of labour became necessary – because of changes in the method of production or in the availability of resources, for example – the family head decided on the new distribution of labour. By assigning as much work as possible to women and younger family members, he could increase family income while reducing his own work burden.

Either custom or the marriage contract stipulated that the wife must do the work that was needed to serve male family members and children. This obligation included not only child care and domestic duties, but also carrying water, gathering fuel, and often caring for domestic animals and processing crops. In most rural communities, women were obliged to work in the fields, and in some communities women and children did nearly all the agricultural work.

Frequent pregnancy and prolonged breastfeeding tax a woman's health. If a woman married early and spent the entire period between puberty and menopause being either pregnant or breastfeeding, and if she also worked hard at multiple tasks in the household and in agriculture, the strain on her health was heavy. Maternal and infant morbidity and mortality, and the frequency of involuntary abortion, were attributable to or aggravated by such patterns of child-bearing and work. Thus, a conflict existed between the family's interest in a large number of surviving children and the family head's interest in obtaining as much work as possible from the adult women.

Rural societies have dealt with this problem in a variety of ways. One is spacing of births, another is polygyny, and a third is customary strictures on women's work in agriculture.

In communities where modern contraception is not practised, a family can prolong the period in which the wife can recover strength between the end of breastfeeding and the onset of a new pregnancy by abstinence or other traditional means of fertility restriction. Traditionally, most African societies had enforced periods of abstinence after each birth, and in many parts of India women moved back to their parents' household after child birth.

The custom of marital abstinence after childbirth provides an inducement to polygyny. Moreover, the conflict between motherhood and work is attenuated when a number of wives share the burden of serving the husband and performing tasks related to domestic duties, child care, and agricultural labour. In sparsely populated regions with free access to cultivation of common land, polygyny is highly advantageous to the family head, because he can combine large family size with a negligible work burden, all the work being done by his wives and children. Where market access is available for surplus products, he can expand the area under cultivation in step with the increase in the family labour force and become rich by means of unpaid family labour. In other words, polygyny is a means to create family wealth in regions without land shortage and without the availability of labour for hire. A likely outcome for the society as a whole is increased income inequality.

The sexual division of labour is different in rural areas where increasing population density has led to the replacement of long-fallow production on common land with more intensive systems of agriculture using animal draught power. The use of animals for land preparation and transport is always a male monopoly. Men perform the operations for which animals are employed, while women and children perform some or all of the tasks for which only human muscle power is used. In this system of agriculture, women and children contribute a smaller share of total agricultural work, and animals and men a larger one. Moreover, since additional land can only be obtained by purchase, if at all, women's agricultural work is less of an economic asset than under common-land tenure. There is less economic motivation for polygyny, which at most is practised only by a small number of rich men.

In many rural communities, men exercise control over women to such an extent that they prevent them from working outside the home. Women who do no work in the fields can devote all their time to child care, domestic work, and other activities that can be performed in or close by home. With this type of family organization, as well, only a small minority of rich men can afford to be polygynous.

The interrelationship between demographic and economic change differs in these various rural settings. The sections that follow describe the relationship between population change, female status and rural development under each of the three basic patterns of rural organization: first, men and women farming common land; second, men farming with women assisting on private land; and third, men farming while women remain secluded. The last section deals with the interrelationship between the status of women and economic and social services available in rural areas.

MEN AND WOMEN FARMING COMMON LAND

In regions where land is held in common, a large increase in the local population results in a major expansion in the cultivated area. If market access is available for cash crops, a share of the increase in the rural labour-force will be absorbed in expanding production of cash crops for urban use or for export. Since men have the right of decision, they leave the production of food crops for family consumption to the women and devote their own labour to cash-crop production. When women are obliged to feed men and children, men can earn money by cash cropping or wage labour. Thus, the first pattern is characterized by a division of labour, with men as producers of cash crops and women as producers of subsistence crops.

Although cash crops are produced mainly by men, who in turn reap the income from sales, men in most cases require their female family members and children to do some of the manual work in production and processing. Many cash crops are produced with the help of large amounts of family labour provided by women and children. Even in cases where women do all the work on a cash crop, men often sell the crop and pocket the income or oblige the women to hand over the money to them.

This organization of family labour, in which male farmers require women and children to do a large share of the work without pay, provides a strong inducement to the expansion of commercial agriculture, but it is a handicap to the production of food crops. When the population in a village increases, some of the surrounding pasture and other uncultivated land are brought under cultivation. The men appropriate the best land for their cash crops, while the women's food crops must be grown on poorer land or land at a greater distance from the village. As the cultivated area is expanded, fuel, wild food, and fodder must be gathered further away from the village. All the additional work is usually the responsibility of women and children. In these circumstances, women may be unable to produce enough food for the family; either the diet deteriorates or imported food is purchased.

Men are unlikely to fill the gap in food production because this low-status activity is women's work and depends on primitive techniques, which the men avoid using whenever possible. Thus, the unequal burden of family labour contributes to the shift from subsistence production to commercialized agriculture and to increased dependency on imported food. Although the main cause of this shift to cash-crop production for export is the distortion of world market prices, due to the farm support policies in the industrialized countries, the subordinate status of women in the exporting countries also contributes to the change in the production pattern.

As population growth and increases in cash-crop production make good land scarce, some family heads migrate to find wage labour on plantations or large farms or in urban areas, leaving the women behind to support the rest of the family. In many villages such deserted wives account for a large share of the agricultural population. A low-status group without male support, female heads of households are usually discriminated against in access to land, agricultural inputs and credit. The female-headed families become a village proletariat with too few resources to produce sufficient food.

Growing population density and increasing cash-crop production cause a gradual change from common-land tenure to private ownership of land. Men who plant trees or intensive cash crops on common land are likely to register this land as their property as the amount of uncultivated land in the area is reduced. When the reduction in uncultivated land shortens fallow periods, a family cultivating the same piece of land with only short interruptions comes to consider the land their own, even when no formal registration of property is undertaken. With few exceptions, privatization of land leads to a deterioration in the status of rural women. Under the system of common tenure, both male and female community members had the right to use the land for cultivation, either by simply farming it or by having it assigned to them by the village chief. But only in exceptional cases is land registered as the property of female cultivators. The right of ownership becomes vested in the husband, as head of the family.

As mentioned earlier, common-land tenure encourages large family size, because women and children represent free labour; the more of them a man has, the more land his family can cultivate. This advantage disappears, of course, when women lose their cultivation rights through privatization. A larger family no longer confers a right to additional land. Moreover, a private landowner can mortgage or sell land to weather emergencies and support his old age, while cultivators of common land have no such recourse, but must rely on help from adult children. Thus, private tenure provides less inducement to large family size than does common tenure.

However, if privatization makes men less dependent on help from adult children, it renders women more dependent on both adult children and spouses. This has wide implications, especially for women who live under the marriage systems that are traditional in Africa. Most African men have no legal obligation to support a wife and children, even while the marriage lasts, and they are free to terminate the marriage at will. The age difference between spouses is large – around eight years in first marriages and much greater when a married man takes additional wives. In a family system based on the principle of an autocratic age-sex hierarchy, a large age difference implies a low status for the wife, especially the youngest wife. A wife's lack of adult status makes her extremely vulnerable, particularly if the husband exercises his right to abandon her.

Because men are the decision-makers, African societies tend to make progress in modernization through routes such as privatization of land, where men win and women lose, but they avoid forms of modernization that would be to the advantage of women, as demonstrated by the nearly total failure to modernize family legislation. Thus, rural African women are more than ever dependent upon adult children for help in old age and in case of abandonment by the husband. For such women, voluntary restriction of fertility is a risky affair, given the persistence of high child mortality and widespread subfecundity in many regions (the latter due to a variety of sexually transmitted diseases).

MALE FARMERS WITH FEMALE LABOUR ON PRIVATE LAND

The second pattern of rural organization is one of private property in land use of animal draught power. The male family head and other male workers use the animals, while female family members perform some or all of the operations for which only human muscle power is used. In communities of this type the main means of accommodating population increase is by intensification of agriculture. Continued population increase in an area with no unutilized land leads to reduction in farm size with subdivision between heirs, and the smaller farm size leads to intensification of land use. High-yielding crops are introduced, and short fallow agriculture is replaced by annual cropping. When this reduces the area available for pasture, fodder crops may be introduced in the rotation. In the most densely populated areas, annual cropping may be replaced by multicropping.

When extensive systems of agriculture are applied and animals gather their own feed, most of the work is concentrated in the sowing and harvesting seasons with long periods in between without any work in the fields. Women's participation is limited to the relatively short peak seasons. But, when population growth results in intensification of agriculture, many traditional operations require more labour, and additional operations that were unnecessary with more extensive production must be introduced in order to obtain high yields or to avoid declines in yields and damage to the land.

When both cultivation and animal husbandry become intensive, many operations must be performed in the dry season, and the growing season may be prolonged by means of irrigation and by cultivation of crops with overlapping growing seasons. Much of the additional work involves hand operations of the type usually done by women, so that women perform agricultural work for a much longer part of the year. Many of the female operations, like weeding and transplanting rice to permit multicropping, are onerous, highly labour-intensive tasks. When intensification results in high crop yields, the work involved in harvesting and processing of crops increases. Usually, women are obliged to do all the additional work.

When infant and child mortality declines, more children survive to an age at which they can produce more than they consume. If children do not attend school, the male head of household can freely deploy the labour-force of several family members and reap considerable benefit from labour-intensive agricultural production with relatively little additional work on his part. The extensive use of women and children for the additional operations required by labour-intensive production provides a greater inducement to intensification than would be the case if the adult male labour-force had to do all the additional work or to hire agricultural workers.

If the availability of female family labour promotes labour intensification of agriculture, it also retards industrial inputs. In some cases, the potential for increasing yields and speeding up seasonal operations that such inputs offer makes them economical, notwithstanding the availability of unpaid female family labour. But in other cases, such changes are prevented or delayed because wives and children work without pay.

Use of mechanized equipment is a status symbol reserved for males. When tools and other techniques are upgraded, female labour is systematically replaced by male labour. The application of chemical inputs is considered high-status work reserved for men. This helps to explain why chemicals are used mainly on cash crops, although such inputs would also raise the yields of subsistence crops, thus saving both land and female labour.

The green revolution in Asia combined labour-intensive and modern inputs. Chemical inputs raised crop yields, and tractors speeded up the operations to allow multicropping; but once green revolution techniques were introduced in rice-farming areas, women had to do much more hand-weeding and transplanting. The availability of female family labour may help to explain why herbicides were little used, while hand-weeding was extensively employed in many regions. In their choice of techniques, the decision-makers, be they male farmers or male agricultural experts and advisers, take little account of the disutility of back-breaking work for the women in the family, and the women themselves have no say in the choice of technique.

Use of tractors, pumps, and other machinery is spreading rapidly in many developing countries. As soon as an operation becomes mechanized, men take over, while women continue to use only hand tools. Examples of this abound in the development literature. In Korea, even transplanting, once exclusively performed by females, became a male operation with the introduction of a rice-planting tractor. A man drives the tractor, while women follow after and hand-plant seedlings. In other agricultural tasks, the same trend is seen; with the introduction of hand-tractors and threshing machines, women became assistants to the male operators. Their work burden was not necessarily reduced by this type of mechanization; it even increased in some cases, because the machine could cover a much larger area than could the old techniques.

In villages where land is held privately, those with small holdings and the landless work for large landholders in the peak seasons. Female family members of these labourers also often work for wages in the peak seasons, still performing traditional female jobs. Because of their inferior status, traditional female jobs command much lower wages than traditional male jobs, although the former are often the most unpleasant.

As mentioned above, when population increase leads to intensification of agriculture, the demand for additional female labour is large. The same is true for diversification of the cropping pattern because most secondary crops rely on hand-labour, while the basic crops use animal-drawn or mechanized equipment, at least for some operations. Low female wages help to make labour-intensive crops profitable even on larger farms, but since the small farms have access to unpaid female labour, while large farms must pay for their marginal labour, small farms are usually more intensively cultivated and have a more diversified cropping pattern. The specialization in labour-intensive crops helps the small farms to survive the competition from larger farms. Female family members on small farms are usually prevented by male heads from accepting employment as wage labourers on large farms.

When farms are subdivided among heirs, some small farmers survive on reduced landholdings by intensification of land use, while others change from full-time to part-time farming, supplemented by wage labour on larger farms. Increasing pressure on agricultural land can lead to land concentration. Larger farmers or persons in non-agricultural occupations buy up small farms, and the former owners become full-time wage labourers. These alternative responses to the problem of increasing man–land ratios have different effects upon demographic trends, because the attitudes of landowning farmers and full-time agricultural workers toward family size are likely to differ.

As mentioned in the previous section, privatization of land weakens motivations for large family size because land ownership provides security against destitution in old age and emergencies, thus making the landowner less dependent on help from adult children. Moreover, if a family has too many male heirs, it risks losing status through subdivision or sale of the farm. Therefore, in communities where land ownership is long established, family-size attitudes are likely to differ from those in communities that have – or until recently had – common-land tenure. Among landowning farmers the parents of a large family are held in high esteem only if the landholding is large enough to support the family. There is evidence in many societies of customary family limitation among landowning farmers, the means ranging from late marriage, celibacy, and prohibition of remarriage of widows to induced abortion and infanticide. Voluntary family-planning programmes in rural areas are most successful in such societies.

The increasing incomes and monetization in rural areas during the spread of green revolution technologies in recent decades permitted a growing share of the population to count on property income and access to credit as security, instead of relying on help from adult children. In Japan, the decline of family size accompanied very high rates of private saving. Where private landownership is the norm, marriages typically are more stable and the wife's right to support from her husband is better secured by legislation than is the case where land is commonly held. In these circumstances, fathers assume greater responsibility for their families, and both men and women are more inclined to practice contraception.

Agricultural workers have less motivation for fertility limitation than landowners in the same community: the workers experience higher child mortality; having no property and less access to credit, they are much more dependent upon adult children as economic support; and they command more help from young children, who rarely go to school. Children of agricultural workers help their parents both by engaging in wage labour for landowning farmers and by assisting in subsistence farming. If population growth results in increasing landlessness, this may retard the fertility decline, unless the harder labour performed by wives substantially increases the number of involuntary abortions.

The relative numbers of landowning farmers and landless workers vary widely among developing countries. In most of Latin America, the share of landless or nearly landless workers in the rural population is high; in most Asian countries it is much lower. This may help to explain why rural fertility is lower in Asia than in Latin America. Another feature that may help to explain the slow pace of fertility decline in much of rural Latin America is the marriage system. Most lower class Latin American women, like African women, live in unstable marriages, and many of them cannot count on much, if any, support from the fathers of their children. Therefore, they must rely on their young children for income support and on adult children for old-age support. Men who feel no obligation to support either their children or the mothers of these children lack motivation to practice contraception, and most rural women in Latin America have recourse to no better means of fertility control than illegally induced abortion.

MEN AS FARMERS, WOMEN SECLUDED

The main purpose of the seclusion of women, or purdah, is to ensure the fidelity of wives and the chastity of daughters and other unmarried women. But this institution is also a radical means of giving priority to motherhood over field work by women. Women who avoid outdoor activities devote their time to child care, domestic work, processing of crops, care of stabled animals, and home crafts. When women are secluded, small farms forgo free labour in the fields – a serious impediment to intensification of agriculture and diversification of the cropping pattern. Agricultural production is usually less intensive in regions without a supply of female labour than in regions with similar conditions in which women do participate in field work. Moreover, where female seclusion is practised, farmers plant mainly crops that use animal draught power, avoiding crops that require the manual labour performed only by women.

When population in a densely settled rural region increases without concomitant intensification of agriculture, the population becomes poorer in the absence of employment opportunities for men on large farms, in rural industries, or through migration. Bangladesh is one such region with severe restrictions on female labour-force participation. In spite of the very high population density, agriculture is less intensive in Bangladesh than in many other parts of Asia. There is more broadcasting and less transplanting of rice, and the cropping pattern is little diversified, being concentrated on rice and jute. Rural poverty is extreme, and the country is heavily dependent upon food imports. India also has regions where the cultivator's wife and other female relatives do not participate in outdoor work. But where these are multi-ethnic communities, the negative effects of lack of female family labour are less severe. Women from landless families belonging to an ethnic group in which both men and women do field work find employment as day labourers for the cultivator families with secluded women.

When women only work indoors, there is little motivation to introduce changes to raise their labour productivity. Food preparation and crop processing are done with primitive equipment and highly labour-intensive methods. Women continue to make clothing and other household items, even after the region has reached a stage of development at which such activities are usually replaced by purchases. In some cases, women in seclusion add to family incomes by engaging in domestic production of, for instance, textile or tobacco products, which are sold in the market by male family members or children. Or such women perform services like hand-weaving or sewing for customers. But if seclusion is widely prevalent in a region, there will be an oversupply of such products and services. Extremely low prices will yield derisory hourly pay, and women's work will contribute little to family income, even though they work exceedingly long hours.

A more profitable solution, much used in rural communities where women are secluded, is for men to migrate to seek work. If the husband migrates and leaves a secluded wife and children behind, he appoints another male family member as guardian for the wife and sends remittances to support the family. Under seclusion, family organization is highly autocratic and the age hierarchy is pronounced. The status of the wife usually deteriorates and she is subjected to even stricter supervision when she is left under the charge of other family members instead of her own husband.

Owners of larger farms can in theory compensate for the lack of female family labour by recruiting male wage labour to do the work done by women in other regions. But in fact, men are often unwilling to do these jobs. Men not only support their higher status by monopolizing the use of mechanized equipment; they also defend their status by refusing to do jobs that are usually performed by women. Here again, multi-ethnic societies may provide a solution. In some regions of India, male wage workers belonging to ethnic minority groups perform the hand-weeding that neither the men nor the secluded women from the landowning majority groups will do.

Men who perform work that is also done by women receive substantially higher wages than the women. The large differences between male and female wages arise from the higher status of men rather than from lower female productivity: it is generally agreed that for many operations, such as transplanting and cotton plucking, female labour is more efficient than male. In communities where seclusion is practised, a competitive labour market between the sexes, which equalizes male and female wages, appears only under particularly acute shortages of labour. Statistics from North India and Egypt reveal that when female labour is crucial for agricultural operations, yet scarce because of widespread seclusion, female wages may be equal to male wages. Because the higher male earnings are status wages and not efficiency wages, female seclusion is a handicap to intensification and diversification of production not only on small farms relying on family labour, but also on large farms relying on wage labour.

When women are secluded, girls are considered an economic burden, because dowries tend to be high and adult daughters cannot provide economic assistance to their parents. Therefore, in communities with restrictive attitudes to use of female labour, preference for sons is strong and in many cases girls are neglected by their parents. Poor nutrition and health care for girls, if not open infanticide, limit family size.

In communities where prejudices concerning women's work are strong, women must rely either on property income or on help from adult sons or other male family members in case of divorce and widowhood. Because of son preference, the risk of divorce is larger, the fewer living sons a women has. Moreover, the earlier a woman begins child-bearing, the more likely she is to have a son old enough to support her in case of widowhood or divorce. So, both parents and daughters have an interest in early marriage. Age differences between spouses are large, thus increasing the risk of early widowhood. School attendance is low for girls in such settings. When women are allowed to work only in the house, education is a luxury that only rich parents may choose for family prestige.

For these reasons, there has usually been little, if any, decline of rural fertility in those Arab and Asian countries in which the secluded wife continues to be the ideal.

STATUS OF WOMEN AND ACCESS TO RURAL SERVICES

The extent to which national and local governments provide services to rural areas varies widely between and within countries. Some governments supply mainly health and educational services; others make large investments in rural transport and communications, large-scale water control, and major land improvement schemes. Some governments have established extensive networks of agricultural services, including research, training, and extension facilities. Of course, agricultural development is much more successful where government investment is higher, with the result that private services and private investment in ancillary rural crafts and industries are also larger in these areas.

Rural women benefit indirectly from agricultural investments and services because of improved family incomes, but the direct benefits of the research, training, and extension facilities have virtually all accrued to men. In this field, as in many others, the lower status of women has been the main cause of the uneven distribution of resources. Male extension agents address themselves only to male heads of households; neither female producers nor female family workers benefit from their advice. Research activities focus on the cash crops produced by men; the secondary crops and subsistence food produced by women are neglected. Finally, trainees have virtually all been men.

The passing on of skills from parents to children is an important part of agricultural training in most developing countries, but when women are bypassed by the extension agents and the recruiters to training courses, they have no knowledge of modern methods to pass on to their daughters, while the sons learn readily from their fathers. Everywhere, the male status in agriculture is enhanced by reserving formal training for men and male youth; women are refused access, or only a token number are admitted. In many countries, agricultural work has little prestige among young men, and attendance at agricultural schools and courses is often low. In spite of this, the concern for male status among local personnel and foreign advisers prevents women from obtaining agricultural training, even in countries where they do most of the agricultural work. Where courses for rural women exist, they provide instruction in health, nutrition, family planning, and domestic skills, not in agricultural or other income-earning skills.

The exclusion of women from agricultural training and extension has been discussed and lamented at numerous international conferences and meetings. As a result, some national governments and multinational and bilateral donors have set up rural projects aimed at better integration of women in agricultural modernization. Some of these projects have been directed at 'women only'; others have been 'general' projects meant to take special account of women. Some projects have been sabotaged by local communities or by governments or donors. In other cases, there has been no open resistance, but women have hardly benefited. Few 'women only' projects have been outstandingly successful, and in most of the 'general' projects the benefits accrued mainly to men.

It is difficult to avoid the conclusion that these projects failed either because the male decision-makers were convinced that women were unable to learn, or because they wanted to preserve the gap in status and prestige between men and women. The projects were unable to stem the general trend toward a widening distance between male and female agricultural qualifications, resulting from the sex discrimination in training in modern methods, and in access to modern equipment and other inputs. It seems that general improvement in female status by means of political action, legal reform of family organization, and female education are preconditions for substantial changes in women's position in the agricultural sector.

If women have reaped few benefits from agricultural services, the situation is quite different with respect to social services. The most important improvement in the lives of rural women was the decline in maternal and child mortality, resulting from the spread of medical and sanitation services. The physical and psychological strain on women is reduced when they produce fewer children for the graveyard. Also, access to modern means of birth control in rural areas of many developing countries reduces the strain of frequent motherhood and of induced abortion.

Health improvements and mortality decline for women and girls have been large nearly everywhere, and girls' use of educational services has increased rapidly. In some countries boys still represent a large majority of students at rural schools, but the gap between the rates of school attendance for boys and girls has been narrowing everywhere. In regions where women do much of the agricultural work, however, they pay a high price in terms of labour input forgone for the education of their children, especially girls.

Many African mothers have been willing to forgo help from their school-age daughters and to pay their school fees in order to improve the girls' future earnings. Under the optimism prevailing in Africa in the period immediately following independence, parents did not view a large family and education of children as incompatible goals. Only later did economic crisis radically change the prospects for the growing numbers of educated young people. It remains to be seen whether the shortage of jobs for the educated will influence the attitude of rural parents toward education or toward fertility control.

As a result of the rapid spread of education, age-power relations between women are changing. Illiterate mothers and mothers-in-law have less authority over literate daughters and daughters-in-law than they did over illiterate ones. But it is uncertain to what extent increasing school attendance of girls contributes to greater equality between the sexes. Most of the development literature concerning female education focuses on the quantitative aspects: how many girls go to school, and for how many years? It is tacitly assumed that school attendance helps to improve women's status whatever the ideological content of the curriculum. But indoctrination in national culture is usually an important element in the curriculum of rural schools, and if the principle of female inferiority is an important feature of the national culture, the influence of school attendance on the attitudes of boys and girls to the status of women is not what might be hoped for. Young women may be more inclined to use their educated status to justify withdrawing from agricultural work than to compete with educated young men for more prestigious employment on farms or in rural services. And women who want to improve their position may be more inclined to migrate to towns than to face the rural community's opposition to changes in the status of women.

The occupational choice of female rural school leavers depends not only on the national ideology, but also on the opportunities for female non-agricultural employment in rural areas. Development of rural services and small-scale industries provides possibilities for accommodating a large family on a small landholding. In parts of Asia, many girls add to family income by means of non-agricultural work in rural areas. They earn money to pay their own dowry, and this may give them more say in the choice of a marriage partner as well as contributing to a rise in the age at marriage, thus reducing fertility.

CONCLUSION

Autocratic methods of family organization, with men as decision-makers and women obliged to obey them, promote adaptation to population growth by labour-intensive methods, and they help small farms to survive the competition with large farms that must pay for their marginal labour supply. The exception is regions in which women are prevented from working in agriculture for status reasons. In these regions, the need to pay male wages for marginal labour provides a disincentive to agricultural intensification. The subsistence crops that are grown by women are likely to be neglected in efforts to improve productivity, with serious effects on nutrition and family welfare in many countries.

Because women in most underdeveloped rural settings are forbidden to use mechanized equipment and other modern inputs, low (or zero) female wages for labour-intensive operations compete with much higher wages for male use of modern inputs, and the resulting distortion of cost calculations is a deterrent to agricultural modernization. Under these conditions, agricultural work has even less attraction for female than for male school leavers, and the former are likely either to migrate to towns, to become housewives without agricultural work, or, in areas where there are such opportunities, to seek local employment in service or processing industries. The incentives to male migration are strongest in areas where women are secluded and where women produce the family food without male help.

The subordinate status of women is conducive to large family size. Women's dependence upon the good will of their husbands and older family members makes them hesitant to practice contraception, and, because their opportunities for self-support in case of divorce and widowhood are limited by labour market restrictions and wage discrimination, they run a great risk of becoming dependent upon help from their children. However, when rural development raises men's interest in family limitation, the inferior status of women may actually serve to reduce fertility, because it is usually the husband who decides on family size.

REFERENCES

The stylized treatment of rural settings and their concomitant family and fertility patterns in this essay is not appropriately tied to specific references. The bibliography following provides general supporting material for the themes and arguments adduced.

Abdullah, T A and S A Zeidenstein (1982) *Village Women of Bangladesh*, Oxford: Pergamon Press.

Ahmed, I, ed (1985) *Technology and Rural Women*, London: Allen & Unwin.

Boserup, E (1980) 'Food production and the household as related to rural development', in *The Household, Women and Agricultural Development*, ed C Presvelou and S S Zwart, Wageningen: Veenman and Zonen.

— (1984) 'Technological change and human fertility in rural areas of developing countries', in *Rural Development and Human Fertility*, ed W A Schutjer and C S Stokes, New York: Macmillan.

— (1985) 'Economic and demographic interrelationships in sub-Saharan Africa', *Population and Development Review* 11, no 3.

— (1986) 'Shifts in the determinants of fertility in the developing world', in *The State of Population Theory: Forward from Malthus*, ed D Coleman and R Schofield, Oxford: Basil Blackwell.

— (1989) *Woman's Role in Economic Development*, London: Earthscan Publications.

Bukh, J (1979) *The Village Woman in Ghana*, Uppsala: Scandinavian Institute for African Studies.

Bunster, B, et al, eds (1977) *Women and National Development*, Chicago: University of Chicago Press.

Buvinic, M, M A Lycette, and W P McGreevey, eds (1983) *Women and Poverty in the Third World*, Baltimore: The Johns Hopkins University Press.

Chipande, G (1984) 'The impact of demographic changes on rural development in Malawi', paper presented at the *Seminar on Population, Food, and Rural Development*, International Union for the Scientific Study of Population.

Epstein, T S and R A Watts, eds (1981) *The Endless Day*, Oxford: Pergamon Press.

Federici, N (1985) The status of women, population and development', *IUSSP Newsletter* 23.

Fortmann, L (1981) 'The plight of the invisible farmer', in *Women and Technological Change in Developing Countries*, ed R Dauber and M L Cain, Boulder, Colo : Westview Press.

Huston, P (1985) *Third World Women Speak Out*, New York: Praeger.

International Rice Research Institute (1985) *Report of the Project Design Workshop on Women in Rice Production*, Los Baños, Philippines.

International Service for National Agricultural Research (1985) *Women and Agricultural Technology*, The Hague.

Jahan, R and H Papanek, eds (1979) *Women and Development: Perspectives from South and South East Asia*, Dacca: Asiatic Press.

Jejeebhoy, S J (1987) 'Reproductive motivation: The extent to which women differ from men', paper presented at the Seminar on *Development, Status of Women, and Demographic Change*, Italian Institute for Population Research.

Loutfi, M F (1980) *Rural Women: Unequal Partners in Development*, Geneva: International Labour Office.

Mason, K O (1985) *The Status of Women: A Review of its Relationship to Fertility and Mortality*, New York: The Rockefeller Foundation.

Mickelwait, D R, M A Riegelman, and C F Sweet (1976) *Women in Rural Development,* Boulder, Colo : Westview Press.

Miller, B D (1981) *The Endangered Sex,* Ithaca: Cornell University Press.

Oppong, C (1980) *A Synopsis of Seven Roles and Status of Women: An Outline of a Conceptual and Methodological Approach,* Geneva: International Labour Office.

Pala Okeyo, A (1985) *Toward Strengthening Strategies for Women in Food Production,* United Nations: INSTRAW.

Papanek, H, and G Minault, eds (1982) *Separate Worlds: Studies of Purdah in South Asia,* Columbia, Missouri: South Asia Books.

Sen, A (1985) *Women, Technology and Sexual Divisions,* United Nations: INSTRAW.

Sharma, K S Hussein, and A Saharya (1984) *Women in Focus,* India: Sangham Books.

'Symposium on law and the status of women' (1977) *Columbia Human Rights Law Review* 8, no 1.

Tinker, I (1985) 'Women's participation in community development of Korea', in *Toward a New Community Life,* ed M G Lee, Seoul: National University.

Utas, B, ed (1983) *Women in Islamic Societies,* London: Curson Press.

Westergaard, K (1983) *Pauperization and Rural Women in Bangladesh,* Comilla: Sambabaya Press.

Chapter 18

Toward a Political Economy of Fertility

Susan Greenhalgh

SOME BASIC PRECEPTS

What, then, is meant by a political economy of fertility? Because each discipline will have its own views on this question, the answer can only be worked out over time, as researchers with different backgrounds read and react to one another's work. I do not attempt here to anticipate the outcome of these interdisciplinary deliberations; my aim, rather, is the modest one of presenting a preliminary and partial formulation of the key precepts from the viewpoint of anthropology.

Precepts are different from assumptions and hypotheses, the building blocks of theory. At least at this early stage, the political economy envisioned here is not a theory. Rather, it is an analytic framework, a set of research questions and strategies that can accommodate and, hopefully, foster the development of a multiplicity of theories – liberal, conservative, and radical; grand, middle-ground, and micro-level.

From the perspective of anthropological political economy, a political economy of fertility might have five key attributes. These relate to: level, time, process, causality, and method.

Level

Taking a leaf from anthropology, demographic political economy might select as its object the location of demographic subjects at the conjuncture of local and global processes. The underlying assumption is the interconnectedness of different parts of the world. Analytically, this means that research must be multi-levelled. While the ultimate objective is to understand local (that is to say, national or subnational) behaviour in some corner of the world, the sources of that behaviour are sought at organizational, community, regional, national, international, and global levels.

Existing research highlights the fertility-enhancing or depressing effects of structures and processes occurring at each of these levels. At the organizational level, for example, the exclusion of children from factories in turn-of-the-century Italy reduced their economic attractiveness to parents, encouraging working-class couples to have fewer children (Kertzer and Hogan 1989). At the international level, British colonialism had ultimately pro-natalist effects on what is now The

Gambia, as the shift to production for the world market increased economic vulnerability, which in turn intensified pressure on women to bear children to enhance the family labour force (Weil 1986). Effects of processes at the community and regional levels are generally appreciated, while consequences of national- and global-level forces are illustrated by the work of Coleman (1983) and Schneider and Schneider (1984), described below.

Time

Because the fertility effects of processes on these multiple levels of organization are usually indirect and take time – often long stretches of it – to work themselves through the system, a political economy of fertility must be an explicitly historical field of inquiry. Students of contemporary transitions are unlikely to discover the ultimate (what I have called the 'remote-remote') determinants of fertility decline without attention to historical context – sometimes decades, but usually centuries. For example, existing research suggests that contemporaneous changes in family economy may precipitate demographic change, but the roots of those changes are likely to lie hidden beneath several layers of historical transformation (Ross 1986). Cultural change in the values of children may foster fertility decline, while deeply rooted familial values hinder the completion of the fertility transition (Stamm and Tsui 1986).

Process

A political economy of fertility must be concerned with the social and cultural, *and* the political and economic forces underlying demographic change. Particular emphasis is placed on the *political-economic*, to wit, the links between political and economic processes, and the political–economic dimensions of social and cultural organization. For example, turning a political–economic spotlight on an Indian household would likely reveal a hornet's nest of interpersonal conflicts revolving around the political inequalities in decision power and resorce control that are grounded in economically based hierarchies of gender and generation.

Because political factors have been largely absent from demographic research, a goldmine of insights awaits those probing political sources of demographic stasis and change. Broadly construed, political forces range from the high politics of international organizations and national bureaucracies lobbying to advance their interests (Finkle and Crane 1976; Warwick 1982; Alonso and Starr 1987; Crane and Finkle 1989) to the humble politics of individual women maneuvering to ensure security in their old age (Bledsoe 1990).

Causality

Political economy generally emphasizes structural determinants of macro-level outcomes. Demographic political economy, whose subject always involves micro-level actions, should follow anthropological political economy in allocating analytic attention to both structure and agency, macro-environment and micro-behaviour. One way to proceed would be to view demographic actors as goal-oriented strategizers operating in an environment of opportunities and constraints (Barlett 1980). Analytic energies are devoted to sketching in both the larger, historically-developed structures and processes that define people's options, and the motivations and strategies, conscious and unconscious, that actors employ to achieve their goals. An approach that relies less on assumptions of rational calculation is a 'practice' perspective, which views actors as 'heavily constrained by both internalized cultural parameters and external material and social limits' (Ortner 1989, p. 14). Whatever approach is adopted, particular attention must be paid to ruling out biological factors as sources of change, perhaps by examining the 'proximate determinants' of fertility (Bongaarts 1978) before proceeding to the more distant ones. For examples of structure-cum-agency approaches, the reader might consult Cleveland (1986) and Weil (1986) on the ties between agricultural intensification and fertility increase in West Africa, or Greenhalgh (1988) on the effects of transformations in the stratification system for fertility in China.

Method

A political economy of fertility must employ both quantitative and qualitative research methods. Quantitative methods are, of course, de rigueur in population research. As Schofield and Coleman put it, 'Demography without numbers is waffle, an amiable kind of social history' (1986, p. 4). In addition to their demographic function, quantitative techniques are useful for measuring and assessing the degree of change in causal variables. Kertzer and Hogan (1989), for example, have made skilful use of data on occupational composition of the labour force to demonstrate the role of proletarianization in the northern Italian fertility decline.

Yet quantitative methods alone will not suffice, for certain types of processes, especially the cultural and political ones, elude even the most determined enumerator, demanding instead the close scrutiny of the ethnographer or social historian. Levine's (1987) portrait of the cultural roots of child neglect among Tibetans in Nepal, or Lesthaeghe and Surkyn's (1988) account of the moral acceptability of birth control in Western Europe make abundantly clear the value of qualitative data in demographic research.

PROJECTS

To illustrate the kinds of insights that can emerge from a political economy of fertility, in this section I describe three studies in anthropological political economy. Spanning Third World and First, rural and urban, fertility and family planning, these studies indicate the spread of anthropological interest in reproductive matters.[1] The three studies included represent differing degrees of historical depth and supra-local contextualization. All, however, are thoroughly political-economic, employ both qualitative and quantitative methods (all fall at the low end of technical sophistication in data manipulation, using quantified data primarily for descriptive purposes), and pay attention to both structure and agency as sources of demographic outcomes.

---

1 Anthropological interest in fertility and family planning is broader than conveyed in this essay. Excluded here, for example, is the research on these subjects by medical anthropologists.

Parental Politicking in Sierra Leone

The value of fine-grained ethnographic research is amply illustrated by Caroline Bledsoe's account (1988, 1990; Bledsoe and Isiugo-Abanihe 1989) of the sociopolitical management of family size among the Mende of Sierra Leone. Focusing on contemporary interhousehold fostering strategies, Bledsoe shows how the social regulation of family size through child fosterage minimizes the costs of raising children to their biological parents, spreading them across regional networks of guardians. Fosterage is also a social mobility strategy of parents, allowing them to build a regional network of ties that enhance their personal power and yield benefits from children who succeed it in the modern sector. Guardians, too, stand to gain, for any contribution made to a child's upbringing is a legitimate basis for claiming assistance from the child in the future. Unlike the families assumed by most demographic theories, in Mende society biological parenthood does not automatically compel future support. Children, rather, are but 'bundle(s) of potentialities' (1990, p.97): to obtain benefits, parents (and guardians) must activate their rights and the children's obligations. Analytically, Bledsoe's research indicates the difficulty of applying traditional cost-benefit analyses of fertility in Africa, where intergenerational rights and duties are likely to be negotiable rather than fixed, and the unit of cost-benefit accounting is a loosely structured and spatially dispersed network whose borders are in constant flux. The fundamentally political nature of intergenerational relations among the Mende suggests that it is not only the cultural, but also the political roots of African fertility regimes that need illuminating.

Bureaucratic Obstructionism in Japan

In a study linking national, organizational, and individual levels of analysis, Samuel Coleman (1983) tackles the puzzle of the dominance of traditional means of birth control in one of today's most affluent societies. Extensive participant observation, semi-structured interviews, and a large-scale clinic survey enable him to put to rest the notion that a putatively pro-abortionist streak in Japanese culture lies behind the heavy reliance on induced abortion by Japanese couples. Rather, he finds that the extraordinary prevalence of abortion and two other traditional methods of birth control – condoms and rhythm – is rooted in the political economics of the Japanese health care and contraceptive marketing system. That system, whose creation in the late 1940s and early 1950s Coleman traces, consists of three elements: first, a body of laws severely restricting the provision of modern contraception; second, a politically powerful organization of gynaecologists, whose members derive substantial income from the performance of abortions and, given their economic stake in the procedure, support the legal status quo and oppose the use of pills, diaphragms, and sterilization; and third, a private family planning association, which is both disinclined to offer modern methods because its lucrative condom sales provide the great bulk of its operating expenses, and technically unable to provide them, because such methods require the service of doctors, with whom the association has distant relations. These organizational obstacles to the provision of modern contraception are deeply entrenched, all the more so because they mesh with the themes of repressed sexuality and sex-segregated

203

conjugal roles that are dominant in Japanese society. Coleman's research suggests that cultural explanations of apparently irrational contraceptive behaviour must be carefully examined. In Japan, and probably elsewhere as well, contraceptive practice is embedded in relationships of power and economic advantage at every level of the family-planning system, from national bureaucracy, to local family-planning organization, to individual couple.

Global Political Economy in Sicily

Spanning multiple organizational levels and a century of time, Jane and Peter Schneider's demographic history of a Sicilian town is the most ambitious of the three studies (Schneider and Schneider 1984, 1989). Analysis of a rich base of archival, vital, ethnographic, and oral historical data revealed sharp divergences in the timing and patterns of demographic transition among the town's for social classes. The Sicilian transition was sequential, occurring around the turn of the century among the gentry, in the period between the World Wars in the artisanry, and in the years following World War II among two strata of the peasantry. In all four cases fertility decline was initiated by expansion or contraction in the opportunity structure. For example, members of the gentry began to limit their families as early as the 1880s, when a depression in agriculture (induced by competition from cheap North American grain) lowered the main source of revenue, and emigration of farm workers depleted the labour force on their farms. With alternative avenues to wealth and prominence for their children relying on expensive higher education, the perception of overpopulation grew, and couples began to restrict their child-bearing by avoiding sexual contact with each other.

The contraceptive practice of withdrawal also varied by class, revealing the differential power of the sexes in upper-and lower-class marriages (Schneider and Schneider 1989). In the upper class, husbands philandered, martyring their wives for their restraint. In the artisan class, a more companionate relationship prevailed, producing a more co-operative set of arrangements. The adoption of withdrawal not only reflected, but also reinforced class differences, empowering groups who adopted early to put social distance between themselves – those with *voluntá* (will power) – and their neighbours – *le bestie* (animals).

The Schneiders' research suggests that fertility transitions may best be construed as products of changes in class-specific opportunity structures in response to transformations of global and regional political economies. Underscoring the central theme of Coleman's study, their work indicates that the adoption of contraception may be an eminently political process, both reflecting and exacerbating power differentials between the sexes and classes.

CONCLUSION: OBSTACLES TO OVERCOME

While readers may agree in principle on the benefits of developing a multidisciplinary research programme, achieving this desired state is another matter. The structure of academia, with its bounded disciplines, each with its own departments, associations, and meetings, greatly discourages communication across the borders.

As for border crossings between anthropology and demography, the historical record suggests that, despite a shared interest in understanding fertility, communication has often been impeded by differences in disciplinary folk culture and *Weltanschauung* (Howell 1986; Caldwell, Caldwell, and Caldwell 1987). Furthermore, to the extent that interdisciplinary sharing has occurred, the relationship has been marked in the main by the one-way transmission of ideas and methods – from demography to anthropology. Despite years of work by the Caldwells and their colleagues, and in spite of the particular value of anthropological theories and methods at this juncture in the development (or dismantling) of demographic transition theory, in 1990 the flow of anthropological ideas into demography remains a trickle at best. Where is the problem?

The view from demography suggests a promising degree of receptivity to anthropological ideas. While some demographers continue to question the reliability of anthropological data (in some cases the scepticism is warranted), and others continue to hold slightly musty ideas of what anthropologists actually do (hopefully this review will have dusted them off), perhaps because of its inherently interdisciplinary character, demography appears to exhibit an openness to novel approaches rarely found in the other social sciences. The formation of a Committee on Anthropological Demography within the IUSSP is a case in point.

The view from anthropology, however, is less encouraging. Historically, anthropological interest in demography has been concentrated in biological and archaeological branches of the field. Reviews and broad overviews of demographic anthropology in the United States indicate a focus of research attention on such issues as primate population structure, palaeodemography, and the role of population in cultural evolution, especially as investigated in small-scale, bounded (sometimes called 'primitive' or 'anthropological') populations (Baker and Sanders 1972; Weiss 1976; Swedlund 1978; Hassan 1979; Schacht 1981; Howell 1986; Hammel and Howell 1987).

Cultural anthropologists have been primarily interested in ecological (Swedlund 1978; Netting 1982; Fricke 1986)[2] or evolutionary (Weiss 1976; Betzig, Mulder and Turke 1987) issues. With a few exceptions (fewer in the 1980s), anthropological interest in social, cultural, economic, and political aspects of the demographic transition has remained marginal (an early review is Nardi 1981).[3]

If the demographic transition has failed to capture the imagination of cultural anthropologists, why might this be so? Moving into the realm of conjecture, I suggest that to most anthropologists 'fertility' is a microscopic piece of behaviour artificially extracted from the larger kinship and family contexts of which it is an integral part. Furthermore, anthropological interests tend to the grand problems of cultural evolution, which dwarf in importance processes as limited in temporal and human scale as fertility decline in a single society (cf. Weiss 1976, p. 371).

Theoretically, a major deterrent has been the dominance of classical demographic transition theory in explanations of fertility decline; to anthropolo-

---

2 Fricke's more recent work on marriage (1990), however, links contemporary marital strategies to historical structures in a political-economic account whose goals are congruent withthose espoused here.

3 A review of four leading journals in general and cultural anthropology (*American Anthropologist, Current Anthropology, American Ethnologist, Man*) indicates that in the five years ending in mid-1988, only 13 articles and 7 short coments were published on the topic of fertility, broadly defined. Of these, only 8 can be loosely classified as social or cultural in content; the remaining 12 deal with palaeodemography or with evolutionary or ecological aspects of population.

gists, especially those who have observed demographic change first-hand in the field, conventional transition theory presents too mechanical and unilineal a picture of transformations in demographic regimes. Additionally, the subject of fertility control is inevitably tainted, in the anthropological mind, by its association with modernization and Westernization, processes that undermine the cultural diversity anthropologists go to the field to discover. Ironically, anthropological interest in demographic matters may also have been dampened by the polemics surrounding Marvin Harris's cultural materialist research programme, which sought to explain complex cultural phenomena in terms of 'demo-techno-econo-environmental' forces (Harris 1979).

Yet another, perhaps even greater, stumbling block is the association of demography with quantification and manipulation of numbers. While the majority of anthropologists have always preferred words to numbers, the anti-quantification bias in the field may be spreading, as various forms of 'interpretivist', 'practice', 'structuralist', and 'postmodernist' anthropologies gain increasing numbers of converts.

If the anthropological aversion to demography is so overdetermined, what is the likelihood anthropologists will want to apply their skills to the development of a demographic political economy? Some hope resides in evidence of a small but growing number of demographic research teams that include anthropologists. In the United States, for example, one could cite the Fricke-Thornton-Axinn team at the University of Michigan, or the Kertzer-Hogan team split up between Bowdoin College and Pennsylvania State University.

Beyond this, the task ahead is to convince students of political economy to turn their attention to population matters. (Since there are more anthropological political economists than anthropological demographers, it makes better sense to convert political economists to demography than vice versa.) Why is population important to political economy? In response to this question one can do no better than direct attention to the abundant role of population processes in Eric Wolf's (1982) *Europe and the People Without History*, undoubtedly the finest exemplar of anthropological political economy at this time. *People* is filled with people, their production, displacement, enslavement, and eradication. How much stronger Wolf's forceful arguments could be were they systematically backed up and perhaps sharpened by quantitative assessments of the levels and trends of fertility, migration, mortality, and population growth. Outside anthropology, one can point to such eloquent statements of the role of population in world history as William McNeill's (1976) *Plagues and Peoples*, Alfred Crosby's (1986) *Ecological Imperialism*, and, more recently, Philip Curtin's (1989) *Death by Migration*. Were more anthropologists to devote their skills to probing issues such as the ones raised in these books, perhaps by focusing on one locality and using survey and archival sources to fill in the numbers and illuminate the processes, how much richer anthropology – and demography – would be.

REFERENCES

Alonso, William and Paul Starr, eds (1987) *The Politics of Numbers*, New York: Russell Sage.

Baker, Paul T and William T Sanders (1972) 'Demographic studies in anthropology', *Annual Review of Anthropology* 1, pp151–178.

Barlett, Peggy F (1980) 'Adaptive strategies in peasant agricultural production', *Annual Review of Anthropology* 9, pp545–604.

Betzig, Laura L, Monique Borgerhoff Mulder, and Paul W Turke, eds (1987) *Human Reproductive Behaviour: A Darwinian Perspective*, Cambridge: Cambridge University Press.

Bledsoe, Caroline (1988) 'The politics of polygyny in Mende education and child fosterage transactions', prepared for *Gender Hierarchies*, ed Barbara D Miller.

— (1990) 'The politics of children: fosterage and the social management of fertility among the Mende', in *Births and Power: Social Change and The Politics of Reproduction*, ed W Penn, Handwerker. Boulder: Westview.

— and Uche Isiugo-Abanihe (1989) 'Strategies of child-fosterage among Mende grannies in Sierra Leone', in *Reproduction and Social Organization in sub-Saharan Africa*, ed Ron J Lesthaeghe, Berkeley: University of California Press.

Bongaarts, John (1978) 'A framework for analyzing the proximate determinants of fertility', *Population and Development Review* 4, no 1, pp104–132.

Caldwell, John C, Pat Caldwell, and Bruce Caldwell (1987) 'Anthropology and demography: the mutual reinforcement of speculation and research', *Current Anthropology* 28, no 1, pp25–43.

Cleveland, David A (1986) 'The political economy of fertility regulation: the Kusasi of savanna west Africa', in Handwerker, ed, pp263–293.

Coleman, Samuel (1983) *Family Planning in Japanese Society: Traditional Birth Control in a Modern Urban Culture*, Princeton: Princeton University Press.

Crane, Barbara B and Jason L Finkle (1989) 'The U.S., China, and the United Nations Population Fund: dynamics of US policy making', *Population and Development Review* 15, no 1, pp23–59.

Crosby, Alfred W (1986) *Ecological Imperialism: The Biological Expansion of Europe, 900–1900.* Cambridge: Cambridge University Press.

Curtin, Philip D (1989) *Death by Migration: Europe's Encounter with the Tropical World in the 19th century*, Cambridge: Cambridge University Press.

Finkle, Jason L and Barbara B Crane (1976) 'The World Health Organization and the population issue: organizational values in the United Nations', *Population and Development Review* 2, no 3/4, pp367–393.

Fricke, Thomas E (1986) *Himalayan Households: Tamang Demography and Domestic Process*, Ann Arbor: UMI Research Press.

— (1990 'Elementary structures in the Nepal Himalaya: reciprocity and the politics of hierarchy in Ghale-Tamang marriage', *Ethnology* 29, no 2, April.

Greenhalgh, Susan (1988) 'Fertility as mobility: Sinic transitions', *Population and Development Review* 14, no 4, pp629–674.

Hammel, E A and Nancy Howell (1987) 'Research in population and culture: an evolutionary framework', *Current Anthropology* 28, no 2, pp141–160.

Handwerker, W Penn, ed (1986) *Culture and Reproduction: An Anthropological Critique of Demographic Transition Theory*, Boulder: Westview Press.

Harris, Marvin (1979) *Cultural Materialism: The Struggle for a Science of Culture*, New York: Random House.

Hassan, Fedki A (1979) 'Demography and archaeology', *Annual Review of Anthropology* 8, pp137–160.

Howell, Nancy (1986) 'Demographic anthropology', *Annual Review of Anthropology* 15, pp219–246.

Kertzer, David I and Dennis P Hogan (1989) *Family, Political Economy, and Demographic Change: The Transformation of Life in Casalecchio, Italy, 1861–1921*, Madison: University of Wisconsin Press.

Lesthaeghe, Ron and Johan Surkyn (1988) 'Cultural dynamics and economic theories of fertility change', *Population and Development Review* 14, no 1, pp1–45.

Levine, David (1987) *Reproducing Families: The Political Economy of English Population History*, Cambridge: Cambridge University Press.

McNeill, William H (1976) *Plagues and Peoples*, Garden City: Anchor.

Nardi, Bonnie A (1981) 'Modes of explanation in anthropological population theory: biological determinism vs self-regulation in studies of population growth in Third World countries', *American Anthropologist* 83, no 1, pp28–56.

Netting, Robert Mc C (1981) *Balancing on an Alp: Ecological Change and Continuity in a Swiss Mountain Community*, New York: Cambridge University Press.

Ortner, Sherry (1989) *High Religion: A Cultural and Political History of Sherpa Buddhism*, Princeton: Princeton University Press.

Schacht, Robert M (1981) 'Estimating past population trends', *Annual Review of Anthropology* 10, pp119–140.

Schneider, Jane and Peter Schneider (1984) 'Demographic transitions in a Sicilian rural town', *Journal of Family History* 9, no 3, pp245–273.

– (1989) 'Not a moment too soon: family limitation by withdrawal in western Sicily', unpubl. ms.

Schofield, Roger and David Coleman (1986) 'Introduction: the state of population theory', in *The State of Population Theory: Forward from Malthus*, ed. David Coleman and Roger Schofield, Oxford: Basil Blackwell, pp1–13.

Stamm, Liesa and Amy Ong Tsui (1986) 'Cultural constraints on fertility transition in Tunisia: a case-analysis from the city of Ksar-Hellal', in Handwerker, ed, pp159–174.

Swedlund, Alan C (1978) 'Historical demography as population ecology', *Annual Review of Anthropology* 7, pp1137–173.

Warwick, Donald P (1982) *Bitter Pills: Population Policies and Their Implementation in Eight Developing Countries*, New York: Cambridge University Press.

Weil, Peter (1986) 'Agricultural intensification and fertility in The Gambia (West Africa)', in Handwerker, ed, pp294–320.

Weiss, Kenneth M. (1976) 'Demographic theory and anthropological inference', *Annual Review of Anthropology* 5, pp351–381.

Wolf, Eric R (1982) *Europe and the People Without History*, Berkeley: University of California Press.

Chapter 19

International Dimensions of Population Policies

Paul Demeny

The topic of this essay represents a relatively small subset of the issues that would be involved in a comprehensive discussion of population policies in the contemporary world. The overwhelming proportion of what might be construed as 'population problems' is located – and dealt with in one fashion or another – within the geographic boundaries of sovereign states. Much of what is often discussed under the loose label 'world population problems' reveals itself, upon closer examination, to be a collection of a multitude of national problems.

Despite their surface diversity, the underlying structure of such national population problems is identical. The myriads of discrete actions that determine demographic processes are governed by a calculus of advantage and disadvantage as perceived by individuals. However, under the existing arrangements regulating social interaction, some of the consequences of individual demographic acts are borne by persons who have had no influence on the process of deliberation that led to a particular demographic decision in the first place. Such 'demographic externalities' which emanate from individual actors are likely to be minute in size in any particular case, but they may be of great significance in the aggregate. Welfare transfers, whether negative or positive, may flow predominantly from individuals of certain demographic or socioeconomic characteristics to others, thus leaving some groups relatively worse off while others experience net gains. Or, the effects may be mutual and symmetrical, each individual or group of individuals both transferring costs to others and bearing costs transferred by others. This may leave relative welfare positions largely unaffected, yet make everybody less well off than they might have been if the costs generated by individual demographic acts were fully borne by the relevant decision-makers. In such situations, there is a potential for mutually agreed-upon social interventions aimed at influencing the outcome of individual-level decision-making in demographic matters – interventions that would enhance the welfare of at least some in the society without diminishing the welfare of others. The intervention may consist of legally binding rules concerning demographic behaviour; education and other forms of normative persuasion; or, most plausibly, changes in the institutional environment that modify the cost calculus individuals make in demographic matters.

Since nations do not live in hermetic isolation, *prima facie* demographic externalities are not fully contained within national boundaries. Indeed, in principle, international population problems possessing the same underlying structure as national problems can be readily identified. Naturally, the significance of international spill-over effects attached to demographic behaviour is not to be taken for granted *a priori*. For instance, it would be reasonable to expect that in many cases sheer geographic distance might be enough to weaken such effects sufficiently to make it doubtful that there is scope for a social welfare improvement on the international level through population policy measures. But, whether countries are adjacent or distant, it is the very existence of international boundaries that tends to constitute the most important barrier to the transmittal of significant demographic spillovers. Such boundaries demarcate the main units within which population externalities can be not only identified but also acted upon. National entities possess the ready machinery of the state for political bargaining and decision-making and for enforcing rules and executing policies once they are adopted. In contrast, supranational organizations endowed with analogous attributes exist today only in rudimentary form, and what powers they do possess are ill-suited for formulating and enforcing population policies on a global or even a regional scale.

Yet, in addressing our assigned topic, we are not searching for content in an empty box. Population issues are not fully confined within national boundaries. On the most obvious level, policies controlling the settlement of foreigners in a national territory have an impact outside the country that exercises the control, even though international law recognizes the right of sovereign states to set such policies at their own discretion. The history of international migration policies is, of course, as old as the nation-state itself. As long as the nation-state remains the basic building block of the world system, the existence of such policies will be a permanent fixture of the regulatory mechanisms that shape global demographic trends. Since the end of the Second World War, national interests in political matters have also become interlinked in a more explicit fashion. A number of governments, concerned with economic and social ills that appeared to be aggravated by an unprecedented surge of political growth in the less developed countries, have taken an open interest in overall demographic trends outside their own borders. A less than disinterested governmental role in international fact-finding and analytic work concerning population change has, of course, numerous historical antecedents. But the direct involvement of national governments in population policy formulation and execution in other countries that has characterized the post-war period can be regarded as wholly novel. This new-found interest has manifested itself in two main forms.

First, bilateral contracts between governments came to involve population policy matters. Increasingly, in intergovernmental discussions of economic and social issues, concerns about the interrelationships between population dynamics and development trends were explicitly raised and, as part of development aid (itself, of course, a new facet of international economic relations), financial assistance and sometimes operational partnership was sought or offered for the establishment and support of 'population programmes'. Second, the issue of world population trends was put on the agenda of international organizations, most notably in the United Nations and its specialized agencies. This initial focus was on promotion of data-gathering and scientific work, but increasingly programme assistance was also made available to states requesting it. In 1969 a special United Nations Fund for Population Activities was established to serve as the main agency for co-ordinating UN activities in the population field and for channelling multilateral assistance to national programmes. More recently, World Bank lending became available to help the financing of national population programmes. Activities under each of these rubrics have grown rapidly in volume and visibility, especially during the last ten years.

Does this increase mark the beginning of a secular trend? Will the success or failure of national attempts to regulate population processes be increasingly subject to international scrutiny? Have national population programmes acquired a long-term claim for financial and technical assistance from abroad? It is the objective of this paper to discern, at least in qualitative terms, the rationale, direction and content of future developments in the international population policy arena. The discussion follows a plan that is both simple and conventional. First, the main international population issues are identified. In the second section, policies that have been adopted in response to these problems are briefly discussed followed by an assessment of options and likely policy choices during the coming decades. The concluding section considers the main sources of uncertainty that render prognostication on future international population policy matters highly uncertain.

INTERNATIONAL POPULATION ISSUES

What are the main factors underlying the increasing attention given to population policies on the international scene? The answer may be approximated by noting four overlapping and interrelated concerns that appear to influence, if unevenly and in varying combinations, the approaches towards international population phenomena embodied in national policies. The concerns have to do with:

1. Shifts in relative demographic size within the family of nations.
2. International economic and political stability.
3. Humanitarian and welfare considerations.
4. Narrowing options with respect to long-term social development.

Each of these concerns is a reflection of measurable or perceived consequences of the extraordinarily rapid growth of the world population during the present century and in particular of the marked acceleration of the growth since the end of the Second World War. None of these concerns has been adequately articulated, either in the academic literature or in international and national forums in which population policies are considered. The general tone of the ongoing policy discussions has been, and remains, intensely pragmatic; discussion is focused on what appears to be feasible at the moment, and aims at patient widening of the existing scope of co-operation between national governments.

Given this orientation, the inclination to be perfunctory concerning the rationale for any particular action or even for a general policy is not unexpected. It reflects the political sensitivity of the issues involved and the fragility of the value consensus, whether between nations or in the domestic arena, on which policies are based. It also reflects what Tinbergen (1975, p24) characterized as a 'pre-scientific stage of understanding the problem and its solution'. Even when demographic patterns and magnitudes can be ascertained (a condition often far from being satisfied), there remains wide disagreement concerning the influence of these patterns on human welfare and the nature of their interaction with other social phenomena.

Resolution of such disagreements has thus far proven elusive. International co-operation in the meantime has proceeded along the line of least resistance. For better or worse, this has entailed a degree of obfuscation concerning policy rationales and goals. Instead of an examination of principles and foundations, there has been a concentration on what was politically attainable: *ad hoc* international co-operation aimed at moderating population growth. The bargains struck typically involve tangible, if thus far decidedly small-scale, transfers between nations – transfers earmarked for encouraging the establishment, and assisting in the execution, of national population programmes whose ends and means meet outside sympathy and concurrence. The goal of a constitutional-level international contract spelling out a code of demographic behaviour applicable to the members of the family of nations has been seen, probably correctly, as out of reach.[1]

Thus, international action in the population field has become a subset of international development assistance. Among the motivating concerns listed above, item 3, humanitarian and welfare considerations, has received most attention, both in marshalling domestic concerns for supporting international assistance in population matters and in underpinning the willingness of recipient nations to co-operate. Considerations of economic and political stability, item 2, also have been often invoked, at least in justifying donor interest. Items 1 and 4, in contrast, have been seldom discussed, owing, no doubt, to the feeling that they touch on sensitive nerves and to the fact that they focus on consequences of population growth that are long-run as well as poorly quantifiable. Nevertheless, a careful reading of the record of the policy discussions of the last few decades leaves little doubt that the influence of these factors has been potent.

Shifts in Relative Population Size

The explosive increase of the world population is perhaps the single most spectacular event of modern history. Global numbers during the last 100 years have trebled. Net population growth between 1900 and the year 2000 will, in all probability, be of the order of 4.5 billion. During the first quarter of the 21st century, an additional net increase of 2 billion is anticipated by the United Nations. Underlying this expansion are sharp differences in observed and anticipated national and regional growth rates. From the point of view of the slower growing nations, this feature of global demographic growth is a source of obvious if ill-articulated long-term concern. In the domain of evolutionary theory, the consequence of any sustained difference between the rates of growth of two populations occupying the same ecological niche is straightforward: the eventual complete displacement of the slower growing population by the faster growing one (Hardin 1960). Since among human populations rates of growth are subject to social adjustment and relative magnitudes may be reversed by conscious action, the biological principle is not directly applicable. Nevertheless, the shifts in relative demographic weights can be remarkably rapid and, barring catastrophic developments (which, of course, may also reinforce the existing trend), non-reversible.

A few examples illustrating the shifts in relative population sizes should

---

1 A somewhat ill-conceived attempt to introduce elements of such was a contract into the 'World Population Plan of Action', which was the focal point of the deliberations of the 1974 United Nations World Population Conference in Bucharest, was decisively rebutted by the Conference.

suffice. Europe's population was 17 per cent of the world total in 1900 and 15.6 per cent in 1950. It is 10.9 per cent today, and this share is virtually certain to fall to 8 per cent or less by 2000. Expected trends in the 21st century are elabourated in a number of recent long-term population projections (World Bank 1981 and Frejka 1981). Europe's population in 2025 is forecast by the UN at 6.4 per cent of the world total; Frejka anticipates eventual stabilization at about 4.4 per cent. The relative ranking of individual countries exhibits similar pronounced shifts. Thus, France, the world's 5th largest independent country in 1900, ranked 10th in 1960, 15th in 1980, and will rank 20th in the year 2000. France's stabilized rank in the 21st century is forecast as 32nd by the World Bank.

Although the countries of Europe represent the most direct instances of declining relative demographic weight, similar shifts are observable elsewhere. For example, the population of northern America (essentially, the US and Canada) in 1950 still exceeded that of Latin America and the Caribbean. Today, the latter region has a larger population by some 120 million; in 2000 the gap will be, according to the UN, 267 million. In 2025 it will exceed 520 million.

It is well known that analogous shifts within the countries that comprise distinct sub-populations (distinguished by, for example, ethnic, linguistic or religious differences) tend to generate great anxiety among the members of the groups suffering relative decline and are a source of social tension or, at least, of perceived potential internal power conflicts. Among the many contemporary examples, reference to the Soviet Union (where between 1970 and 1979 the population of the Slavic republics grew by 6 per cent and that of the Central Asian republics by 28–31 per cent) and to such small countries as Lebanon, Sri Lanka, and Malaysia should suffice.

Transposing such anxieties to the international scene is not straightforward, but the general disinclination to discuss the issue is probably deceptive. Historical experience certainly suggests that, in the long run, relative demographic weights tend to translate into relative political and economic power. The contrasting fates of the European colonization in the Americas and Australia, on the one hand, and in Asia and Africa, on the other, are instructive. Of the two great European wars in the 20th century, the first ended with an extensive redrawing of the political map to better approximate demographic boundaries. More ominously, the second established an historical precedent for redrawing the political map to reflect massive demographic shifts imposed through force.

Clearly, the stability of the existing division of the world among nation-states rests ultimately on relative military power. It is equally evident that such power in the contemporary world is poorly correlated with demographic growth rates or even with absolute demographic size. But in a long-term perspective, the eventual emergence of a strong, positive correlation is an entirely plausible expectation. Sharp differences, especially between adjacent countries, with respect to population size, density and population-to-natural resource ratios are a potential source of instability as they create the temptation to achieve equalization of differences through force.

Thus, the present pattern of demographic growth differentials in the world represents a serious long-term problem from the point of view of the slower growing nations. Sustaining these differentials for a long period would tend to lead to increasing international tensions and perhaps even to the eventual imposition of adjustments of national boundaries. The elimination of such demographic growth differentials, through a reduction in the rate of increase of the rapidly growing nations, may therefore appear as a condition of long-term peace and overall stability within the international system.

There is strong reticence on the part of slow-growing nations to stake out such a claim. However, in a muted way, the objective of equalizing rates of demographic increase internationally is implicit in the population projections cited above. Ostensibly, these projections are artefacts of demographic analysis, reflecting the best guesses on the future evolution of demographic behaviour. Yet, the grounding of the governing assumption of the projections – that replacement-level fertility will be attained in all countries within a relatively short span of time and from then on will be sustained infinitely – is plainly tenuous. The projections of demographic developments in the 21st century are best described as normative: they express a hope and spell out a suggested timetable against which the actual time-path of demographic variables can henceforth be measured.

International Economic and Political Stability

Concern with the deleterious consequences of rapid population growth on domestic economic development and, by extension, on the health of the world economy is a major factor in explaining international interest in population matters. Reduced to the most basic terms, economic improvements in the less developed world require rapid accumulation and effective application of human and physical capital. Human capital growth assumes achievement of adequate standards of health and nutrition, the elimination of illiteracy, and the acquisition of technical and entrepreneurial skills through formal education and through work experience in productive activities. Capital accumulation calls for postponement of current consumption. Each of these requirements is rendered more stringent and more difficult of achievement under conditions of rapid population growth. Societies experiencing such growth have an age structure heavily biased in favour of youth, with proportions under age 15 of around 40 per cent and often higher. The high youth dependency burden tends to dilute both parental and collective provision of health care, nutrition and education for children, with harmful eventual consequences for their productivity as adults. The rapid growth of the population of working age depresses capital-to-labour ratios, interferes with the adoption of modern technologies and aggravates unemployment, while making capital accumulation more difficult. Elimination of the structural imbalance characterizing underdevelopment in the contemporary world – the coexistence of a technologically advanced subsector with a traditional low-productivity economy – is retarded by rapid demographic growth, which both causes the rate of growth of the modern component to be lower than would otherwise be possible, and expands the size of the traditional economy.

The considerations just noted have to do with rates of change and structural characteristics. In a number of developing countries these problems are also aggravated by the excessive size of the existing population relative to resources and available technology. When such circumstances prevail, even in the absence of demographic growth, development is hindered by the need to exploit resources that require the application of large amounts of capital per unit of output – for example, in making marginal lands suitable for agricultural production, in conducting offshore mineral exploration, or in maintaining or achieving a given standard of environmental sanitation. The spatial redistribution of populations necessitated by development also entails various diseconomies, such as those associated with urban concentrations beyond a certain scale. Population growth amplifies such problems greatly.

Whether a given population size or a given growth rate is deemed excessive, the problem generally perceived is not that these demographic factors will lead to catastrophic events within a historically short span of time, nor even that such growth precludes material improvement.[2] Although the possibility of demographic growth-induced localized breakdowns cannot be ruled out, the effects of rapid population growth according to most analyses are relative: a slower rate of improvement than would otherwise be feasible. There is a broad consensus among economists that, save for special circumstances seldom found in the economies of the contemporary world, very rapid population growth – of the order of 2 per cent per year or more – is likely to exert a major hindrance on development.[3]

At the level of the international economy, differential demographic growth contributes significantly to maintaining and even widening the prevailing large income differentials between rich and poor countries. It is virtually certain that such income differentials will persist during the coming 50 years, in no small measure owing to demographic growth patterns.[4] In view of the initial disparities in income per capita, as long as there is substantial positive growth in the high-income countries, a widening of the gap between rich and poor countries is, of course, an arithmetic necessity as far as absolute differences are concerned. To narrow income differentials reflected in the more relevant measure – the relative size of per capita incomes – requires a faster rate of improvement among the less well-off countries. In the last 20 years, high rates of population growth greatly narrowed, and in many instances more than wiped out, the relative gains that developing countries could otherwise have realized from their generally high rates of growth in terms of aggregate income.

The disparities in demographic patterns between the broad categories of developed and developing countries manifest themselves in many important facets of economic performance. Thus, for example, differential demographic growth tends to shift the terms of trade against many primary products exported by developing countries. Similarly, contrasting growth trends in the population of labour force age accentuate the differences in employment opportunities and in relative factor prices between developing and developed countries. At present, as a result of past demographic trends, the effect is particularly strong with respect to the prospects faced by persons in the young labour-force ages. For example, between 1980 and 2000, the age group 20–39 will be increasing at the annual rate of 2.45 per cent in the developing countries, in contrast to a rate of 0.24 per cent in the developed world. (Excluding China, the rate ranges between 2.8 and 3.2 per cent in the

---

2 When such forecasts are made, disagreement is apt to be vocal. The dominant negative reaction of economists to the *The Limits of Growth* report is epitomized in Carl Kaysen (1972). More recently, the massive US government study, *The Global 2000 Report to the President* (1980), elicited equally harsh dissent despite its more guarded formulations. The titles of two reviews are indicative: Julian Simon characterized the report as 'Global Confusion, 1980' (in *The Public Interest*, winter 1981); more succinctly, Herman Kahn termed it 'Globaloney' (in *Policy Review*, spring 1981).
3 For a review of the relevant literature see Robert Cassen (1976).
4 Analyses that reach such a conclusion in examining expected development patterns during the next 20 years include Wassily Leontief et al. (1977), and Interfutures (1979). See also Nathan Keyfitz (1976).

major developing regions.) In absolute terms, the net increase during this period will be 17 million in the developed countries as a whole and 600 million in the developing world.[5]

Although the great diversity of development performance within the so-called Third World makes generalization difficult, it is clear that the ongoing process of rapid demographic growth puts heavy additional pressure on the changing social and economic fabric of most developing countries. Amplified by rising expectations that result from increased exposure to the outside world, dissatisfaction of significant segments of the population with their status is likely to grow. Almost by definition, development implies differential improvement in material conditions, leading to sharpened class conflicts and regional antagonisms. The weakening and eventual breakdown of social institutions that have accommodated poverty and mediated between conflicting interests in the traditional society expose some groups to particularly harsh conditions. The loss of political cohesion that results tends, in turn, to worsen economic performance. Great Power rivalries feed on the general conditions of economic and political weakness of Third World countries, and this interferes with the development of stable trade relations and the international flow of capital, further hindering material progress.

It follows from the foregoing that policies that would reduce population growth could have highly beneficial economic and political returns. On this issue – unlike that discussed in the preceding section – the perspectives of the developing and developed countries are likely to overlap. Thus, scope for co-operation between nations can be found, aimed at promoting policies that promise to reduce undesirably rapid population growth. From the point of view of individual countries, the perceived payoffs are primarily domestic, economic and social gains. In contrast, the perspective of the developed countries on the matter is international. For them, the appeal of such policies lies in the hoped-for result of greater political tranquillity in friendly countries, greater stability of international relations, security of export markets and sources of needed imports, and reduced pressures for unilateral international wealth transfers from developed to developing countries. International organizations that seek to reduce income differentials between member countries also have strong reason to support such policies.

The macro-level benefits discussed in this section do not of course follow immediately upon such policies. For instance, significant alleviation of employment problems would follow a reduction of fertility with a time lag of only some 15–20 years. Even so, economic and political returns to investments in supporting population programmes, if such programmes are effective in moderating demographic growth, compare favourably with the returns expected from investments in many fields of conventional economic assistance.

Humanitarian and Welfare Considerations

Concern with poverty has always been an important force for international action involving unilateral resource transfers between nations. The earliest beginnings of foreign aid were ad hoc expressions of human solidarity towards victims of disasters, natural or manmade. Following the Second World War, in an increasing

---

5 For a more extended discussion see Paul Demeny (1979).

number of countries some of the arguments of distributive justice that made the nation-state an engine of domestic income redistribution were extended to support systematic assistance to economically less developed countries. In enlisting domestic support for foreign assistance, humanitarian considerations for the welfare of the poor living outside the national boundaries continue to be stressed and have proven effective to a degree.

There are, however, crucial differences between domestic redistribution and international income transfers. Within states, modifications of the patterns of primary income distribution through compulsory levies are the outcome of a participatory political process that creates individual entitlements and rights, backed up by corresponding obligations that are enforced through appropriate institutions. Internationally, the corresponding element of participation is missing: decisions are made unilaterally by the donor state and reflect donor values and political judgements. In a further difference, domestic income transfers, although mediated by the state, are from individual to individual, assuring a pattern of benefits and sacrifices that are unambiguously linked to individual characteristics. International transfers are largely between sovereign states, with the donor exercising only limited control over ultimate use. This creates the virtual certainty that some of the individuals supporting the transfers as taxpayers are less well off than some of the recipients.

These characteristics have tended, first, to set fairly narrow limits to international assistance without a tangible *quid pro quo*. Transfers between states based on humanitarian concerns are a small fraction of the size of income flows generated by internal redistribution schemes. Indeed, much of the domestic debate concerning the socially desirable patterns of income distribution makes no reference to international differences between incomes, even though these differences are often far wider than differences within countries.

Second, foreign transfers predicated on humanitarian considerations, as distinct from development aid in general, tend to emphasize particular end uses so as to secure greater assurance that aid does benefit the poorest segments of the recipient population. Among the types of aid seen as most effective in this respect, population assistance has ranked high: on a par with, or just below, health assistance or food distribution schemes. The concern with aiding the poor through population programmes springs to some extent from the notion of macro-economic gains expected from successful programmes: slowing down population growth should accelerate overall development, and this should benefit the poorest segments of the population. But the main focus of the humanitarian argument is on direct welfare assistance, especially the provision of goods and services to poor people who otherwise would not have access to such services; and on the attendant benefits accruing to particular groups, such as women and young children, in terms of greater freedom, better health or greater emotional and personal well-being.

The attitude of recipient governments towards foreign assistance motivated by humanitarian considerations tends to be ambivalent. Such grants are seen as justified by existing international income differentials, and this interpretation accords well with the influential view that such differentials in and of themselves establish a moral claim for international transfers. On the other hand, in practice such aid necessarily carries strong paternalistic overtones and tends to create relationships of dependency rather than a partnership of equals based on the expectation of mutual gains from exchange.

To some extent, international institutions resolve the dilemma posed by these

conflicting perspectives. They reallocate funds contributed by national governments through grants that favour poor countries and that are more akin to
entitlements than to international charity. It is sometimes suggested that further
development of such institutions should lead to a supranational authority with
powers of taxation and endowed with redistributive functions analogous to those
of nation-states.[6] There is little evidence, however, that the international system is
moving towards the degree of integration and solidarity that would be a necessary
condition for the emergence of such an authority.

Options for Development

Discussions of the welfare implications of rapid population growth tend to be
dominated by narrow economic considerations. In evaluating future economic
gains, the usual reference point for comparisons is the current level of consumption, with tastes implicitly assumed constant. But development not only brings
higher levels of income; it also changes preferences. Although it should be possible in every country to satisfy the basic needs of a much larger population,
satisfaction of higher-level needs is likely to prove more difficult. As population
increases, the range of developmental options available becomes narrower. One
broad class of options concerns preservation of desirable characteristics of the
natural environment. The accommodation of large populations at high-income
levels entails a steady accumulation of manmade artefacts, leading to the disappearance of certain environmental amenities. *Ceteris paribus*, increased
population size in a given territory means reduced per capita availability of natural
assets that are in fixed supply. The effect is amplified by economic growth, which
tends to reduce the land area not claimed by human habitation or by industry.

The consequences of such changes affect primarily the inhabitants of the
country in which the changes take place, but there is also an international dimension to the problem. Even if the rate of use – current or prospective – of natural
amenities by non-nationals is low, the increasing scarcity or outright destruction
of such amenities does represent a loss to them. Most inhabitants of London or
Cairo may never plan to visit unspoiled nature in the American West, or the
foothills of the Himalayas, or the Amazon Basin. Significant psychic benefits are
derived, however, from the simple awareness that such places exist and are potentially accessible. The narrowing of such options diminishes welfare.

Another class of relevant options concerns the conditions of contact with
people living in countries other than one's own. One of the likely domestic implications of rapid population growth in any given country is greater governmental
regulation of people's lives. Combined with the differences in national economic
and social development, in turn caused partly by differential demographic growth,
such a trend tends to reduce interaction with citizens of other countries. It is
certain to contribute, for example, to the perpetuation of the system of nation-
states. Despite the expected further advances in the ease of transport and
communication that in effect diminish the size of the planet, 'spaceship earth' is
likely to remain partitioned into many cubicles. Within the foreseeable future, the
option for convergence into an integrated human society is likely to remain effec-

---

6 The most recent proposal for such a plan is put forward in the Brandt Commission Report (1980).

tively out of reach. It is not suggested, of course, that demographic factors necessarily have a dominant influence on the prevailing forms of domestic political organization and on the patterns of international intercourse; but it would be clearly implausible to assume that development paths that would have been open to a world of numbering, say, 3 billion persons – the world total in 1960 – will also be open to a population three or four times that size.

One option that is likely to be lost as a result of population growth is population growth itself. As noted above, the standard assumption concerning long-term demographic prospects posits the universal achievement of replacement-level fertility by 2000 or within a few decades thereafter. Thus, the feast of very rapid population growth in the second part of the 20th century is to be replaced by the famine of no growth at all later. Although such a cessation of population growth is likely to be, on balance, highly desirable, the necessity to maintain a stationary population (presumably permitting only minor fluctuations around the zero-growth fertility level) will mean forgoing the obvious social amenities provided by a relatively young age distribution. The even greater amenity of parental freedom of choice concerning the number of children may also become a casualty of rapid demographic growth. It should be noted in this context that the nature of the social mechanisms that will be necessary to achieve and thereafter maintain replacement-level fertility is not at all clear. Indeed, the issue is not addressed in the literature presenting the projections. It is highly unlikely that the stipulated aggregate behaviour will be the fortuitous outcome of voluntary individual choices. Often, to make the projections at all plausible, an intrusive governmental role in shaping fertility decisions will have to be assumed. If so, this further illustrates the validity of the point made in the preceding paragraph.

POPULATION POLICY RESPONSES

To what extent can population policies mitigate the problem of rapid demographic growth, and, in particular, what is the likely scope of international action in population policy matters during the coming decades? The potential role of two types of policies – relating to international migration and to mortality – would seem to be narrowly circumscribed. The prospects for useful action in the matter of fertility are more promising.

Policies Concerning International Migration

International migration changes the distribution of the population between nation-states. It can have an important effect on national growth rates, but can affect aggregate growth on the world level only indirectly – through mortality and fertility. Quite likely, in the sending countries the indirect demographic effects generated by large-scale migration could be quite significant. In the short run, international migration tends to reduce mortality and increase fertility, thus increasing the rate of natural population growth. Still, the growth-reducing effect of outmigration is likely to be dominant: international migration can be an important safety valve relieving population pressures. In the receiving countries, the main demographic effect of migration is, of course, to increase population growth.

The aggregate economic effect is also fairly straightforward. International migration, by bringing about a better adjustment of the world's population to world economic resources, should result in a higher total world product. This potential economic effect is quite large. The existing distribution of the world population between countries is poorly related to relative resource endowments. For example, the current population of southern and eastern Asia represents 50 per cent of the estimated total world population. Yet the area occupied by this population possesses only 16.5 per cent of the world's total energy resources (Revelle 1980). If China is excluded, the contrast is even more pronounced: 30 per cent of the world's population possesses 3.2 per cent of estimated total energy resources. Prospective demographic trends are likely further to increase such inequalities with respect to the natural resource base. The distribution of manmade physical productive assets and of human capital shows equally sharp inequalities.

If there were no barriers to the international movement of people, it is virtually certain that the existing great differences in factor endowments would generate massive migration flows, significantly affecting relative demographic and economic characteristics of many nations. Disregarding the complicated issue of the brain drain (which, in any event, is not usefully discussed as a population policy matter), the economic effects, in terms of changes in income per head, would be generally beneficial both for the sending and the receiving countries. However, in the receiving countries, the competition created by the migrants would tend to reduce the relative income shares accruing to labour and, quite possibly, absolute wage levels in less skilled occupations as well.

There are, of course, heroic simplifications lurking behind these bland propositions, rendering them largely meaningless. Thus, for example, large-scale immigration might generate cultural and political tensions that would drastically reduce the real and perceived economic advantages both for immigrants and for the receiving country. But the point is academic. International migration is not free; hence its current volume, while large by most historical standards, is insignificant by comparison with the net annual increase of the world population. National policies in most countries that would be potentially attractive destination points for international migrants either completely bar entry to foreigners for permanent settlement or keep such movements within narrow limits.

Policies of communist states, of course, are uniformly in the first category. The logic of comprehensive state planning is clearly hostile to movements of labour across frontiers, even to and from states with similar economic and political arrangements. The Chinese–Soviet border, for example, marks one of the sharpest gradients between neighbouring states as regards population-to-resource ratios. There is, of course, no significant migration across that frontier now, but even at the time of Chinese–Soviet amity, there was no expectation that such movements would materialize in the future.

A strictly enforced stance against permanent labour migration is not the exclusive property of communist states. Japan is an outstanding example of a market economy that follows such a policy. Judging from the tone of recent policy discussions concerning migration, the majority of Western European states are also moving in that direction as far as migration from outside the European Economic Community is concerned. Any return to the more liberal attitudes that characterized European migration policies during the early post-war decades is expected to be partial, limited to labour movements under term contracts. Owing to low fertility in the past, a return to economic buoyancy may of course re-create a situation of acute labour shortages in Western Europe. (For example, between 1990 and 2000 the size of the population between ages 20 and 40 will decrease by more than 4 million.) But emerging technological trends suggest that, through automation, the demand for labour could be significantly reduced. More importantly, in future decisions concerning immigration policy, social rather than economic considerations are likely to be increasingly influential. This will tend to favour restrictive policies.

As to the United States, which remains the most important country of immigration, the direction and the outcome of the current debate on immigration policy is less easily predictable. The seeming confusion of that debate reflects not only the conflicting economic interests involved, but also the fact that the size of what is probably the largest component of US immigration – illegal migration – can be estimated only within very broad limits. It is reasonable to assume, however, that, as in Europe, non-economic considerations will be given increasing weight in determining policy. Since concern about the social impact of immigration tends to increase disproportionately beyond some threshold level of the number of recent migrants, public resistance to the costly and onerous measures that would be required to enforce the existing immigration laws is likely to weaken in the future. Since those laws – now easily flouted – are fairly restrictive and are likely to remain so, such a development would tend to reduce immigration to the US substantially.[7]

It seems safe to conclude that in the coming decades international migration policies are not likely to make a significant contribution to the solution of problems caused by rapid population growth. Proposals for radical new initiatives towards population redistribution across international frontiers – for example, through transfer of administrative control (but not sovereignty) over designated territories from one state to another for purposes of colonization seem to lack realism.[8]

Policies Affecting Mortality

Levels of mortality are a major factor in influencing rates of population growth. The rapid reduction of death rates in the developing world since the Second World War (to a significant degree achieved through health policies supported by foreign assistance) was the primary cause of the 'population explosion'. Since Third World mortality levels are still significantly above those achieved in the economically advanced countries, much further improvement is still possible. To the extent that such improvements are realized, population growth rates will increase. It has often been suggested that lowering infant and childhood mortality will contribute to reduced fertility, compensating for the initial growth-promoting effect. The scientific debate on this issue is not fully resolved, but, on balance, the evidence does not confirm that such compensation in fact takes place (Preston 1978). However, past decisions concerning health policies were not influenced by the expected impact of mortality reduction on population growth. In view of the

---

7 Occasionally a return to the pre-First World War open-door U.S. immigration policy is advocated. For an uncompromising statement of this position, see chapter 14 in David Friedman (1973).
8 See, for example, Alfred Sauvy (1978). Sauvy's examples for ceding administrative control through 'treaties of solidarity' include the United States, France and Australia, on the one hand, and Mexico, the Mahgreb and South-east Asia, on the other hand.

overriding value of health in its own right, it is unlikely that policy-makers will take a different stance in the future. In so far as rapid population growth is deemed socially undesirable, there is a sound consensus that the full burden of adjustment ought to be placed on fertility.

Policies Affecting Fertility

Government efforts in the developing countries aimed at reducing population growth through reduction of fertility have received much international attention during the past two decades. The policy approaches have been thoroughly debated and widely publicized. Only the briefest reminder of the contending viewpoints need be given here to serve as a background to the issue at hand: the expected international dimension of such fertility-reducing policies during the coming decades.

By way of a rather drastic simplification, two main positions concerning fertility policy may be distinguished. The first sees high levels of fertility as an aberration that reflects the inability of potential parents to apply efficient birth-preventing measures, either because of ignorance or because of the high cost of acquiring the needed services. In this view, a large proportion of parents in high-fertility countries desire no more children than they already have; indeed, some of their existing children have resulted from pregnancies that were unwanted. The policy prescription corresponding to this diagnosis is straightforward. Programmes are to be organized to inform people about birth-control techniques, and subsidized (or preferably free) services are to be offered providing access to efficient contraceptive technology.

The other position explains high fertility as a fairly accurate expression of prevailing parental preferences for children. These preferences are seen as deeply rooted in parents' emotional needs and are strongly supported by cultural norms. Fertility behaviour also reflects, *inter alia*, children's positive economic contribution to productive activities of the family and their insurance value as old age support for parents. According to this view, in order to achieve a decline in fertility, policies must change the social and economic arrangements that bear on parental reproductive behaviour. Access to improved contraceptive technology is a factor in shaping that behaviour but, in and by itself, it is unlikely to be a significant one.

Under conditions of rapid socio-economic change, the programmatic implications of these two positions need not be contradictory. One result of such a change will be the emergence of increasing demand for birth control. Family-planning programmes can cater to that demand by providing access to contraceptive technology and by reducing the costs of its adoption. The question of the relative importance of the causal factors is moot: the aim is to ease the onset of fertility decline and accelerate its pace.

Not surprisingly, strong international support for such programmes has been forthcoming. The improved contraceptive methods that became available in the 1960s were a natural candidate for organized technology transfer: they were new, relatively inexpensive, and manufactured only in the developed countries. Voluntary acceptance of birth-control services certifies that programme clients derive a personal benefit from their participation while at the same time contributing to the social objective of the programmes: reduction of the rate of population growth. Thus, harmony of individual and collective interests tend to make such programmes politically non-controversial, and hence a natural choice for favoured treatment in foreign assistance programmes.

Family-planning programmes have performed well in the relatively advanced developing countries, but not so in situations of economic backwardness and slow social change. Under such conditions, available remedies for the problem of rapid population growth are more painful and difficult. The policy remedies are of two distinct types, although in practice they tend to be jointly applied. First, governments may seek to overrule individual reproductive motivations and demand conformity to socially determined rules concerning proper fertility behaviour. The Chinese objective of reducing the size of all families to no more than two children – and even pressing for the adoption of the single-child norm – is an extreme example of policies of this type. Second, as part of the overall design of development policy (which under conditions of backwardness may aim at a radical restructuring of social institutions), demographic considerations can be explicitly recognized. Thus, when a reduction of population growth is a social desideratum, development policy may be given a bias that creates micro-level pressures favouring the adoption of low-fertility. Once again, the policies pursued by China provide the most apposite reference.

It can be readily appreciated that neither of these lines of attack on socially objectionable patterns of fertility behaviour offers a large scope for international assistance, let alone for close foreign involvement in policy execution. To promote such policies, there are no tangible goods that can be helpfully transmitted from donor to recipient: the 'technology' of new institutional design is necessarily homegrown. Even when foreign assistance could be helpful, political considerations tend to dictate reticence either in accepting or in offering it. Outsiders' judgements on human rights matters are bound to differ from domestic interpretations.

Significant international involvement in fertility policies is likely therefore to continue to be limited to assistance in the relatively non-controversial field of family-planning programmes. Given the large numbers of people who are potential clients of family-planning programmes, such assistance could grow rapidly as fertility decline spreads to more and more countries. However, once such a decline has started in any particular country, the case for assistance will tend to become less compelling. Developing countries experiencing fertility decline are likely to be the economically most successful ones. Such countries are likely to be increasingly able and willing to finance domestic service programmes whenever such programmes are demanded by the population. Domestic willingness fully to underwrite the costs of family-planning programmes is likely to be more than matched by donor reluctance to extend assistance indefinitely. In the 'difficult' countries, international population assistance will continue to have limited scope, at least until a large-scale demand for family-planning services emerges. International attention will have to focus, instead, on creating the economic and social preconditions of fertility decline. In such situations, the issue of population policy merges with the broader issue of development policy. To discuss that vast subject is outside the scope of the present paper.

PROSPECTS FOR FERTILITY DECLINE

The magnitude of the international problem of rapid population growth, and its hold on the attention of policy-makers in the coming decades, depend mainly on future fertility trends. On this score, the message implicit in present global projections is, in part, discouraging. It illustrates the momentum of population growth: in the developing world, further rapid demographic increase in the 1980s and 1990s is a virtual certainty. The confidently expected speedy and universal convergence of the projections to replacement level fertility anticipated during the coming decades, in contrast, has a soothing effect, since it implies a rapid decline of demographic growth by the early 2000s. In recent years, this prospect of quasi-automatic decline has come to dominate discussions of population issues. But, in fact, no claim can be made that such convergence is assured or even highly proba-ble. Numerous features of the contemporary demographic situation could be cited to demonstrate this point. Sixty years of socialist rule have left the fertility of the Muslim populations of the Soviet Union virtually unchanged. In 1980, World Bank projections anticipated that Iran's population would stabilize at 102 million; in 1981 the figure was changed to 140 million, presumably to reflect the hostility of the new regime towards family planning. In sub-Saharan Africa and in much of South Asia, fertility decline has not yet begun, and no solid theory explains why it should start tomorrow. If the past is a guide to the future, a significant reversal of recent Chinese fertility trends is by no means impossible. There is, of course, a broad negative correlation between levels of 'development' and levels of fertility, and this does suggest that successful development eventually will reduce popula-tion growth. But such correlations do not rule out the possibility that in many developing countries future increases in income and in food production will be used, partly or entirely, simply to sustain further rapid demographic expansion. Policy-makers' ability to influence fertility trends remains tenuous within countries; the proposition applies with double force to the global scene. The prevailing mood of optimism about long-term world demographic prospects notwithstanding, the 'solution' of the international problem created by rapid population growth is not yet at hand.

REFERENCES

Brandt Commission Report (1980) *North–South: A Program for Survival*, Cambridge, Mass: MIT Press.

Cassen, Robert H (1976) 'Population and Development: a survey', *World Development* 4 (nos 10/11), pp785–830.

Demeny, Paul (1979) 'Patterns of population growth and structural change in the world economy', in *Conference on Economic and Demographic Change: Issues for the 1980s, Helsinki*, Liège: IUSSP.

Frejka, Tomas (1981) 'World population growth prospects', Center for Policy Studies Working Papers no 72, The Population Council, New York.

Friedman, David (1973) *The Machinery of Freedom*, New York: Harper and Row.

The Global 2000 Report to the President (1980) Washington, DC: Council on Environmental Quality and the Department of State.

Hardin, Garrett (1960) 'The competitive exclusion principle', *Science* 131 (29 April), pp1292–7.

Interfutures (1979) *Facing the Future*, Paris: Organization for Economic Co-operation and Development.

Kahn, Herman (1981) 'Globaloney', *Policy review* (Spring).

Kaysen, Carl (1972) 'The computer that printed W*O*L*F', *Foreign Affairs* 50, pp660–8.

Keyfitz, Nathan (1976) 'World resources and the world middle class', *Scientific American* no. 235 (July), pp28–35.

Leontief, Wassily et al (1977) *The Future of the World Economy*, New York: Oxford University Press.

Preston, Samuel H, ed (1978) *The Effects of Infant and Child Mortality on Fertility*, New York: Academic Press.

Revelle, Roger (1980) 'Economic dilemmas in Asia: the needs for research and development', *Science* 209 (4 July), pp.164–174.

Sauvy, Alfred (1978) *La question de l'espace et la population sous l'angle de la solidarité*, Geneva: Institut International d'Études Sociales. (Série de Recherche no 36.)

Simon, Julian (1981) 'Global Confusion, 1980', *The Public Interest* (Winter).

Tinbergen, Jan (1975) 'Demographic development and the exhaustion of natural resources', *Population and Development Review* 1 (September), pp23–32.

World Bank (1981) *World Development Report 1981*, Washington DC.

Part IV

Resources and the Environment

Popular discussions of population problems in the contemporary world are typically concerned with emerging or predicted scarcities of natural resources and with degradation of the natural environment. In a finite world and holding other things equal, more people lead to more resource use and less environmental amenity. The resource picture was sketched two centuries ago by Malthus, at a time when resources still principally meant arable land. The amenity case was made eloquently by J.S. Mill in the mid-nineteenth century.

Development performance can clearly be affected by resource scarcities, though the relationship is not simple. Moreover, conventions in national income accounting have allowed depletion of natural resources to be disregarded, masking this process in the standard measures of economic performance. The masking problem is even greater in assessing effects of changes in the natural environment (or in the 'environmental services' it provides); these may be seen as a significant ingredient of human welfare, but yet remain statistically invisible. Aesthetic criteria generally, and hence a whole range of quality distinctions – in production and consumption as well as in environmental conditions – tend to be neglected when it comes to measurement. See Spengler (in this Part), and on the significant issue of biodiversity, Wilson (1992); environmental valuation issues are treated from an economic perspective in Costanza (1991). (Note that the valuations applied in most of the social science literature on the environment are anthropocentric; the non-human realm is valued for the immediate amenity it offers to humans, now and in the future, and for the environmental services it supplies to human societies and economies. The 'biocentric' stance of the deep ecologists, with its radically different value orientation, is not considered.)

Resource scarcity and environmental crisis, with population growth deeply implicated, are proclaimed in the 'limits to growth' modelling of Meadows et al. (1992) and in the ecological analyses of Ehrlich and Ehrlich (1990). Hardin (1993), Harrison (1994), Myers (1991), and World Resources Institute (1994) also write in this vein. However, other writers take strong issue with any alarmist tone. Alternative, more optimistic accounts, stressing the frequent transitoriness of non-renewable resource constraints in the past, though acknowledging potentially serious existing or coming problems with certain renewable resources, are given by Barnett and Morse (1963), Johnson and Lee (1987), Simon (1995), and Preston (in this Part).

Resource-dependence has been steadily reduced as technology has advanced and human capital has grown. Non-renewable resources have found vastly expanded supplies in some cases and ready substitutes in others, banishing fears of an era of diminishing returns and rendering earlier worries about the imminent exhaustion of particular resources (coal, for instance) almost quaint. As Barnett and Morse (1963) wrote: 'the social heritage consists far more of knowledge, equipment, institutions, and far less of natural resources, than it once did.' Cases where scarcity may be less readily dealt with include petroleum and various environmental 'sinks' for waste products (such as the atmosphere as a sink for carbon dioxide). So-called positional goods, such as unique environments, are by definition scarce (see Hirsch 1976).

General treatments of population, resources and the environment include Colombo et al. (1996), Davis and Bernstam (1991), Kiessling and Landberg (1994), Ramphal and Sinding (1996), World Bank (1992), and Zaba and Clarke (1994). A historical treatment of views of the subject in Western thought is given by Teitelbaum and Winter (1989), showing the many antecedents of current debates.

Will the future be different? Resource constraints are potential impediments to the sustainability of development as industrialization spreads around the world, a matter that became a focus of research and policy attention following the publication of the Brundtland Report (World Commission on Environment and Development 1987; see also Daly 1996). Daly (in this Part) argues that not all resource constraints can be eluded by invoking substitutability. There may be important complementarities of human with natural capital, so that an increasing abundance of the former could not substitute for scarcities of the latter. The resource requirements of food production for a rapidly expanding world population are a perennial matter of concern: arable land availability, soil quality, and water (especially aquifers) for irrigation. Brown (1996) finds the current position cause for worry; many other experts – Smil (1994), Dyson (1996), Bongaarts (in Part V) – are cautiously optimistic. Overall human demands on the world's products of photosynthesis, of which foodcrops are only one, are appraised by Vitousek et al. (1986), with the sobering though controversial finding that 40 per cent of the terrestrial total is already in some sense appropriated for human use. The numerous assessments of the 'carrying capacity' of the Earth have yielded wildly disparate results (see Cohen 1995).

Population–resource interactions are mediated by human institutions: markets or management regimes that serve to ration access to the resource by potential users. In some circumstances, these procedures break down, or possibly they never emerged in the first place, leading to depletion or degradation as the demands on the resource increase. A classic stylized account of this, intended to model possible external effects (externalities) of population growth, is Garrett Hardin's (1968) 'tragedy of the commons'. The tragedy is the decline through overuse – and through institutional incapacity – of an open-access, common-property resource. Harold J. Barnett and Ronald D. Lee (both in this Part) discuss the transfers of costs away from those incurring them that are entailed in this and similar cases. Partha Dasgupta (1993) analyses a range of further instances of population-linked externalities. Analogues of these local-level transfer problems may exist at higher levels of social organization, even internationally. The possiblity of political violence as a consequence is discussed by Thomas Homer-Dixon (1991) and Norman Myers (1996). But the outcomes may also be invisible: to be found in a long-term development path that is inferior in both economic and environmental respects to what could have been attained under a more restrained pace of population growth (see Demeny, in this Part).

REFERENCES

Barnett, Harold J. and Chandler Morse (1963) *Scarcity and Growth: The Economics of Natural Resource Availability*, Johns Hopkins Press, for Resources for the Future, Baltimore.

Brown, Lester R. (1996) *Tough Choices: Facing the Challenge of Food Scarcity*, Earthscan, London.

Cohen, Joel E. (1995) *How Many People Can the Earth Support?*, W.W. Norton, New York.

Colombo, Bernardo, Paul Demeny, and Max F. Perutz, (eds.) (1996) *Resources and Population: Natural, Institutional, and Demographic Dimensions of Development*, Clarendon Press, Oxford.

Costanza, Robert (ed.) (1991) *Ecological Economics: The Science and Management of Sustainability*, Columbia University Press, New York.

Daly, Herman E. (1996) *Beyond Growth: The Economics of Sustainable Development*, Beacon Press, Boston.

Dasgupta, Partha (1993) *An Inquiry into Well-Being and Destitution*, Clarendon Press, Oxford.

Davis, Kingsley and Mikhail S. Bernstam, (eds.) (1991) *Resources, Environment, and Population: Present Knowledge, Future Options*, Oxford University Press, New York.

Dyson, Tim (1996) *Population and Food: Global Trends and Future Prospects*, Routledge, London and New York.

Ehrlich, Paul, and Anne Ehrlich (1990) *The Population Explosion*, Simon and Schuster, New York.

Hardin, Garrett (1968) 'The tragedy of the commons', *Science*, 162: pp1243–48.

Hardin, Garrett (1993) *Living within Limits: Ecology, Economics, and Population Taboos*, Oxford University Press, New York.

Harrison, Paul (1994) *The Third Revolution: Environment, Population and a Sustainable World*. rev. ed, Penguin Books, London.

Hirsch, Fred (1976) *Social Limits to Growth*, Harvard University Press, Cambridge, Massachusetts.

Homer-Dixon, Thomas (1991) 'On the threshold: Environmental changes as causes of acute conflict', *International Security*. 16:7 pp6–116.

Johnson, D. Gale and Ronald D. Lee (eds.) (1987) *Population Growth and Economic Development: Issues and Evidence*, The University of Wisconsin Press, Madison.

Kiessling, Lidahl, and Ann Landberg (eds.) (1994) *Population, Economic Development and the Environment*, Oxford University Press, Oxford.

Meadows, Donella H., Dennis L. Meadows, and Jørgen Randers (1992) *Beyond the Limits: Confronting Global Collapse, Envisioning a Sustainable Future*, Earthscan, London.

Myers, Norman (1991) *Population, Resources and the Environment: The Critical Challanges*, UNFPA, New York.

Myers, Norman (1996) *Ultimate Security: The Environmental Basis of Political Stability*, Island Press, New York.

Ramphal, Shridath and Steven W. Sinding (1996) *Population Growth and Environmental Issues*, Praeger, Westport, Connecticut and London.

Simon, Julian L. (ed.) (1995) *The State of Humanity*, Blackwell, Oxford and Cambridge, Massachusetts.

Smil, Vaclav (1994) 'How many people can the Earth feed?' *Population and Development Review*, 20: pp255–292.

Teitelbaum, Michael, and Jay Winter (eds.) (1989) *Population and Resources in Western Intellectual Tradition*, Cambridge University Press, New York.

Vitousek, Peter M. et al (1986) 'Human appropriation of the products of photosynthesis', *BioScience* 36: pp368–373.

Wilson, Edward O. (1992) *The Diversity of Life*, Harvard University Press, Cambridge, Massachusetts.

World Bank (1992) *World Development Report* (1992: Environment and Development, Oxford University Press, New York.

World Commission on Environment and Development (1987) *Our Common Future*, Oxford University Press, New York.

World Resources Institute (1994) *World Resources 1994-95: People and the Environment*, Oxford University Press, New York.

Zaba, Basia, and John Clarke, (eds.) (1994) *Environment and Population Change*, Ordina Editions, Liège.

Chapter 20

The Aesthetics of Population

Joseph J Spengler

Under the title, the aesthetics of population, I shall attempt to deal with certain of the interrelations obtaining between population movements, on the one hand, and the content of the aesthetic component of our system of values, on the other. In as much as these interrelations often manifest themselves in economic form, a considerable part of my address has to do with such economic manifestations. Moreover, as this is a presidential address and not a report of research findings, I shall allow myself the luxury of some population grumbles, since, in what men write of population, there is much to grumble about.

You may be asking yourself, What has aesthetics to do with population? I shall supply an answer as I go along. Again, if your overwhelming interest lies in mensuration, you may be saying, What is there to measure in aesthetics? I might, by way of reply, list works dealing with the quantitative aspects of aesthetic matter. I prefer, however, an answer given to a similar question by W.F. Lloyd a century and a quarter ago: 'It does not follow that because a thing is incapable of measurement, therefore it has no real existence.'[1]

PROFESSIONALIZATION AND AESTHETIC VALUE

Aesthetics is concerned with aesthetic value – above all, with beauty, with the beautiful. Whether this value is autonomous, or whether it must somehow be harmonized with ethical and utilitarian considerations, is not my primary concern. It is to be noted, however, that the capacity of the beautiful to affect human conduct need not depend significantly upon its appeal to utilitarian self-interest. Aesthetic value is, nonetheless, a part of reality. In essentially materialist societies, however, it may tend, along with other values, to be subordinated to things as such. Even so, use and ornament may be combined; beauty and utility may flow from the same object.

My concern is not with the beautiful as such, but with the disregard of beauty, in popular and technical writings about population – and they must be voluminous – into which beauty might properly enter as a subject of consideration. It may be true, as Whitehead has contended, that actualized beauty exists 'even

---

1 In a lecture on the notion of value, London, 1834 (Lloyd 1837).

though no percipient organism fully appreciates it'.[2] It is also true, however, that when the percipient organism, man, fails to appreciate beauty, the days of that in which it is actualized may be numbered, and there must follow other effects consequent upon the disregard of beauty.

Disregard of aesthetic value by those who write about population is easier to explain than to condone. It is not necessary to fall back upon complex explanations. This disregard is largely the outcome, as Whitehead has implied, of professionalization. Ours has become an age of high specialization and professionalization. On this has rested the progress of demography, as of other sciences. But progress consequent upon high specialization exacts its price; it grooves the science and it grooves the practitioner; it produces, in science as in business, 'a celibacy of the intellect', an imperviousness to abstractions requisite 'for the comprehension of human life.' It results in a superficial treatment of all aspects of life except those which fall within the groove of the specialist's 'science.' It results also in a virtual abdication, by the scientific elite, to politicians, journalists, and mere data-manipulators, of the task of interpreting, co-ordinating, and applying the findings of science, be it demography or something else. A by-product of this grooving and perhaps also of the associated lenity of practitioners of demography toward its misinterpreters is the current neglect of aesthetic value in writings and policies having to do with population.[3]

This outcome might have been avoided had these same forces of specialization produced a really firm critical elite, capable of articulating a sensitivity to aesthetic values and of communicating this sensitivity to a significant fraction of our population. Of this élite, however, there is little sign, and there is even less sign of media through which their critical evaluations might be widely propagated. Most of the media formerly suitable have given place to periodicals of a sort better suited to accommodate contemporary tastes and the more modish efforts of today's hucksters. In consequence, few spokesmen exist outside the environs of demography to draw the attention of its practitioners to the significance and the role of aesthetic values.[4]

ADEQUACY OF MEASURES OF IMPACT OF POPULATION GROWTH

Having suggested why aesthetic value is currently assigned so little weight in literature and policies having to do with population movements, I shall touch upon a statistico-economic aspect of my fundamental thesis, that undue population growth is currently tending to debase aesthetic values and to be fostered by such debasement. Our notions of what is taking place in the country and in the

---

2 See A.H. Johnson (1994), p20. The above paragraphs have been influenced also by Whitehead's observations in *Science and the Modern World* (1947 [1925]), pp281–82, 287, 291: and by George Santayana's remarks in his *The Sense of Beauty* (1899), pp49ff, 161–67, 208–220. At one point later on I have followed E. Jordan's approach in *The Aesthetic Object*, (1937), chaps 15–16.
3 I have drawn on A N Whitehead's comments on professionalization, in *Science and the Modern World*, chap 13, esp pp282ff Cf also José Ortega Y Gasset (1932).
4 Cf W H W, 'The art of the presentation', in *Fortune*, March, 1957. pp130–131: Ortega Y Gasset, *op cit*, chaps 7–8.

world at large are formed by the reports that we receive of what is happening. Of necessity, these reports are not only quantitative, but also summary in character; they tend therefore to illude the uncritical reader into believing them to be more concrete and more complete than in fact they are. What I have said is applicable to our notions of the movement of real income and to the impact of population growth upon income and welfare. Preference scales suitable to the task are not being used to evaluate effects consequent upon the growth and spread of population. Indices currently in use neglect aesthetic values and imperfectly represent the consequences and the concomitants of population growth. Presumably, the index-maker looks upon himself as equipped with at least a dipper; frequently, however, he is armed with little more than a sieve.

The growth and spread of population affect the magnitude and the composition of the average quantum of environment at the disposal of the individual. Population growth is a process involving the conversion of substances and services into the origination, development, repair, replacement, and increase of members of the human species. This process is accompanied, therefore, by transformation and dissipation:

1. by the transformation of a given population, together with its replaceable and its irreplaceable environment, into a successor population and environment;
2. by the permanent dissipation of at least that part of the environment which is not susceptible of replacement or increase, even in an effective surrogate sense.

What this process precipitates may be translated into terms, either of the flow of goods and services, or of the stock of environment available; this flow or this stock may then be measured.

The flow of goods and services is measurable in a number of ways; but no widely used measure adequately reflects the impact of population growth upon this flow and hence upon man's material well-being. Even the measures usually employed by statisticians – many of whom seem to be more interested in counting what they can find than in discovering what is important – mask some of the adverse influences of population growth and concentration. By way of example we may consider gross and net national product. Each includes outlays that have passed the test of the market and outlays that have had the approval only of a governmental or other bureaucracy. Of especial concern to demographers, however, is the failure of this measure to allow for the fact that, with the growth and agglomeration of population, there are associated disadvantages which must be offset through the use of productive powers that might otherwise have been employed to increase the flow of final goods and services. Yet these uses are represented as eventuating in real product – in the sense of the stuff that a husbandman puts upon his customer's table – even though they do not do so any more than do outlays upon an exploded hydrogen bomb. These outlays might be even greater – for example, if commuters were fully compensated for time spent in travelling to and from work.

How defective gross and net national product are on the ground indicated has not been determined. Careful estimates have not yet been made. We do not know to what extent these measures include offsetting outlays that are really costs, or in what degree such costs are imputable to population growth. Moreover, the cost-

233

effects of urbanization and/or population growth have not been sharply distinguished from concomitant redistributive effects. Kuznets' findings suggest, however, that these costs and redistributive effects make up a considerable fraction of gross national product; they include sizeable outlays upon 'extensive transportation and intensive handling in distribution, credit, and other service channels', together with excessive expenditures upon housing and other services by urban residents.[5] Conceivably, between 5 and 10 per cent of US gross national product, of which perhaps half was imputable to past population growth, consisted of costs, or offset-outlays already in the early 1930s. Whatever the correct figures, they are average values. The corresponding marginal values would be higher, since both urbanization and its costs are increasing functions of size of population. Today's average values must be appreciably higher, therefore, than were those of the 1930s.

Having pointed to one flaw in gross and net national product, considered as measures of the impact of population growth – namely, its treatment of certain costs as if they represented income – we may note a second, to wit, disregard of effects consequent upon decline in the amount of free resources available per head. Well-being depends upon both free and scarce goods and services; yet only those which are scarce command a price and are counted. So long as a good or service is free and hence of zero price, its contribution to well-being is not included in gross and net national product; it enters the hallowed environ of the income calculator only by becoming scarce and hence of positive price. Or in H J Davenport's (1918) inimitable words, 'the distribuendum does not include all of the values in life, but only those which, being adapted to the price denominator, are submitted to it and received under it' (pp489–90).

Consider a natural resource such as land, and suppose the average amount used per head does not exceed a. When population grows beyond the size at which each and all may have quantity a at zero price, the quantity obtainable per head will have to be cut down to what is available, say, a' per capita, and this will have to be done by putting such price on the use of land as will reduce the average share from a to a' and impute corresponding prices and income-yields to land. We thus have two effects. First, there is a redistribution of product to the owners of land from the owners of other factors of production; thus, a considerable fraction of what urban dwellers pay for services is made up of such redistributed rental income – of income, that is, which might otherwise have appeared in gross national product as wages, etc. The flaw we refer to, however, is not this redistributive effect; it is the fact that the reduction in the amount of land-service supplied per head, from a level of a to one of a', is not reflected in changes in gross or net national product.

Before turning to the suitability of asset-change as a measure, it is to be noted that the recent behaviour of gross and net national product, together with related measures, reveals, despite their shortcomings, that current opinion regarding an economic breakthrough is somewhat myth-ridden. For, in the words of the Red Queen, we are not doing a great deal more than enough running 'to keep in the same place.' Between 1946 and 1955 our gross national product increased, in real terms, about 38 per cent. Expressed in per capita terms, this becomes only about 18 per cent, or just over 1.75 per cent per year. Net national product per

---

5 See Simon Kuznets (1953), pp159–65, 185–87.

head has increased at something like the same rate. If, however, we turn to what matters even more to most of us, namely, to real 'personal disposable income', to what is left of personal income after taxes, we find that it has increased no more than 10 per cent, if that much. Whatever else this rate of increase of 1 per cent or less per year may mean, it can hardly be said to signify a breakthrough.[6]

One may argue, much as has Boulding (1949–50), that the movement of physical assets per head affords a better measure of the impact of population growth upon welfare than does the movement of net national product per head. This measure is not perfect, of course. It may not take adequately into account increases in assets which are analogous to the costs of urbanization discussed earlier. It is subject to the qualification that some mortality is essential, in the world of assets and ideas as in the world of men and values, if we are to have, not Struldbruggian stagnation, but Odyssean flux. The principle underlying this measure does, however, guard us against certain forms of error and confusion. It stresses the utilization and increase rather than the consumption of assets. It recognizes that consumption entails destruction. It does not endorse deliberate acceleration of obsolescence, or purposeful shortening of the life of consumer durables and housing, or asset-squandering under the guise of supposedly useful consumption, a guise more easily sembled in countries where pennies need not be watched. Above all, it reflects the tendency of the growth of assets per head to be retarded, usually by population growth under present-day circumstances, and always by high reproduction. Emphasis upon the movement of assets instead of upon that of national product is of peculiar interest to demographers; it implies that expenditure is a better index of an individual's tax-paying capacity than is income, and taxes based upon expenditures appear to be at least potentially less favourable to population growth than are taxes based upon income.

CURRENT ASSESSMENT OF THE IMPACT OF POPULATION GROWTH ON WELL-BEING

Having argued that the measures of output which we employ do not adequately reflect the impact of population growth upon material well-being, I shall touch upon some of the assessments currently being made of the impact of population growth upon man's well-being. These assessments are of two sorts: those encountered in scientific literature and those appearing in popular and special-interest media. The content of these assessments arises in varying degree from disregard of aesthetic and related values, and from failure to utilize preference scales which are really suited to measure and assess the impact of the growth and the spread of population.

Disregard of aesthetic and related values, together with failure to develop and make use of suitable preference scales, is of multiple origin. It arises in part from a diversity of conditions – for example, that population literature is shot through with radical empiricism; that the theory of economic growth has not been effectively integrated with that of population growth; and that minutiae too frequently are the subject of excessive concern. It arises also from a disposition, even on the

---

6 Data on income, etc, are reported in the *Survey of Current Business*, July, 1956. See also E L Rauber (1956) and (1957, pp2–9). Rauber puts the rate per year at about 0.5 per cent per year.

part of Malthus' critics, to accept his main posing of the population question. For his way of putting the problem led many to infer, when food and/or other kinds of output continued to outstrip numbers in England and Western Europe, that Malthus's ghost had been laid. Subsequent commentators have reasoned similarly when they have indicated that production has been rising faster than population; or when they have urged that the earth could continue to support its inhabitants, almost irrespective of their rate of multiplication; or when they have asked, in the words of a recent title, *Must Man Starve?*, and have given the obvious answer, No! It is possible even that this way of putting the question has led to misinterpretation of such correlation as may at times seem to exist between the rate of population growth and the rate of increase per capita income. For Kuznets' statistical findings bear out theoretical reasoning that, because of the divers relationships and intervening variables present, such correlations as exist are without much, if any, significance (Kuznets 1956, pp. 28–31).

More extreme by far is the population booster, now as ever extemporizing after the manner of Carver's fox, who recommended 'large families to the rabbits.' In the Middle Ages the population booster, then a lord, found in his serfs' goodly 'litters', as they were then plainly designated, a source of 'surplus value' (Coulton 1955, pp. 76–7, 82). Today's population booster is a less rational fellow than his mediaeval forbear; often he is a politician, an unwitting businessman, a local chamber-of-commerce spokesman, or a journalist; sometimes he is a land or other speculator in search of a quick promoter's profit. He writes optimistically of the market expansion to which population growth supposedly gives rise, apparently oblivious to the fact that, since every recruit to a population is eventually a producer as well as a consumer, the amount of market available per producer is affected little if at all. The modern booster behaves as if he depended for sight entirely upon a monocle that gave sight only to the eye through which he looked at consumption and demand whilst leaving totally blind the other eye through which alone supply might be made visible. Our booster seems to be unaware that he is implicitly endorsing the very stagnation theory, which he found so unpalatable in the 1930s when it was being asserted that the entrepreneur had lost his élan, with the result that business prosperity was made to depend largely upon the behaviour of the stork instead of upon the intelligence of man. Our businessman booster may also be unaware that, when he talks so optimistically of the empty spaces and the unused resources remaining to be exploited, he is but repeating remarks common among communist dialecticians. The population boosters of old – the nationalists and the imperialists – are no longer as vocal as in the past, having succumbed perhaps to the humanitarian sentiments of the day; and yet, in most countries, it is only on nationalist and imperialist grounds that a strong case can be made, it being given that the stork sometimes is the ultimate arbiter of national destiny.

To the arguments of the population boosters, as to those of writers who underestimate the adverse effects of population growth, various answers are possible. One may infer that humans no more thrive when crowded than do crappies. One may remark on the unfavourableness of the age composition of a growing population. One may point out that a rate of population growth of 1 per cent per year offsets an annual savings rate of 4–5 per cent of national income, and thereby appreciably reduces the rate of growth of per capita income. Or one may observe that, even should Lil Abner's 'schmoos' allay man's hunger for food, other of his hungers would not only remain, but would be made more unsatisfiable by population growth; for, of the elements present in man's environment and upon which his well-being depends, many are fixed or depletable in nature, with the result that the amount available per head must decline as population increases, thus imposing limitations upon the augmentability of various goods and services.

A better and more intelligent answer was given 33 years ago by A B Wolfe, when he was considering the question, whether America could support 500 million people on a diet substantially free of meat and waste. His answer was, *cui bono?* To what purpose? For whose good? Mill had expressed a somewhat similar view already in 1848; and so had Matthew Arnold in 1867, when he remarked, apropos authors who talked solemnly of large English families and looked upon them as meritorious *per se*, that these authors reasoned 'as if the British Philistine would have only to present himself before the Great Judge with his twelve children, in order to be received among the sheep as a matter of right'.[7]

Exponents of optimum-population theory are agreed that the amount of mundane 'welfare' available per capita, howsoever defined, almost invariably depends upon the size and the rate of population growth. They disapprove of population growth which makes this welfare less than it otherwise would have been. As economists, they are bound to look at children as prospective sources of satisfaction to their parents much as newly acquired durable goods are prospective sources of satisfaction to their owners. Accordingly, if economists set great store by consumer sovereignty and freedom of choice (and one can hardly fail to do so and yet remain in the Western liberal tradition), they cannot condone economic institutional arrangements – arrangements apparently based upon the principle of need set forth in the Parable of the Vineyard rather than upon the principle of productivity endorsed in the Parable of the Talents – which interfere with consumer sovereignty and so bias the allocation of resources as to give undue stimulus to population growth. This bias has been introduced into almost all Western countries and is partly responsible for the post-war increase in the rate of population growth.

In the United States and elsewhere the rate of growth would not be so high were potential parents required to meet nearly all of the costs of procreating and rearing children, costs which at present are being shifted in considerable part to others. For, while it may be true that natality has been stimulated in America by the development of a quasi-matriarchate, whereunder the young male passes early from the suzerainty of 'Mom' to that of a spouse bent upon establishing herself similarly, this stimulus would be appreciably weakened if the costs of such behaviour were made incident upon the responsible parties instead of upon the forgotten taxpayer. So long as population policy is not based upon optimum theory and upon a predominance of consumer sovereignty and freedom of choice, population growth is likely to be excessive, at least on economic and 'welfare' grounds.

Whether the American people will remove economic stimuli making for excessive growth – say, by adopting an expenditures tax and doing away with hidden subsidies to natural increase and with tax exemptions for living children beyond the second (except perhaps for parents with high IQs) – remains to be seen. We live in an age of egalitarian sentiment, in an age in which the silk purse and the sow's ear are commonly rated of nearly equal importance, and in such an age it is

---

7 See Arnold (1925 [1869]), p. 49. For Wolfe's remark, see his essay 'The optimum size of population' (1925), p. 65.

hard to maintain consumer freedom, or to base rewards wholly upon economic productivity. It is of interest to note, however, that the *US News & World Report*, which had been reporting approval of the US high rate of population growth, recently reported Americans as asking, when they learned that there might be 300 million Americans by 1993, 'How long can this go on? How many more people can this country handle without overcrowding?[8] This concern would be all the greater if they realized that increase in population density beyond a critical level is likely to be unfavourable to economic and other forms of liberty to which Americans and others attach a high degree of importance.

INTERRELATION OF AESTHETIC VALUE AND POPULATION GROWTH

I come now to aesthetic values proper. I shall touch upon the significance of variation in the importance of aesthetic values for variation in the rate of natural increase, and upon the significance of variation in the rate of natural increase for variation in the importance attached to aesthetic values. I take it for granted that the precise content of artistic expression of beauty tends to vary in time, and that artistic expression sometimes becomes decadent (Sorokin 1937). For the sake of expositive convenience, therefore, I shall mean by beauty, conformity with relevant aesthetic criteria, and by ugly, extreme deviation from such conformity. I shall argue, in general, that an overworked stork is the enemy of the beautiful, and that, when men no longer prize the beautiful highly, the stork is likely to be given too much rein.

The overworked stork is the enemy of the beautiful because satisfaction of the demands of the stork absorbs resources which might otherwise have been devoted to satisfying the criteria of beauty and to meeting the requirements of excellence. Population growth entails diversion of resources from the elevation of people above what has been the common level to mere multiplication of those at or near the common level. A people that worships the stork cannot escape paying the piper. Witness the average non-rural school child: viewed as an object of improvement, he often is worse off today than in the 1930s, in part because population growth is diluting the amount of resources we are willing and able to devote to the disciplined and skill-incorporating upbringing of the average child. More generally, agents of production required to support population growth might otherwise have been used to improve the health, education and cultural attainment of the given self-replacing population. A probable outcome, I like to think, would then have been increase in the conformity of man's behaviour and artefacts with aesthetic criteria.

Population growth not only absorbs resources; it also accelerates their dissipation and intensifies many kinds of scarcity. For, since aggregate demand depends upon per capita demand as well as upon the number of demanders, it grows both as population grows and as average requirements grow. Poverty, in the sense of particular forms of relative shortage, thus arises both because there are many demanders, as in India, and because every demander wants so much, as in America. Population growth, because it increases the rate at which gross national product expands, intensifies the rate at which depletable resources are

---

8 See *US News & World Report* for March 1, 1957, pp30–31.

used up. Illustrative of this class of resources are inorganic substances of use to man, but subject to reduction to a state of non-utilizability by the relentless march of economic entropy consequent upon use (Spengler 1948, pp238–9, 257).

Of perhaps greater significance is steady diminution in the amount available per head of factors essential to production and well-being, but in approximately fixed supply. Illustrative are water, land, and suitably situated space, the last itself largely dependent upon accessible landed area. Water, long the economist's stock example of a free good, has become scarce, a factor presently setting limits to economic growth in various parts of the United States. This shortage will be felt increasingly as population growth augments both water pollution and water requirements; it will be intensified if underground water-tables fall. Recourse to widespread use of purified salt water would prove expensive at best, as would migration of the inhabitants of water-short areas to other lands.[9]

Turning to land, we shall soon find our population numbering 60 per square mile, and by the close of the century, perhaps around 100 per square mile, a figure not far below that of Indo-China, or that of Eire whence people have been emigrating for the past 125 years. By the close of the century, per capita landed acreage, now about 11, may have fallen to 6 or less. The growing shortage of land will be increasingly felt as numbers increase, for the consumption pattern of America is already the most space-oriented in the world. At present every year 1.1 million acres reportedly are taken permanently out of crop use by urban and suburban development, together with the expansion of industry, airports, military establishments, and new highways; and another 700,000 acres are lost annually through soil erosion, tree planting, waterlogging, salt deposits, and other contamination.[10] Much of this land is lost also to those uses which prompted John Ruskin to call land 'the most precious "property" that human beings can possess'. He would probably have found operative a Gresham's law of aesthetics in the continuing replacement of Arcadian beauty by car-dominated, bill-boarded, neon-signed shabbiness.[11]

The figures I have given indicate that currently nearly 0.5 per cent of our limited crop land – 409 million acres in 1950 – is being lost to crop use every year, even as other land is being lost to uses that fail to take into account the intrinsic worth of natural environment. For these and related reasons, Americans may expect increasingly to feel the lash of land famine. Eventually, there will be too little land to provide the kind of diet we prefer. Our seashore, a priceless scenic and scientific resource, will be given over more and more to the often uglifying hands of profit-seeking subdividers, and therewith the fate of our wildlife, the future of our shoreline, and access to beaches, already a diminishing quantity at best.[12] Within the interior, along rivers and lakes, similar constrictive forces will operate, with water pollution also exacting an increasing toll. Replacement of ugly human rabbit warrens, common in many American metropolitan areas, by clusters of human habitations which better satisfy aesthetic criteria, will prove

---

9 For summary accounts of data relating to land and other natural resources see Spengler (1949) and (1956, pp337–351).

10 See Charles Grutzner's report, the first of a series, 'Changes ahead in city and suburban living', appearing in the *New York Times*, January 27 to February 3, 1957. See also J F Dewhurst et al, (1955), chapters 17, 22, and US Department of Agriculture (1957).

11 See his *Essays on Political Economy*, in Fuchs (1926), p48. See also Dan Jacobson (1957), pp18ff.

12 U.S. Department of Interior (1956). One may consult also data relating to the use of our national parks.

ever more costly. Access to playgrounds and parks, public and otherwise, will prove increasingly difficult, as a rule. In short, all the amenities – and they are many – into the satisfaction of which land and space enter, will become more and more scarce; and men will feel increasingly, as Longfellow would feel, were he to return to the present-day environs of the great university with which he once was associated. Nor will there be much opportunity to substitute under-ground or above-ground space for surface-space; suitably situated space of this sort is very limited in amount and costly of access. From the eventual threat of an approximation to standing-room only, there is thus but one effective means of escape – namely, limitation of numbers. One cannot get rid of excess numbers after they have come into being. Only if numbers are duly limited can men give effective expression to the beautiful and the excellent.

Having argued that an overworked stork is the enemy of the beautiful, I shall now argue that we have given so much rein to the stork because we do not prize the beautiful, because we may be afflicted with what Mencken called 'the libido for the ugly'; for this attitude causes us to disregard the destructive impact of population growth upon beauty and excellence. Of this tendency to neglect beauty, excellence, and related values, there are various manifestations. For example, critics of manners in America are beginning to look upon the behaviour of the American Leviathan as being under the empire of something like ancient Rome's Fortuna, which, in Voltaire's words, makes all 'blindly play her terrible game', and which seemingly inspires many of Leviathan's leaders to behave as figurines in a ballet under the governance of a similar but not very foresightful élan. Moralists might assert that wealth is possessing its possessors, or that the chase is outweighing the quarry, or that men hold with Samuel Butler that progress has its origin in an 'innate desire on the part of every organism to live beyond its income'.[13] Whatever the forces at work, ethical and aesthetic values play but a small part in ordering the behaviour of many of those upon whom largely depends the aggregate growth, demographic as well as economic, of the American Leviathan. Our recent economic-demographic growth, for all its phenomenal character, has some of the quality of a megalomaniac's dream; it appears to be too much dominated by a kind of blind dinosaurism, and too little by the discipline of ethical and aesthetic values.

All this is well illustrated in Russell Lyne's (1957) acutely perceptive *A Surfeit of Honey*. Herein the average American is represented as intent on being in fashion and yet shuddering 'at the idea of being fashionable'. Our servo-mechanistically minded executives are portrayed as having 'built-in ulcers' and as buying 'two-hundred-and-forty horsepower cars' fitted 'with built-in safety belts?' Our American society is described as equipped 'with more built-in tranquilizers of more different sorts than any that has ever existed' (pp1, 84–5). Were Thomas Carlyle still alive he might be prompted to repeat his evaluation, exaggerated of course, made in 1843, of the impact of England's growing wealth. 'No man of you shall be the better for it; this is enchanted fruit' (Carlyle 1932 [1843], bk 1, ch 1). Mr. Lynes's portrait would hardly have occurred, even to a social critic, were aesthetic values in the saddle in American society. For then premium would be attached to real excellence, to beauty, and behaviour and production would gener-

---

13 This sentence has been partly inspired by Gelett Burgess's 'A Prayer' and by Robert Burton, *Anatomy of Melancholy*; and the preceding, by Wyndham Lewis's *The Demon of Progress in the Arts*, London, 1954. p51.

ally be so oriented. Presumably, many would agree that, 'in the wisdom of our choice of purposes to be achieved',[14] we have hardly even marked time.

I should like to refer again to my earlier observation that increases in gross and net national product per head, especially when accompanied by population growth, are partly offset by the adverse effects of changes in the composition of this product. These effects, whilst expressible in economic terms, may also be reduced to terms of aesthetic debasement. Although some of these adverse effects accompany income growth, even in the absence of population growth, they are very greatly accentuated by population growth. Population growth entails both urban concentration and an essentially escapistic suburbanward dispersal of people, together with a usurpation of land for conversion into suburbs and highways, and for diversion to various analogous purposes. All of these uses chew up and uglify the countryside, and some of them intensify the spread of 'urban blight' within metropolitan areas.

The dissipative process tends to be more powerful when gross national product per head is relatively high, as in the United States; and it is accelerated when product per head is rising. It is possible, of course, that the spread of urban blight may be prevented through heavy expenditure on urban renewal, as in parts of Manhattan; but a sufficiency of resources is seldom provided for this purpose, and when it is provided, it is made available through the non-satisfaction of many other important wants, such as education, health, the preservation of natural beauty, and so on. It cannot be validly argued, therefore, that when population growth is accompanied by increases in product per head, these increases are improving the well-being of the average individual as much as they would have improved it in the absence of such population growth. For the countryside is necessarily much more chewed up than it would have been in the absence of population growth, and the amount of urban blight is almost invariably much greater. These dissipative effects, reflected in adverse changes in the composition of gross national product, thus offset, in part if not wholly, supposed increments in measured product per head.

If American production and behaviour were oriented to real excellence and beauty, aesthetic quality would be stressed far more, and mere quantity far less, than it is in present-day American society. Moreover, if aesthetic and related values were given greater support than at present, resources would be diverted away from population growth – much of it blind and pointless – and to the service of beauty and excellence. In consequence, the rate of population growth, underpinned as it is in part by band-wagon attitudes, would fall, here as well as abroad, and now instead of in the future when growing scarcity of growth-limiting factors had finally made itself felt.

Were there greater emphasis upon questions stressed by exponents of optimum theory, and were their modes of thought more common, adequate attention might be given to the role of aesthetic values in economic-demographic development. It would then be recognized that the aesthetic component might be an important element in a system of values, in which event this element might be both an important determinant of population growth and a variable modifiable through population growth.[15]

Before I close I must indicate how the qualitative composition of a population

14 A.J. Lotka used these words in a slightly different connection: see Lotka (1939), pp625–26.
15 On the optimum see H. Leibenstein (1954), Chapter 9; also Spengler (1954), pp128ff, 166ff.

tends to be affected when the tastes of its elite undergo proletarianization and their values become vulgarized. This vulgarizing process, to which Toynbee (1939, vol 5, pp188ff, 445–79) has called attention, entails a decline in the importance that a people attaches to the creative and value-imposing role of the élite, and to excellence in general as distinguished from excellence in a restricted number of particulars. Such a pseudo-orthogenetic drift, once it gets under way, becomes cumulative, particularly in societies of the sort that Pareto has described as fox-dominated: lowered tastes permeate environments in which children are reared, and these environments in turn produce children with perhaps even lower tastes. When this state of affairs becomes widespread, it is not easy to give selective preference to excellence, whether of genetic or of euthenic origin. Eugenic programmes are not likely to prove effective, therefore, in the face of a declension in popular emphasis upon excellence and aesthetic values. Jefferson's natural aristoi are not likely to flourish in a world of mass-men. Under the circumstances, it is hardly to be expected that reproductive selection will be of a sort to favour the maintenance of excellence, or the strengthening of aesthetic values.

REFERENCES

Arnold, Matthew (1925 [1869]) *Culture and Anarchy*, New York.

Boulding, K E (1949–50) 'Income or welfare', *Review of Economic Studies* 17, pp77–86.

Carlyle, Thomas (1843) *Past and Present*, Oxford.

Coulton, G C (1955) *Medieval Panorama*, New York.

Davenport, H J (1918) *Economics of Enterprise*, New York.

Dewhurst, J F et al (1955) *America's Needs and Resources*, New York.

Fuchs, James, ed (1926) *Ruskin's Views of Social Justice*, New York.

Jacobson, Dan (1957) 'Cars, cars, cars, roads, roads, roads', *Reporter*, February 21.

Johnson, A H (1944) '"Truth, beauty and goodness" in the philosophy of A N Whitehead', *Philosophy of Science* 11.

Jordan, E (1937) *The Aesthetic Object*, Bloomington.

Kuznets, Simon (1953) *Economic Change*, New York.

– (1956) 'Quantitative aspects of the economic growth of nations', *Economic Development and Cultural Change* 5.

Leibenstein, H (1954) *A Theory of Economic–Demographic Development*, Princeton.

Lloyd, W F (1837) *Lectures on Population, Value, Poor Laws and Rent*, London. (Reprint: A M Kelley, New York, 1968.)

Lotka, A J (1939) 'Contact points of population study with related branches of science', *Proceedings of the American Philosophical Society* 80, no 4.

Lyne, Russell (1957) *A Surfeit of Honey*, New York: Harper and Brothers.

Ortega Y Gasset, José (1932) *The Revolt of the Masses*, New York.

Rauber, E L (1956) 'The realm of the red queen', *Monthly Review* of the Federal Reserve Bank of Atlanta, January 31.

– (1957) 'Population and economic growth', *Population Bulletin* 13 (February).

Santayana, George (1899) *The Sense of Beauty*, New York.

Sorokin, P A (1937) *Social and Cultural Dynamics*, New York.

Spengler, J J (1948) 'Aspects of the economics of population growth', *Southern Economic Journal* 14.

– (1949) 'The World's Hunger...Malthus, 1948', *Proceedings of the Academy of Political Science* 23, January, pp53–72.

– (1954) 'Welfare economics and the problem of overpopulation', *Scientia* 89.

– (1956) 'The population problem: dimensions, potentialities, limitations', *American Economic Review* 46, no. 2 (May), pp337–351.

Toynbee, A J (1934–61) *A Study of History*, London.

US Department of Agriculture (1957) *Major Uses of Land in the United States*, Agricultural Research Service, Bulletin no 168. Washington, DC.

US Department of Interior (1956) *Our Vanishing Shoreline*, Washington, DC.

Whitehead, A N (1925) *Science and the Modern World*, New York.

Wolfe, A B (1925) 'The optimum size of population', in *Population Problems*, ed L I Dublin, New York.

Chapter 21

Population Problems: Myths and Realities

Harold J Barnett

A great deal is being written today about population growth, its economic and social effects, and the prospects for these. Much of what is written is nonsense. This is unfortunate. Misplaced alarms divert attention from more urgent social questions. From invalid diagnosis, wrong prescriptions are concocted. The serious problems relating to population are obscured by fuzzy thinking and colourful propaganda. The propensity for slogans, lack of objectivity, and absence of scientific analysis is disturbing to social scientists – as Gunnar Myrdal has put it, academicians have a professional peculiarity, 'a faith that illusions are dangerous and truth is wholesome'.

My design in this paper is to identify several major ideas concerning population problems and to analyse them. Some I find to be valid and some not. For most of the paper I confine discussion to the developed countries. The reason, as I elabourate later, is that I believe the economically underdeveloped nations will develop during the next couple of generations and will then share the population problems of developed countries.

THE 'LAW OF DIMINISHING RETURNS'

Much contemporary and historical writing fears economic impoverishment over the long run due to the 'law of diminishing returns'. One form of the basic notion, deriving from Malthus, is that agricultural land and other natural resources are scarce. Population growth presses against the limited land, and therefore man's level of living is impoverished from increase in his numbers. A somewhat different concept of natural-resources limitation, from Ricardo, is that resources are used in the order of declining quality. As population grows, diminishing returns result from this fact. Both the Malthusian and Ricardian concepts are generally thought to be reinforced by resource exhaustion and ecological damage, thus aggravating the diminishing-returns tendency. For example, in 1863 W S Jevons wrote on the dangers of coal depletion and G P Marsh on attrition of ecological systems.

Diminishing-returns notions derive from classical economic models. In these, economic output is conceived to depend on the quantities of labour, capital, and useful natural resources. The natural-resource factor is viewed as being fixed or even declining in quantity or quality, while the labour factor increases without end. Ergo, declining product per labourer and per capita.

In the advanced nations, diminishing-returns doctrine is quite erroneous in explanation of long-term economic growth. The errors are pervasive in the assumptions and logic of the classical growth model and in our records of the economic history of these nations over the past 100 years or so. First, birth rates have slowed down as compared with the biological maximum rates which Malthus and Ricardo had contemplated. It cannot be assumed that an increasing population factor will inevitably press harder and harder, endlessly, on limited natural resources. There is no natural law which requires this. Second, the capital stock has increased much faster than population numbers. An increase in capital per worker obviously exerts force contrary to diminishing returns per worker. Third, natural resources have not been fixed in volume as an economic factor, nor have they declined in economic quality. Increased knowledge has greatly improved the availability, access, and usability of natural resources and therefore the products derived from them. The assumption that man will utilize best resources first and then lesser ones, thereby descending a quality gradient as population grows, is erroneous in a dynamic world.

Ricardian economic scarcity requires that society be able to array the physically varying natural resources in a declining order of *economic* qualities and that the order remain invariant through time; that it use them in this order; and that the decline in economic quality not be permanently interrupted by access to indefinitely great expanses of unused resources of unchanging marginal economic quality. We consider these propositions:

1. Ordering resources according to economic quality clearly requires relating known and stable physical properties of resources to known and stable socio-technical parameters in such a way as to arrive at a unique and permanent economic ordering. Yet historically, for example, copper and tin came into use early, iron later, and the light metals last. There is no reason to believe this is an order of declining economic quality. Consider, similarly, the order of use of energy commodities – first, dung and wood, then peat, then coal, later oil and gas, now nuclear energy. If we view both knowledge (ignorance) and the stability (instability) of production parameters with hindsight, it would seem that success in translating physical properties into economic qualities should not be viewed as a fact.
2. Even if transition of physical properties into economic qualities were always successful, does society necessarily use resources in this order? For a number of reasons, the answer would seem to be, 'not always'. Impediments are international trade barriers, modern governmental reservations of resources, distances from population centres (recognized by Ricardo as an influence distinct from intrinsic physical properties), and institutional obstacles. But this is not to deny that where economic quality can be determined to be a function of physical properties there is powerful economic motivation to use resources in order of physical properties.
3. Assume now use in declining order of economic quality. Is the decline necessarily an economic continuum? It is relatively so for certain things, particularly if these are defined narrowly, like north-eastern cherry wood or high-grade manganese in Virginia. But it is not for others, such as seawater, magnesium, taconite, aluminum clays, low-grade manganese ores, lateritic nickel, uranium in granite, solar energy, etc. Many of our modern mineral resources are quality plateaus of enormous extent.

245

4. The composition of output has changed greatly. Some newer types of output are less resource-intensive. Economic pressures on the more fixed types of resources have moderated or diminished and have shifted to more plentiful resources.

Finally, and in summary, pervasive changes in knowledge, technology, social arrangements, economic institutions, market sizes, and the overall socio-physical environmental context have occurred in the advanced nations. The classical economists omitted socio-technical change from their economic growth models or underrated its significance and powers.

In Malthus's and Ricardo's time, and to a considerable extent through the 19th century, a considerable part of 'final' or virtually final output was agricultural goods – foodstuffs, natural fibres, timber, game, etc. To this extent, increase in these outputs could be, and was, viewed as identical with economic growth. Again, there was a simple answer as to how these goods would be further processed. They would be *mechanically* shaped from the gifts of nature – the wheat grain would be taken out; the hide separated from the meat; the timber sawed to size; the fibres combed, twisted, and woven; etc. Turning to the derivation of the basic substances from nature, man's role here also was a *mechanical one*. Thus, if a man stood on a square mile of land, or a nation on 3 million, the natural resources relevant for economic activity could be easily identified and measured. They were acres of cropland or pasture, board-feet of standing timber, etc.

What has since happened in advanced nations to the meaning of final goods, the methods by which they are produced, and the definition of natural resources is so profound that we find the novelty difficult and seek simplification in possibly archaic analogies. With respect to the meaning of goods, more than 90 per cent of the increase in real gross national product in the United States since 1870 has been of non-agricultural origin. As to the method of transforming materials into final goods, this has become far less a purely mechanical one and to a considerable degree, a controlled heat or electrochemical process. Finally, the natural-resource building-blocks have changed radically – they are atoms and molecules. The natural-resource input is to a far less degree acres, and to a far greater degree particular atmospheric and other molecules.

This has changed the meaning of 'natural resources' for societies which indeed have modern technologies and access to capital. We now look more at contained molecules of iron, magnesium, aluminum, coal, nitrogen, etc, and at their naturally existing chemical combinations, than at acres or board-feet. While in a sense the same ultimate world limits still exist, in a more significant sense they do not. How many taconite iron atoms or seawater magnesium atoms and bromine molecules constitute plenitude and how many scarcity? Further, in a significant degree even the ultimate limits are different from Malthus' and Ricardo's. Their natural resources were conceived for a two-dimensional world nourished by acreage. Ours is a three-dimensional world sustained by subsurface resources. Their society could reach natural resources only significant distances above and below the acres. We have multiplied our 'reach' by a factor of many thousands.

None of the foregoing proves that increases in population numbers are 'desirable', or that non-increases would be undesirable. Rather, our need is to controvert simple-minded diminishing-returns views with logic and facts. The fact is that, in virtually all of the developed or developing nations for which we have long-term economic growth data, increases in economic output per capita have occurred and almost always have accompanied increases in population.

PROSPECTIVE CHILDREN – THEIR USE OF AND CONTRIBUTION TO ECONOMIC RESOURCES

Visualize prospective children as users of and contributors to economic output. If children are conceived and born, what effect would they have on economic output and incomes per capita in advanced nations?

In such economies the child is a consumer of economic resources for the first 15 to 20 years or so of his life, but he is not a producer. His parents can thus expect to be poorer in their own consumption if they conceive and bear him. The contemporary society in general will also be poorer in consumption per capita; it will have to devote to him public resources – for example, for schools – which otherwise the adults could have used for themselves. We see that children reduce the level of economic living for the parents and the *contemporary* society which produces and rears them.

But it is not true that the next or later generations are impoverished by births in the current generation. The current generation's children grow into working adults. In the absence of diminishing returns, they at least meet their own needs. More likely, they produce more economic goods than they consume during their working lives. We reach an important conclusion: only the generation which produces the children experiences adverse economic impact from having these children. Future generations are not adversely affected by the increase in numbers. When grown up, the extra bodies work as well as consume. In the absence of diminishing returns, real output per capita does not decline.

INDIVIDUAL FAMILY PLANNING

In this section we discuss individual family costs and benefits from children; in the next, society's costs.

We have just seen that the begetting of children reduces the goods and services real income level per capita of the family during the period of childhood and adolescence relative to what it would otherwise have been. Then why do people have children? The reason is that total welfare – economic plus all other aspects of welfare – is likely to have increased for the parents.

We reason thus: the great bulk of adults in the United States and other developed nations is literate, educated, and at least somewhat individualistic. Birth-control techniques have been developed very rapidly in efficiency and economic availability in the past several decades. In each case of sexual intercourse, the couple usually has a very clear choice as to whether or not to avoid conception of a child. That is, the couple may be expected to have the will and the wit to make a sensible decision and the opportunity to do so. In the great majority of families, the number of children does not exceed the number desired. If the couple chooses to expose the woman to pregnancy, this will usually be done deliberately. It will be because, in the great bulk of the cases, the anticipated pleasure of having another child exceeds the anticipated sum of economic and all other costs. The economic costs to the family are rather readily apparent and probably well anticipated. Parents will not choose to have more children than they can economically provide for in their view of economic adequacy. While couples with no children may underestimate the psychic burdens of raising children, couples with one or more children are likely to anticipate these difficulties rather well.

What this leads to for developed nations are these conclusions:

(a) couples are likely to make rational benefit and cost decisions as to whether to avoid conception;
(b) the means of avoidance are readily available now and are becoming even more universally available; and therefore
(c) the production of children as determined by the parents, at whatever number they choose, is likely to be a rational and appropriate decision for the parents.

In summary to this point, then, we have reasoned that the production and rearing of children can reduce income per capita. But it will do so only for the period from children's birth to their entrance into the work-force. The advent of children will not reduce income per capita in the future generations. The family decision to have children in an advanced country such as the United States is likely to be a rational one in the sense that there will not be more children in a family than the parents can economically care for on standards which the family views as appropriate.

SOCIAL COSTS NOT BORNE BY THE PARENTS

The parents' rational, foresighted decision, however, may not be rational for society. The reason is that there are costs for society in the production and rearing of children which are borne by the contemporary society but not by the specific parents. Such costs are public service expenditures for education, health, recreation and other public goods.

Visualize a couple with two children and contemplating having a third. In a significant sense they are casting up for the family the accounts for economic and psychic benefits versus economic and psychic costs. If they think the family benefits will exceed their family costs, they decide to have another baby. The difficulty is that they have omitted from consideration a large volume of costs which society will bear for them. Nor will they properly assess these costs against their decision on the grounds that they pay taxes and are members of society. Their tax bill will be no smaller if they refrain from having the child (indeed, if they do beget him their tax bill may be smaller because of tax exemptions and deductions).

It is not my purpose to assess the volume of social costs omitted from the family calculation beyond indicating that they are substantial in size. Society's education cost alone may total $15,000 per child, at current price levels. Society allocates considerable sums in aid to dependent children, public and clinic health services, etc. We have thus identified an important respect in which an advanced society of rational, foresighted, individualistic people will tend to beget too many children. How serious is this dilemma, and is it likely to get better or worse?

The strong trend toward improved social services in advanced countries operates to cause overpopulation, relative to numbers which rational, foresighted families would choose if they individually carried all the costs of their begetting decisions. As society advances and becomes more affluent, it calls for more than proportionate increases in social services – education, health, parks, highways. We desire to buy more of our economic needs communally with tax dollars. The tax assessments tend much more to be levied against income and wealth than against numbers of children.

Each family, rich or poor, experiences, relatively, a smaller cost per child of its own than the costs which the child inflicts on society. That is, the tax bill the family experiences is virtually the same whether *that family* has another child or not. But while the error in calculation occurs in every family, it is of much greater influence for poor families than for rich ones. In the rich family the economic elements of the calculation of benefit versus cost in having another child are of smaller importance to family welfare as compared to psychic elements, simply because economic income is very high and marginal dollars of small utility. In the poor family, contrariwise, the availability of public services for children at no cost, particularly education and health, make it possible for them to decide to have children whom otherwise they would not choose to bear and raise. Also, in addition to the stronger incentive from low cost, the children of families of low income are a substitute for pecuniary income and the pleasures money can buy.

In summary, on the above reasoning, overpopulation may result, *ceteris paribus*, in an individualistic society in which the overall society bears a significant portion of the cost of their rearing.[1]

OBLIGATION TO CONSERVE NATURAL RESOURCES FOR ECONOMIC WELFARE OF FUTURE GENERATIONS

In this section we concentrate on productivity and economics. In the next, we consider environmental damage.

It is widely believed that natural resources should be physically conserved by all means, for otherwise the future will be economically impoverished. Renewable resources should not be drawn down but should be used at the highest possible level of sustained physical yield. Non-renewable resources should be used only after renewable resources are fully employed – water power before coal, for example. Physical waste should be reduced wherever it is found. Current production should be constrained to retard the depletion of non-renewable resources. So far as it is necessary to achieve these objectives, the economic freedom of private property owners, producers, and consumers – specifically freedom to engage in those short-horizon, self-interested behaviour patterns which destroy resources or deplete them rapidly under laissez faire – should be restricted in favour of government regulation or ownership.

All of the foregoing is based on the premise that each society should leave the next generation economically as well off as possible and no less well off than it is. But for this objective preservation of specific natural resources is unlikely to be the efficient means. Resource reservation, if not economically meritorious on current calculations, will reduce the economic value of output through time. It may, by curbing research and capital formation, have a perverse effect on future output and welfare.

It is by no means necessary to reduce production today in order to increase production tomorrow. If, instead, current production is maintained and consumption is reduced in favour of research and investment, future production will be increased. Higher production today, if it also means more research and invest-

---

1 We have ignored the possibility that there might be social benefits beyond those counted by the specific family. Da Vinci, Beethoven, Einstein, and other geniuses have enriched society beyond the pleasures which they provided for themselves and their immediate families.

ment today, thus will serve the economic interest of future generations better than reservation of resources and lower current production.

The premise that the economic heritage will shrink in value unless natural resources are conserved is wrong for a progressive world. The opposite is true. In the United States, for example, over the period for which data exist, the economic magnitude of the estate each generation passes on – the income per capita the next generation enjoys – has been approximately double that which it received. Therefore, resource reservation to protect the economic interest of future generations is unnecessary. There is no need for a future-oriented ethical principle to replace or supplement the economic calculations that lead modern man to accumulate primarily for the benefit of those now living. The reason, of course, is that the legacy of economically valuable assets which each generation passes on consists only in part of the natural environment. The more important components of the inheritance are knowledge, technology, capital instruments, and economic institutions. Far more than natural resources, these are the determinants of real income per capita. Even with respect to natural-resource wealth alone, as Edmund Jones remarked at the White House Conference of Governors which dealt with conservation in 1908, 'we shall add far more to our natural resources by developing our ability to increase them than we can ever do by mere processes of saving'.

If those now living devote themselves to improving society's productive power and also its capacity to reach decisions concerning the use of that power which will increasingly benefit themselves and their children, the value of the economic heritage will grow continually. To increase current real income, physical capital is accumulated. To satisfy his curiosity, man adds to society's intellectual capital. To enrich its own life, each generation strives to improve the health and education of its children, thereby augmenting society's human capital. And, in consequence of efforts to improve society's functioning as a productive enterprise, economic institutions and standards are rendered more effective. By devoting itself to improving the lot of the living, therefore, each generation whether recognizing a future-oriented obligation to do so or not, transmits a more productive world to those who follow.

CONGESTION AND ENVIRONMENTAL DAMAGE

A more productive world is not necessarily a better world, however. In a progressive society, current rational calculations may suffice to serve the purely economic interests of the future as well as the present. But a serious non-economic problem – environmental damage – has become of major concern, concurrent with man's strong progress in solution of his economic problems. Indeed, it is largely because of the economic and technological successes of modern industrial societies and the processes by which they occur that environmental damages have become obtrusive and oppressive.

John Stuart Mill foresaw this difficulty more than a century ago in the following gentle plea:

> *There is room in the world, no doubt, and even in old countries, for a great increase of population, supposing the arts of life to go on improving, and capital to increase. But even if innocuous, I confess I see very little reason for desiring it... A population may be too crowded, though all be amply supplied with food and raiment. It is not good for man to be kept perforce at all times*

in the presence of his species. A world from which solitude is extirpated, is a very poor ideal. Solitude, in the sense of being often alone, is essential to any depth of meditation or of character; and solitude in the presence of natural beauty and grandeur, is the cradle of thoughts and aspirations which are not only good for the individual, but which society could ill do without. Nor is there much satisfaction in contemplating the world with nothing left to the spontaneous activity of nature; with every rood of land brought into cultivation, which is capable of growing food for human beings; every flowery waste or natural pasture ploughed up, all quadrupeds or birds which are not domesticated for man's use exterminated as his rivals for food, every hedgerow or superfluous tree rooted out, and scarcely a place left where a wild shrub or flower could grow without being eradicated as a weed in the name of improved agriculture.[2]

Alan Paton and Henry Beston have posed the dilemma for modern industrial societies poetically:

The grass is rich and matted, you cannot see the soil. It holds the rain and the mist, and they seep into the ground, feeding the streams in every kloof. It is well tended, and not too many fires burn it laying bare the soil. Stand unshod upon it, for the ground is holy being even as it came from the Creator. Keep it, guard it, care for it, for it keeps men, guards men, cares for men, Destroy it and man is destroyed.[3]

For man is of a quickening spirit and the earth, the strong, incoming tides and rhythms of nature move in his blood and being; he is an emanation of that journeying god the sun, born anew in the pale South and the hollow winter, the slow murmur and the long crying of the seas are in his veins, the influences of the moon, and the sound of rain beginning. Torn from earth and unaware, without the beauty and the terror, the mystery, and ecstacy so rightfully his, man is a vagrant in space, desperate for the inhuman meaninglessness which has opened about him, and with his every step becoming less than man. Peace with the earth is the first peace.[4]

The essence of the population-environmental damage problem is this. A couple implicitly tallies its prospective benefit-cost accounts in considering whether to have another child. It counts in the cost or disadvantage column the fact that the home will be a bit more crowded, that more clothes will have to be washed, that the plumbing will be worked a bit harder, etc. But it does not take into account in its decision to have a child the fact that the child may make the city more crowded, that a grove of trees will be cut to provide more housing, that more highways will have to be built. Even less will the accounts comprehend that, in order to avoid diminishing returns concurrent with increasing population, society will undertake industrial and technological changes which further increase congestion, the volumes of pollutants, and land disfigurement. These costs will not significantly enter the decision calculus on having a child for two reasons. First, that particular prospective child will contribute only imperceptibly to the city crowding, the increase in pavements, the loss of forests, etc. And second, the burden of even that tiny increase in city congestion will be shared by all the inhabitants of the

---

2 J S Mill, *Principles of Political Economy*, Book 4, Chapter 6.
3 Alan Paton, *Cry, the Beloved Country*, Chapter 1, p3.
4 Henry Beston, *Herbs and the Earth*, quoted by David McCord in *Harvard Today* (spring 1969).

city, not carried alone by the parents who beget him.

Each family will count no social cost in environmental deterioration in deciding to have another child. But from the aggregate of their decisions will indeed come congestion, pollution, etc, if the parents more than reproduce their own numbers. It is as if each person would stand on tiptoe in a parade so *he* could see better; or throw *his* candy wrapper in the street because obviously his candy wrapper alone would not clutter the landscape; or burn his leaves since obviously his doing so will not pollute the air much.

Some private actions – leaf burning or littering – which inflict social costs or burdens on society can be prevented by law. Other private actions are impossible or extraordinarily difficult to prevent by law. Begetting children is in the latter category. Laws which deny parents the opportunity to have children are not present in modern societies. The decision is virtually always a private, parental one.

However, society, through government actions and private groups, can exert substantial persuasion upon couples to limit their begetting. Indeed, most modern governments, religions, and medical groups, and a number of foundations and other private agencies strongly encourage and assist couples in family planning or planned parenthood. Undoubtedly, these efforts do significantly reduce the number of births, and from that the extent of environmental deterioration is somewhat reduced. But family planning has as its purpose encouraging couples to have only the number of children *they* personally desire and they personally can care for. Rational family planning does not treat or solve at all the dilemma in which environmental damage from a family decision to have a child will be borne by the whole society and not by the family which made the decision.

In summary, *ceteris paribus*, there is a very great likelihood that population growth will not be adequately restrained by the fact of environmental deterioration. There is no reason for the individual family to believe that the damage it experiences in its environment will be less if *it* refrains from having a child. Families will therefore not restrain their begetting children for this reason. This applies even if individual family planning or planned parenthood becomes universal and highly rational. Aside from enacting laws to overcome the population over-pressure on environment, it appears that governments, religions, and foundations have not even recognized that this is a problem which cannot be handled by present concepts of rational family planning or planned parenthood.

Finally, we must note that the problem of population over-production causing environmental problems has a most troublesome time dimension. If the problem is a serious one at all, then it is serious for future generations as well as present ones and indeed a greater threat to the future than to the present. Each pair of children now born in excess of the number which merely stabilizes population increases congestion by two people during their childhoods. The congestion continues for their whole lives. And then they further increase congestion in their adulthood by the number of children which they in turn beget in excess of the population maintenance rate. In this sense the environmental damage consequence of population growth is a threat which is more harsh than the effects of population growth on output per capita. We noted earlier that society's output per capita was reduced only during the period of childhood, *ceteris paribus*, and was then restored when children became workers. This is not so for environmental congestion and damage, which endures as long as the incremental people do.

UNDERDEVELOPED COUNTRIES

To this point we have discussed only the advanced nations. But the world's population problem includes the underdeveloped countries as well. Indeed, much more than half of the world's population lives there. How should we modify and supplement the foregoing analysis to account for population in underdeveloped countries?

Three attributes of such economies cause us to be greatly concerned about their population increases during the next few generations. These are:

1. The desperate shortage of capital, as a factor of production and carrier of improved technology.
2. The high birth rate.
3. The great increase in population from gains in longevity.

We discuss each attribute in turn:

1. *Capital shortage.* In the advanced countries, increased capital per worker and improved capital devices are major in overcoming diminishing returns when population increases. In the underdeveloped countries, shortage of capital limits the extent to which increased population can be accommodated without significantly retarding gains in worker productivity. If population increases too fast, there is too little gain in capital per worker, and also too much of the scarce capital must be diverted to providing public services. Even as in an advanced economy, children absorb resources during childhood. But in the underdeveloped economy the impact of this diversion on worker productivity, technological change, and improved education is much harsher. There results, if population accretions are large, a much slower rate of gain in output per capita than would otherwise be the case.
2. *High birth rates.* The birth rates in underdeveloped countries are high for a variety of reasons, including less rationality, capacity, and will for family planning. Also, children are social insurance for the parents' old age, and they provide psychic income in the families who are poor in economic goods. And there are other reasons, such as a decline in family responsibility when a peasant economy is disrupted by outside contacts. The high birth rates impede capital formation for industry and education, technological advance, and progress toward low birth rates. They also increase more than proportionately the size of the dependent, non-working population.
3. *Longevity.* The average length of life in underdeveloped countries is now quite low. From worldwide public health measures and medical advances, as well as from the beginnings of economic development, longevity is trending upward. From longevity gains, ceteris paribus, we can anticipate very great increases in population in these countries over the next few generations. If life expectancy at birth increased from say, 30 years to 50 or 60 years, it is obvious that the leverage on population numbers is very great. This is so even if the birth rate were to fall to two children per female child ever born, a rate which, in the absence of longevity change, would merely maintain the population at a constant level. However, as just discussed, birth rates in these countries considerably exceed this maintenance level and thus populations will increase from births and longevity. While the longevity gains are

253

favourable in the sense that they provide more workers, they also provide more parents of child-bearing age, and there is also more capital needed to maintain and improve productivity.

4. *Summary.* Populations in underdeveloped countries will be subject to considerable increase in the next couple of generations due to large longevity gains, high birth rates, and slow rates of economic progress. Assume that there is no severe thermonuclear war. Assume also that advanced nations will continue to assist the underdeveloped ones in public health and economic aid. Then it is virtually impossible that the population of presently underdeveloped nations would not increase enormously. The increase relative to the populations of the presently advanced countries will be large.

Despite the economic development-population increase difficulty, the economic history of the past 100 years tells us that economic advance does occur in the underdeveloped nations. The burst in world population size until each nation achieves a literate, educated, and economically advanced society is likely to be the end of the population explosion. Population may increase thereafter, but it will be at a more deliberate pace and with more deliberation. For, with literacy, education, and economic development, and the ready availability of safe and efficient contraceptives, should come the rationality of family planning or planned parenthood, as it has already come to couples in the presently advanced nations. It would seem inevitable that the individual family would come to see advantage in limiting children's births to the number they could economically and psychologically properly care for. This is what has been happening in the presently advanced nations to all races, religions, and colours as contraceptive technology and availability have improved. Why should it not occur in the newer nations as they develop? It may be that population will not stabilize, but if it advances the increase will not be heedless on the part of couples.

The social and political world structures will, however, be much changed from today. Longevity gains are of trivial size, and the birth rates are lower in the advanced countries, The international political, social, economic, and racial consequences of the disparity in rates of growth among nations could be substantial. Far more than now the future world population will be Asiatic and African, yellow or brown or black, ambitious and aggressive in the new nations, experimental in economic systems, and quite divergent from the political philosophy of Bentham, Mill, or Jefferson, and of the United States and Western Europe.

TIME DIMENSIONS

It is frequently stated that population growth must be quickly brought under control; that the population bomb which can destroy the world has a short fuse. As compared with my view that populations will eventually level off or rise only slowly, others claim that there is not time.

Let us consider the time problem. We use the present rate of annual world population growth of about 2 per cent per year. This gain rate includes both the effects of improved longevity and of birth rates in excess of what would be required merely to replace deaths and hold population constant if there were no changes in length of life. At this rate, population would double in about 35 years. Thus, the present world population of almost 3.5 billions would become almost 7 billions in the year 2005. Relatively, more of the increases would occur in the presently underdeveloped countries. For example, population in Asia and Africa is increasing at about 2 per cent per year and in Latin America at 3 per cent per year. At the time that longevity reaches 60 or 70 years in these underdeveloped areas, population gain from increase in length of life will become unimportant, and the rate of population increase will be much lower.

What of birth rates? Each decade more countries climb the development ladder. As they progress, according to the record of economic history, literacy and education improve, knowledge of and access to birth control become available, family incentives to planned parenthood increase, and individual families tend to move toward rationality in family planning. Thus, as we move through time, we also move in development, education, social change, and all other attributes of progressive societies. Increasingly, as literacy, education, and access to contraceptives improve, so does rational family planning. More and more does reproduction take on attributes we call 'humane and rational' – that is, foresight, compassion, and deliberation.

How, then, can we believe that 'there is not time'? How can we believe that in a developed society parents will choose to have children whom they expect to be unable to support, care for, sustain? Increasingly, each child is born out of a specific act of will. If only there be rationality in the intent, future population increase is no greater economic danger than it has been over the past 100 years or so in Europe, the United States, and other advanced societies where the economic standard of living has risen steadily. Growth of population numbers is not, in itself, an evil. It is only if there are, on balance, adverse effects that it merits social concern.

We conclude that an average population growth rate of any size does not march on with independent force all of its own. Malthus and Ricardo thought it did, to the very limit of animal existence. But this was because the great bulk of their society, recently torn and disrupted by the Industrial Revolution, had not yet emerged from its brutal state, from brutish satisfaction of subsistence and sexual hungers, and because there was absence of contraceptive devices, knowledge, or reason. The birth rate in advanced societies will be what people decide it to be, each night, each year, each generation. Intelligent, rational people will determine the statistic; the statistic does not generate the people. In modern societies, the biological and psychological forces toward reproduction are tempered by contraceptives and intelligence. It is not reproduction which should be feared, but inadequate knowledge, lack of reason, and mind-dulling poverty.

If we play out the numbers we began with earlier, from a growth rate of 2 per cent per year, the 7 billions of year 2005 would, *if the growth rate held constant*, that is, assumedly overcoming cessation of gains from improved longevity by large increase in birth rate), become almost 14 billions in 2040. This seems like a large figure to me. If I were present (in spirit) and were to be asked, I would advise the grandchildren of my great-grandchildren that it seemed to me that there were a lot more people in the world than there were when I was a boy and more than I would have thought desirable.

A major point, however, is that each future generation will choose its own birth rate. It will do so, not mindlessly as a grasshopper horde, without regard for available vegetation, but individually, with explicit regard to its own and its children's welfare. As our generation in this rich country has chosen to change the relation of man, society, and nature, so may our descendants in their own

255

fashion change this relation. It is naïve to expect future societies to choose a statistical birth rate according to our preferences. Neither their birth rate nor their environmental management is our decision. We have enough to do in sensibly managing our own birth rates and our own environments without presuming we are or should be making these decisions for future generations. The fear that there is not time because of diminishing returns is not well placed. The difficulty is not diminishing returns.

The difficulty is that the world, states, and even cities are becoming ungovernable, because of pressures which advanced technology and economic power place on political systems and governmental structures conceived in an earlier age. The real problem, I suggest, is that the technologically advanced world which has given us increasing returns has also released problems which so far our societies and governments have not learned to handle. These include, for example, international disorder and holocaust, revolution and civil wars in nations, and violence in cities. They also include environmental congestion and damage related in part to greatly increased population numbers.

CONCLUSIONS

For a technologically advanced world there is no reason to believe, because of population growth, that diminishing returns will have set in, that there will be a shortage of natural resources for production of extractive goods, or that income per capita will not be at high levels. The economic future, as I see it, will have a much larger world population, literate and educated populations in all nations, and incomes per capita ranging from the present levels in Western Europe upward.

In summary, I foresee the world with a population problem of the type which presently exists in the advanced countries. The population difficulties will be:

(a) that very large availabilities of public and social services for children without explicit cost to the children's specific parents induces a larger birth rate than would otherwise occur;
(b) that national societies do not have the governmental capabilities to restrict the birth rate in order to avoid undue environmental congestion and deterioration; and
(c) that in the world society composed of sovereign nation-states, there exist no world governmental capabilities for limiting population growth, just as there are not in the world society effective capabilities for limiting arms, or reliably preventing nuclear war, or avoiding other catastrophes or serious problems.

REFERENCES

Beston, Henry (1935) *Herbs and the Earth*, Garden City, NY: Doubleday.
Mill, John Stuart (1848) *Principles of Political Economy*, London.
Paton, Alan (1950) *Cry, the Beloved Country*, New York: Charles Scribner.

Chapter 22

Population and the Environment: The Scientific Evidence

Samuel H Preston

INTRODUCTION

My assigned task is to review the scientific evidence linking population growth and environmental change. Clearly, I can only provide a brief introduction to this vast topic.

I will focus on the broad sweep of what we think we know and why we think we know it. The emphasis is on the quality of evidence available, evaluated according to what I take to be conventional scientific standards. This seems an appropriate emphasis in a meeting of the world's scientific academies. Unfortunately, the subject of population growth is one in which evidence is often intermingled with sentiment, strained metaphors, and apocalyptic visions.

As in any scientific evaluation, when we are examining evidence, we are dealing with the past. We look to the historical record in search of demographic footprints. We cannot look to the future for evidence. Computer simulations and projections of relations among populations, environments, and economies are useful for many purposes, but they are not evidence in the conventional sense; they are collections of hypotheses. Whether the hypotheses make any sense, individually or collectively, can only be evaluated by examining the historical record.

We have to begin by recognizing that the subject with which we are dealing is not one where investigators are permitted the luxury of controlled experimentation: thank goodness, I might add. Instead, they must attempt to interpret naturally-occurring events using research designs that come as close as possible to recapitulating the logic of experimental methods, so that they can try to establish cause and effect relationships. I have to say, however, that research designs in this area have not been notably ambitious. Most of what we know or think we know is a result of what can be called 'informed observation' – that is, observation informed by what are usually very primitive, though often serviceable, models of human behaviour. The data on which these observations are based are usually very slim in the environmental area.

Nevertheless, I believe that what we know at present supports the position that population growth has contributed and is contributing to a variety of environmental changes. Some, but not all, of these changes would be classified as ailments or degradations. These undoubtedly include the destruction of forests, especially tropical forests; soil erosion and degradation in certain major regions, especially within sub-Saharan Africa, and the loss of species of plants and animals.

BIOLOGICAL MODELS

Food Production and Agrarian Resources

Let me be as explicit as possible about the model and evidence that supports the conclusion that the expansion of human numbers contributed to deforestation, soil degradation, and species loss. The basic element of the model recognizes man's prodigious need for food. To support more people, more food must be produced. To produce more food, more resources are required in food production. Some of these resources – in fact, the most important – are men's and women's labour, which is available in rough proportion to population size. But other resources include land and water. With more people, more of these resources will be devoted to food production, and fewer will be permitted to remain in their natural state or used for other purposes.

This model is so commonsensical that describing it may seem gratuitous, but I think that it is useful to acknowledge that what we think we know is based not only on empirical evidence but on evidence interpreted in light of this primitive model. The evidence on which the conclusion is based is, first of all, that patterns of land use have changed dramatically as human numbers have expanded. Forests that covered nearly all of Europe in AD900 had virtually disappeared by 1900. They were converted primarily into agricultural fields and pastures to feed Europe's growing population (Wolman 1993). A similar process is occurring on a much-compressed time scale in most developing countries today. Sixteen million square kilometres of tropical forest have been reduced to eight over the last four decades, according to Norman Myers. The most significant agent of forest destruction is the encroachment of slash-and-burn cultivators (Myers 1991).

So there is clearly an association over time between population growth and loss of forest. There is also an association over space. During the 1970's, the correlation between a nation's rate of population growth and its proportionate change in forested area was –0.56 for 41 counties in the humid tropics (Grainger 1990; Mather 1987). These associations are what we would expect if population growth were driving the search for additional resources to be used in food production.

Associations do not establish causation, of course. We are convinced that we understand the direction of causation because we interpret it in light of the model I described. One alternative explanation of these associations is that both population growth and changes in land use were a product of a third factor, a change in productive technology. This interpretation is implausible, however, because the technology of forest clearance for food production is one of the oldest known to man. Furthermore, the acceleration in population growth rates is not for the most part attributable to changes in productive technology, but to the development and diffusion of methods to combat man's greatest natural enemy, disease-inducing microbes: bacteria, viruses, and parasites (Preston 1980). These were nature's first line of defence against the expansion of *Homo sapiens*. That line has been decisively breached. What we are essentially talking about at this meeting is man's assault on nature's second line of defence, the physical environment.

The changes in landscape that I have noted are not an unalloyed disaster for humans, although they certainly are for many other species. In traditional Western thought, the wilderness was the useless and threatening home of wolves and bandits. Civilization came with the clearing of forests for permanent cultivation. It was only with the Romantic movement that the wilderness became potentially attractive and amusing (McNicoll 1993). Furthermore, the transformation of forest and swamp into cultivated land in Europe was not accompanied by soil degradation but, in general, by maintenance or improvement of soil quality (Wolman 1993; Ruttan 1993).

The situation is quite different in tropical areas. The population is growing at 2–3 per cent a year, rather than less than 1 per cent a year, a rate that was typical of Europe during its period of landscape transformation. This slower pace permitted the evolution of institutions and practices aimed at soil protection – for example, the enclosure movement (North and Thomas 1973). Furthermore, food production is less receptive to intensification in tropical areas because the soil is less responsive to additional applications of fertilizer (National Research Council 1986) and, in many cases, capital that would be necessary for agriculture intensification is lacking. The result is that, relative to Europe, the response to population growth in these areas more often takes the form of occupying new land rather than of intensifying production on old land (Grainger 1990). Not infrequently, these new lands are located in ecologically sensitive areas that are unusually vulnerable to permanent degradation, but the old lands are also more vulnerable to intensification in tropical areas because of soil and climatic conditions (Lele and Stone 1989). The combined effects of extensification and intensification, as estimated by the World Resources Institute (1993), are that agricultural activities have removed about 15 per cent of organic carbon from the world's soil. Some 70,000 square kilometres of farmland are being abandoned each year because of soil exhaustion.

Data on species loss are notoriously poor (Simon and Wilavsky 1984), but the logic of accelerated loss is nevertheless compelling. Tropical forests have a much greater abundance of plant and animal species than do temperate forests, and it is tropical forests that are now disappearing most rapidly. In most cases, no agency is present to protect other species, in part because tropical forests are at the outer bounds of administrative structures. This is not evidence so much as it is theory, but the theory is sound. Nevertheless, the huge range of estimates of the rate of species loss is troublesome. For most purposes, even ethical accountancy, it matters whether the rate of loss is 100 per year or 100,000.

Industrial Production

Man does not live by bread alone, and expanded human numbers are also accompanied by increased demand for other goods and services. The production and consumption of these goods and services very frequently has environmental implications as well. In particular, air and water resources often serve as a repository or sink for the by-products of production. How much population growth contributes to the pollution of these resources has not, however, been established with any degree of precision.

Most analysts approach this question with the I = PAT equation, wherein the environmental impact is expressed as a product of population size, production per capita, and impact per unit of production. There are many problems with the way this equation has been used. It ignores interactions among the elements – for example, the effect of population growth on per capita production (Demeny 1991) and the clear tendency of more affluent nations to choose technologies that are less polluting. The World Bank's *World Development Report* for 1992 focused on the environment. Contrary to the implications of this formula, it concluded that higher levels of affluence were associated with lower levels of pollution and resource degradation. The formula is also very sensitive to the level of aggregation at which it is implemented. At present, population growth is concentrated in those regions where the impact multiplier of population growth is very low. Wolfgang Lutz (1992) has shown that failure to account for this regional pattern will lead to an overestimation of population's impact on carbon dioxide emissions by a factor of four.

But the most disappointing feature of this formula is that it defines away the issue. Whatever impact is on the left-hand side, the contribution of population growth to it will always be the same, equal to whatever the proportionate change in population is. The formula could have been written in terms of total production and the impact of each unit of production, in which case population would disappear from the accounting altogether. This kind of arbitrariness clearly violates normal standards of science.

Why this analytic problem is much less acute for analysis of food production and the resources devoted to it goes back to our recognition of biological requirements. People require at least 2200 calories a day for metabolism and basic activities, and resources *must* be reshuffled to ensure that these requirements are met. Otherwise, the population could not expand. This requirement simply does not come into play when we are dealing with automobile emissions or chlorofluorocarbons. We are left with the vague feeling that population growth is probably related to environmental pollution, but unable to say exactly how. Our research designs simply have not been up to the task.

SOCIAL MODELS

But we have gone about as far as a primitive biological model can take us. *Homo sapiens* is an intelligent, problem-solving, sociable and co-operative species. These features vastly complicate analysis of the relationship between population growth and environmental change. For example, food demands need not be satisfied within the ecological system whose population is growing but can be met by trade with other regions. People tend to move from areas with fewer economic opportunities to those with more. The smaller the area under study, the more confused these relations become, in part because local features influence population change. It is often no longer possible to treat population change as entirely exogenous, the feature that allows us to approximate the experimental method and to speak with more confidence at the global or highly aggregative level.

Institutions

In moving beyond the biological model, it is important to recognize that humans create institutions that can mitigate the environmental impact of population growth. The most important of these institutions are those that govern ownership and access to natural resources, especially land. Over and over again in the literature, one finds that land tenure systems, which in many instances provide incentives for resource preservation, are a key variable conditioning the relationship between population growth and land use changes. These are stressed, for example, in a recent World Bank (1990) report on the population/agriculture/environment nexus in sub-Saharan Africa. In some places in Africa, ownership rights are acquired simply by clearing land. In other places, farmers who let their land lie fallow risk losing their ownership rights. In still other places, incentives for high fertility are provided by systems in which the allocation of land is a function of family size. In all of these instances, land tenure systems are not functioning effectively to preserve land resources for future generations. Examples are also provided where granting land ownership outright to farmers has led to the development and improvement of land resources by virtue of the incentives that owners acquire for land preservation.

Perhaps the most vivid such example is Michael Mortimore's (1993) careful analysis of environmental change in northern Nigeria. Mortimore has taken extensive samples of soil quality in a densely settled agrarian zone of rapid population growth in 1977 and 1990. He finds no evidence of soil deterioration during this period. Furthermore, the soil quality is equivalent to that in an uncultivated area with comparable ecological features. He concludes that 'population growth and high population density are compatible with sustainable resource management by smallholders' (Mortimore 1993, p62). Where soil preservation is less successful, he suggests, incentives must be found for small holders to invest in it, above all by providing secure ownership rights.

This is not the only example where population growth has proven compatible with sustainable resource management. The padi system for growing rice in Asia was developed in the 11th and 12th centuries and provided not only constant but increasing yields for nearly a thousand years (Wolman 1993). The potential for increased yields may now, however, be nearly fully exploited in the highest yield regions of Japan (Ruttan 1993).

The role of social institutions in environmental protection is also highlighted by a comparison of forest resources in China and Japan (Mather 1986). In China, the pressure of population on land resources, combined with weak administrative structures, led peasants to pursue short-term strategies of forest clearance. By the 19th century, the country had been almost entirely denuded of its forest cover. In Japan, on the other hand, the increasing demand for timber beginning in the 17th century was accompanied by an awareness of the adverse effects of deforestation. First the lords and later the imperial government prevented extensive depletion of forest cover. Since 1900, two-thirds of the forests have been in the hands of public institutions where they have been effectively preserved. Establishing clear lines of resource ownership is hardly a panacea, however. In many parts of Latin America, for example, the best land is heavily concentrated in the hands of large landowners whose output is sold mainly to the United States. Population growth must be accommodated disproportionately in marginal areas where resources are more vulnerable to degradation (Stonich 1989; Durham 1979).

In addition to land tenure systems that may provide incentives for land preservation, a second factor that affects the preservation of resources is the availability of credit. If farmers must borrow at real interest rates of 20 per cent, or cannot borrow at all, they will not undertake the investments required to maintain soil fertility, especially if the return from such investments is only 15 per cent.

Unfortunately, ownership rights are typically most ambiguous, administrative structures weakest, and credit markets most inefficient in the frontier areas of developing countries where forests are being destroyed. While it is useful to note that human institutions can intervene to prevent degradation, it is not realistic to suppose that such institutions will flourish in these areas. Mortimore (1993), in fact, suggests that resource degradation is actually more common in low-density areas and is often reversed when higher densities are achieved. While this claim holds out hope for the longer term, there is little doubt that continued population growth in the shorter term increases the risk of continued deforestation and resource degradation in marginal areas.

Other Factors and Policy Options

Population growth is not the only factor capable of affecting the extent of resource degradation. Depending on time, place, and criterion, it may not be the most important factor. The World Bank's (1990) review of population/environment/agriculture linkages in sub-Saharan Africa lists a huge array of obstacles to expanded food production and better resource management. These include not only land tenure and credit systems, but also biased agricultural prices and exchange rates, adverse tax policies, weak agricultural extension services, excessive government control, and civil wars; but few if any of these problems will be resolved through rapid population growth. They are the context on which this growth will be imposed. According to the Bank, they have the effect of compelling growing populations to exploit ever more extensively the resources available.

Because they have multiple origins, it would be foolhardy to think that problems of food production and resource maintenance can or should be solved by population policy alone. There are times when certain biologists and ecologists appear to take this position. The reason is, I think, they are too wedded to the primitive, biological model of human beings, whereby humans are distinguished from ants or seagulls only by their greater capacity for ecological destruction. While this model helps us understand certain features of resource use, it is entirely inadequate as a guide to policy because it ignores the vast repertoire of social arrangements that humans have constructed to govern their behaviour. Problems of poverty and resource degradation have multiple sources and admit to multiple forms of intervention.

The attractiveness of population policy in this array – and here I refer specifically to voluntaristic family-planning programmes – is that they are relatively cheap and, by assisting couples to have the number of children they desire, help to advance private goals as well as social goals. It is easy to forget in these large-scale discussions of population issues that private goals and social goals are often one and the same. For excellent reasons, most of the world's vital resources are privately owned and managed. The most important questions of population and resource balance in India should ultimately be answered not by the government's deciding whether it wants 1.4 or 1.6 billion people in 2040, but by millions of Indian couples deciding whether they want to divide their plot and patrimony among two, three or four heirs. Family-planning programmes provide the means whereby population size and resources can be better balanced at the family level. They will not resolve all issues of population and environmental relations, but they surely deserve a prominent place in the array of policy initiatives.

REFERENCES

Demeny, P (1991) 'Tradeoffs between human numbers and material standards of living', in *Resources, Environment, and Population: Present Knowledge, Future Options*, ed K Davis and M. Bernstam, New York: Oxford University Press.

Durham, W (1979) *Scarcity and Survival in Central America: The Ecological Origins of the Soccer War*, Stanford, Calif.: Stanford University Press.

Grainger, A (1990) 'Population as a concept and parameter in the modelling of tropical land use change', presented at the Population–Environment Dynamics Symposium, University of Michigan, Ann Arbor, Oct 1-3.

Lele, U and S W Stone (1989) *Population Pressure, the Environment and Agricultural Intensification: Variations on the Boserup Hypothesis*. MADIA Discussion Part 4, Washington DC: World Bank.

Lutz, W (1992) 'Population and environment: what do we need more urgently, better data, better models, or better questions?' presented at the Annual Conference of the British Society for Population Studies, Exeter College, Oxford University, September 9-11.

Mather, A S (1987) 'Global trends in forest resources', *Geography* 72, no 1 (January), pp1-15.

McNicoll, G (1993) 'Malthusian scenarios and demographic catastrophism', Research Division Working Paper no 49, The Population Council, New York.

Mortimore, M (1993) 'Northern Nigeria: land transformation under agricultural intensification', in *Population Growth and Land Use Change in Developing Countries: Report of a Workshop*, ed C Jolly and B B Torrey, Washington DC: National Academy Press.

Myers, N (1991) 'The world's forests and human populations: the environmental interconnections', in *Resources, Environment, and Population: Present Knowledge, Future Options*, ed K Davis and M Bernstam, New York: Oxford University Press.

National Research Council (1986) *Population Growth and Economic Development: Policy Questions*, Washington, DC: National Academy Press.

National Research Council, (1991) *Policy Implications of Greenhouse Warming*, Washington, DC: National Academy Press.

North, D D and R P Thomas (1973) *The Rise of the Western World: A New Economic History*, Cambridge: Cambridge University Press.

Preston, S H (1980) 'Causes and consequences of mortality change in less developed during the twentieth century', in *Population and Economic Change in Developing Countries*, ed. R. Easterlin, Chicago: University of Chicago Press.

Ruttan, V (1993) 'Population Growth, environmental change, and innovation: implications for sustainable growth in agriculture', in *Population Growth and Land Use Change in Developing Countries: Report of a Workshop*, ed. C. Jolly and B B Torrey, Washington DC: National Academy Press.

Simon, J and A Wildavsky (1984) 'On species loss, the absence of data, and risks to humanity', in *The Resourceful Earth: A Response to Global 2000*, ed J Simon and H Kahn, New York: Basil Blackwell.

Stonich, S C (1989) 'Processes and environmental destruction: a Central American case study', *Population and Development Review* 15: pp269-296.

Wolman, M (1993) 'Population, land use, and environment: a long history', in *Population Growth and Land Use Change in Developing Countries: Report of a Workshop*, ed C Jolly and B B Torrey, Washington DC: National Academy Press.

World Bank (1990) *The Population, Agriculture and Environment Nexus in Sub-Saharan Africa*. Working Paper, World Bank Africa Region. Washington, DC

 – (1992) *World Development Report: Development and the Environment*, Washington, DC

World Resources Institute (1993) *Population and the Environment*, Washington, DC

Chapter 23

The Second Tragedy of the Commons

Ronald D Lee

Some people justify population-control policies on the grounds that population growth reduces economic well-being. It is not clear, however, whether population growth strongly affects such economic variables as prices, incomes, unemployment, balance of trade, saving and investment, and economic growth. Recent assessments find the evidence weak and conflicting (World Bank 1984; National Research Council 1986; Kelley 1988). Of course, many potential consequences of population growth would not be caught in the net of economic statistics, which mainly reflect the goods and services passing through markets. The most serious consequences of population growth may well be those afflicting non-market resources, particularly environmental resources and amenities. While pressure on such resources, if unabated, must eventually affect production and the economy, it need not do so discernibly for a considerable time. Analysis is further complicated because many environmental consequences are global and therefore are not evident in international comparisons of performance.

In any event, even if population growth were known to reduce the well-being of future generations, it would not automatically follow that such growth should be slowed. After all, individual couples choose their family size with full knowledge that children are costly, and that more children mean fewer parental resources available for each, and lower per capita income in the household. Is the societal view of the trade-off between numbers and well-being, now and in the future, anything beyond the sum total of the parental views, which are implicitly represented in their individual decision-making about fertility? Some may argue 'yes', that society should take a better informed, less selfish, intergenerationally more egalitarian, and longer run view than individual parents. Perhaps this is so. But we will see that laissez-faire in family size can lead to a socially undesirable outcome even when social goals are no different from those of parents.

The discrepancy between the laissez-faire outcome and the socially optimal outcome arises because of 'externalities to child-bearing' – that is, costs and benefits of children that are passed on by the parents to society at large. When all assets are privately owned and there are no public sector and no public goods, then such externalities do not arise.[1] In the real world there are many exceptions to these conditions (see Lee, 1988a), and externalities to child-bearing are perva-

---

1 Actually, even in this case externalities may arise because the birth rate alters the population growth rate and age distribution, which influence the rate of interest. See Lee (1980 and 1988b), and Eckstein and Wolpin (1985). However, when a recursive altruistic utility function is assumed, as in Willis (1987) and Nerlove et al (1987), externalities do not occur in this case.

sive. Among the most important are environmental externalities, since many enjoyable and productive aspects of the environment are not privately owned: air-shed, water-shed, ozone layer, parks, climate, freedom from noise, and so on.

What are the connections among future well-being, family size externalities, and the environment? Garrett Hardin sketched them in a seminal 1968 article, writing eloquently of the 'tragedy of the commons' as a metaphor for the population problem. At one time, he suggested, all villagers could freely graze their cattle on the commons. Self-interest led each villager to add more cattle until the incremental private gain to doing so fell to zero. Although each additional cow reduced the food for all other cows and thereby diminished their value, this total reduction was spread thinly over the many individual villagers, so that those adding cows bore only a small fraction of the cost. In this way, the social gains from adding cows were always less than the individual gains, and they turned negative well before the individual gains did. Consequently, the commons was overused and degraded, and each villager fared worse than he or she could have, if use had been generally lower. In this case, even if the social goal is nothing other than maximization of individual welfare, rational individual behaviour will not lead to the social optimum, which can be reached only by collective regulation of use.

'Common property resources' are often taken to be those for which markets are absent or poorly developed, as in Hardin's parable. In fact, in the past such resources have typically been efficiently managed by the communities that shared their use (Runge, 1981). The problems described by Hardin arise primarily after traditional management has been weakened by modernization or after increasing intensity of use, often due to population growth, makes previously abundant resources scarce, or innocuous behaviours harmful. Such is the case today for many resources shared by communities at local, national, and global level, including water-sheds and air-sheds. Common property resources have special significance, for when they are present (and ineffectively managed), social and individual interests diverge, and a laissez-faire policy does not lead to socially or individually optimal outcomes.[2] Thus, Hardin's metaphor of too many cows on the commons could provide a powerful rationale for an interventionist population policy.

Crowding of cities, highways, and parks, pollution of air and water, overfishing, deterioration of the ozone layer, global warming from the greenhouse effect – these problems, which are certainly exacerbated by population growth, testify to Hardin's insight. For many, they appear sufficient reason for policies to limit fertility and population. Yet the logic is not entirely clear, and this view is open to a straightforward rebuttal: that the problems are not caused by population growth per se, but rather are due to faulty institutional arrangements. They arise because many common-property resources are anachronistically treated as free access, with the predictable consequence that they are overused and degraded. Rather than tackle these problems indirectly and inefficiently through population policy, which is highly uncertain and at best brings change only in the long run, we should tackle them directly through optimal resource management. This might take the form of privatization, or imposition of user fees, or rationing and licensing, taxes and subsidies for users, or outright legislated levels of use. According to this view, once the common property resources are optimally managed, they pose no greater problem for laissez-faire reproduction than do privately owned

---

2 That is, to a Pareto optimal outcome, in which no one can be made better off without making someone else worse off. This sort of optimality leaves aside the question of income distribution and focuses instead on efficiency.

resources.[3] Why not, then, adopt policies of the sort just listed and allow people to make their own fertility decisions unhindered?

In fact, though, there are two distinct problems, two tragedies of the commons. The first problem is that, with a given population size, a free-access resource is subject to overuse and degradation, such that the existing population could be made better off on its own terms if use of the resource were limited.[4] This problem arises because of the institutional arrangements and can best be addressed by altering these arrangements to establish the optimal level of use. Once this is done, however, a second problem remains, for even if the level of use is regulated for the existing population, there is still free access to the resource through reproduction. The optimal level of use per person depends on the number of people. Under optimal management, when the population is larger each person will be entitled to use the resource less – to visit Yosemite less often, to turn up the volume on his stereo less high, to burn less firewood, to discharge less waste. Furthermore, with a larger population, the optimal level of total use will generally be slightly higher (although less than proportionately so), and so each person will have to live with slightly more congestion, pollution, and degradation. Because each additional person is born with a birthright to public resource use, each birth inflicts costs on all others by reducing the value of their environmental birthright. Free access through reproduction is the second tragedy of the commons.

I have said that the first tragedy of the common is appropriately remedied by direct policies restricting access, such as user fees or regulation. What of the second? We must pause here to consider how we may evaluate the trade-off between numbers of people and quality of life, for pointing out that a trade-off exists does not establish that smaller populations are better than larger ones. Much has been written on this issue, but one appealing approach is to view the trade-off through the eyes of the parents (see Nerlove *et al* 1987). This approach also permits the problem to be formulated in much the way in which Hardin originally formulated the tragedy of the commons. We assume that parents care about both the number of children they have and the future welfare of their children. Thus parents, in deciding how many children to have, take into account the consequences for the future welfare of their children, and strike a balance between conflicting aims, a balance reflecting their own values and circumstances. The societal goal is taken to be nothing other than to benefit the current generation of parents on the parents' own terms, and therefore to care about future welfare exactly to the extent to which they do. Under certain circumstances, including private ownership of all resources, it can be shown that no divergence of social and private interests occurs in this case – that is, individuals cannot, through collective decision-making, improve on the laissez-faire outcome. When there are common property or free-access resources, however, the laissez-faire outcome is suboptimal, and collective decision-making about reproduction will enable all parents to achieve a higher level of satisfaction by restricting fertility, just as the cattle owners in the original tragedy of the commons could all do better by collectively agreeing to reduce their herds.

---

3 A number of economic analyses have concluded that externalities to child-bearing do not occur when all resources are privately owned (Ng 1986; Willis 1987; Nerlove et al 1987; Lee 1988a). Of course, externalities transcending national borders require international co-operation on policy-making and enforcement.

4 Historically, it appears that common-property resources were communally managed in one way or another, to avoid such problems. In other words, common property resources were not free-access resources.

Some economists have argued that the problem of free access through reproduction is effectively remedied by optimal resource management policies for the
existing population – say, user fees. A stiff charge for the use of Yosemite National
Park, for example, would convey to all potential parents a message about the
constraints their children would face, and this message would provide the optimal
disincentive to reproduce.[5] But this argument is fallacious. The user fees provide
no child-bearing disincentive, since they are a fee on use and not on procreation.
The prospective child's net wealth is not reduced by the fee he or she will pay in
the future, for the fees, once collected, must be used to defray park management
costs or general governmental costs, or be returned to the public in one way or
another. These fees simply substitute for taxes that would otherwise be raised by
some other means.

If the optimal management policy does not also constitute an optimal fertility
policy, then some other policy must be found. Many kinds are possible, but if a
financial disincentive is chosen, it must be applied directly to the fertility decision
– that is, it must be a tax of some sort on births. The appropriate level of the tax
would depend on how much an additional birth reduces the satisfaction of all
other persons through their use of non-private resources, and on the number of
people so affected.

So many problems pertain to a heavy tax on child-bearing that I believe it is
useful only as a conceptual tool, and not as a practical policy. Yet the idea might
provide a useful guide to thinking about alternative, more practical policies. Here
are a few of the problems raised:

* Would such a tax leave the rich free to have as many children as they
  wished, and deter only the poor?
* Would it be applied globally?
* Should the same tax be levied on a birth in Bangladesh as in the United
  States?

Certainly, the environmental impact of a birth would depend on the wealth of the
parents to whom it was born, and therefore the tax should vary with social class
and nationality. Also, while the appropriate tax might make children very costly
indeed, it would also lead to a disbursement of funds to the population. Other
things equal (including fertility), the poor would gain at the expense of the rich,
for the tax and transfer system should recognize that the children of the rich
would consume a disproportionate share of the environmental birthright of the
poor.[6] Within each income stratum of each nation, income would be redistributed
from those with many children to those with few; and across strata and across
nations, income would be redistributed from the rich to the poor.

Herman Daly (1991) asserts that 'the market cannot find an optimal scale any
more than it can find an optimal distribution'[7] and suggests that in a finite world,
public policy should recognize explicitly the limits of resources and the environ-

---

5 See, for example, Willis (1987), p671 and Ng (1986).
6 Of course, the environmental cost of child-bearing is only one of many costs, both positive and
negative, that are not borne by the parents. In a recent paper, I have attempted to address more
generally the issue of externalities to child-bearing (Lee 1988a).
7 Daly goes on: 'The latter requires the addition of ethical criteria; the former requires the further
addition of ecological criteria... In theory whether we double the population and the per capita
resource use rate, or cut them in half, the market will still grind out a Pareto optimal allocation for
every scale. Yet the scale of the economy is certainly not a matter of indifference.'

ment and choose an optimal sustainable scale for the global economy. It is not clear what 'optimal' would mean in this context. Given any sustainable level of aggregate consumption, one would still have to choose the appropriate population size and corresponding per capita level of consumption. Such decisions would be very difficult to make, defend, and enforce. But setting aside the question of optimality, it is certainly not true that the market economy is indifferent to scale. The classical economists described the convergence of the economic system to the stationary state, at which population, capital, and incomes would all cease to grow. This convergence depended on assumptions about the behaviour of parents and capitalists. Many neoclassical theoretical systems likewise converge to stationary states when they include natural resources, although in fact they often ignore such resources.[8] Assumptions about the reproductive behaviour of parents would determine the qualities of the end-point of economic growth, and under the assumption of inclusive markets and altruistic parental choice, the end-point could indeed be claimed to be an optimal scale. In this view, parents vote on the optimal scale through reproductive choice, and we, unlike Malthus in his early writings, may hope that this decision is governed by rational minds, concerned about the future welfare of their children. However, in the presence of environmental (or other) externalities, the outcome of the vote would *not* have optimal properties – and this is the thrust of Hardin's story of the commons, and of the argument I have advanced here.

Imagine, now, a policy equivalent to the hypothetical system of taxes on births, with taxes chosen to internalize the environmental costs of child-bearing. Individual couples could choose a number of children consistent with their individual tastes, values, and circumstances. No particular sustainable population size or individual level of fertility would be imposed by central authorities. It is not immediately clear to what kind of equilibrium size and level of economic activity such a policy would steer the population. For that matter, it is not clear that the long-run outcome would be a stationary state at all. Whatever its nature, the evolution of the system would ultimately reflect the preferences of the people in it. Whatever the trade-off implicitly chosen between numbers and environmental quality of life, it would be theirs. This much cannot be said of the current situation, in which we are ineluctably driven to an environmental standard lower than we would choose for our descendants if we were able.

REFERENCES

Daly, Herman (1991) 'Sustainable development: from concept and theory to operational principles', in *Resources, Environment, and Population: Present Knowledge, Future Options*, ed Kingsley Davis and Mikhail S Bernstam, New York: Oxford University Press.

Eckstein, Zvi and Kenneth I Wolpin (1985) 'Endogenous fertility and optimal population size', *Journal of Public Economics* 27 (June), pp93–106.

Hardin, Garrett (1968) 'The tragedy of the commons', *Science* 162 (13 December), pp1243–48.

Kelley, Allen C (1988) 'Economic consequences of population change in the Third World', *Journal of Economic Literature* 26, no 4 (December), pp1685–728.

---

8 See Pitchford (1974), for a detailed discussion of these issues.

Lee, Ronald D (1980) 'Age structure, intergenerational transfers and economic growth: an overview', *Revue Économique* 31, no 6 (November), pp1129–56.

— (1988a) 'Evaluating externalities to child-bearing in developing countries: the case of India', forthcoming in proceedings of the UN-INED Conference on Population and Development, New York, August 1988.

— (1988b) 'Declining fertility and aging population: consequences for intergenerational transfers within and between households', manuscript of the Graduate Group in Demography, University of California, Berkeley.

National Research Council (1986) *Population Growth and Economic Development: Policy Questions*, Washington, DC: National Academy Press.

Nerlove, Marc, Assaf Razin, and Efraim Sadka (1987) *Household and Economy: Welfare Economics of Endogenous Fertility*, Orlando, Florida: Academic Press.

Ng, Yew-Kwang (1986) 'On the welfare economics of population control', *Population and Development Review* 12, no 2 (June), pp247–66.

Pitchford, J D (1974) *Population in Economic Growth*, New York: American Elsevier.

Runge, Carlisle Ford (1981) 'Common property externalities: isolation, assurance, and resource depletion in a traditional grazing context', *American Journal of Agricultural Economics* 63, no 4 (November), pp595–606.

Willis, Robert (1987) 'Externalities and population', in *Population Growth and Economic Development: Issues and Evidence*, ed D Gale Johnson and Ronald D Lee, Madison: University of Wisconsin Press, pp661–700.

World Bank (1984) *World Development Report 1984*, New York: Oxford University Press.

Chapter 24

From Empty-world Economics to Full-world Economics

Herman E Daly

The thesis argued here is that the evolution of the human economy has passed from an era in which human-made capital was the limiting factor in economic development to an era in which remaining neutral capital has become the limiting factor. Economic logic tells us that we should maximize the productivity of the scarcest (limiting) factor, as well as try to increase its supply. This means that economic policy should be designed to increase the productivity of natural capital and its total amount, rather than to increase the productivity of human-made capital and its accumulation, as was appropriate in the past when it was the limiting factor. This chapter aims to give some reasons for believing this 'new era' thesis, and to consider some of the far-reaching policy changes that it would entail, both for development in general and for the multilateral development banks in particular.

REASONS THE TURNING-POINT HAS NOT BEEN NOTICED

Why has this transformation from a world relatively empty of human beings and human-made capital to a world relatively full of these not been noticed by economists? If such a fundamental change in the pattern of scarcity is real, as I think it is, then how could it be overlooked by economists whose job is to pay attention to the pattern of scarcity? Some economists – for example, Boulding (1964) and Georgescu-Roegen (1971) – have indeed signalled the change, but their voices have been largely unheeded.

One reason is the deceptive acceleration of exponential growth. With a constant rate of growth, the world will go from half full to totally full in one doubling period – the same amount of time that it took to go from 1 per cent full to 2 per cent full. Of course, the doubling time itself has shortened, compounding the deceptive acceleration. If we take the per centage appropriation by human beings of the net product of land-based photosynthesis as an index of how full the world is of humans and their furniture, then we can say that it is 40 per cent full because we use, directly and indirectly, about 40 per cent of the net primary product of land-based photosynthesis (Vitousek *et al*, 1986).

Taking 35 years as the doubling time of the human scale – that is, population times per capita resource use – and calculating backwards, we go from the present 40 per cent to only 10 per cent full in just two doubling times or 70 years, which is about an average lifetime. Also 'full' here is taken as 100 per cent human appropriation of the net product of photosynthesis, which on the face of it would seem to be ecologically quite unlikely and socially undesirable (only the most recalcitrant species would remain wild – all others would be managed for human benefit). In other words, effective fullness occurs at less than 100 per cent human preemption of net photosynthetic product, and there is much evidence that long-run human carrying capacity is reached at less than the existing 40 per cent (see Goodland 1991). The world has rapidly gone from relatively empty (10 per cent full) to relatively full (40 per cent full). Although 40 per cent is less than half, it makes sense to think of it as indicating relative fullness because it is only one doubling time away from 80 per cent, a figure that represents excessive fullness.

This change has been faster than the speed with which fundamental economic paradigms shift. According to physicist Max Planck, a new scientific paradigm triumphs not by convincing the majority of its opponents, but because its opponents eventually die. There has not yet been time for the empty-world economists to die, and meanwhile they have been cloning themselves faster than they are dying by maintaining tight control over their guild. The disciplinary structure of knowledge in modern economics is far tighter than that of the turn-of-the-century physics that was Planck's model. Full-world economics is not yet accepted as academically legitimate; indeed, it is not even recognized as a challenge.[1]

Another reason for failing to note the watershed change in the pattern of scarcity is that in order to speak of a *limiting* factor, the factors must be thought of as complementary. If factors are good substitutes, then a shortage of one does not significantly limit the productivity of the other. A standard assumption of neoclassical economics has been that factors of production are highly substitutable. Although other models of production have considered factors as not at all substitutable – for example, the total complementarity of the Leontief model – the substitutability assumption has dominated. Consequently the very idea of a limiting factor was pushed into the background. If factors are substitutes rather than complements, then there can be no limiting factor and hence no new era based on a change of the limiting role from one factor to another. It is therefore important to be very clear on the issue of complementarity versus substitutability.[2]

---

1 For an analysis of economics as an academic discipline, see Part I of Daly and Cobb (1989).
2 The usual Hicks-Allen definition of complementarity and substitutability is: 'if a rise in the jth factor price, which reduces the use of the jth factor, increases (resp. reduces) the use of the ith factor for each fixed (level of output), i is a substitute (resp. complement) for j' (Takayama 1985). In a model with only two factors, it follows from this definition that the factors must be substitutes. If they were complements, then a rise in the price of one of them would reduce the use of both factors, while output remained constant, which is impossible. The customary diagrammatic use of two-factor models thus reinforces the focus on substitutability by effectively defining complementarity out of existence in the two-factor case. In the Leontief model of L-shaped isoquants (fixed coefficients), the above definition simply breaks down because the reduction in use of one factor inevitably causes a reduction in output, which the definition requires must remain constant. For the argument of this chapter, we need appeal only to 'complementarity' in the sense of a limiting factor. A factor becomes limiting when an increase in the other factor(s) will not increase output, but an increase in the factor in question (the limiting factor) will increase output. For a limiting factor, all that is needed is that the isoquant become parallel to one of the axes. And for the practical argument of this chapter, 'nearly parallel' would also be quite sufficient.

The productivity of human-made capital is more and more limited by the decreasing supply of complementary natural capital. Of course in the past when the scale of the human presence in the biosphere was low, human-made capital played the limiting role. The switch from human-made to natural capital as the limiting factor is thus a function of the increasing scale and impact of the human presence. Natural capital is the stock that yields the flow of natural resources – the forest that yields the flow of cut timber; the petroleum deposits that yield the flow of pumped crude oil, the fish populations in the sea that yield the flow of caught fish. The complementary nature of natural and human-made capital is made obvious by asking what good a saw-mill is without a forest; a refinery without petroleum deposits; a fishing-boat without populations of fish.

Beyond some point in the accumulation of human-made capital it is clear that the limiting factor on production will be remaining natural capital. For example, the limiting factor determining the fish catch is the reproductive capacity of fish populations, not the number of fishing boats; for gasoline the limiting factor is petroleum deposits, not refinery capacity; and for many types of wood it is remaining forests, not saw-mill capacity. Costa Rica and peninsular Malaysia, for example, now must import timber to keep their saw-mills employed. One country can accumulate human-made capital and deplete natural capital to a greater extent only if another country does it to a lesser extent – for example, Costa Rica must import timber from somewhere. The demands of complementarity between human-made and natural capital can be evaded within a nation only if they are respected between nations.

Of course, multiplying specific examples of complementarity between natural and human-made capital will never suffice to prove the general case. But the examples given above at least serve to add concreteness to the more general arguments for the complementarity hypothesis given in the next section.

Because of the complementary relationship between human-made and natural capital, the very accumulation of human-made capital puts pressure on natural capital stocks to supply an increasing flow of natural resources. When that flow reaches a size that can no longer be maintained, there is a big temptation to supply the annual flow unsustainably by liquidation of natural capital stocks, thus postponing the collapse in the value of the complementary human-made capital. Indeed, in the era of empty-world economics, natural resources and natural capital were considered free goods (except for extraction of harvest costs). Consequently, the value of human-made capital was under no threat from scarcity of a complementary factor. In the era of full-world economics, this threat is real and is met by liquidating stocks of natural capital to temporarily keep up the flows of natural resources that support the value of human-made capital. Hence the problem of sustainability.

MORE ON COMPLEMENTARITY VERSUS SUBSTITUTABILITY

The main issue is the relation between natural capital that yields a flow of natural resources and services that enter the process of production, and the human-made capital that serves as an agent in the process for transforming the resource inflow into a product outflow. Is the flow of natural resources (and the stock of natural capital that yields that flow) substitutable by human-made capital? Clearly, one resource can substitute for another – we can transform aluminium instead of copper into electric wire. We can also substitute labour for capital, or capital for labour, to a significant degree, even though the characteristic of complementarity is also important. For example, we can have fewer carpenters and more power saws, or fewer power saws and more carpenters and still build the same house. But more pilots cannot substitute for fewer aircraft, once the aircraft are fully employed.

In other words, one resource can substitute for another, albeit imperfectly, because both play the same qualitative role in production – both are raw materials undergoing transformation into a product. Likewise, capital and labour are substitutable to a significant degree because both play the role of agent of transformation of resource inputs into product outputs. However, when we come to substitution across the roles of transforming agent and material undergoing transformation (efficient cause and material cause), the possibilities of substitution become very limited and the characteristic of complementarity is dominant. For example, we cannot construct the same house with half the lumber no matter how many extra power saws or carpenters we try to substitute. Of course, we might substitute brick for lumber, but then we face the analogous limitation – we cannot substitute bricklayers and trowels for bricks.

THE COMPLEMENTARITY OF NATURAL AND HUMAN-MADE CAPITAL

The upshot of these considerations is that natural capital (natural resources) and human-made capital are complements rather than substitutes. The neoclassical assumption of near-perfect substitutability between natural resources and human-made capital is a serious distortion of reality, the excuse of 'analytical convenience' notwithstanding. To see how serious, just imagine that in fact human-made capital was indeed a perfect substitute for natural resources. Then it would also be the case that natural resources would be a perfect substitute for human-made capital. Yet, if that were so, then we would have had no reason whatsoever to accumulate human-made capital, since we were already endowed by nature with a perfect substitute. Historically, of course, we did accumulate human-made capital long before natural capital was depleted, precisely because we needed human-made capital to make effective use of the natural capital (complementarity!).

It is quite amazing that the substitutability dogma should be held with such tenacity in the face of such an easy *reductio ad absurdum*. Add to that the fact that capital itself requires natural resources for its production – that is, the substitute itself requires the very input being substituted for – and it is quite clear that human-made capital and natural resources are fundamentally complements not substitutes. Substitutability of capital for resources is limited to reducing waste of materials in process, for example, collecting sawdust and using a press (capital) to make chip-board. And no amount of substitution of capital for resources can ever reduce the mass of material resource inputs below the mass of outputs, given the law of conservation of matter-energy.

Substitutability of capital for resources in aggregate production functions reflects largely a change in the total product mix from resource-intensive to different capital-intensive products. It is an artefact of product aggregation, not factor substitution (i.e. along a given product isoquant). It is important to emphasize that it is this latter meaning of substitution that is under attack here – that is, producing a given physical product with less natural resources and more capital. No one denies that it is possible to produce a different product or a different product mix with less resources. Indeed, new products may be designed to provide the same or better service while using fewer resources, and sometimes less labour and less capital as well. This is technical improvement, not substitution of capital for resources. Light-bulbs that give more lumens per watt represent technical progress, qualitative improvement in the state of the art, not the substitution of a quantity of capital for a quantity of natural resource in the production of a given quantity of a product.

It may be that economists are speaking loosely and metaphorically when they claim that capital is a near-perfect substitute for natural resources. Perhaps they are counting as 'capital' all improvements in knowledge, technology, managerial skills, etc – in short, anything that would increase the efficiency with which resources are used. If this is the usage, then 'capital' and resources would by definition be substitutes in the same sense that more efficient use of a resource is a substitute for using more of the resource. But to define capital as efficiency would make a mockery of the neoclassical theory of production, where efficiency is a ratio of output to input, and capital is a quantity of input.

The productivity of human-made capital is more and more limited by the decreasing supply of complementary natural capital. Of course, in the past when the scale of the human presence in the biosphere was low, human-made capital played the limiting role. The switch from human-made to natural capital as the limiting factor is thus a function of the increasing scale of the human presence.

MORE ON NATURAL CAPITAL

Thinking of the natural environment as 'natural capital' is in some ways unsatisfactory, but useful within limits. We may define capital broadly as a stock of something that yields a flow of useful goods or services. Traditionally, capital was defined as produced means of production, which we are here calling human-made capital in distinction to natural capital, which, though not made by people, is nevertheless functionally a stock that yields a flow of useful goods and services. We can distinguish renewable from non-renewable, and marketed from non-marketed natural capital, giving four cross categories. Pricing natural capital, especially non-marketable natural capital, is so far an intractable problem, but one that need not be faced here. All that need be recognized for the present argument is that natural capital consists of physical stocks that are complementary to human-made capital. We have learned to use a concept of human capital that departs even more fundamentally from the standard definition of capital. Human capital cannot be bought and sold, though it can be rented. Although it can be accumulated, it cannot be inherited without effort by bequest, as can ordinary human-made capital, but must be learned anew by each generation. Natural capital, however, is more like traditional human-made capital in that it can be bequeathed. Overall, the concept of natural capital is less a departure from the traditional definition of capital than is the commonly used notion of human capital.

There is a troublesome subcategory of marketed natural capital that is intermediate between natural and human-made, which we might refer to as 'cultivated natural capital', consisting of such things as plantation forests, herds of livestock, agricultural crops, fish bred in ponds, etc. Cultivated natural capital supplies the raw material input complementary to human-made capital, but does not provide the wide range of natural ecological services characteristic of natural capital proper (for example, eucalyptus plantations supply timber to the saw mill and may even reduce erosion, but they do not provide a wildlife habitat nor do they preserve biodiversity). Investment in the cultivated natural capital of a forest plantation, however, is useful not only for the timber, but as a way of easing the pressure of timber interests on the remaining true natural capital of real forests.

Marketed natural capital can, subject to the important social corrections for common property and myopic discounting, be left to the market. Non-marketed natural capital, both renewable and non-renewable, will be the most troublesome category. Remaining natural forests should in many cases be treated as non-marketed natural capital, and only replanted areas treated as marketed natural capital. In neoclassical terms the external benefits of remaining natural forests might be considered 'infinite' thus removing them from market competition with other (inferior) uses. Most neoclassical economists, however, have a strong aversion to any imputation of an 'infinite' or prohibitive price to anything.

POLICY IMPLICATIONS OF THE TURNING POINT

In this new full-world era, investment must shift from human-made capital accumulation towards natural capital preservation and restoration. Also, technology should be aimed at increasing the productivity of natural capital more than human-made capital. If these two things do not happen then we will be behaving *uneconomically* – in the most orthodox sense of the word. That is to say, the emphasis should shift from technologies that increase the productivity of labour and human-made capital to those that increase the productivity of natural capital. This would occur through market forces if the price of natural capital were to rise as it became more scarce. What keeps the price from rising? In most cases natural capital is unowned and consequently non-marketed. Therefore it has no explicit price and is exploited as if its price were zero. Even where prices exist on natural capital the market tends to be myopic and excessively discounts the costs of future scarcity, especially when under the influence of economists who teach that accumulating capital is a near perfect substitute for depleting natural resources! Natural capital productivity is increased by:

(a) increasing the flow (net growth) of natural resources per unit of natural stock (limited by biological growth rates);
(b) increasing product output per unit of resource input (limited by mass balance); and especially
(c) increasing the end-use efficiency with which the resulting product yields services to the final user (limited by technology).

We have already argued that complementarity severely limits what we should expect from (b), and complex ecological interrelations and the law of conservation of matter-energy will limit the increase from (a). Therefore the focus should be mainly on (c).

The above factors limit productivity from the supply side. From the demand side, tastes may provide a limit to the economic productivity of natural capital that is more stringent than the limit of biological productivity. For example, game ranching and fruit-and-nut gathering in a natural tropical forest may, in terms of biomass be more productive than cattle ranching. But undeveloped tastes for game meat and tropical fruit may make this use less profitable than the biologically more productive use. In this case, a change in tastes can increase the biological productivity with which the land is used.

Since human-made capital is owned by the capitalist we can expect that it will be maintained with an interest to increasing its productivity. Labour power, which is a stock that yields the useful services of labour, can be treated in the same way as human-made capital. Labour power is owned by the labourer who has an interest in maintaining it and enhancing its productivity. But non-marketed natural capital (the water cycle, the ozone layer, the atmosphere, etc) is not subject to ownership, and no self-interested social class can be relied upon to protect it from over-exploitation.

If the thesis argued above were accepted by development economists and the multilateral development banks, what policy implications would follow? The role of the multilateral development banks in the new era would be increasingly to make investments that replenish the stock and that increase the productivity of natural capital. In the past, development investments have largely aimed at increasing the stock and productivity of human-made capital. Instead of investing mainly in saw-mills, fishing-boats and refineries, development banks should now invest more in reforestation, restocking of fish populations and renewable substitutes for dwindling reserves of petroleum. The latter should include investment in energy efficiency, as it is impossible to restock petroleum deposits.

Since natural capacity to absorb wastes is also a vital resource, investments that preserve that capacity (eg pollution reduction) also increase in priority. For marketed natural capital this will not represent a revolutionary change. For non-marketed natural capital, it will be more difficult, but even here economic development agencies have experience in investing in complementary public goods such as education, legal systems, public infrastructure and population control. Investments in limiting the growth-rate of the human population are of greatest importance in managing a world that has become relatively full. Like human-made capital, labour power is also complementary with natural resources and its growth can increase demand for natural resources beyond the capacity of natural capital to sustain supply.

Perhaps the clearest policy implication of the full-world thesis is that the level of per capita resource use of the rich countries cannot be generalized to the poor, given the current world population. Present total resource use levels are already unsustainable, and multiplying them by a factor of 5 to 10 as envisaged in the Brundtland Report, albeit with considerable qualification, is ecologically impossible. As a policy of growth becomes less possible, the importance of redistribution and population control as measures to combat poverty increase correspondingly. In a full world, both human numbers and per capita resource use must be constrained. Poor countries cannot cut per capita resource use, indeed they must increase it to reach a sufficiency, so their focus must be mainly on population control. Rich countries can cut both, and for those that have already reached demographic equilibrium the focus would be more on limiting per capita consumption to make resources available for transfer to help bring the poor up to sufficiency. Investments in the areas of population control and redistribution therefore increase in priority for development agencies.

Investing in natural capital (non-marketed) is essentially an infrastructure investment on a grand scale and in the most fundamental sense of infrastructure – that is, the biophysical infrastructure of the entire human niche, not just the within-niche public investments that support the productivity of the private investments. Rather, we are now talking about investments in biophysical infra-structure ('infra-infrastructure') to maintain the productivity of all previous economic investments in human-made capital, be they public or private, by invest-ing in rebuilding the remaining natural capital stocks that have come to be limitative. Indeed, in the new era the World Bank's official name, The International Bank for Reconstruction and Development, should emphasize the word recon-struction and redefine it to refer to reconstruction of natural capital devastated by rapacious 'development', as opposed to the historical meaning of reconstruction of human-made capital in Europe devastated by the Second World War. Since our ability actually to re-create natural capital is very limited, such investments will have to be indirect – that is, conserve the remaining natural capital and encour-age its natural growth by reducing our level of current exploitation. This includes investing in projects that relieve the pressure on these natural capital stocks by expanding cultivated natural capital (plantation forests to relieve pressure on natural forests), and by increasing end-use efficiency of products.

The difficulty with infrastructure investments is that their productivity shows up in the enhanced return to other investments, and is therefore difficult both to calculate and to collect for loan repayment. Also in the present context these ecological infrastructure investments are defensive and restorative in nature – that is, they will protect existing rates of return from falling more rapidly than otherwise, rather than raising their rate of return to a higher level. This circum-stance will dampen the political enthusiasm for such investments, but will not alter the economic logic favouring them. Past high rates of return to human-made capital were possible only with unsustainable rates of use of natural resources and consequent (uncounted) liquidation of natural capital. We are now learning to deduct natural capital liquidation from our measure of national income (see Ahmad *et al* 1989).

The new era of sustainable development will not permit natural capital liqui-dation to count as an income, and will consequently require that we become accustomed to lower rates of return on human-made capital – rates on the order of magnitude of the biological growth rates of natural capital, as that will be the limiting factor. Once investments in natural capital have resulted in equilibrium stocks that are maintained but not expanded (yielding a constant total resource flow), then all further increase in economic welfare would have to come from increases in pure efficiency resulting from improvements in technology and clari-fication of priorities. Certainly, investments are being made in increasing biological growth-rates, and the advent of genetic engineering will add greatly to this thrust. However, experience to date – for example, the green revolution – indicates that higher biological yield rates usually require the sacrifice of some other useful quality (disease resistance, flavour, strength of stalk).

In any case the law of conservation of matter-energy cannot be evaded by genetics – that is, more food from a plant or animal implies either more inputs or less matter-energy going to the non-food structures and functions of the organ-ism. To avoid ecological backlashes will require leadership and clarity of purpose on the part of the development agencies. To carry the arguments for infrastruc-ture investments into the area of biophysical/environmental infrastructure or natural capital replenishment will require new thinking by development economists. Since much natural capital is not only public but globally public in nature, the United Nations seems indicated to take a leadership role.

Consider some specific cases of biospheric infrastructure investments and the difficulties they present. First, a largely deforested country will need reforestation to keep the complementary human-made capital of saw-mills (carpentry, cabinet-making skills, etc.) from losing their value. Of course the deforested country could for a time resort to importing timber. To protect the human-made capital of dams from silting up the lakes behind them, the water-catchment areas feeding the lakes must be reforested or original forests protected to prevent erosion and siltation. Agricultural investments depending on irrigation can become worthless without forested-water catchment areas that recharge aquifers.

Second, at a global level enormous stocks of human-made capital and natural capital are threatened by depletion of the ozone layer, although the exact consequences are too uncertain to be predicted. The greenhouse effect is a threat to the value of all coastal and climatically dependent capital, be it human-made (port cities, wharves, beach resorts) or natural (estuarine breeding-grounds for fish and shrimp). And if the natural capital of fish populations diminishes due to loss of breeding-grounds, then the value of the human-made capital of fishing-boats and canneries will also be diminished in value, as will the labour power (specialized human capital) devoted to fishing, canning, etc. We have begun to adjust national accounts for the liquidation of natural capital, but have not yet recognized that the value of complementary human-made capital must also be written down as the natural capital that it was designed to exploit disappears. Eventually, the market will automatically lower the valuation of fishing boats as fish disappear, so perhaps no accounting adjustments are called for. But *ex ante* policy adjustments aimed at avoiding the *ex post* writing down of complementary human-made capital, whether by market or accountant mechanisms, are certainly called for.

REFERENCES

Ahmad, Y J; S El Serafy; E Lutz, eds (1989) *Environmental Accounting for Sustainable Development*, Washington DC: World Bank.

Boulding, K (1964) *The Meaning of the Twentieth Century*, New York: Harper and Row.

Daly, H E, and J B Cobb (1989) *For the Common Good*, Boston: Beacon Press.

Georgescu-Roegen, N (1971) *The Entropy Law and the Economic Process*, Cambridge: Harvard University Press.

Goodland, R (1991) 'The case that the world has reached limits', in *Environmentally Sustainable Economic Development: Building on Brundtland*, ed R Goodland et al, Paris: UNESCO.

Takayama, A (1985) *Mathematical Economics*, 2nd ed, New York: Cambridge University Press.

Vitousek, P M; P R Ehrlich; A H Ehrlich; P A Matson (1986) 'Human appropriation of the products of photosynthesis', *BioScience* 34, no 6, pp368–73.

Chapter 25

Population Size and Material Standards of Living

Paul Demeny

Nature exists without human presence, as it did before *Homo sapiens* appeared on Earth, or as it does on Mars where inhabitants from a neighbouring planet have yet to set foot. Environment, in contrast, is nature seen through the eyes of humans, experienced by them, and evaluated by human criteria. Humans are dependent on a biophysical environment that permits survival and reproduction. Improved human welfare requires success in shaping this environment and in using its renewable and non-renewable resources, so as to better satisfy human material and spiritual aspirations. These aspirations have meaning only if seen as lodged in persons now alive: in members of present human societies. Values persons hold, however, incorporate a regard for the interests of future generations. Such values may also be sensitive to the perceived interests of non-human sentient beings.

A coherent perspective on the impact of population on the environment presupposes clarity about the identity of the evaluator. In God's eyes, presumably, plutonium and oxygen are just two of many elements, an eagle is no more beautiful than a mosquito, and the climate of the moon is no less agreeable than that of Tuscany. Humans make more biased judgements. To point out this distinction is important, since there is a strong current in the contemporary discussion of environmental issues that, albeit with varying consistency, rejects the validity of the anthropocentric approach. In what follows, in line with standard utilitarian doctrine, I will assume that the criterion of environmental preservation is subordinate to the criterion of improved human welfare at large.

Human valuations concerning either of these desiderata – *environment*, defined in a narrow sense as the agreeableness of people's physical surroundings and their capacity to satisfy human wants, or *welfare*, defined in a comprehensive fashion, balancing environmental goods and values against all other human needs and values – are apt to differ. If such differences affected only the immediate actors, the legitimate public policy interest they could elicit would be nil. How tidy one's neighbour's living-room is nobody's business but the neighbour's. But humans live in society, not in isolation, and the sphere of strictly private behaviour – private in the sense that no significant external effects are attached to a person's acts – is narrow. All too commonly, the interests of individuals and of their various social groupings in transforming and exploiting the environment are in conflict. Reconciling these differences so as to attain a development path that is socially optimal – that best serves the separate interests of the individual members that compose society – is the task of human institutional design and public policy.

In shaping institutions and adopting public policies that aim at enhancing human welfare, the size and composition of a society's membership list are of eminent interest. The intuitively obvious existence of trade-offs between human numbers and material welfare is easily envisaged by making extreme assumptions – picturing, say, Japan with a population size equal to that of China or, alternatively, to that of Iceland. Such extremes suggest the putative existence of an optimum population size – a point (or a more or less narrow size-band) somewhere in between: neither too large nor too small. But a search for such an optimum is rather pointless. Population size in a given polity at a given time is inherited from history. Social interest in aggregate human numbers therefore is naturally focused on *change*: on the rules that ultimately govern the rate at which population is growing or decreasing. This brief essay discusses some of the considerations concerning the human environment and bearing on policy decisions related to demographic growth. Do they provide arguments that would justify attempts to influence aggregate change in population numbers through deliberate collective action? The scope of the discussion is narrowed somewhat by a focus on situations characterized by rapid population growth – growth at the historically unprecedented rates of change that still prevail in most contemporary developing countries.

POPULATION AND THE ENVIRONMENT

Sheer human presence and all human activities modify the environment. The extent of the impact tends to be strongly related to human numbers, the scope and intensity of their exertions, and the technology at their disposal. Significant and lasting impact pre-supposes fairly large numbers and a technology advanced at least beyond that employed by hunter-gatherers. A simple classification of the impacts on the environment distinguishes between outcomes that were the intended fruits of deliberate human action, and those that were necessary, if typically unintended and often unwelcome or unforeseen, byproducts of such action. The notion of 'environmental impact', by convention, focuses not on the purposeful achievement but on its undesired side-effects – not on the goods created but on the 'bads'; not on the cathedral but on the marred hillside from which the stone for building it was quarried.

The potential importance and pervasiveness of such 'negative goods' amply justify interest in environmental impacts defined in that narrow sense. The demise of a number of ancient civilizations – for example, those of Mesopotamia and Greece – can be traced, at least in part, to ecological damage wrought by human activities, resulting in the exhaustion of some critical resource upon which those civilizations depended. Neither modern industrial economies nor technologically backward contemporary societies with unfavourable population-resource ratios and rapidly growing populations can consider themselves safely exempt from analogous ecological ambushes.

As a generalized example of negative environmental impacts, consider 'pollution'. In a formulation first suggested by Paul Ehrlich, pollution, at a given time-period and defined for the appropriate spatial unit, may be thought of as the combined product of population size, income per capita, and the pollution-intensity of income. The following equation expresses a definitional identity:

$$\text{Pollution} = \text{Population} \times \frac{\text{Income}}{\text{Population}} \times \frac{\text{Pollution}}{\text{Income}}$$

The formula is applicable for consideration of numerous specific environmental impacts. Thus, for example, use of a non-renewable resource – say, oil – can be factored as:

$$\text{Resource use} = \text{Population} \times \frac{\text{Income}}{\text{Population}} \times \frac{\text{Resource use}}{\text{Income}}$$

The formula is readily extended to characterize changes in environmental impact over time. Thus, if income per capita and the pollution-intensity (or the resource use-intensity) of income are held constant, the size of the environmental impact will change in direct proportion to change in population size. Other things equal, and as a first approximation, doubling population size will double pollution and resource use.

The assumption of independence between the three factors in the right-hand side of the equations above is, however, invalid. For example, changes in population size and changes in income per capita may be partly compensating. In particular, slower population growth may be accompanied by more rapid increase in income per capita. The interaction of each of these two terms with the third term, the resource intensity of income use, may be even more important. The latter is affected by the state of the technology characterizing the production and consumption of income. It is also affected by the individual and collective choices that govern the particular uses through which income is expended. Both of these factors are strongly affected by the level of income per capita and, more relevant in the present context, by the relation of population size to the environment and by the rate of population growth. A significant change in the demographic parameters is bound to cause shifts in these relationships, sometimes compensating and sometimes reinforcing the environmental impact a given demographic change in and by itself could be expected to generate. In particular, over time, non-linearities to scale may appear. Quantitative increases can generate qualitative changes; thresholds separating, for example, tolerable levels of pollution from levels that generate unacceptable risks for human health may be crossed. Up to a certain level, damage to a renewable resource, such as a forest ecosystem, may be corrected by a spontaneous and relatively rapid biological process; beyond that level, the damage may be irreparable, or the natural recovery or the human-engineered repair of the ecosystem in question may require a very long time or entail exorbitant cost. Thus, a doubling of population size, even if the other terms on the right-hand side of the equation remain constant, could more than double the environmental impact. In some other instances, scale economies would make the effect less than proportionate.

Simple applications of the formulas above, nevertheless, are broadly suggestive of plausible orders of magnitude of environmental impacts and of the relative importance of the different factors identified in the equations. They explicate and confirm the intuitively obvious – for example, that rapid demographic growth since mid-century (which between 1950 and the late 1980s doubled the world's population) must have been a major contributor to the introduction of pollutants into the human environment and to the use of non-renewable resources.

This is not to discount the importance of the second and third terms in the equations above. Their impacts on the environment and on non-renewable resource use were highly important during recent decades. From mid-century to the late 1980s, global income per capita increased approximately two-and-a-half-fold. Rapid technological change, while beneficial in contributing to the increase in labour productivity that permitted such rapid income growth, entailed the adoption of industrial processes that introduced a new range of toxic chemicals and noxious byproducts into the environment. Thus, deleterious environmental effects can be observed even if demographic growth is moderate or nil. For example, the especially severe environmental deterioration in Eastern Europe during recent decades, which is now being documented in increasing detail, seems largely unrelated to rapid demographic growth (although not unrelated to changes in the spatial distribution of the population). Between 1950 and 1990, Eastern Europe's population increased by only 28 per cent, and, in some of the environmentally worst affected countries, much more slowly than that. The lion's share of the explanation in this instance appears to be attributable to the drastic rise in the pollution- and resource use-intensities of income that accompanied rapid industrialization in the region. But to ignore the effects of population growth because of such examples is clearly illogical. The examples merely serve as a reminder that situations differ depending on demographic characteristics.

CONTRASTING DEMOGRAPHIC-ECONOMIC PATTERNS

With an admittedly heroic abstraction from the multiplicity of intermediate situations, two contrasting patterns of demographic-economic characteristics may be usefully identified, patterns that are also distinguished by greatly differing significance of population growth for the human environment. The distinction corresponds to the conventional division of countries as belonging to the 'developed' (DC) or the 'developing' (LDC) world.

In the aggregate, the DC group is characterized by an absolute population size that is large by historical standards – roughly equivalent to the population of the entire globe around the middle of the 19th century – even if this population of 1.2 billion (in 1990) constitutes just 23 per cent of the world's total. The rate of population growth in the developed countries as a whole is low: currently 0.5 per cent per year and declining. On the assumption that DC fertility rates will reverse the steady downward trend exhibited during the last four decades and will actually increase somewhat from 1990 to 2025, the United Nations population projections (medium variant) anticipate an average annual growth of 0.33 per cent during that period. (The assumption of a future fertility increase is less than convincing. Actual population growth rates may well turn out to be much closer to zero than is projected.) The population of the developed countries in 2025 thus would exceed its 1990 level by 12 per cent. In that year, it would constitute 16 per cent of the global population.

Further characteristics of the DC group include a per capita income that is extraordinarily high by historical standards. Based on World Bank estimates (with modest extension to countries not covered by the Bank's statistics), gross national product per capita in DCs in 1987 was slightly over $10,000, measured in 1987 dollars. Production of that income (which during the last quarter century has been increasing at an annual rate of over 2 per cent per capita) is facilitated by the use of science-based modern technology that is dependent on heavy use of energy derived primarily from fossil fuels, but also and increasingly from nuclear fission; on modes of transportation and communication permitting rapid and low-cost movement of materials, people, and information over large distances; on extensive use of machinery, including machinery capable of markedly changing surface vegetation and topographic features of the land; and on industry producing or making use of an ever-widening array of chemicals and toxic materials.

Conditions in the LDCs are markedly different. In 1990, the aggregate population in these countries was 4 billion – twice as large as the entire global population around 1930. The current rate of expansion of the population exceeds 2 per cent per annum. The United Nations projections assume that fertility rates in the developing countries as a whole during the next 35 years will drop by 40 per cent. Although, again, this assumption is less than compelling (actual growth rates may be higher than projected because in a number of countries the assumed generalized fertility decline is not yet supported by observed evidence), it would still lead (in combination with moderate assumptions as to the further decrease of mortality) to a 2025 LDC population of 7.1 billion, or an increase of 74 per cent over its current level. At that time, population increase in these countries would still exceed 1.1 per cent, or nearly 80 million persons per annum. The share of the population of the countries now classified as less developed will have risen from its present 77 per cent to 84 per cent of the global total.

These demographic characteristics of the LDCs are at present accompanied by per capita income levels markedly lower than in the DCs. Based again on World Bank estimates, average GNP per capita in 1987 was $780, or less than 8 per cent of the estimated GNP per capita in the DCs. Certainly, this implied 1:13 ratio between average per capita incomes in LDCs and DCs cannot be taken as an accurate estimate of differences in material levels of welfare. A correction of the estimated figures, making them more closely reflect purchasing-power parities, would appreciably narrow the income gap. Nevertheless, the striking contrast between LDCs and DCs with respect to income per capita would remain after any statistically defensible adjustment. The low-income levels, in turn, reflect a state of the LDC economies characterized by only a shallow and partial spread of the advanced technology applied in DCs. The economic structure of most LDCs remains numerically dominated by technologically backward and highly labour-intensive agriculture and by low-productivity handicraft and service sectors. Average per capita use of energy sources dominant in modern industrial economies is still low in LDCs, with use of fuel-wood representing a significant fraction of total energy use.

Abstracting from the significant complications introduced by differences in technology between DCs and LDCs with respect to the pollution- and resource use-intensity of income, the current levels of population-related environmental impacts in these two categories of countries may be approximately characterized by the comparative product of the first two terms in the above equations: population size times income per capita.

Using the relevant estimates noted in the preceding paragraphs, the gross world product (GWP) in 1987 can be put at $15 trillion. Eighty per cent of this sum, $12 trillion, was income produced in the DCs. Within GWP, approximately $11 trillion, or 73 per cent of the total, was income produced in the OECD countries, which, in combination, represent somewhat less than 15 per cent of the world's population. OECD income per capita in 1987 was $14,700, or nearly

20 times the corresponding overall LDC figure. Within the latter group, the countries classified by the World Bank as 'low income' comprised 56 per cent of the world's population, had an average annual income of $290 (or one-fiftieth of the OECD average), and produced less than 6 per cent of GWP. Even allowing for significant error in these figures, the estimated composition of GWP by country of origin provides a strong presumptive identification of the DCs as the dominant current source of whatever deleterious environmental impact is attendant upon economic activity. Apart from differences in the ways in which income is produced and expended (differences that partly reinforce, partly weaken this presumption), two considerations modify the portent of the claim. The first concerns change over time, the main topic of the present discussion. The second consideration is related to the geographic-political unit within which environmental impact is experienced: most of the impact is not global but is contained within national boundaries – indeed, within subnational units. In what follows, these two points will be discussed briefly.

The present size of the world population is a given, as are the differing levels of economic development associated with its component parts. The status quo is effectively beyond the reach of policy: deliberate human action can hold sway only over the future. The striking DC–LDC contrasts in anticipated demographic dynamics were noted above. They suggest that population growth *per se* during the coming decades, and most likely beyond, will virtually cease contributing to changing environmental impact in the DCs. Virtually all such change in these countries will be due to the dynamics of income per capita and the technology applied in producing and expending it.

Demographic growth, in contrast, will continue to be rapid in LDCs. But, as noted above, such growth is currently lightly weighted by income per capita, thus moderating the potential environmental impact. The low incomes now prevailing in LDCs, however, should be seen as anomalous and, it is to be hoped, temporary. Certainly, they do not reflect the aspirations of the LDCs themselves, nor their determination to narrow and eventually to close the gap that separates them from the level of affluence now enjoyed by the developed countries. The populations of the less developed world made no vow of permanent poverty – indeed, their economic policies are oriented toward maximum feasible material growth. Should LDC income per head rise in a rapid and sustained fashion (as has been spectacularly the case in a number of successful LDCs in recent decades), these countries would not only generate virtually all environmental impact attendant upon future demographic growth, but the massive demographic weight of their expanding populations would eventually dominate the global economic picture, including the environmental impact of GWP. Assessment of the size and character of such impact thus crucially depends on expectations about the prospects of LDCs for increasing levels of material welfare. Further considerations that enter into such assessment concern the anticipated feed-back of development on demographic change – might it modify the scenario incorporated in the standard UN projections? – and, of course, on judgement about the severity and intractability of the deleterious environmental impact associated with increasing per capita income.

On each of these issues, informed opinion continues to reflect startlingly wide disagreement. It is difficult to avoid concluding that the fields of study bearing on the subject remain in a pre-scientific state, with experts defending positions and making forecasts that are often diametrically opposed. Signs of convergence between conflicting interpretations of empirical evidence or between contending theoretical constructs are largely absent. For the sake of mnemonic convenience and brevity, although with some injustice to disciplinary labels, two salient and conflicting perspectives may be distinguished. They may be characterized as 'ecological' and 'economic'.

ECOLOGICAL PERSPECTIVES

In the ecological perspective, the dominant tone in discussing the impact of demographic and economic growth (and of modern technology) on the environment tends to be deeply pessimistic. There is a vast and rapidly expanding literature identifying and documenting damage generated by such growth upon terrestrial and aquatic ecosystems and their various specific components, and demonstrating growing atmospheric pollution. Indeed, a plausible discussion of the impact of rapid demographic change could be offered by reporting salient findings culled from the literature discussing changes in the human environment – as is done, in fact, albeit in non-population-centred contexts, in numerous specialized reports. Accounts of environmental issues in the mass media also largely consist of retailing such findings.

But, at least for practitioners of the social sciences, and especially for economists and historians, the accumulation of ecological studies resists such use. For all their scientific underpinnings and admirable empirical bent, the findings in the ecological literature thus far lend themselves poorly to generalizations that would aid understanding of overall developmental trends. Reflecting, no doubt, the vast complexity of ecosystems susceptible to damage from economic activity and the great variety of means through which such damage can be inflicted, the findings offered tend to be episodic, often plainly focused on the untypical and the extreme, and often simply eclectic or even merely anecdotal. The list of documented dire ecological consequences attendant upon human activity, each more or less loosely linked or linkable to population growth, seems, at least to the non-expert, endless. Loss of topsoil, desertification, deforestation, toxic poisoning of drinking water, oceanic pollution, shrinking wetlands, overgrazing, species loss, shortage of firewood, exhaustion of oil reserves and of various mineral resources, siltation in rivers and estuaries, encroachment of human habitat on arable land, dropping water tables, erosion of the ozone layer, loss of wilderness areas, global warming, rising sea levels, nuclear wastes, acid rain – these and many other problems cover the range from the dubiously conjectural through the plainly marginal to the disturbing but evidently exceptional, all the way to the potentially cataclysmic. These catalogues of man-inflicted damages are seldom relieved by reports of agreeable ecological-environmental change, thus arousing lay suspicion that their muster is directed to support a preconceived analytic conclusion and a political agenda: that sustained material growth is impossible, or rather that it necessarily leads to decay, deterioration, and ultimately to ecological collapse. These latter propositions, *qua* long-run propositions, are universally accepted, as indeed they are self-evident. But findings about ecological changes, to be relevant for shaping public policy, would need to be fitted into broader conceptual models that can plausibly accommodate and organize disparate facts, including human behavioural responses, and provide adequate parametrization for identifying time-scales and for assessing relative importance of deleterious effects – issues critical for taking corrective action. In the absence of this, the findings poorly support the sweeping policy conclusion that is not only hostile to demographic growth, but often explicitly urges responses that would be apt to drastically slow or even preclude future economic growth.

ECONOMIC PERSPECTIVES

Economists' interpretations of salient issues of population change, development, and the environment, despite the notable divergences in detail and emphasis between expert positions, differ significantly from those derived from the ecological perspective. While economists recognize that, other things equal, sustained population growth would lead to an ultimate low-level Malthusian equilibrium or, alternatively, to systemic collapse, with few exceptions (more vocal in the 1960s and 1970s than in the 1980s) economists see such outcomes as sufficiently remote in time so as not to qualify as a guide for prediction or ground for policy intervention in the near and medium-term future. Even with no further progress in state-of-the-art technology, including organizational skills, economists see large hidden reserves for growth in the existing inefficiencies with which production is carried out in LDCs, and in the extent of unused technological knowledge. Tapping these reserves by adopting the institutional arrangements and production practices of the most successful economies should permit substantial material improvement in virtually all LDCs, even if they have to accommodate further major population increases.

This expectation is reinforced in the light of historical experience, which suggests that assuming cessation of technological-organizational progress is plainly unrealistic. Indeed, most economists tend to read the lessons of the past as ground for optimism concerning the overall direction of world economic development. Taking measured changes in average material conditions over long periods of time as the criterion of welfare improvement, the last 200 years, and especially the last 40 years, can be fairly described as an historically unprecedented success story in material progress. This claim is not contradicted by the recognition that the rate of advance has been uneven, both geographically and between social strata within countries. Nor is it necessarily negated by the fact that, along with rapidly increasing total population size, the absolute number of people in poverty may have also been increasing. The relevant measures of success are the decreasing proportion of the poor and progress toward material improvement among those who are still in poverty. In a process of secular transition, widening relative differentials of income are an expected concomitant of the differing time of entry, by country and by social strata, in the process of modern economic growth – a process characterized by the adoption of institutions and policies permitting the increasing application of science, technology, and physical and human capital in expanding society's capacity to satisfy human wants. As that process spreads, geographically and between social strata, the rate of material progress among the highest-income population segments slows down and the late-comers eventually are able to catch up with them. As to demographic growth, its initial acceleration is a natural byproduct of such economic transformation since, predictably, the fruits of economic improvement are in part used for obtaining better health and lowered mortality. Malthusian outcomes, however, need not be the inevitable result of rapid population growth. Such growth is transitory: given economic success, the spontaneous onset of 'demographic transition' can be confidently expected. Pressures built into the reward mechanisms of modern industrial society induce behavioural changes that eventually lead to low fertility, hence to low or no population growth.

The economic perspective also offers a more benign and optimistic interpretation of environmental changes. This holds both for past trends and for anticipated future developments. Improving environmental quality and securing the best possible environmental outcome are objectives that people pursue not single-mindedly but in competition and along with other desirable goals. They seek an overall welfare optimum, rather than maximize satisfaction in particular domains without regard to cost in terms of opportunities foregone. Their choices are constrained by their income within a set of preferences, and are conditioned by their knowledge, access to information, and cultural background.

ENVIRONMENTAL CHOICES

The environmental choices of individuals or individual families that do not significantly affect other persons are instructive in this regard. They show wide variations in their environment-affecting practice, even at given levels of income and knowledge. There are individuals who are tidy and highly safety-conscious; and there are individuals who are not. But both types are optimizers according to their best lights, rather than maximizers of any particular component within their preference sets: even in Swiss households pianos may not be dusted off twice a day. Depending on tastes, environmental choices may vary considerably, yet make equally good sense. When incomes also differ, optimal trade-offs between environmental and other objectives will naturally differ as well. Someone with modest means will rationally choose to live in an environment of lower quality than a rich person, and accept greater risks to his safety and health. Such trade-offs also shift with increasing knowledge about the true environmental risks and qualities attached to available options. Some environmental actions are not highly knowledge-intensive. Thus, garden-variety household pests are easily recognized, eliciting the correct remedies – for example, the acquiring of a cat. But detecting radon gas is not possible without scientific instruments, and acting upon relevant findings requires sophisticated understanding of possible dangers.

The homey examples just cited intimate the essential nature of environmental choices and their crucial dependence on income levels, knowledge, and preferences. But they deal with problems whose solution entails costs and benefits that affect essentially the person or persons who decide how to deal with the problem. The most difficult, and often the most important, environmental issues arise from individual and group actions whose benefits accrue to the actors but whose costs are borne, entirely or disproportionately, by someone else. To seek to privatize the benefits of one's actions and to transfer the costs of those actions to the rest of society is a universal human tendency. In modern societies and under conditions of rapid economic development, this tendency, as a rule, is too weakly kept in check by social norms and moral precepts alone. When such is the case, the damage generated by environmental 'externalities' may get out of hand, with grave consequences for human welfare. Solution of the problem calls for recourse to social technologies: the adoption or development of institutional frameworks permitting efficient negotiation and effective enforcement of mutually acceptable standards and modes of behaviour. In a complex society, the difficulties of devising appropriate institutional arrangements – low-cost mechanisms for reaching and enforcing private contracts, tort laws, taxes and bounties discouraging undesirable patterns of consumption and promoting desirable modes of conduct, government regulations limiting or prohibiting socially disapproved behaviour, collective action aimed at producing or protecting public environmental amenities, and so on – are enormous. So are the potential environmental and general welfare benefits which success in that endeavor can secure for the members of a society. But seeking solutions to environmental problems through institutional changes and legal-political arrangements is itself a potentially error-prone process, with great opportunities for social mischief.

POPULATION GROWTH AND MATERIAL PROGRESS

It follows from the above discussion that three major factors will largely determine future environmental trends. Each is a potentially powerful lever for ameliorative intervention through appropriate public policies, especially in LDCs. The first factor is economic growth. Higher incomes would broaden the range of available choices and permit satisfaction of needs beyond basic necessities. The income elasticity of demand for environmental quality is high. Economic growth and environmental improvement are not enemies. To the contrary, they go hand-in-hand: controlling pollution and purchasing improved environmental quality are value-producing charges on income. Only reasonably affluent societies can afford adequate levels of such spending. In low-income countries rapid economic growth is especially indispensable for creating a capacity that would permit protecting and improving the environment.

The second factor is knowledge, embodied in a widely diffused form in the citizenry at large, accumulated in public agencies, and concentrated at the state-of-the-art level in well-established scientific and educational institutions. Better monitoring of environmental changes and clearer understanding of environmental options, risks, and benefits permit more enlightened and efficient choices both by private individuals and by public bodies.

The third factor is least easily measured but by all evidence is the most important. It involves social technology: improved institutions and related socio-political arrangements capable of generating efficient, co-ordinated responses to recognized social problems. Preventing environmental problems from getting out of hand and devising ways of acquiring and protecting the level and quality of environmental amenities best suited to citizens' preferences are crucial tasks for the public agenda.

The brief enumeration above of the factors playing the most influential roles in setting future environmental trends brings us back to the issue of rapid population growth in LDCs. As was noted above, according to mainline economic thinking rapid population growth, given reasonably enlightened economic and social policies in the countries experiencing such growth, need not be inconsistent with continuing economic improvement. Contemporary LDCs also have a special asset: they can exploit the advantages of being late-comers to modern economic growth. They can adopt, at relatively low cost, technologies developed elsewhere, bypass technological detours pioneers unwittingly had to follow, learn from other countries' policy mistakes, attract foreign capital and expertise, relieve domestic natural resource constraints through access to foreign markets, and so on. Thus, most LDCs should be able to attain rates of economic growth that are faster than their rates of population growth, hence increase their incomes per capita. Only egregiously misguided public policies could bar this avenue of steady material improvement. As in earlier development experience, economic growth would eventually bring about the onset of fertility decline. Where fertility is already decreasing, continued economic growth would in due course bring the demographic transition to its ultimate conclusion.

But avoiding disaster and making slow improvement may fall far short of what should be not only a desirable but also an attainable rate of material progress. Countries experiencing rapid population growth are necessarily forced to devote a disproportionate share of their economic and social efforts to keeping pace with sheer demographic expansion. There is a long list of problems whose solution is rendered more difficult and more onerous under conditions of rapid population growth. The central task of development – the structural transformation of the traditional economy into a high-productivity modern industrial economy – will require far greater investments and take more time than would be the case with slower demographic growth. The absorption of large youth cohorts that seek entry into the labour force will be more difficult, as will be lowering the existing levels of unemployment and underemployment. Urbanization will be a greater burden as cities grow faster, and economies of scale will be exhausted earlier than would be the case with slower population growth. In many LDCs with relatively unfavourable land-population ratios, attainment of self-sufficiency in food, even if strongly desired, is likely to be delayed or rendered technically unfeasible. With rapidly increasing absolute numbers, a country's capacity to finance its development through exports drawing on the domestic natural resource-base is bound to be lowered. These and similar problems would tend to slow economic development in terms of income growth per capita. Thus, when population growth is rapid, countries' ability, both on private and on public account, to address environmental problems is weakened, and private and collective spending on positive environmental improvements receives low priority. Progress towards greater knowledge and sophistication in handling environmental problems is hindered due to countries' impaired capacity to provide good quality education to all young persons and to support a strong state-of-the-art scientific base that is needed to accurately assess and successfully address environmental issues. Finally, rapid population growth further overloads the typically weak administrative-political structures found in LDCs, and makes reform of institutional arrangements affecting the efficacy of environmental and other development-related policies more difficult.

Developing countries with rapid population growth, and international organizations that seek to assist the development efforts of such countries, including their efforts to improve the environment, thus can ill afford to ignore the issue of population change. In particular, the timing of the onset of fertility decline and the tempo of that decline are unlikely to be optimal under a laissez-faire national fertility policy. Exceptional situations apart, the demographic predicament in LDCs during the next few decades is not the inability of these countries to upgrade economic performance and to effect environmental improvements if population growth remains rapid and fertility declines but slowly. The problem, rather, is the likelihood of an increasing demographic saturation that is successfully accommodated, but which locks LDCs into a long-term development path that is distinctly inferior in terms of standards of material welfare and its environmental component to what would be attainable with a rapid decline of fertility to replacement level or, temporarily, even below it.

The welfare and environmental consequences of a failure to achieve effective social control of fertility at present are still largely contained within individual countries. For this reason, the trade-offs that must be made between continuing population growth and gains in material progress are primarily for each country to decide, in light of their own preferences. Population-generated spill-overs crossing international borders, however, are increasing in importance and this trend is bound to continue in the future, particularly as growing LDC populations achieve higher levels of income per capita. Assessing such trade-offs and acting upon the findings will have to move increasingly also to the international political and economic agenda.

Part V

Futures

In broad outline, the global economic and demographic trends observed over the last several decades would support an expectation over the next decades of continued, if uneven, improvement in economic conditions and, partly in consequence, an approaching completion of the demographic transition. That demographic outcome, indeed, is the future built into the medium-variant population projections of the United Nations, which (in the 1996 revision – see United Nations 1997a) portray the world's fertility dropping from 2.8 children per woman in the 1990s to 2.1 ('replacement level') by around 2040, and life expectancy increasing in the same period from 66 years to 76 years. The world population, under this scenario, would rise from 6 billion in 2000 to 9 billion in 2040, but by then the annual increment would have dropped from 80 million people to below 50 million – and zero (and perhaps negative) population growth would be in sight. Closely tied to these trends would be a substantial aging of population, continued rapid urbanization in the less developed regions (United Nations 1997b), and continuation of the major shift in the balance of world population toward the South. (Longer range projections are given in United Nations 1992 and a wider spectrum of input assumptions in Lutz 1996.)

Both in evaluating this scenario and in probing its ingredients, consensus quickly wanes. The range of views on population and development presented in the earlier sections above are echoed and even magnified in looking ahead. The most sanguine outlook may be represented by Richard A. Easterlin (1996) or, in this Part, by F.A. Hayek. For Easterlin, the population explosion is a passing phenomenon, ushering in a future of sustained economic growth led by ever-higher material aspirations. For Hayek, population growth both promotes and responds to increasing differentiation and more intensive interaction among individuals in an 'extended order' of human society. Population problems simply do not arise in these circumstances: what we see is erstwhile poor countries successively building the complex economies and settlement densities already found in the rich countries.

More cautious or circumspect assessments of societal futures extrapolate emerging problems as well as favourable trends. Such problems include: supporting the necessary scale of transfer payments to the aged as their numbers multiply (World Bank 1994); accommodating changed relations between men and women and between parents and children, but avoiding fertility collapse to levels far below replacement, with its eventual implication of radical population decline (Davis et al. 1987, Preston 1984, Folbre 1994); maintaining the quality of socialization and education of children in the face of crumbling families and local communities (Coleman 1993); lessening the ecological damage associated with rising average consumption levels (Durning 1992); and coping not only with the large remaining public health agenda in poor regions but also with the health implications of extended lifespans worldwide and with new or re-emerging infectious disease threats (World Health Organization 1992). The future food situation, though in the aggregate far from dire by many informed accounts, is increasingly technology-dependent and regionally disparate (see Alexandratos 1995, and Bongaarts, in this Part). The greenhouse effect, the atmospheric warming caused by increased amounts of carbon dioxide and other 'greenhouse' gases, has the potential to create ramifying changes in the environment, affecting crop production (perhaps positively), disease vectors, natural ecosystems, sea levels, and weather patterns. Greenhouse gas emissions are linked to population growth as well as to industrialization.

Population change can have political consequences and political developments, in turn, clearly have the capacity to modify future economic and demographic trends. 'Failed states', according to Robert D. Kaplan (1996), owe their ungovernability partly to population growth and the resource scarcities and urban congestion tied to it. Environmentally-related political instability, Myers (1994) argues, will become common in many regions. But while examples of economic retrogression and associated political turbulence will surely continue to be found in the future, so too will cases of recovery and eventual return to paths of stable positive growth. At the international level, the drastic changes in population-size relativities among countries that are in train must have major political implications. Hedley Bull (in this Part) discusses how Western governments must adjust their perceptions and responses to these realities (see also McRae 1994). International migration from poor to prosperous countries is another politically sensitive issue that will not lessen in importance. This migration fills the demographic gap created by very low fertility, and in doing so creates increasingly polyethnic populations in the industrialized world – the topic explored by William H. McNeill, in this Part. The larger possibilities for international conflict along religious, cultural and ethnic fault-lines in the post-Cold War era are discussed by Samuel P. Huntington (1996).

What is the likelihood that the UN's medium demographic scenario is seriously awry? Ronald D. Lee (1991) and Griffith Feeney (in this Part) note that the uncertainties of population projections increase rapidly once the projection period exceeds a few decades. Behavioural patterns underlying human fertility can change with remarkable rapidity, aided by the ease of cultural transmission in the modern world. Some events in the natural world, connected or perhaps wholly unconnected to human activity, can potentially reach the scale at which they could impinge on global demographic trends. Nuclear war would have been of that nature, and may become so again; C.S. Holling (1986) writes of the unpredictability and possible suddenness of climate change; Joshua Lederberg (in this Part) imagines catastrophic new disease organisms. A raft of more exotic if remoter cases is described by John Leslie (1996).

Most disasters are local, however. Even such a massive event as the Chinese famine of 1959–61, with its 30 million deaths, barely shows up in the Asia-wide, let alone global, population trajectory. Hence there is the possibility, elaborated by Fred Hoyle (in this Part), of a world population continuing to ratchet upwards as technological and organizational advances remove the obstacles to its doing so. In the far distance Hoyle sees not an approach to equilibrium, and not a Malthusian resource crisis, but an organizational collapse engendered by population overload. His conclusions on the human future, he remarks, are 'in some ways more horrible, in some ways more hopeful, and certainly in all ways less dull' than those of Malthus.

REFERENCES

Alexandratos, Nikos (ed.). 1995) *World Agriculture: Toward 2010. An FAO Study*, John Wiley and Sons, Chichester.

Coleman, James (1993) 'The rational reconstruction of society', *American Sociological Review* 58: pp1–15.

Davis, Kingsley, Mikhail S. Bernstam, and Rita Ricardo-Campbell (eds.) (1987) *Below-Replacement Fertility in Industrial Countries: Causes, Consequences, Policies*, Cambridge University Press, Cambridge.

Durning, Alan Thein (1992) *How Much is Enough? The Consumer Society and the Future of the Earth*, Earthscan, London.

Easterlin, Richard A. (1996) *Growth Triumphant: The Twenty-first Century in Historical Perspective*, University of Michigan Press, Ann Arbor.

Folbre, Nancy (1994) *Who Pays for the Kids? Gender and the Structures of Constraint*, Routledge, London.

Holling, C.S. (1986) 'The resilience of terrestrial ecosystems: Local surprise and global change', in *Sustainable Development of the Biosphere*, William C. Clark and R.E. Munn, (eds.), Cambridge University Press, Cambridge.

Huntington, Samuel P. (1996) *The Clash of Civilizations and the Remaking of World Order*, Simon and Schuster, New York.

Kaplan, Robert D. (1996) *The Ends of the Earth: A Journey at the Dawn of the 21st Century*, Random House, New York.

Lee, Ronald D. (1991) 'Long-run global population forecasts: A critical appraisal', in *Resources, Environment, and Population: Present Knowledge, Future Options*, Kingsley Davis and Mikhail S. Bernstam, (eds.), Oxford University Press, New York.

Leslie, John (1996) *The End of the World*, Routledge, London.

Lutz, Wolfgang (ed.) (1996) *The Future Population of the World: What Can We Assume Today?*, revised and updated edition, Earthscan, London.

McRae, Hamish (1994) *The World in 2020: Power, Culture and Prosperity*, Harvard Business School Press, Boston.

Myers, Norman (1994) *Ultimate Security: The Environmental Basis of Political Stability*, W.W. Norton, New York.

Preston, Samuel H. (1984) 'Children and the elderly: Divergent paths for America's dependents', *Demography* 21: pp435–457.

United Nations (1992) *Long-Range World Population Projections: Two Centuries of Population Growth 1950–2150*, United Nations, New York.

United Nations (1997a). *World Population Prospects: The 1996 Revision*, United Nations, New York.

United Nations (1997b). *World Urbanization Prospects: The 1996 Revision*, United Nations, New York.

World Bank (1994) *Averting the Old Age Crisis: Policies to Protect the Old and Promote Growth*, Oxford University Press, New York.

World Health Organization (1992) *Our Planet, Our Health: Report of the WHO Commission on Health and the Environment*, WHO, Geneva.

Chapter 26

The Extended Order and Population Growth

F A Hayek

The modern idea that population growth threatens worldwide pauperisation is simply a mistake. It is largely a consequence of oversimplifying the Malthusian theory of population; Thomas Malthus' theory made a reasonable first approach to the problem in his own time, but modern conditions make it irrelevant. Malthus' assumption that human labour could be regarded as a more or less homogeneous factor of production – that is, wage labour was all of the same kind, employed in agriculture, with the same tools and the same opportunities – was not far from the truth in the economic order that then existed (a theoretical two-factor economy). For Malthus, who was also one of the first discoverers of the law of decreasing returns, this must have indicated that every increase in the number of labourers would lead to a reduction of what is now called marginal productivity, and therefore of worker income, particularly once the best land had been occupied by plots of optimum size. (On the relation between Malthus' two theorems, see McCleary 1953, p111.)

This ceases to be true, however, under the changed conditions we have been discussing, wherein labour is not homogeneous but is diversified and specialized. With the intensification of exchange, and the improving techniques of communication and transportation, an increase of numbers and density of occupation makes the division of labour advantageous, leads to radical diversification, differentiation and specialization, makes it possible to develop new factors of production, and heightens productivity. Different skills, natural or required, become distinct scarce factors, often manifoldly complementary; this makes it worthwhile to workers to acquire new skills which will then fetch different market prices. Voluntary specialization is guided by differences in expected rewards. Thus labour may yield increasing rather than decreasing returns. A denser population can also employ techniques and technology that would have been useless in more thinly occupied regions; and if such technologies have already been developed elsewhere, they may well be imported and adopted rapidly (provided the required capital can be obtained). Even the bare fact of living peacefully in constant contact with larger numbers makes it possible to utilize available resources more fully.

When, in such a way, labour ceases to be a homogeneous factor of production, Malthus's conclusions cease to apply. Rather, an increase of population may now, because of further differentiation, make *still further* increases of population possible, and for *indefinite periods* population increase may be both self-accelerating and a prerequisite for any advance in both material and (because of the individuation made possible) spiritual civilization.

It is, then, not simply more men, but more different men, which brings an increase in productivity. Men have become powerful because they have become so different; new possibilities of specialization – depending not so much on any increase in individual intelligence, but on growing differentiation of individuals – provide the basis for a more successful use of the earth's resources. This in turn requires an extension of the network of indirect reciprocal services which the signalling mechanism of the market secures. As the market reveals ever new opportunities of specialization, the two-factor model, with its Malthusian conclusions, becomes increasingly inapplicable.

The widely prevailing fear that the growth of population that attends and fosters all this is apt to lead to general impoverishment and disaster is thus largely due to the misunderstanding of a statistical calculation.

This is not to deny that an increase of population may lead to a reduction of average incomes. But this possibility is also misinterpreted – the misinterpretation here being due to conflating the average income of a number of existing people in different income classes with the average income of a later, larger number of people. The proletariat are an *additional* population that, without new opportunities of employment, would never have grown up. The fall in average income occurs simply because great population growth generally involves a greater increase of the poorer, rather than the richer, strata of a population. But it is incorrect to conclude that anybody needs to have *become* poorer in the process. No single member of an existing community need to have become poorer (though some well-to-do people are likely, in the process, to be displaced by some of the newcomers and to descend to a lower level). Indeed, everyone who was *already* there might have grown somewhat richer; and yet average incomes may have decreased if large numbers of poor people have been added to those formerly present. It is trivially true that a reduction of the average is compatible with all income groups having increased in numbers, but with higher ones increasing in numbers less than the lower ones. That is, if the base of the income pyramid grows more than its height, the average income of the increased total will be smaller.

But it would be more accurate to conclude from this that the process of growth benefits the larger number of the poor more than the smaller number of the rich. Capitalism created the possibility of employment. It created the conditions wherein people who have not been endowed by their parents with the tools and land needed to maintain themselves and their offspring could be so equipped by others, to their mutual benefit. For the process enabled people to live poorly, and to have children, who otherwise, without the opportunity for productive work, could hardly even have grown to maturity and multiplied; it brought into being and kept millions alive who otherwise would not have lived at all and who, if they had lived for a time, could not have afforded to procreate. In this way, the poor benefited more from the process. Karl Marx was thus right to claim that '*capitalism' created the proletariat: it gave and gives them life.*

Thus the whole idea that the rich wrested away from the poor what, without such acts of violence would, or at least might, belong to them, is absurd.

The size of the stock of capital of a people, together with its accumulated traditions and practices for extracting and communicating information, determine whether that people can maintain large numbers. People will be employed, and materials and tools produced to serve future needs of unknown persons, only if those who can invest capital to bridge the interval between present outlay and future return will gain an increment from doing this which is at least as great as what they could have obtained from other uses of that capital.

Thus without the rich – without those who accumulated capital – those poor who could exist at all would be very much poorer indeed, scratching a livelihood from marginal lands on which every drought would kill most of the children they would be trying to raise. The creation of capital altered such conditions more than anything else. As the capitalist became able to employ other people for his own purposes, his ability to feed them served both him and them. This ability increased further as some individuals were able to employ others not just directly to satisfy their own needs but to trade goods and services with countless others. Thus property, contract, trade, and the use of capital did not simply benefit a minority.

Envy and ignorance lead people to regard possessing more than one needs for current consumption as a matter for censure rather than merit. Yet the idea that such capital must be accumulated 'at the expense of others' is a throw-back to economic views that, however obvious they may seem to some, are actually groundless, and make an accurate understanding of economic development impossible.

THE REGIONAL CHARACTER OF THE PROBLEM

Another source of misunderstanding is the tendency to think of population growth in purely global terms. The population problem must be seen as regional, with different aspects in different areas. The real problem is whether the numbers of inhabitants of particular regions tend, for whatever reason, to outgrow the resources of their own areas (including the resources they can use to trade).

As long as an increase in population has been made possible by the growing productivity of the populations in the regions concerned, or by more effective utilization of their resources and not by deliberate artificial support of this growth from outside, there is little cause for concern. Morally, we have as little right to prevent the growth of population in other parts of the world as we have a duty to assist it. On the other hand, a moral conflict may indeed arise if materially advanced countries continue to assist and indeed even subsidize the growth of populations in regions, such as perhaps the Sahel zone in Central Africa, where there appears to exist little prospect that its present population, let alone an increased one, will in the foreseeable future be able to maintain itself by its own efforts. With any attempt to maintain populations beyond the volume at which accumulated capital could still be currently reproduced, the number that could be maintained would diminish. Unless we interfere, only such populations will increase further as can feed themselves. The advanced countries, by assisting populations such as that in the Sahel to increase, are arousing expectations, creating conditions involving obligations, and thus assuming a grave responsibility on which they are very likely sooner or later to default. Man is not omnipotent, and recognizing the limits of his powers may enable him to approach closer to realising his wishes than following natural impulses to remedy remote suffering about which he can, unfortunately, do little if anything.

In any case, there is no danger whatever that, in any foreseeable future with which we can be concerned, the population of the world as a whole will outgrow its raw material resources, and every reason to assume that inherent forces will stop such a process long before that could happen. (See the studies of Julian L Simon (1977, 1981a and b), Ester Boserup (1981), Douglass North (1973, 1981) and Peter Bauer (1981), as well as my own, 1954, p15 and 1967, p208.)

For there are, in the temperature zones of all continents except Europe, wide regions which can not merely bear an increase in population, but whose inhabitants can hope to approach the standards of general wealth, comfort, and civilization that the 'Western' world has already reached only by increasing the density of their occupation of their land and the intensity of exploitation of its resources. In these regions the population must multiply if its members are to achieve the standards for which they strive. It is in their own interest to increase their numbers, and it would be presumptuous, and hardly defensible morally, to advise them, let alone to coerce them, to hold down their numbers. While serious problems may arise if we attempt indiscriminately to preserve all human lives everywhere, others cannot legitimately object to an increase in numbers on the part of a group that is able to maintain its own numbers by its own efforts. Inhabitants of countries already wealthy hardly have any right to call for an 'end to growth' (as did the Club of Rome or the later production of *Global 2000*), or to obstruct the countries in question, which rightly resent any such policies.

Some notions that attend such recommended policies for restricting population – for example, that advanced peoples should turn parts of the territories inhabited by still undeveloped people into a sort of nature park – are indeed outrageous. The idyllic image of happy primitives who enjoy their rural poverty and will gladly forgo the development that alone can give many of them access to what they have come to regard as the benefits of civilization is based on fantasy. Such benefits do, as we have seen, demand certain instinctual and other sacrifices. But less advanced people decide for themselves, individually, whether material comfort and advanced culture is worth the sacrifices involved. They should, of course, not be forced to modernize; nor should they be prevented, through a policy of isolation, from seeking the opportunities of modernization.

With the sole exception of instances where the increase of the numbers of the poor has led governments to redistribute incomes in their favour, there is no instance in history wherein an increase of population reduced the standards of life of those in that population who had already achieved various levels. As Simon had convincingly argued, 'There are not now, and there never have been, any empirical data showing that population growth or size or density have a negative effect on the standard of living' (1981a, p18, and see his major works on this subject, 1977 and 1981b).

DIVERSITY AND DIFFERENTIATION

Differentiation is the key to understanding population growth, and we should pause to expand on this crucial point. The unique achievement of man, leading to many of his other distinct characteristics, is his differentiation and diversity. Apart from a few other species in which selection artificially imposed by man has produced comparable diversity, man's diversification is unparalleled. This occurred because, in the course of natural selection, humans developed a highly efficient organ for learning from their fellows. This has made the increase of man's numbers, over much of his history, not, as in other instances, self-limiting, but rather self-stimulating. Human population grew in a sort of chain reaction in which greater density of occupation of territory tended to produce new opportunities for specialization and thus led to an increase of individual productivity and in turn to a further increase of numbers. There also developed among such large numbers of people not only a variety of innate attributes but also an enormous variety of streams of cultural traditions, among which their great intelligence enabled them to select, particularly during their prolonged adolescence. The greater part of humankind can now maintain itself just because its members are so flexible, just because there are so many different individuals whose different gifts enable them to differentiate themselves from one another even further by absorbing a boundless variety of combinations of differing streams of traditions.

The diversity for which increasing density provided new opportunities was essentially that of labour and skills, of information and knowledge, of property and incomes. The process is neither simple nor casual nor predictable, for at each step increasing population density merely creates unrealized possibilities which may or may not be discovered and realized rapidly. Only where some earlier population had already passed through this stage and its example could be imitated, could the process be very rapid. Learning proceeds through a multiplicity of channels and pre-supposes a great variety of individual positions and connections among groups and individuals through which possibilities of collabouration emerge.

Once people learn to take advantage of new opportunities offered by increased density of population (not only because of the specialization brought about by the division of labour, knowledge and property, but also by some individual accumulation of new forms of capital), this becomes the basis of yet further increases. Thanks to multiplication, differentiation, communication and interaction over increasing distances, and transmission through time, mankind has become a distinct entity preserving certain structural features that can produce effects beneficial to a further increase of numbers.

So far as we know, the extended order is probably the most complex structure in the universe – a structure in which biological organisms that are already highly complex have acquired the capacity to learn, to assimilate, parts of suprapersonal traditions, enabling them to adapt themselves from moment to moment into an ever-changing structure possessing an order of a still higher level of complexity. Step by step, momentary impediments to further population increase are penetrated, increases in population provide a foundation for further ones, and so on, leading to a progressive and cumulative process that does not end before all the fertile or richly endowed parts of the earth are similarly densely occupied.

THE CENTRE AND THE PERIPHERY

And it may indeed end there: I do not think that the much-dreaded population explosion – leading to 'standing room only' – is going to occur. The whole story of population growth may now be approaching its end, or at least approaching a very new level. For the highest population growth has never taken place in developed market economics, but always on the peripheries of developed economics, among those poor who had no fertile land and equipment that would have enabled them to maintain themselves, but to whom 'capitalists' offered new opportunities for survival.

These peripheries are, however, disappearing. Moreover, there are hardly any countries left to enter the periphery: the explosive process of population expansion has, during the last generation or so, very nearly reached the last corners of the earth.

Consequently there is strong reason to doubt the accuracy of extrapolating the trend of the last several centuries – of an indefinitely increasing acceleration of population growth – into the indefinite future. We may hope and expect that once the remaining reservoir of people who are now entering the extended order is exhausted, the growth of their numbers, which distresses people so much, will gradually recede. After all, no fairly wealthy group shows any such tendency. We do not know enough to say when the turning-point will be reached, but we can fairly assume that it will be very long indeed before we approach the horrors which the fancy of the ineluctable indefinite increase of mankind conjures up.

I suspect that the problem is already diminishing: that the population growth rate is now approaching, or has already reached, its maximum, and will not increase much further but will decline. One cannot of course say for certain, but it appears that – even if this has not already occurred – some time in the last decade of this century population growth will reach a maximum and that, after-wards, it will decline, unless there is deliberate intervention to stimulate it.

Already in the mid-1960s, the annual rate of growth of the developing regions peaked at around 2.4 per cent, and began to decline to the present level of around 2.1 per cent. And the population growth rate in the more developed regions was already on the decline by this same time. In the mid-1960s, then, population seems to have reached, and then retreated from, an all-time high annual growth rate (United Nations 1980, and J E Cohen 1984, p50-1). As Cohen writes: 'humankind has begun to practice or to experience the restraint that governs all its fellow species'.

The processes at work may become more comprehensible if we take a closer look at the populations at the peripheries of the developing economics. The best examples are perhaps to be found in those fast-growing cities of the developing world – Mexico City, Cairo, Calcutta, São Paulo or Jakarta, Caracas, Lagos, Bombay – where the population has doubled or more over a short span and where old city centres tend to be surrounded by shanty towns or 'bidonvilles'.

The increase of population taking place in these cities stems from the fact that people living on peripheries of market economics, while already profiting from their participation in them (through, for example, access to more advanced medicine, to better information of all sorts, and to advanced economic institutions and practices), have nonetheless not adapted fully to the traditions, morality and customs of these economics. For example, they still may practice customs of procreation stemming from circumstances outside the market economy where, for instance, the first response of poor people to a slight increase of wealth had been to produce a number of descendants at least sufficient to provide for them in their old age. These old customs are now gradually, and in some places even quickly, disappearing, and these peripheral groups, particularly those closest to the core, are absorbing traditions that allow them better to regulate their propagation. After all, the growing commercial centres become magnets, in part just because they provide models of how to achieve through imitation what many people desire.

These shanty towns, which are interesting in themselves, also illustrate several other themes developed earlier. For example, the population of the country-side around these cities has not been depleted at the expense of the shanty towns; usually it too has profited from the growth of the cities. The cities offered suste-nance to millions who otherwise would have died or never been born had they (or their parents) not migrated to them. Those who did migrate to the cities (or to their peripheries) were led there neither by the benevolence of the city folk in offering jobs and equipment nor by the benevolent advice of their better-off country 'neighbours', but rather by following rumours about other unknown poor folk (perhaps in some remote mountain valley) who were saved by being drawn into the growing towns by news of paid work available there. Ambition, even greed, for a better life, not beneficence, preserved these lives: yet it did better than beneficence could have done. The people from the countryside learned from market signals – although they could hardly have understood the matter in such abstract terms – that income not currently consumed by rich men in the cities was being used to provide others with tools or livelihood in payment for work, enabling people to strive who had not inherited arable land and the tools to cultivate it.

Of course, it may be hard for some to accept that those living in these shanty towns deliberately chose them over the countryside (about which people have such romantic feelings) as places of sustenance. Yet, as with the Irish and English peasants Engels found in the Manchester slums of his own time, that is what happened.

The squalor of these peripheral areas is primarily due to the very economic marginality that dictated residence there rather than in the countryside. Also not to be ignored are the adverse 'cyclical' effects of third-world governments' attempts to manage their economies, and of the ability of these governments to remove employment opportunities from peripheral groups as concessions to established labour interests or misguided social reformers.

Finally – and here one may sometimes witness the selection process at something like first hand, and in its most naked form – the effects of commercial morals do not fall most harshly and visibly on those who have already learnt to practice them in a relatively more advanced form, but rather on newcomers who have not yet learnt how to cope with them. Those who live on the peripheries do not fully observe the new practices (and thus are almost always perceived as 'undesirable' and often thought even to border on the criminal). They are also experiencing personally the first impact that some practices of more advanced civilization exert on people who still feel and think according to the morality of the tribe and village. However painful for them this process may be, they too, or they especially, benefit from the division of labour formed by the practices of the business classes; and many of them gradually change their ways, only then improving the quality of their lives. At least a minimal change of conduct on their part will be a condition for their being permitted to enter the larger established group and gradually to gain an increasing share in its total product.

For the numbers kept alive by differing systems of rules decide which system will dominate. These systems of rules will not necessarily be those that the masses (of which the shanty-town dwellers are only a dramatic example) themselves have already fully adopted, but those followed by a nucleus around whose periphery increasing numbers gather to participate in gains from the growing total product. Those who do at least partially adopt, and benefit from, the practices of the extended order often do so without being aware of the sacrifices such changes will also eventually involve. Nor is it only primitive country folk who have had to learn hard lessons: military conquerors who lorded over a subject population and even destroyed its elite often later had to learn, sometimes to their regret, that to enjoy local benefits required adopting local practices.

CAPITALISM GAVE LIFE TO THE PROLETARIAT

We may in our remaining sections perhaps draw together some of our main arguments and note some of their implications.

If we ask what men most owe to the moral practices of those who are called capitalists the answer is: their very lives. Socialist accounts which ascribe the existence of the proletariat to an exploitation of groups formerly able to maintain themselves are entirely fictional. Most individuals who now make up the proletariat could not have existed before others provided them with means to subsist. Although these folk may *feel* exploited, and politicians may arouse and play on these feelings to gain power, most of the Western proletariat, and most of the millions of the developing world, owe their existence to opportunities that advanced countries have created for them. All this is not confined to Western countries or the developing world. Communist countries such as Russia would be starving today if their populations were not kept alive by the Western world – although the leaders of these countries would be hard put to admit publicly that we can support the current population of the world, including that of the communist countries, only if we maintain successfully and improve the basis of private property which makes our extended order possible.

Capitalism also introduced a new form of obtaining income from production that *liberates* people in making them, and often their progeny as well, independent of family groups or tribes. This is so, even if capitalism is sometimes prevented from providing all it might for those who wish to take advantage of it by monopolies of organized groups of workers, 'unions', which create an artificial scarcity of their kind of work by preventing those willing to do such work for a lower wage from doing so.

The general advantage of replacing concrete particular purposes by abstract rules manifests itself clearly in cases like these. Nobody anticipated what was going to happen. Neither a conscious desire to make the human species grow as fast as possible nor concern for particular known lives produced that result. It was not always even those who first initiated new practices (saving, private property, and such like) whose physical offspring thus gained better chances of surviving. For these practices do not preserve *particular* lives but rather increase the *chances* (or prospects or probabilities) of more rapid propagation of the *group*. Such results were no more desired than foreseen. Some of these practices may indeed have involved a decrease in esteem for some individual lives, a preparedness to sacrifice by infanticide, to abandon the old and sick, or to kill the dangerous, in order to improve the prospects of maintaining and multiplying the rest.

We can hardly claim that to increase mankind is good in some absolute sense. We submit only that this effect, increase of particular populations following particular rules, led to the selection of those practices whose dominance has become the cause of further multiplication. (Nor...is it suggested that developed morals that restrain and suppress certain innate feelings should wholly displace these feelings. Our inborn instincts are still important in our relations to our immediate neighbours, and in certain other situations as well.)

Yet if the market economy did indeed prevail over other types of order because it enabled those groups that adopted its basic rules the better to multiply, then *the calculation in market values is a calculation in terms of lives*: individuals guided by this calculation did what most helped to increase their numbers, although this could hardly have been their intention.

THE CALCULUS OF COSTS IS A CALCULUS OF LIVES

Though the concept of a 'calculus of lives' cannot be taken literally, it is more than a metaphor. There may be no simple quantitative relationships governing the preservation of human lives by economic action, but the importance of the ultimate effects of market conduct can hardly be overrated. Yet several qualifications have to be added. For the most part, only *unknown* lives will count as so many units when it is a question of sacrificing a few lives in order to serve a larger number elsewhere.

Even if we do not like to face the fact, we constantly have to make such decisions. Unknown individual lives, in public or private decisions, are not absolute values, and the builder of motor roads or of hospitals or electric equipment will never carry precautions against lethal accidents to the maximum, because by avoiding costs this would cause elsewhere, overall risks to human lives can be much reduced. When the army surgeon after a battle engages in 'triage' – when he lets one die who might be saved, because in the time he would have to devote to saving him he could save three other lives (see Hardin 1980, p59, who defines 'triage' as 'the procedure which saves the maximum of lives') – he is acting on a calculus of lives. This is another instance of how the alternative between saving more or fewer lives shapes our views, even if only as vague feelings about what ought to be done. The requirement of preserving the maximum number of lives is not that all individual lives be regarded as equally important. It may be more important to save the life of the doctor, in our example above, than to save the lives of any particular one of his patients: otherwise none might survive. Some lives are evidently more important in that they create or preserve other lives. The good hunter or defender of the community, the fertile mother and perhaps even the wise old man may be more important than most babies and most of the aged. On the preservation of the life of a good chief large numbers of other lives may depend. And the highly productive may be more valuable to a community than other adult individuals. *It is not the present number of lives that evolution will tend to maximize but the prospective stream of future lives.* If in a group all men of fertile age, or all such women, and the required numbers to defend and feed them, were preserved, the prospects of future growth would hardly be affected, whereas the death of all females under 45 would destroy all possibility of preserving the strain.

But if for this reason all unknown lives must count equally in the extended order – and in our own ideals we have closely approached this aim so far as government action is concerned – this aim has never governed behaviour in the small group or in our innate responses. Thus, one is led to raise the question of the morality or goodness of the principle.

Yet, as with every other organism, the main 'purpose' to which man's physical make-up as well as his traditions are adapted is to produce other human beings. In this he has succeeded amazingly, and his conscious striving will have its most lasting effect only so far as, with or without his knowledge, it contributes to this result. There is no real point in asking whether those of his actions which do so contribute are really 'good', particularly if thus it is intended to inquire whether we *like* the results. For, as we have seen, we have never been able to choose our morals. Though there is a tendency to interpret goodness in a utilitarian way, to claim that 'good' is what brings about desired results, this claim is neither true nor useful. Even if we restrict ourselves to common usage, we find that the word 'good' generally refers to what tradition tells us we ought to do without knowing why – which is not to deny that justifications are always being invented for particular traditions. We can however perfectly well ask which among the many and conflicting rules that tradition treats as good tend, under particular conditions, to preserve and multiply those groups that follow them.

LIFE HAS NO PURPOSE BUT ITSELF

Life exists only so long as it provides for its own continuance. Whatever men live *for*, today most live only *because* of the market order. We have become civilized by the increase of our numbers just as civilization made that increase possible: we can be few and savage, or many and civilized. If reduced to its population of 10,000 years ago, mankind could not preserve civilization. Indeed, even if knowledge already gained were preserved in libraries, men could make little use of it without numbers sufficient to fill the jobs demanded for extensive specialization and division of labour. All knowledge available in books would not save 10,000 people spared somewhere after an atomic holocaust from having to return to a life of hunters and gatherers, although it would probably shorten the total amount of time that humankind would have to remain in such a condition.

When people began to build better than they knew because they began to subordinate concrete common goals to abstract rules that enabled them to participate in a process of orderly collabouration that nobody could survey or arrange, and which no one could have predicted, they created situations unintended and often undesired. We may not like the fact that our rules were shaped mainly by their suitability for increasing our numbers, but we have little choice in the matter now (if we ever did), for we must deal with a situation that has already been brought into being. So many people already exist; and only a market economy can keep the bulk of them alive. Because of the rapid transfer of information, men everywhere now know what high standards of living are possible. Most of those who live in some more thinly settled places can hope to reach such standards only by multiplying and settling their regions more densely – so increasing even further the numbers that can be kept alive by a market economy.

Since we can preserve and secure even our present numbers only by adhering to the same general kinds of principles, it is our duty – unless we truly wish to condemn millions to starvation – to resist the claims of creeds that tend to destroy the basic principles of these morals, such as the institution of several property.

In any case, our desires and wishes are largely irrelevant. Whether we *desire* further increases of production and population or not, we must – merely to maintain existing numbers and wealth, and to protect them as best we can against calamity – strive after what, under favourable conditions, will continue to lead, at least for some time, and in many places, to further increases.

While I have not intended to evaluate the issue whether, if we had the choice, we would want to choose civilization, examining the issues of population raises two relevant points. First, the spectre of a population explosion that would make most lives miserable appears, as we have seen, to be unfounded. Once this danger is removed, if one considers the realities of 'bourgeois' life – but not utopian demands for a life free of all conflict, pain, lack of fulfilment, and, indeed, morality – one might think the pleasures and stimulations of civilization not a bad bargain for those who do not yet enjoy them. But the question of whether we are better off civilized than not is probably unanswerable in any final way through such speculation. The second point is that the only thing close to an objective assessment of the issue is to see what people do when they are given the choice – as we are not. The readiness with which ordinary people of the Third World – as opposed to Western-educated intellectuals – appear to embrace the opportunities offered them by the extended order, even if it means inhabiting for a time shanty towns at the periphery, complements evidence regarding the reactions of European peasants to the introduction of urban capitalism, indicating that people will usually choose civilization if they have the choice.

REFERENCES

Bauer, Peter (1981) *Equality, the Third World and Economic Delusions*, Cambridge, Mass: Harvard University Press.

Boserup, Ester (1981) *Population and Technological Change: A Study of Long Term Trends*, Chicago: University of Chicago Press.

Cohen, J E (1984) 'Demographic doomsday deferred', *Harvard Magazine.*

Hardin, Garrett James (1980) *Promethean Ethics: Living with Death, Competition and Triage*, St. Louis: Washington University Press.

Hayek, F A (1954/1967) 'History and politics', in *Capitalism and the Historians*, ed F A Hayek, London: Routledge & Kegan Paul. Reprinted in F A Hayek, *Studies in Philosophy, Politics and Economics* (London: Routledge & Kegan Paul, Ltd, 1967).

– (1967/1978), 'The confusion of language in political thought', address delivered in German to the Walter Euken Institute in Frieburg im Breisgau and published in 1968 as an Occasional Paper by the Institute of Economic Affairs, London. Reprinted in F A Hayek, *New Studies in Philosophy, Politics, Economics and the History of Ideas* (London: Routledge & Kegan Paul, 1978).

McCleary, G F (1953) *The Malthusian Population Theory*, London: Faber & Faber.

North, D C (1973) and R P Thomas, *The Rise of the Western World*, Cambridge: Cambridge University Press.

– (1981) *Structure and Change in Economic History*, New York: W. W. Norton.

Simon, Julian L (1977) *The Economics of Population Growth*, Princeton: Princeton University Press.

– (1981a) 'Global confusion, 1980: a hard look at the Global 2000 Report', *The Public Interest* 62.

– (1981b) *The Ultimate Resource*, Princeton: Princeton University Press.

United Nations (1980) 'Concise report of the world population situation in 1979: conditions, trends, prospects and policies', *United Nations Population Studies*, no 2.

Chapter 27

Can the Growing Human Population Feed Itself?

John Bongaarts

Demographers now project that the world's population will double during the next half-century, from 5.3 billion people in 1990 to more than 10 billion by 2050. How will the environment and humanity respond to this unprecedented growth? Expert opinion divides into two camps. Environmentalists and ecologists, whose views have been widely disseminated by the electronic and print media, regard the situation as a catastrophe in the making. They argue that in order to feed the growing population farmers must intensify agricultural practices that already cause grave ecological damage. Our natural resources and the environment, now burdened by past population growth, will simply collapse under the weight of this future demand.

The optimists, on the other hand, comprising many economists as well as some agricultural scientists, assert that the earth can readily produce more than enough food for the expected population in 2050. They contend that technological innovation and the continued investment of human capital will deliver high standards of living to much of the globe, even if the population grows larger than the projected 10 billion. Which point of view will hold sway? What shape might the future of our species and the environment actually take?

Many environmentalists fear that the world food situation has reached a precarious state: 'Human numbers are on a collision course with massive famines....If humanity fails to act, nature will end the population explosion for us – in very unpleasant ways – well before 10 billion is reached', write Paul R Ehrlich and Anne H Ehrlich of Stanford University in their 1990 book *The Population Explosion*. In the long run, the Ehrlichs and like-minded experts consider substantial growth in food production to be absolutely impossible. 'We are feeding ourselves at the expense of our children. By definition, farmers can overplow and overpump only in the short run. For many farmers the short run is drawing to a close', states Lester R Brown, president of the Worldwatch Institute, in a 1988 paper.

Over the past three decades, these authors point out, enormous efforts and resources have been pooled to amplify agricultural output. Indeed, the total quantity of harvested crops increased dramatically during this time. In the developing world, food production rose by an average of 117 per cent in the quarter of a century between 1965 and 1990. Asia performed far better than other regions, which saw increases below average.

Because population has expanded rapidly as well, per capita food production generally has shown only modest change; in Africa it actually declined. As a consequence, the number of undernourished people is still rising in most parts of the developing world, although that number did fall from 844 million to 786 million during the 1980s. But this decline reflects improved nutritional conditions in Asia alone. During the same period, the number of people having energy-deficient diets in Latin America, the Near East and Africa climbed.

Many social factors can bring about conditions of hunger, but the pessimists stress that population pressure on fragile ecosystems plays a significant role. One specific concern is that we seem to be running short on arable land suitable for cultivation. If so, current efforts to bolster per capita food production by clearing more fertile land will find fewer options. Between 1850 and 1950 the amount of arable land grew quickly to accommodate both larger populations and stronger demand for better diets. This expansion then slowed, and by the late 1980s ceased altogether. In the developed world, as well as in some developing countries (especially China), the amount of land under cultivation started to decline during the 1980s. This drop is largely because spreading urban centres have engulfed fertile land or, once the land is depleted, farmers have abandoned it. Farmers have also fled from irrigated land that has become unproductive because of salt accumulation.

Moreover, environmentalists insist that soil erosion is destroying much of the land that is left. The extent of the damage is the subject of controversy. A recent global assessment, sponsored by the United Nations Environment Programme and reported by the World Resources Institute and others, offers some perspective. The study concludes that 17 per cent of the land supporting plant life worldwide has lost value over the past 45 years. The estimate includes erosion caused by water and wind, as well as chemical and physical deterioration, and ranks the degree of soil degradation from light to severe. This degradation is least prevalent in North America (5.3 per cent), and most widespread in Central America (25 per cent), Europe (23 per cent), Africa (22 per cent), and Asia (20 per cent). In most of these regions, the average farmer could not gather the resources necessary to restore moderate and severely affected soil regions to full productivity. Therefore, prospects for reversing the effects of soil erosion are not good, and it is likely that this problem will worsen.

Despite the loss and degradation of fertile land, the 'green revolution' has promoted per capita food production by increasing the yield per hectare. The new, high-yielding strains of grains such as wheat and rice have proliferated since their introduction in the 1960s, especially in Asia. To reap full advantage from these new crop varieties, however, farmers must apply abundant quantities of fertilizer and water.

Environmentalists question whether further conversion to such crops can be achieved at reasonable cost, especially in the developing world, where the gain in production is most needed. At the moment, many farmers in Asia, Latin America and Africa use fertilizer sparingly, if at all, because it is too expensive or unavailable. Fertilizer use in the developed world has recently waned. The reasons for the decline are complex and may be temporary, but clearly farmers in North America and Europe have decided that increasing their already heavy application of fertilizer will not further enhance crop yields.

Unfortunately, irrigation systems, which would enable many developing countries to join in the green revolution, are often too expensive to build. In most areas, irrigation is essential for generating high yields. It also can make arid land cultivable and protect farmers from the vulnerability inherent in natural varia- tions in the weather. Land brought into cultivation this way could be used for growing multiple crops each year, thereby helping food production to increase.

Such advantages have been realized since the beginning of agriculture: the earliest irrigation systems are thousands of years old. Yet only a fraction of arable land in the developing countries is now irrigated, and its expansion has been slower than population growth. Consequently, the amount of irrigated land per capita has been dwindling during recent decades. The trend, pessimists argue, will be hard to stop. Irrigation systems have already been built in the most afford- able sites, and the hope for extending them is curtailed by rising costs. Moreover, the accretion of silt in dams and reservoirs and of salt in already irrigated soil is increasingly costly to avoid or reverse.

Environmentalists Ehrlich and Ehrlich note that modern agriculture is by nature at risk wherever it is practised. The genetic uniformity of single, high-yield- ing crop strains planted over large areas makes them highly productive, but also renders them particularly vulnerable to insects and disease. Current preventive tactics, such as spraying pesticides and rotating crops, are only partial solutions. Rapidly evolving pathogens pose a continuous challenge. Plant breeders must maintain a broad genetic arsenal of crops by collecting and storing natural varieties and by breeding new ones in the labouratory.

The optimists do not deny that many problems exist within the food-supply system. But many of these authorities, including D Gale Johnson, the late Herman Kahn, Walter R Brown, L Martel, the late Roger Revelle, Vaclav Smil and Julian L Simon, believe that the world's food supply can dramatically be expanded. Ironically, they draw their enthusiasm from extrapolation of the very trends that so alarm those experts who expect doom. In fact, statistics show that the average daily caloric intake per capita has climbed by 21 per cent (from 2063 calories to 2495 calories) between 1965 and 1990 in the developing countries. These higher calories have generally delivered greater amounts of protein. On average, the per capita consumption of protein has risen from 52 grams per day to 61 grams per day between 1965 and 1990.

According to the optimists, not only has the world food situation improved significantly in recent decades, but further growth can be brought about in various ways. A detailed assessment of climate and soil conditions in 93 developing countries (excluding China) shows that nearly three times as much land as is currently farmed, or an additional 2.1 billion hectares, could be cultivated. Regional soil estimates indicate that sub-Saharan Africa and Latin America can exploit many more stretches of unused land than can Asia, the Near East and North Africa.

Even in regions where the amount of potentially arable land is limited, crops could be grown more times every year than is currently the case. This scenario is particularly true in the tropics and subtropics where conditions are such – relatively even temperature throughout the year and a consistent distribution of daylight hours – that more than one crop would thrive. Nearly twice as many crops are harvested every year in Asia than in Africa at present, but further increases are possible in all regions.

In addition to multicropping, higher yields per crop are attainable, especially in Africa and the Near East. Many more crops are currently harvested per hectare in the First World than elsewhere: cereal yields in North America and Europe averaged 4.2 tons per hectare, compared with 2.9 in the Far East (4.2 in China), 2.1 in Latin America, 1.7 in the Near East and only 1.0 in Africa.

Such yield improvements, the enthusiasts note, can be achieved by expanding the still limited use of high-yield crop varieties, fertilizer and irrigation. In *World Agriculture: Toward 2000*, Nikos Alexandratos of the Food and Agriculture Organization (FAO) of the United Nations reports that only 34 per cent of all seeds planted during the mid-1980s were high-yielding varieties. Statistics from the FAO show that at present only about one in five hectares of arable land is irrigated, and very little fertilizer is used. Pesticides are sparsely applied. Food output could be drastically increased simply by more widespread application of such technologies.

Aside from producing more food, many economists and agriculturalists point out, consumption levels in the developing world could be boosted by wasting fewer crops, as well as by cutting storage and distribution losses. How much of an increase would these measures yield? Estimates vary widely. Robert W. Kates, director of the Alan Shawn Feinstein World Hunger Program at Brown University, writes in *The Hunger Report: 1988* that humans consume only 60 per cent of all harvested crops, and some 25–30 per cent is lost before reaching individual homes. The FAO, on the other hand, estimates lower distribution losses: 6 per cent for cereals, 11 per cent for roots, and 5 per cent for pulses. All the same, there is no doubt that improved storage and distribution systems would leave more food available for human nutrition, independent of future food production capabilities.

For optimists, the long-range trend in food prices constitutes the most convincing evidence for the correctness of their view. In 1992–93 the World Resources Institute reported that food prices dropped further than the price of most non-fuel commodities, all of which have declined in the past decade. Cereal prices in the international market fell by approximately one-third between 1980 and 1989. Huge government subsidies for agriculture in North America and Western Europe, and the resulting surpluses of agricultural products, have depressed prices. Obviously, the optimists assert, the supply already exceeds the effective demand of a global population that has doubled since 1950.

Taken together, this evidence leads many experts to see no significant obstacles to raising levels of nutrition for world populations exceeding 10 billion people. The potential for an enormous expansion of food production exists, but its realization depends of course on sensible governmental policies, increased domestic and international trade and large investments in infrastructure and agricultural extension. Such improvements can be achieved, the optimists believe, without incurring irreparable damage to global ecosystems.

Proponents of either of these conflicting perspectives have difficulty accepting the existence of other plausible points of view. Moreover, the polarity between the two sides of expert opinion shows that neither group can be completely correct. Finding some common ground between these seemingly irreconcilable positions is not as difficult as it at first appears if empirical issues are emphasized and important differences in value systems and political beliefs are ignored.

Both sides agree that the demand for food will swell rapidly over the next several decades. In 1990, a person living in the developing world ate on average 2500 calories each day, taken from 4000 gross calories of food crops made available within a household. The remaining 1500 calories from this gross total not used to meet nutritional requirements were either lost, inedible or used as animal feed and plant seed. Most of this food was harvested from 0.7 billion hectares of land in the developing world. The remaining 5 per cent of the total food supply came from imports. To sustain this 4000-gross-calorie diet for more than twice as many residents, or 8.7 billion people, living in the developing world by 2050, agriculture must offer 112 per cent more crops. To raise the average Third World diet to 6000 gross calories per day, slightly above the 1990 world average, food production would need to increase by 218 per cent. And to bring the average Third World diet to a level comparable with that currently found in the developed world, or 10,000 gross calories per day, food production would have to surge by 430 per cent.

A more generous food supply will be achieved in the future through boosting crop yields, as it has been accomplished in the past. If the harvested area in the developing world remains at 0.7 billion hectares, then each hectare must more than double its yield to maintain an already inadequate diet for the population of the developing world. Providing a diet equivalent to a First World diet in 1990 would require that each hectare increase its yield more than six times. Such an event in the developing world must be considered virtually impossible, barring a major breakthrough in the biotechnology of food production.

Instead, farmers will no doubt plant more acres and grow more crops per year on the same land to help augment future crop harvests. Extrapolation of past trends suggests that the harvested area will increase by about 50 per cent by the year 2050. Each hectare will then have to provide nearly 50 per cent more tons of grain or its equivalent to keep up with current dietary levels. Improved diets could only result from much larger yields.

The technological optimists are correct in stating that overall world food production can substantially be increased over the next few decades. Current crop yields are well below their theoretical maxima, and only about 11 per cent of the world's farmable land is now under cultivation. Moreover, the experience gained recently in a number of developing countries, such as China, holds important lessons on how to tap this potential elsewhere. Agricultural productivity responds to well-designed policies that assist farmers by supplying needed fertilizer and other inputs, building sound infrastructure and providing market access. Further investments in agricultural research will spawn new technologies that will fortify agriculture in the future. The vital question then is not how to grow more food, but rather how to implement agricultural methods that may make possible a boost in food production.

A more troublesome question is how to achieve this technological enhancement at acceptable environmental costs. It is here that the arguments of those experts who forecast a catastrophe carry considerable weight. There can be no doubt that the land now used for growing food crops is generally of better quality than unused, potentially cultivable land. Similarly, existing irrigation systems have been built on the most favourable sites. Consequently, each new measure applied to increase yields is becoming more expensive to implement, especially in the developed world and parts of the developing world such as China, where productivity is already high. In short, such constraints are raising the marginal cost of each additional ton of grain or its equivalent. This tax is even higher if one takes into account negative externalities – primarily environmental costs not reflected in the price of agricultural products.

The environmental price of what in the Ehrlichs' view amounts to 'turning the earth into a giant human feedlot', could be severe. A large inflation of agriculture to provide growing populations with improved diets is likely to lead to widespread deforestation, loss of species, soil erosion and pollution from pesticides, and run-off of fertilizer as farming intensifies and new land is brought into production. Reducing or minimizing this environmental impact is possible but costly.

Given so many uncertainties, the course of future food prices is difficult to chart. At the very least, the rising marginal cost of food production will engender steeper prices on the international market than would be the case if there were no environmental constraints. Whether these higher costs can offset the historical decline in food prices remains to be seen. An upward trend in the price of food some time in the near future is a distinct possibility. Such a hike will be mitigated by the continued development and application of new technology and by the likely recovery of agricultural production and exports in the former Soviet Union, Eastern Europe and Latin America. Also, any future price increases could be lessened by taking advantage of the underutilized agricultural resources in North America, notes Per Pinstrup-Andersen of Cornell University in his 1992 paper 'Global perspectives for food production and consumption'. Rising prices will have little effect on high-income countries or on households possessing reasonable purchasing power, but the poor will suffer.

In reality, the future of global food production is neither as grim as the pessimists believe nor as rosy as the optimists claim. The most plausible outcome is that dietary intake will creep higher in most regions. Significant annual fluctuations in food availability and prices are, of course, likely; a variety of factors, including the weather, trade interruptions and the vulnerability of monocropping to pests, can alter food supply anywhere. The expansion of agriculture will be achieved by boosting crop yields and by using existing farmland more intensively, as well as by bringing arable land into cultivation where such action proves economical. Such events will transpire more slowly than in the past, however, because of environmental constraints. In addition, the demand for food in the developed world is approaching saturation levels. In the US, mounting concerns about health have caused the per capita consumption of calories from animal products to drop.

Still, progress will be far from uniform. Numerous countries will struggle to overcome unsatisfactory nutrition levels. These countries fall into three main categories. Some low-income countries have little or no reserves of fertile land or water. The absence of agricultural resources is in itself not an insurmountable problem, as is demonstrated by regions, such as Hong Kong and Kuwait, that can purchase their food on the international market. But many poor countries, such as Bangladesh, cannot afford to buy food from abroad and thereby compensate for insufficient natural resources. These countries will probably rely more on food aid in the future.

Low nutrition levels are also found in many countries, such as Zaire, that do possess large reserves of potentially cultivable land and water. Government neglect of agriculture and policy failures have typically caused poor diets in such countries. A recent World Bank report describes the damaging effects of direct and indirect taxation of agriculture, controls placed on prices and market access, and overvalued currencies, which discourage exports and encourage imports. Where agricultural production has suffered from misguided government intervention (as is particularly the case in Africa), the solution – policy reform – is clear.

Food aid will be needed as well in areas rife with political instability and civil strife. The most devastating famines of the past decade, known to television viewers around the world, have occurred in regions fighting prolonged civil wars, such as Ethiopia, Somalia and the Sudan. In many of these cases, drought was instrumental in stirring social and political disruption. The addition of violent conflict prevented the recuperation of agriculture and the distribution of food, thus turning bad but remediable situations into disasters. International military intervention, as in Somalia, provides only a short-term remedy. In the absence of sweeping political compromise, widespread hunger and malnutrition will remain endemic to these war-torn regions.

Feeding a growing world population a diet that improves over time in quality and quantity is technologically feasible. But the economic and environmental costs incurred through bolstering food production may well prove too great for many poor countries. The actual course of events will depend crucially on their governments' ability to design and enforce effective policies that address the challenges posed by mounting human numbers, rising poverty and environmental degradation. Whatever the outcome, the task ahead will be made more difficult if population growth rates cannot be reduced.

REFERENCES

Alexandratos, Nikos, ed (1988) *World Agriculture: Toward 2000*, New York: New York University Press.

Brown, Lester (1988) 'The changing world lfood prospect: the nineties and beyond', *Worldwatch Paper* no. 85, Washington, DC: Worldwatch Institute.

Ehrlich, Paul R and Anne H Ehrlich (1990) *The Population Explosion*, New York: Simon and Schuster.

Kates, Robert W, et al (1988) *The Hunger Report: 1988*, Providence, RI: World Hunger Program, Brown University.

Pinstrup-Anderson, Per (1992) 'Global perspectives for food production and consumption', paper prepared for the Techno Vision Conference on Technology, Food, People: Technological Challenges in Food Production, Copenhagen.

Simon, Julian L and Herman Kahn, eds (1984) *The Resourceful Earth*, Oxford: Basil Blackwell.

Smil, Vaclav (1987) *Energy, Food, Environment: Realities, Myths, Options*, Oxford: Clarendon Press.

World Bank (1986) *Poverty and Hunger: Issues and Options for Food Security in Developing Countries*, Washington, DC.

World Resources Institute (1992) *World Resources 1992-93*, New York: Oxford University Press.

Chapter 28

Population and the Present World Structure

Hedley Bull

POPULATION AND THE DISTRIBUTION OF POWER

In the course of the last half-century a massive shift has taken place in the distribution of power in the world toward the states, peoples, and political movements of Asia, Africa, and Latin America, however unevenly this has occurred as between one and another.

No doubt the countries of North America, Western Europe, and Japan still represent the dominant centres of wealth and technology in the world today, and along with the Soviet Union, the dominant centres of military strength. No doubt also the advances that have been made by third world peoples and movements since World War II still fall far short of their aspirations and of the goal of a world society in which wealth and power may be said to be justly or fairly distributed. But the third world's own rhetoric on the theme of continued domination by the Western powers or by the superpowers tends to obscure the changes that have taken place. By gaining control of sovereign states and of their political and administrative apparatus, third world leaders have indeed been able to promote the identity and cohesion of their people, to foster national economic development, and to assert local control of economic life against external influences. The idea that legal and political independence leaves peoples helpless in the face of a world economic system of dominance and dependence neglects the fact that it is through the exercise of state power and universally acknowledged rights of sovereignty that many developing states have been able to limit their involvement in the world economy or improve the terms of their participation in it.

In extending their influence third world peoples have benefited from the prestige of their numbers – the numbers not merely of their states but collectively of their peoples. It has been the fashion in Western thinking about international relations in recent decades to discount the importance of population factors, or at all events of sheer size of population, as a source of power. Neither the economies nor the armed forces of contemporary states are labour-intensive to the degree that would justify the treatment of population size as the crucial determinant of state power, as it was taken to be among European states in the 18th and 19th centuries. We recognize that today factors of technology and capital may be much more important than factors of population in determining the economic and the military performance of a modern nation; that where a nation's population is a significant consideration, its size may be less important than its cohesion, the level of its education, its competence in technology or the capacity of the nation's resources to sustain it; that for some contemporary states a large population is more of a liability than an asset; that in relation to economic, military, or other standards of performance, it makes sense to speak of an optimum rather than of a maximum size of population, however difficult this may be to estimate.

Nevertheless, our perceptions of the political weight or importance of a nation or state, and even of its rights, are determined in part by the size of its population. Nations as colossal as China and India are generally acknowledged to have an importance in world affairs that they would still enjoy, even if economically and militarily they were weaker than they are. A population of 100 million or more today is not sufficient to confer superpower status upon a nation, but it is widely thought to be necessary for this status. Given the ambitions of contemporary Brazil or Nigeria, it is not clear that their pro-natalist policies are misconceived, even if they are not sufficient in themselves for the end in view.

The fear of superior numbers, especially when linked to differences of culture, of race, and of level of development, and reinforced by consciousness of a history of antagonism, is far weaker today among the Western peoples than it was at the turn of the century, when white Europeans, North Americans, and Australians spoke freely of the Yellow Peril. The change reflects not only the decline of belief in population as a factor of power, but also the weakening of racial exclusiveness owing to the processes of internal change by which all Western societies except South Africa have become multiracial societies. Nevertheless, it would be wrong wholly to discount this old fear. It focuses today as much or more on the threat posed by more populous countries to living standards and national cohesion than on threats to security. It is more noticeable on the periphery of the old white world (Australia in relation to South-east Asia, Israel in relation to its Arab neighbors, South Africa in relation to black Africa, the Soviet Union in relation to China) than at its centre. But though diminished, fear is still one of the unstated premises of Western concern about rapid population growth in the third world.

What is especially important in the present connection is that the significance of sheer population size is enhanced by the incipient cosmopolitanism in present-day thinking about world affairs. We believe that all human beings are equal in rights. We dimly perceive a world society of human beings possessed of these equal rights stretching over the globe, regardless of differences of race, sex, culture, or creed, their rights undiminished by state boundaries or sovereignty. This perception is rooted in 18th-century visions of the rights of man to which both liberals and Marxists are heir, and which are proclaimed in UN protocols and conventions giving them legal or quasi-legal status. These instruments lack machinery for effective implementation and enforcement, and the actual practice of governments in many parts of the world is a mockery of them. Nor are there grounds for assuming that a groundswell is in progress that will lead inevitably to the dissolution of the system of sovereign states and the emergence of a cosmopolis or functioning world society. But the idea of a world society of equal human beings has a sufficient place in our perceptions of world affairs to have already had a profound influence on questions of right or entitlement.

When in the rich Western countries an assessment is made of moral claims to our position of power and wealth, three considerations have to be taken into account today that would not have had to be raised, say, half a century ago. One is what I have called the emergence of cosmopolitanist perspective, which invites us to consider the condition of individual persons across the globe rather than of states. A second is the progress of egalitarianism, which suggests at least a presumption in favour of an equal distribution of power and wealth (leaving aside for the present the question of what precisely this means). And a third is expanded demographic consciousness, which presents us with a clear picture of our dwindling numbers in the West. All of these considerations point toward the moral vulnerability of the Western countries' present position.

THE OBLIGATIONS AND INTERESTS OF THE RICH

Not only does the growing power of developing countries compel attention to the proposition that the control of world population be related to the development of poor countries; the rich countries' own sense of obligation, reinforced by a sense of their long-term interests, must lead them to the same conclusion.

The Western democracies, which by World War II were accepting the degree of responsibility for the basic economic and social welfare of their citizens implicit in the phrase 'the welfare state', in the years since the war have come to recognize that this responsibility, although in diminished or attenuated form, extends beyond their citizens to mankind as a whole. Non-citizens were not thought, and still arc not thought, to have the same claims upon the state as do citizens; they do not have legal rights but only moral rights to assistance from rich states, and even these moral rights are regarded as imperfect rather than as perfect – that is, they leave the state with some choice as to whether to respond to them or not. By itself the Western states' sense of moral responsibility would not have been enough to cause them to pursue the policies of development assistance they have in fact pursued; these policies also reflect the perceived interests of the Western countries. Moreover, the sense of moral responsibility that does exist toward poor people beyond the state's frontiers is not felt equally toward all of them; it is distorted by historical associations (for example, of former colonial powers and their dependencies), cultural links, and present patterns of connection. Nevertheless, this sense of responsibility is a real factor in world affairs. It is also a new factor. Although it has immediate roots in the responsibilities assumed by colonial powers for economic and social welfare in their dependencies in the last phase of colonial rule, and more distant roots in the anti-slavery movement and ultimately in the natural law tradition of a moral community of mankind, it is a sympathetic response to the greater recent awareness of poverty, suffering, and oppression throughout the world as a whole.

However, the sense of obligation that is felt in the rich countries not only does not always bring them into alignment with third world governments on matters of development assistance, but leaves them divided on a number of basic principles. The sense of obligation in the rich, Western countries is felt towards individual persons within the less developed countries (LDCs), more particularly toward those that are poor or suffering. Third world governments, on the other hand, place their emphasis upon the rights of poor states rather than on individuals.

It is, of course, hazardous to generalize both about Western and about third world policies. The policies that have been described, moreover, are not strict opposites: the transfer of resources to poor individuals within third world states has to be done through the agency of the governments of these states, and Western opinion generally recognizes that improving the lot of individuals requires the strengthening of the economic, social, and political structures. Nevertheless, there is a contrast of emphasis between a rich country's concern with the welfare of individuals, the relief of suffering, and the meeting of basic needs (none of which goals necessarily implies any change in the relationship between donors that are strong and recipients that are weak), and the third world's concern with the development of local structures, the transfer of resources to local governments, and the freedom of these governments to determine the uses made of these resources (goals which imply that the relationship of dependence between donor and recipient states will be brought to an end).

The Western sense of obligation thus does not imply an equalization of wealth or standards of living (any more than the commitment of Western countries to minimum standards of welfare for their own citizens necessarily implies commitment to a more equal distribution of wealth domestically). Many third world governments, by contrast, are committed – at least rhetorically – to goals of equality beyond the measures of redistribution necessary to meet basic needs. This does not mean that third world governments are committed to equal distribution of wealth among their own citizens (like Western governments, they vary widely in their practices in this respect), still less to any conception of an equal distribution of wealth among individual persons in the world as a whole. But it is part of the common doctrine of the third world coalition that existing inequalities should be removed between rich and poor countries in respect of degree of development and average per capita income.

Western and third world perspectives also differ on the ideological justification for a transfer of wealth and resources; whereas the Western thinkers place the emphasis on the present and future needs of third world peoples, together with the goal of harmony in the international community, the spokesmen for the LDCs sometimes emphasize a right of compensation for past exploitation. The doctrine of a right of compensation for exploitation during the past colonial or present neocolonial era involves a number of assumptions that are widely rejected in Western countries: that the wealth of the advanced industrial countries derives significantly, or in the past derived, from exploitation of non-Western countries; that the less developed status of the latter is a consequence of colonial rule or of neocolonial exploitation; that the alleged wrongs of past exploitation are to be singled out from the vast catalogue of wrongs done by nation unto nation throughout history; that the responsibility is a collective one, of colonialist or Western peoples as a whole, and not simply of those that were directly involved; and that the responsibility is passed on from generation to generation.

Third world governments frequently portray the present international economic order as the source of their underdevelopment, poverty, and need, while the Western governments emphasize local or domestic causes, such as government corruption or inefficiency, political instability, social attitudes unfavourable to modernization, or lack of natural resources. For third world governments the international economic order serves as a scapegoat for local failures and difficulties, just as for the advanced countries the idea that the problems of the poor countries are brought about by local factors appears to absolve them from responsibility.

Finally, whereas opinion in the Western countries conceives of the objective in relation with the third world as a redistribution of wealth and the amenities of living that go with it, for third world opinion the objective is not so much the redistribution of wealth as the redistribution of power. For third world peoples and movements, an important part of what is objectionable about the present state of the world is their dependence on others, their vulnerability to the effects of decisions taken by outsiders. The poor countries do seek more power to resist outside forces as a means of securing a redistribution of wealth (thus the preoccupation that developed in the 1970s with the strengthening of third world 'bargaining strength'), but they also seek it as an end in its own right. A redistribution of wealth is necessary ultimately because without it there can be no effective redistribution of power. For the Western countries, development assistance and transfer of resources are thought of as taking place within the existing structure of power; for the third world countries, a vital objective is to change the structure of power.

The sense of obligation that leads the rich countries to assist the development of poor countries is complicated, but not extinguished, by the above conflicts of perspective; on the other hand, it is reinforced by Western considerations of national or state interest. The interests that are advanced by development assistance have been variously and often unconvincingly described – at different times it has been said that the purpose of assistance was to make the recipients more impregnable to radical political change, or better markets for export. One interest that has been consistently pursued is the very simple and old-fashioned one of purchasing compliance and goodwill with subsidies, but this is not an interest that can explain or justify a permanent commitment.

The paramount interest of the Western countries in promoting third world development is, I would argue, the construction of a viable international order. No world order can have any prospect of enduring into the next century unless the countries which represent a majority of the states and most of the world's population come to feel that they have a stake in its continuance. To develop a sense of a stake in the system, they must have an adequate share of its economic rewards and adequate participation in the shaping of political decisions.

As the poor countries become richer and more powerful, the Western powers will be called upon to make uncomfortable adjustments (as in the retreat from colonial rule, neocolonial domination, or white supremacist privilege). They will have to distinguish between what is a timely concession to necessary and just change, and what may be weakness in defence of a vital principle (as in relation to third world acts of aggression, violations of human rights, or assaults on freedom of information). There is no guarantee that when third world countries acquire power and riches, they will use them to exert influence within the established international system rather than to pursue their objectives outside its framework. A world in which third world countries dispose of relatively more power and wealth is also one in which the countries of the Western world have relatively less power. As we might learn from the history of American policy, it is one thing to espouse the power and prosperity of other states as an ideal, but another to come to terms with it in reality.

POPULATION AND MIGRATION

One way to relieve population pressure on the resources of poor countries may be through migration to places where resources are more plentiful. Some third world governments seek to encourage migration of their surplus population to Western countries, or to other areas in the third world such as the oil-producing states of the Middle East. Some, like Mexico, not merely demand entry into the United States for their surplus population, but speak as if entry were a moral right conferred by history or by present poverty. Such claims, moreover, do gain some recognition in those circles in the West in which there is sensitivity to global economic injustice.

From the point of view of the sending countries the benefits of this migration are clear enough. The migrants themselves escape from deprivation to a better standard of life, and if they have gone voluntarily, by their going at least show that they themselves believe that they will benefit. The families left behind may benefit from remittances, from no longer having to provide sustenance for the ones who have departed, and from reduced burdens of welfare. The sending country as a whole will have lost actual or potential labour and, in the case of highly skilled migrants, may suffer the effects of the 'brain-drain', but it may stand to gain from the export of unemployment, the acquisition of revenue and foreign exchange from remittances, and a safety valve for the release of social tensions. High growth rates like those following mass emigration from southern European countries in the post-war period and advantages like those derived by South Asian countries from migration to the Gulf area in the 1970s provide illustrations of these benefits.

Emigration from third world countries today has reached massive proportions, but does not in itself necessarily contribute to the goal of a just geographical distribution of population in relation to available resources, nor imply any demand for it. The causes of this emigration in the post-1945 era have been as much political as economic in nature: anti-colonial wars (as in Africa in the 1960s and 1970s), the oppression and sometimes expulsion of minorities by newly independent states dominated by particular ethnic groups (as of the Chinese in Indochina, Asians in East Africa, non-Amharic-speaking peoples in Ethiopia), civil wars coinciding with foreign intervention (as in East Pakistan in 1971 or Afghanistan at present). The countries that have received the greater part of the migrants are not those of the West, nor indeed the oil-rich ones, but other poor third world countries (at present Sudan, Zaire, Somalia, Thailand, Pakistan, Jordan, Mexico).

The issues raised by these population movements almost invariably take us back to the perception that the present geographical distribution of population in relation to wealth, as between the West and the third world, is an unjust one. The great demand in third world countries for migration into the rich Western countries is fed by the urge to escape from poverty, oppression, and instability, and by the lure of economic opportunity, liberty, and security in the West. It is facilitated and encouraged by the spread of information about the differences of conditions in different parts of the world, by the growth of social networks that facilitate the movement of migrants and their settlement in receiving countries, by the increasing ease and declining cost of long-distance transport, by the removal of barriers of racial and ethnic discrimination in the immigration and internal social policies of the receiving Western states, by the responsibilities recognized by Western countries toward migrants acknowledged to be 'refugees', and by the inability or unwillingness of Western governments to cope effectively with illegal migrants. The fact that the Western countries receive only a small proportion of total emigrants from the third world reflects the barriers to migration rather than lack of pressure for it.

Even where entry into the Western countries is not directly at issue, these states are often expected – by themselves as well as by others – to assume the responsibilities imposed by their wealth and resources, especially when the migrants involved may be regarded as refugees. By long tradition, refugees are a privileged class of migrants (if in other respects underprivileged), in respect both of their claims of entry into receiving states (the so-called right of asylum) and of their claims to just treatment after entry. But the concept of the refugee – a person outside his or her homeland, unable or unwilling to return to it because of persecution or well-founded fear of persecution – once applied principally to small numbers of individuals, usually political activists. In the 20th century, it has come to be applied to millions of people. Again, earlier in this century the refugees were mainly European; today they are chiefly African and Asian. Where once the persecution for which they were regarded as refugees was necessarily political in nature, today there is a tendency to speak also of economic persecution (meaning, moreover, not persecution by economic acts of the state, but rather the mere existence of economic conditions that fail to satisfy standards of human rights). It has even been suggested that for a person to be regarded as a refugee it may be enough that in the sending country there was an absence of positive rights, and that no actual infringement of positive rights is pre-supposed.

Along with refugees in the strict sense, we have thus come to speak of de facto refugees, economic refugees, internal refugees, and crypto-refugees. The widening of the concept of the refugee reflects not only the extension of public sympathies in the rich countries to wider categories of third world emigrants believed to have been denied rights of one kind or another, but also a certain artfulness on the part of the emigrants themselves: the availability of refugee services tends itself to swell the number of refugees. The privileges enjoyed by designated refugees as recipients of special assistance in the West, compared with other migrants in third world countries and indeed with ordinary citizens of the home countries, have sometimes generated resentment.

As the concept has expanded to embrace new categories of migrant, the responsibilities of the international community toward third world emigrants are thought to have expanded also. The principal bearers of these responsibilities are the Western powers – the countries that have the strongest tradition of providing asylum to refugees. They have the most wealth in relation to their populations; in some cases (the United States, Canada, Australia, New Zealand, South Africa) they are accustomed to viewing themselves as countries of immigration; they harbor the chief international non-governmental organizations active in this field and provide the bulk of the funds for the intergovernmental organizations. The responsibilities they are thought to have, in particular, are to be generous themselves in providing asylum to refugees; to provide generous assistance to 'countries of first asylum', in cases where neither repatriation nor resettlement in third countries is an option; and to contribute by means of development assistance or transfer of wealth to changing the conditions in the sending countries that have led to the exit of the refugees.

The Western countries' acceptance of migrants from the third world has not made any great contribution to relieving the pressures of rapid population growth in poor countries. The number of migrants accepted by Western countries from the third world in recent decades has constituted only a tiny proportion of world population growth in that period. Although substantial numbers of refugees have been accepted for resettlement – the most notable example being the million or so Indo-chinese accepted in the United States, Canada, Australia, New Zealand, and European countries – the great majority of refugees in the world are in third world countries. While the economic growth of the European countries in the 1950s and 1960s was built in part on cheap immigrant labour (Commonwealth immigration in the United Kingdom, guest-workers in West Germany and Switzerland), the recession of the early 1970s led to the virtual cessation of legal immigration, apart from acceptance of refugees. In the United States, Canada, and Australia, the trend has also been towards restriction of entry. There is a new concern for developing tougher measures to control illegal entry, 'interdiction of access', and measures to promote 'return migration'.

Yet in the receiving countries, pressures to relax barriers to third world immigration are still significant. A demand for cheap labour remains, especially in relation to work which local labour is unwilling to perform. This need is illustrated by employers' lobbying for Hispanic immigration into the United States. Political or ideological factors still operate in favour of particular immigrant groups, such as refugees from Cuba in the United States or from Vietnam in the United States and Australia. Campaigns are mounted by established ethnic groups, such as Indian and Pakistani communities in the United Kingdom, on behalf of particular individuals or families. In most Western countries, the diplomatic requirements or relationships with particular third world countries operate to moderate what would otherwise be harsher policies (for Britain's relations with Commonwealth countries, for Australia with ASEAN states, for the United States especially with Latin American countries). But for the present, the pressures to keep the doors closed are stronger. They include recession and the defence of jobs by organized labour; concern about the welfare burdens imposed by immigration; concern about social consequences, especially where (as in the case of Mexican immigration into the United States) the possibilities of successful integration are lessened by a 'temporary migrant mentality', linguistic separatism, and alienation resulting from repression of illegal immigration.

The flow of migration from poor to rich countries – and, more generally, all international migration – is impeded by the division of the world into sovereign states which claim the right and, by and large, possess the power to control the movement of persons across their frontiers. The right of individuals to leave their own country, or indeed any country, is asserted by liberal doctrine, proclaimed in the Universal Declaration of Human Rights and the 1975 Helsinki Final Act. In practice, this right is on the whole respected by Western states, but in Communist states there is no right of exit, and in many non-Communist states outside the West exit is a privilege rather than a right. Conversely, freedom of entry into countries is universally denied as a legal right, even (indeed especially) by the Western democracies. It is generally recognized that a state has obligations to admit certain categories of persons, such as its own nationals, diplomatic agents, and representatives of international organizations. There is widespread recognition among Western, African, and Latin American countries of the rights of refugees to asylum; but this is not taken to entail a corresponding duty to admit them to one's own country; on the other hand, the positive duty not to return refugees to the country from which they have fled is widely recognized.

The right to determine the entry of persons into one's territory, and thus the character of one's population, is a matter of the deepest sensitivity for most states; it touches not merely on the prosperity and security of a community, but also on its identity and control of its own destiny. For some peoples, like the Japanese, the goal of preserving their social homogeneity has led to a virtual prohibition of permanent immigration. People like the Malays, the Fijians, or the Sinhalese under British rule that have lost control of their immigration policy have paid dearly for it, and people fight to win or to defend their sovereign independence partly in order to regain this control.

Migration is also impeded by failure of the sovereign state to accord immigrants equal treatment with established inhabitants or citizens. Again, liberal doctrine proclaims an ideal of the maximum interchangeability of civil rights as between one citizenship and another, and their conformity with wider standards of human rights. But in practice immigrants and other aliens are seldom accorded equality of rights with citizens, and indeed the rights of citizenship may vary between a core national group and peripheral groups, as in the British system of tiered gradations of nationality. In many countries deep social distinctions lie behind these distinctions in law as between natives, or sons of the soil, and immigrants, even those of long standing. These distinctions are not uncommonly expressed in the oppression of the migrants, which at its worst takes the form of mass expulsion or genocide.

It is sometimes suggested that the sovereign state's control of migration is breaking down in the face of a 'tidal wave' of pressure from poor countries. This may be true of the US–Mexican or US–Caribbean cases, but these arise from special circumstances. The broad situation is that the Western countries, the most attractive targets for third world immigration, and the countries the most able to contribute to a global equilibrium between population and resources, have used their sovereign powers effectively to stem the flow.

POPULATION AND DEVELOPMENT

The Western countries might respond to third world views on population matters by intensifying their efforts to promote development in those countries which account for most of the world's growth in population. Such a strategy might serve to check population growth both by invoking the presumed contraceptive properties of development and by making direct policies of population control more widely acceptable in third world countries, while promoting a more equitable distribution of wealth and resources over the world as a whole. The means available for working toward such objectives are those that have been debated for many years, and in some cases implemented: improvements in the terms of trade for LDCs, such as preferences for their manufacturers and funds to raise and stabilize the price of primary exports; improved access to lending institutions; transfer of technology; increased official aid and private foreign investment; schemes for income taxation of the rich countries or of persons working in them; the proposed brain-drain tax.

Good reasons exist for questioning whether measures of this kind would be sufficient to cause dramatic changes in the development of poor countries, even if they were to be implemented on a massive scale. It may be doubted that today's differences between countries in wealth and level of development have much to do with the terms on which they participate in the international economy. Domestic differences in political stability, administrative efficiency, managerial and entre-preneurial skills, and adaptability to change, seem to account for the superior economic performance of those societies, especially in East and South-east Asia, that are today moving out of the ranks of the 'less developed.' Massive transfers of capital through official aid or private investment can promote development only to the extent that there is local capacity to absorb it or harness it to developmental purposes. The very conception that what is at issue between the North and South is 'the distribution of wealth' is in some measure misleading: some of the basic sources of the wealth of nations cannot be distributed among them in the way that capital can be; moreover, before wealth can be distributed, it has first to be produced, and proposals for arrangements to transfer wealth to poor countries have to deal also with the effects of these arrangements on the production of wealth, in which poor countries have a stake too.

There are special reasons for scepticism about redistribution of wealth through a brain-drain tax. Under this proposal, skilled or professional migrants from poor to rich countries would pay a supplementary tax on their earned incomes, to be levied by their countries of origin, collected by the host governments, and transferred to a UN fund for development purposes. The advantages of this scheme, which has something in common with the exit tax imposed by the Soviet Union on emigrants, are that it would provide compensation to poor countries for the effects of the 'reverse transfer of technology' they suffer as a consequence of the departure of highly skilled persons trained at their expense. It would also force rich countries to provide compensation for their interference with international mobility of labour in shutting their doors to unskilled migrants, and extend the principle of progressive taxation within poor countries across frontiers. On the negative side, the proposed tax would clearly infringe on the liberty of skilled migrants from third world countries, and handicap them in competition with others in the world labour market. It would discriminate against them within the host countries, and is likely to be in violation of anti-discrimination laws in the United States, the United Kingdom, and elsewhere. It would set aside the advantages which sometimes accrue to the countries of origin through remittances, the ultimate return in some cases of the migrants with their skills enhanced, and services which the migrants sometimes provide to the country of origin while still abroad. It would raise awkward questions as to what would count as a poor country and what as a rich country, which would be particularly hard to deal with for the very large professional migration which occurs among third world countries. Finally, it would tend to institutionalize distinctions between poor and rich countries, and between persons reared or educated in one or the other, distinctions that might otherwise become blurred, to the best interest of the international community.

If measures of development assistance are unlikely to be decisive in themselves, they may nevertheless contribute to the generation of wealth where local factors are favourable. Massive foreign investment of the kind proposed by the Brandt Report is technically possible and did play a vital role in the regeneration of Europe and Japan in the post-1945 era. What is clear, however, is that the Western countries do not at present have the inclination to undertake measures of this kind. The wellsprings of generosity of spirit toward the third world, and even of enlightened self-interest, have largely dried up in the West, and especially in the United States, during this long recession. The reluctance of the Western countries to face reductions in their living standards, always the basic factor making for a negative attitude toward proposals for an international redistribution of wealth, is felt more keenly at a time when these standards are already under threat. Further, the rich countries' reluctance to provide funds whose use they will not control has increased with mounting evidence of corruption and inefficiency in third world countries. Yet at the same time the successes of some third world countries in acquiring a degree of political and military power, or in competing effectively in international trade, together with the rhetorical assault that they have collectively mounted on Western positions over the last decade, have also left their mark on Western attitudes. The 1980s have seen a shift away from egalitarianism and welfarism and a renewal of faith in the operations of the free market in several major Western countries, and this has left them less than ever disposed to look favourably on proposals to interfere in the workings of international market forces. As the degree of hostility between the Western powers and the Soviet Union has intensified, the importance attributed to relations with third world countries has diminished, except in so far as they can be shown to be an aspect of relations with the Soviet Union.

Transferring wealth and resources to where the people are, like allowing people to move to where the wealth and resources are, is made difficult by the system of sovereign states, which claim and accord to one another the right to determine what is to be done with their wealth and resources, just as they claim the right to control their immigration policies. The developing countries may proclaim the rights of poor countries to development assistance and to a just share of the earth resources, as in the Charter of Economic Rights and Duties of States of 1974, but the rich countries insist on their sovereign right to judge for themselves what their response to such proclamations will be. Nor are the developing countries in any position to dispute this, for they are themselves the strongest defenders of the rights of states to sovereign independence.

POPULATION IN COSMOPOLIS

A solution to the problem of world population would be easier to find in a world that gave up the constraints of the sovereign state system in favour of a cosmopolitan society in which individual human rights were paramount, except in so far as they were limited by a beneficent world authority charged with the responsibility to achieve control of population growth, just distribution of the world's wealth and resources, and guaranteed minimum standards of welfare. Labour would be free to leave countries or enter them and enjoy equal rights after entry, subject to the determination by the world authority as to what the proper geographical allocation of population should be (as once suggested by Albert Thomas, the director of the International Labor Office). Capital would be free to move to where it was needed, but required to do so if it did not; the world authority would impose taxation for redistributive purposes on the rich and ensure that the funds transferred to the poor were used for purposes of development. The rights of persons to control the size and spacing of their families would be respected but limited by the goal of an optimum size, rate of growth, and geographical distribution of the world's population.

The world we actually inhabit, however, is one in which we have to reckon with the constraints not simply of the sovereign state system, but of the divisions in human society – political, economic, ideological, ethnic, historical – of which that system is merely an expression. Human rights are not implemented in practice not merely because of the claims of states to sovereignty, but more basically in many communities because of lack of will to respect them, agreement as to what they are, or even belief that they exist. Today, as much as long before modern notions of state sovereignty were conceived (the book of *Exodus* is instructive here), communities are determined themselves to control exit, entry, and the treatment afforded to aliens. In the world we live in capital is invested not where it is needed, but where it is profitable; rich nations are not willing to be taxed for purposes to which they have not consented, and poor nations in the first flush of independence are not willing to be told how they should spend their money; and in the unlikely event that a contemporary world authority were to be established, it would not necessarily be committed to individual human rights, minimum standards of welfare, and population equilibrium.

Yet from another perspective, in a divided world the system of sovereign states can play a positive role. This system, for all of its shortcomings, provides the possibility of coexistence or minimum order, in which diverse political communities respect one another's independence and spheres of jurisdiction, and without which the pursuit of more ambitious goals is not possible. It provides the basis for international co-operation, which through the UN system has reached unprecedented heights. But it does not imply (and should not be allowed to imply) the right of states and nations to disregard their responsibilities to one another and to the international community; whatever rights they have derive from the international community and are not held apart from it.

We can advance only by making use of the sovereign state system and its forms of institutionalized co-operation, inching forward toward solutions for these problems. Advances at the margin have in fact taken place: world population growth has slowed down, migration to the rich countries has had some impact, a shift of wealth and power to third world countries has occurred. Mention has been made of the growth in recent decades of a cosmopolitanist perspective. We should cultivate this perspective and seek to ensure that the policies of states are informed by it. The role of the UN system is crucial in this connection in spreading awareness, fostering debate, and building consensus. In matters of population, as in many others, it is worth promoting the idea that states can behave not merely as custodians of the interests of their own peoples, but also as the agents of the common interests of mankind, even in the face of much historical evidence to the contrary.

Chapter 29

On the Uncertainty of Population Projections

Griffith Feeney

The uncertainty of long-run population projections, by which we mean projections extending 50 to 100 years or more, is great. Ronald Lee begins his interesting review of the subject by telling us that there is 'reassuringly close agreement' on the 21st century population trends. He ends with the observation that, although a world population between 10 and 11 billion is projected for 160 years hence, the chances are only two in three that the actual figure will lie between 5 and 22 billion. Or, to put it another way, there is one chance in three that world population at that distant time will be less than 5 billion or more than 22 billion.[1]

That is a remarkable devolution, from reassuring agreement to uncertainty bordering on total ignorance. What does this say about the relevance of such long-run projections for the discussion of population and resources? At one level, the relevance is clearly nil. At another, the projections are relevant precisely because their uncertainty conflicts with widely held convictions about world population.

Consider, for example, the long-run history of human population growth as it has frequently been portrayed in graphic form. The upper curve in Figure 1 shows world population growth between 1950 and 1985 (time-scale above). The lower curve shows growth between the birth of Christ and 1985 (time-scale below).[2] If we look at the upper curve for clues to the future, the conclusion is uncertain. It is both natural and appropriate to extrapolate the recent trend, suggesting continued population growth at recent rates. At the same time, nothing in the picture rules out a gradual levelling off of the numbers, or a renewed increase.

The lower curve is not so reticent. The growth in the recent past appears so great as to rule out anything but continued sharp increases. This plot really does suggest a 'population explosion'. The problem with this conclusion is that both plots show exactly the same data, as indicated by the dashed lines connecting the common points. The 'explosion' suggested by the lower plot is an artefact of the choice of the time scale.[3]

---

1 Lee (1991). The 2-to-1 odds are based on systematic analysis of the errors in past projections. See Nathan Keyfitz (1981).
2 The data plotted in the upper curve are from United Nations (1988), Table 5, p19. The data for earlier years are from Cook (1962), Tables II and III, pp10 and 12, respectively.
3 This tendentious representation has been displayed repeatedly over the years in articles and textbooks. See for example Figure 1, p111, of John D Durand (1968); Figure 5-1, p182, of Paul R Ehrlich et al (1977); Figure 2.1, p24, of Robert H Weller and Leon F Bouvier (1981); Figure 3-1, p38, of David Yaukey (1985); Figure 3.1, p53, of John R Weeks (1986). Most recently it appeared in *Parade Magazine* in an article by Carl Sagan, 'The secret of the Persian chessboard' (1989). The only instance I have seen that clearly indicates the distorting effect of the time scale is Ansley J Coale (1974).

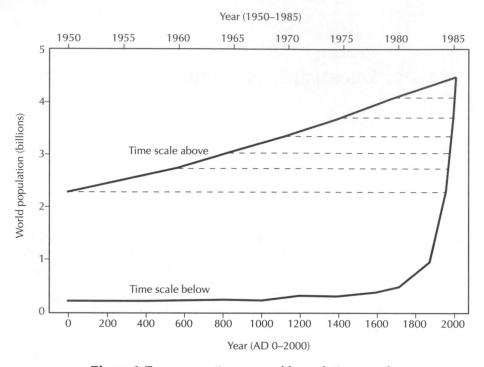

Figure 1 *Two perspectives on world population growth*

If data plotted by the upper curve in Figure 1 can be made to look explosive, so can virtually any other series that increases over time. A plot of doctoral degrees awarded over the past 2000 years would appear to argue for immediate closure of graduate schools. Similar plots might have been used at various points in history to suggest runaway growth of anything from papyrus to buggy whips.

The idea that rapid future population growth is a virtual certainty derives as well from the notion that the world is in the grip of a rapacious mathematical monster called 'exponential growth'. The purely mathematical statement here is that human population growth at any (positive) constant rate would eventually overwhelm the earth. This is true, but the rate of human population growth, like everything else involving human action, is variable. The expectation is not that it will remain constant, but that it will change. Nor does a past increase in growth rates imply a continued increase in the long-term future. Population growth rates are useful in forecasting population for as many as several decades, and, more importantly, for comparing growth in populations of different sizes. They contain no information whatever about population growth a century from now.

Short-term population projections are a different matter, for the simple reason that most of the persons whose numbers are forecast already exist and have high and relatively well-known chances of surviving into the future. This observation was made long ago by John Hajnal in a classic paper that anyone interested in the topic would do well to reread at intervals.[4] It is also true that the current age

---

4 'The prospects for population forecasts' (Hajnal 1955).

distribution of world population embodies a demographic momentum that makes substantial growth highly likely for the next several decades.[5] Whether this constitutes a problem is another matter. The population growth rate is not large in relation to past and present rates of economic growth.

Some will argue that the world is already overpopulated, that no further growth is required. It is, of course, every person's right to venture his own opinion of what world population should be, and to campaign as vigorously as he may wish on its behalf. If we are to recommend imposing our ideas on the rest of the world, however, something more is required. On what grounds is it claimed that the world is overpopulated? Few people doubt that population pressure exists in particular areas, or that local population crises, perhaps very severe ones, may develop. Lee's (1991) juxtaposition of data on population and agriculture suggests danger for 'Bangladesh and Egypt, everyone's favourite examples of countries with serious population problems'. The argument is inherently difficult to make for the world as a whole, however, because conditions in different parts of the world are so divergent.

Is there a biological measure that would neatly circumvent what Paul Demeny has called these 'difficult and stubbornly unresolved' questions? One obvious candidate is human expectation of life at birth, arguably a significant indicator of human welfare, and a statistic widely known, understood, and available. It is, as we all know, higher in the world as a whole today than it has ever been, and by a substantial margin. On this evidence, the world is not overpopulated, whatever else may be wrong with it.

---

5 The phenomenon of momentum may be illustrated with a few population numbers taken from a recent United Nations projections (United Nations 1985, p141). They are, for total world population in millions, as follows:

Age	1990	1995	2000	2005	2010
0–4	599	–	–	–	–
5–9	555	584	–	–	–
10–14	524	550	579	–	–
15–19	527	520	546	575	–
20–24	495	522	515	542	571
25–29	**435**	489	520	510	537
30–34	**393**	**430**	484	512	505
35–39	341	387	**424**	478	506
40–44	278	335	381	**418**	471
45–49	**230**	**272**	**327**	**373**	**410**

The number of persons aged 45–49 nearly doubles between 1990 and 2010, but this has nothing to do with fertility during these years. It reflects the shape of the 1990 age distribution. Because few persons die in adult ages, the decrease in numbers of persons as we move down the table from the 25–29 to the 45–49 age group in 1990 (boldfaced entries in first column) translates into a nearly corresponding increase in numbers of persons aged 45–49 as we move forward in time from 1990 to 2010 (boldfaced entries in last row; boldfaced diagonal entries indicate survivorship). The increasing numbers of persons aged 20–24 between 1990 and 2010 likewise reflect the numbers of persons in the age groups 0–4 to 20-24 in 1990. Increases in the reproductive ages mean larger numbers of births, and hence increases in younger age groups. Because the shape of the 1990 age distribution is primarily the result of rapid population growth in previous years (past growth means larger numbers of births in recent years and fewer in more distant years). We think of the age distribution as embodying a 'momentum' that tends to make the population grow in the future.

The pleasures and satisfactions of working in demography are many. One of the disappointments is the frequency with which one encounters flimsy arguments, often passionately advanced, that there is a world population problem, or that there are no population problems at all.

REFERENCES

Coale, Ansley J (1974) 'The history of human population', in *The Human Population*, San Francisco: W H Freeman, 1974.

Cook, Robert C (1962) 'How many people have ever lived on Earth?' *Population Bulletin* 18, no 1 (February), pp1–19.

Durand, John D (1968) 'The modern expansion of world population', in *Population and Society*, ed Charles B Nam, Boston: Houghton Mifflin

Ehrlich, Paul R et al (1977) *Ecoscience: Population, Resources, Environment*, San Francisco: W H Freeman.

Hajnal, John (1955) 'The prospects for population forecasts', *Journal of the American Statistical Association* 50 (June), pp309–22.

Keyfitz, Nathan (1981) 'The limits of population forecasting', *Population and Development Review* 7, no 4 (December), pp579–93.

Lee, Ronald D. (1991) 'Long-run global population forecasts: a critical appraisal', in *Resources, Environment, and Population: Present Knowledge, Future Options*, ed Kingsley Davis and Mikhail S Bernstam, New York: Oxford University Press.

Sagan, Carl (1989) 'The secret of the Persian chessboard', *Parade Magazine*, Sunday, 5 February.

United Nations (1985) *World Population Prospects: Estimates and Projections as Assessed in 1982*, Population Studies No 86. New York.

United Nations (1988) *World Population Trends and Policies: 1987 Monitoring Report*. New York.

Weeks, John R (1986) *Population: An Introduction to Concepts and Issues*, Belmont, Calif: Wadsworth Publishing Company.

Weller, Robert H and Leon F. Bouvier (1981) *Population: Demography and Policy*, New York: St. Martin's Press.

Yaukey, David (1985) *Demography: The Study of Human Population*, New York: St Martin's Press.

Chapter 30

The Politics of Declining Populations

William H McNeill

Stable human populations have never existed, so far as one can tell from the admittedly defective historic record, and are entirely unlikely in time to come. Instead, growth and decay always prevailed. Some populations flourished and expanded at the expense of others that either lost their corporate identities after being engulfed by an expanding neighbor or were biologically extinguished. That is how civilizations spread across the face of the earth – an unmistakable and dominating trend of human history throughout the past five millennia.

Civilizations also depended on an internal circulation of population, bringing surplus youths from the countryside into cities and armies which could not sustain themselves demographically without such rural reinforcement. Other peasants were allowed or compelled to move away from the cities' sometimes overcrowded hinterlands toward frontiers of settlement, whenever fertile fields became available thanks to military and/or epidemiological aggression. Modern times, with which we have been principally concerned, saw these trends accelerate and magnify themselves at first, because improved transport and communications altered the impact of epidemics in civilized societies and exposed isolated peoples to epidemiological destruction more rapidly than before.

Then, beginning about a hundred years ago, and in practice affecting most of the earth only since 1950, this traditional demographic circulation between town and country was profoundly altered when doctors learned how to check the ravages of most infections, so that cities and armies have ceased to be population sink-holes as they used to be. The extraordinary rates of natural increase that now prevail in much of Africa, Latin America, and Asia reflect this combination of circumstances. Consequently, even if birth control were to become universal tomorrow, the dynamics of the present situation assure decades of continued population growth. That is because so many children, already born, will come of age, marry, and beget children of their own in time to come unless something interferes. Only an external catastrophe, arising independently of conscious or unconscious adjustments of birth and death rates, is likely to make much difference in the short run. And, of course, catastrophe is, almost by definition, unlikely to generate a steady state in its wake.

To discredit the notion of steady state still further: even if some populations in some parts of the earth were somehow to succeed in attaining the goal of zero growth, they would do so in a world where other populations were still expanding

– or mayhap suffering sudden catastrophic collapse. In such a world, a numerically stable population in one country or region could not expect to isolate itself so as to prevent destabilizing encounters with other parts of the earth where drastic population changes were still in course.

Growing populations do not voluntarily leave their neighbours alone and at ease within existing economic, political, and social frameworks. The history of European and Japanese imperialism in the modern age of population growth surely attests to this propensity; and the long record of civilized expansion into frontier areas in the deeper past tells us the same thing. Indeed, competition for food and other sources of energy and jostling for space in which to grow are characteristic of all forms of life. We cannot hope to escape these ecological realities any more than we can call a halt to history and to biological evolution simply because we are tired of so much change.

Alternating bursts of growth and decay, differing from place to place but trending slowly, very slowly upward, was the way human populations behaved in the deeper past. It is the way other successful plants and animals propagate their kind in the balance of nature. When and if accommodation to the demographic explosion of modern times is attained, one might therefore expect a regimen of modest ups and downs to assert itself again, though a big disturbance to ecological relationships, like the modern growth of human populations, is liable to trigger a correspondingly big collapse and may require a long time to settle toward minor fluctuations around some future equilibrium.

What will happen is therefore opaque, even for demographers, and it is doubly so for anyone interested in the social and political implications of a demographic regime different from what has prevailed since 1750. One can, of course, look to the past to see what can be learned about human reactions to declining population. Examples are not far to seek, despite the fact that defeated and decaying populations do not usually write history or leave impressive public records behind them.

As we have seen, innumerable isolated peoples were discriminated and even entirely destroyed in modern times as a consequence of contacts with infections carried by disease-experienced strangers. The prevailing response to such disaster was to try to escape the scourge of disease by getting on the right side of the supernatural power that seemed clearly responsible for unleashing such new and unprecedented epidemics. For peoples so suddenly and severely afflicted, their familiar deities and tutelary spirits were obviously useless. Instead it was the God who kept the strangers from harm who had to be reckoned with, appeased, and obeyed. The success of Christian and Islamic missionaries among previously isolated populations in the Americas, Pacific islands, and some parts of Africa clearly reflected this sort of reasoning among their converts.

Political and cultural implications were considerable. Established élites and religious leaders were discredited by their inability to cope with lethal disease; and even if acceptance of the foreign faith did not halt epidemics (as, of course, it did not), the bewildered and often demoralized remnant found it hard to regain cultural or political autonomy.

Yet efforts to do so abounded and characteristically took the form of millenarian movements, combining motifs from Christian teaching with a vision of the restoration of a purified ancestral way of life from which the intrusive strangers would be entirely excluded. The ghost dance, which spread like wildfire among Plains Indians of the United States in 1889–90 conformed to this pattern, and so did the cargo cults of Oceania. Many other parallel 'crisis cults' arose in modern times among peoples who found themselves dying out in ways that seemed both unjust and mysterious.[1]

Millenarian hope for miraculous restoration of the past easily boiled over into the violence of desperation. This is what happened among the Sioux, whose reception of the ghost dance religion was swiftly followed by a final armed encounter with the United States Army in the battle of Wounded Knee, even though the teachings of Wovoka, the prophet who proclaimed the ghost dance, were thoroughly pacific. Sometimes, suicidal behaviour became explicit, as when a prophetess persuaded the Xhosa of South Africa in 1856 that if they slaughtered their cattle and destroyed their seed corn, the whites would disappear and a new and better world come miraculously into being. As a result, thousands starved, and resistance to further white aggression became even more hopeless than before (Bohannan and Curtin 1988, pp372–3).

Such desperate and unavailing efforts to restore a lost world deserve to be counted among the costs of civilized expansion; but, of course, they affected only a few.[2] Population decay among civilized and far more massive populations might be expected to leave greater marks upon the historic record, and in fact that is almost certainly the case. But population statistics for ancient times are so imprecise that definite assertions become highly speculative about, for example, the fate of the Sumerians in the third millennium BC when their language disappeared from everyday speech in Mesopotamia, or of the Mongols in the 14th century AD, whose empire broke up into disparate fragments after the ravages of the plague. In modern times, declining civilized populations are rather hard to find, for reasons we have already explored.

Differential birth rates among rich and poor have been apparent ever since modern statistics started to be collected; and in a sense, all that is happening in the last decades of the 20th century is that this pattern has begun to reach across ethnic and cultural boundaries. As a whole nation becomes rich and urbanized, reproduction dwindles. Replacement then must come by recruitment from afar, not from the countryside nearby, as aforetime, and from a rural population that already shares most of the cultural characteristics of the dominant group. Turks in Germany, Algerians in France, Pakistanis and other 'New Commonwealth' immigrants in Great Britain, and central Asian Muslims in the Soviet Union all constitute culturally indigestible recruits to the work-forces of these countries. Their importance is already considerable, and if prevailing demographic trends continue, their share in the total population of these lands will increase in time to come simply because they reproduce themselves at a higher rate than the dominant ethnic groups, which are, in fact, failing to maintain themselves. In the United States, Mexican, Central American, and Caribbean immigrants, mostly Spanish-speaking, play a parallel role, though the fact that they are not marked off from the dominant population by an alien religion makes assimilation into a common body politic perhaps a bit easier than in the European case.

Official statistics often glide over the ethnic shifts that are in train among the

---

1 Weston LaBarre (1971) surveys the theme admirably. His category of crisis cults includes examples from groups made desperate not by declining but by rising populations like the Taipings of China. Either circumstance, when accustomed ways of life became impossible, can generate crisis cults. Convergences in ideas and political-military behavior among both sorts of sectarians are very close.
2 Millenarianism among peoples made desperate by rising population pressure, on the other hand, has had enormous and enduring consequences, as the history of Judaism between 168 BC and AD 135 and the history of early Christianity both illustrate.

rich countries of the earth, and for those countries where statistics do not discriminate between ethnic groups, it is hard to find accurate figures. In Germany, however, Turks and other aliens entered the country as so called *Gastarbeiter* on the assumption that they would go back home when their work contracts expired. *Gastarbeiter* are therefore not counted a part of the German population even though many families have now lived in Germany for more than two decades and are unlikely to return to their birthplaces willingly.

As a result, changing ethnic balances in Germany are quite clear. German population started to decrease in 1973; simultaneously, population counted as foreign increased from 2.98 million in 1970 to 4.36 million in 1985, of which 32.7 per cent was Turkish. German birth rates are far below replacement level; Turkish birth rates are far above, and children of Turkish parents, born in Germany, have the right to stay. If vital rates were to remain as they are, Germany would therefore eventually become predominantly Turkish, for the other immigrants (mainly Yugoslavs, Italians, and Greeks) have a birth rate close to or below replacement rates.[3]

To be sure, such an outcome is a very unlike prospect. Demographic behaviour is changeable, and Turkish immigrants living in German cities and working in German factories will not beget so many children when they cease to be youthful newcomers from rural Anatolia. But even if Turkish birth rates in Germany diminish in time to come, the current situation still presents the Germans with an awkward choice between trying to achieve effective assimilation through improved schooling and other civic initiatives, or else inducing or compelling the Turks to go back home according to the original *Gastarbeiter* scheme in order to bring other newcomers in to do the nastier jobs which Germans are now unwilling to undertake. If existing ethnic relationships are simply allowed to drift, a two-tiered caste society would arise on German soil, with Germans occupying the managerial and privileged positions, whereas Turks and other aliens would do all the dirty work without enjoying full civic rights.

Very similar patterns exist also in France where, however, the children of Algerians and others of foreign descent born in France are counted as French and have all the legal rights of French citizens. One result is that French statistics make it more difficult to distinguish what is happening demographically between French residents and citizens with a North African Moslem heritage and other sorts of Frenchmen.[4] According to the census of 1982 there were about 1.4 million Moslems from North Africa in France, and demographers believe that a good many others escaped official enumeration. No one doubts that Moslem numbers are growing rapidly, both by immigration and by natural increase, or that they constitute a minority whose members are almost as sharply segregated from the rest of French society as the Turkish *Gastarbeiter* are from their German self-styled hosts.[5]

Great Britain's census returns show more clearly what has been happening there in recent years. Total population has been almost steady since 1973, with some years of growth and some of decrease; but what forestalls a record of

---

3 Jurgen Bahr and Hans Gans (1986), pp142–6, 156–61. The situation has provoked considerable debate, as for instance, Lutz Franke and Hans W Jurgens (1978) and Vrena McRae (1981).
4 The further fact that many French settlers withdrew to France after 1962 when Algeria became independent means that Algerian birth does not always signify Moslem identity.
5 See, for example, André Chazalette and Pierre Michaud (1977) and Philip Ogden and Hilary Winchester (1986).

absolute decline, like that of Germany, is the flow of immigrants from what is known as the 'New Commonwealth'. These newcomers are distinguished from the rest of the population by the colour of their skins and by a variety of cultural differences as well. Not all of them occupy menial posts, but most do. In 1981 their total number amounted to about 2.2 million, or 4 per cent of the British population as a whole. Ten years earlier, they numbered only 1.4 million, or 2.5 per cent of the entire population. It is entirely their increase that kept the population total from shrinking.[6]

In the Soviet Union, statistics available to me show a rate of growth slightly greater than that for the United States.[7] But such overall figures, even if accurate, obscure differences between the fertility of central Asian Moslems and those of the European populations of the Soviet Union, whose demography in fact conforms very closely to that of west Europeans. It follows that ethnically Russian populations are on the verge of failing to reproduce themselves or have perhaps already passed that point (Coale et al 1979). Estonians are even further along the slippery slope of demographic decay; but the political effect, so far, has been to enhance Estonian national consciousness. Efforts to protect their ethnic identity by erecting legal barriers against the Russians recently provoked public demonstrations. The surprising boldness of such action presumably indicates the strength of feeling generated by their fear of ethnic dilution and eventual dissolution.

United States statistics also make it difficult to figure out what is happening as between different ethnic groups who share the label 'White' in official returns. Immigration, legal and illegal, has been substantial; and barriers to assimilation between newcomers and established elements in the American citizenry are perhaps smaller than in the countries of western Europe where polyethnicity is a new and, for many, an unwelcome situation. But there is no doubt that the portion of the United States citizenry that is of European descent is failing to reproduce itself; and if demographic rates remain unchanged, Hispanics will eventually become numerically predominant.

I should hasten to point out that demographic rates prevailing today will certainly not continue unchanged into the future, though no one can say for sure which way changes will go. Once before, in the depression years of the 1930s, both British and American birth rates dipped below the replacement level; and I am old enough to remember predictions by demographers about how our national population would begin to decline at just about the point in time when in fact the post-war baby boom got under way, thereby utterly confounding the prophets. Similarly, sudden shifts of demographic behaviour among the privileged may occur in the future, and probably will, though as populations age, fewer remain in the reproductive age bracket. This means that change would have to be very sharp indeed to reverse the downward trend of total numbers in a country like Germany.

Changes at the bottom of the social hierarchy are even more likely. Poor immigrant populations may not long persist in begetting large families. All depends on whether they accept the prevailing ideals and family mores of the dominant groups and begin to seek (and attain) a higher standard of living for themselves, or whether they hold fast to their own customs and patterns of demographic behaviour and become a self-perpetuating underclass.

---

6 Anthony Champion (1986), p228.
7 United Nations, *Demographic Yearbook, 1985*, Table 4, attributes a natural rate of increase of 8.8 per thousand to the USSR as against a rate of 7.0 for the United States.

There are obvious difficulties besetting either of these paths toward the future. Assimilation involves betrayal of old values and ways of life. Second-generation immigrants, embarked on this course, may find their way blocked by the unwillingness of older elements in the population to accept them as equals and fellow citizens. Such experiences are liable to generate a culture of defiance among the young, who may find themselves alienated from their parents and from the land of their parents' origin, as well as from the host country in which they find themselves. Signs of defiant, often self-destructive, behaviour abound in Europe (Castles et al 1984, pp159–89) as well as in the United States, and lie behind at least part of the drug epidemic that afflicts American cities. Costs for all concerned, and especially for those who find themselves caught between two worlds and belonging to neither, are very great.

On the other hand, remaining loyal to ancestral ways in a new environment creates a caste system reserving different occupations for particular ethnic groups. Urban societies constructed on this principle are in fact very old. Indeed, one may argue that polyethnicity organized on caste lines is the characteristic norm of civilized urban society, reflecting the necessity, under traditional, pre-modern demographic conditions, of replenishing city populations by welcoming recruits from distant and alien lands – or taking them as slaves when voluntary immigration fell short.

From this perspective, the expectation that immigrants would and should assimilate to a dominant culture became more or less of a reality in the recent past only because general population growth supplied an ample number of recruits for cities from within the radius of a few score of miles. Because such immigrants already shared most of the cultural characteristics of the established urban classes to which they were then expected to assimilate their ways, legal equality and a career open to talent regardless of origins became an attractive and plausible ideal. It was more or less realized in practice in western European lands from the 18th century or before, but in eastern Europe the ideal of ethnic uniformity cost much bloodshed and political violence before it was achieved (more or less) in the wake of World Wars I and II.

The troubled ethnic history of eastern Europe should be of special interest to Americans because our polyethnicity partially recapitulated the historic experience of eastern Europe. Urban ethnic pluralism in eastern Europe dated back to the later Middle Ages, when that part of the Continent was a rapidly developing frontier land. Accordingly, rulers of Poland, Transylvania, and other states extended special privileges to Jews and to German merchants and artisans in order to accelerate urban development and thereby improve state revenues. (The Turks, a little later, were hospitable to Jews, Armenians, and Greeks for similar reasons; the Russians lagged a little behind, allowing enclaves of foreign merchants and professionals to arise in their cities after about 1600.) This official strategy of encouraging deliberate urban development had the unforeseen result of establishing enduring urban castes that were insulated by religious and cultural differences from the environing population. Some of them still survive.

In modern times, the frontier role played by the United States and other countries of European settlement overseas also established ethnically diverse populations. They, too, were organized along caste lines, publicly embedded not so much in religion (though that mattered, too, when Irish immigration first flooded into Protestant New England) as in differences of skin colour. For a long time, American ideals of freedom and equality did not extend to blacks and

Indians; and despite repeated legal enactments since 1863, the gap has never been fully bridged. American cities have indeed been melting pots for many European immigrants; but whether they will be for Mexican, Caribbean, and Central American newcomers remains to be seen, just as it remains to be seen how ethnic relationships will develop in Europe when recruits to their cities come not from a culturally contiguous hinterland but from Moslem and other sharply contrasting cultural backgrounds.

Politically speaking, one must expect considerable volatility in public responses to what is still a new and perhaps unstable demographic regime in the rich, urbanized countries of the earth. Getting used to having foreigners around may be harder for Europeans and Japanese than for Americans and other inhabitants of the erstwhile frontier lands where ethnic mingling has existed for generations. Interestingly enough, the cessation of population growth in the industrialized heartlands of the European continent coincides with changes in European Community regulations which aim at eliminating legal barriers to migration among the European nations themselves. It is conceivable that in time to come people within the EC will begin to identify themselves less as members of a particular nation than as Europeans. That, of course, would significantly alter the boundary between 'us' and 'them', but it would still exclude Moslem and other strangers who are already on the ground, increasing in number and themselves in a very unstable state, both culturally and demographically. The one thing that seems certain is that the difference between European and American society will diminish as both become more obviously polyethnic than in times past.

Shrinking populations are not likely to sustain expansion abroad. Keeping what one has already is a more appropriate preoccupation for governments presiding over an ethnic mix in which the dominating element of the population is diminishing in number. But offence may sometimes be the best defence. I referred a moment ago to recent Estonian efforts at aggressively defending themselves. The parallel behaviour of French Canadians is rather better known. Before World War II, rural *habitants* were prolific enough to maintain the French proportion of the population of Canada at about 30 per cent, even though most immigrants chose to assimilate to the English-speaking style of Canadianism. Some even looked ahead to an ultimate victory of the cradle that might some day restore French preponderance in the whole country or at least in several provinces beyond the stronghold of Quebec itself. But the cultural integument that had sustained large families among the French since colonial times collapsed rather abruptly during and after World War II, when young people decided to disregard the teaching of the Catholic church about birth control. Accordingly, in the 1960s French Canadian birth rates sank below those of English-speaking Canadians and fell far short of replacement rates (Kalback and McVey 1971).

All of a sudden, the French position in the country seemed endangered. The response was an exacerbated French nationalism, seeking either to withdraw from the Canadian confederation entirely or, at a minimum, to safeguard French language and culture by legal proscription of the use of English in many accustomed situations in the province of Quebec. This and the parallel Estonian example show that acquiescence in loss of status in face of diminishing numbers ought not to be taken for granted, even among a people that had formerly been a rather quiet minority.

The tendency toward aggressive self-assertion in face of diminishing numbers may also be recognized in nativist rhetoric directed against Algerians in France,

Turks in Germany, and West Indians and Pakistanis in Britain. So far, such themes have remained on the fringes of national politics in each of these countries. Memory of Nazi crimes and the continuing momentum of European integration pull in an opposite direction, just as the United States' tradition of civil rights and opportunity for all has damped back attacks on blacks and Hispanics. But no one can be sure that some surge of anger may not break through such barriers in time to come, especially if the dominant ethnic group of each country begin to feel really threatened.

Ethnic frictions and rivalries are far nearer the surface in the Soviet Union. Efforts by Great Russians to sustain their hegemony in the absence of the abundant flow of peasant manpower that supplied the needs of the state from the time of Ivan the Terrible to that of Stalin face obstacles that make the situation of Germans in Germany look positively comfortable. Bruises arising from Russian aggressions of the past remain fresh in the recollection of Ukrainians and other European nationalities of the Soviet Union; while in central Asia large Turkish and Iranian populations remain socially and culturally distinct and at least vaguely Moslem, despite decades of ideological blandishment by atheistic Communist propaganda and considerable technical change in both urban and rural life.

Reflecting upon the demographic changes that seem to be in train in the world, I am tempted to recognize some deep-seated natural rhythm whereby a growing population, after 200 years (say, six to eight generations) of successful expansion at the expense of rivals, ceases to reproduce itself and so in turn gives way to others. In ancient Greece and Rome, it was perhaps the disruptive effect of military service and urban living on rural family patterns that halted population growth and invited the wholesale resort to slavery that Marx took as the characteristic form of labour relations in the ancient world.

In modern times, medical science made urban living safe from ordinary lethal infections, and even armies became immune from all but wounds, which in former times were a comparatively minor cause of campaign deaths. Yet, urbanism remains inimical to child-bearing and rearing in a way that rural living is not, and with modern methods of birth control young women are able to regulate births to suit themselves. Most city-dwellers prefer a style of life that is incompatible with what St Augustine once described as the 'incessant squalor of babes'. Having given birth to one or two demanding infants, they want no more, even though for statistical reasons an average of a little more than two children per woman of breeding age is needed to replace each generation as it ages and dies.

Thus it may be true that even though the triumphs of modern medicine eliminated infections as a major factor in urban die-off, the success with which other medical researchers discovered easy and effective methods of birth control may restore the age-old pattern of demographic circulation between town and country, rich and poor, upon which civilized society has depended ever since the third millennium BC.

Globally, there remain billions of peasants and ex-peasants who are ready and eager to move into places vacated by wealthier, urbanized populations. Supply indeed far exceeds demand for labour, even of the humblest sort. One can therefore recognize that the traditional circulation of populations remains very much in working order, with the difference that now, as in the early phases of civilized history, it has become necessary to cross cultural demarcation lines to find recruits for the most powerful and richest cities of the earth.

Let me close with a biblical text. 'Blessed are the meek', said Jesus, 'for they shall inherit the earth' (Matthew 5:5). He uttered these words in an overcrowded Roman province where rebellion simmered among a rural population that could not find enough land to live on in traditional ways. In the course of the next century, the Jews of Palestine did not remain meek. Instead, repeated risings and Roman repression almost emptied the land of its Jewish inhabitants. Those who listened to the Sermon on the Mount therefore did not themselves inherit very much of the earth. But in the longer run, the saying was and still is perfectly true, with this additional gloss: those who succeed in inheriting the earth cease to be meek and thereby open a path for successors to come behind them and sustain the circulation between wealthy town and poverty-stricken countryside that has maintained human society since cities first appeared.

The really surprising thing is that this ancient pattern still looks as though it might maintain itself in spite of all our clever interventions in natural ecological processes. But all the cleverness in the world cannot emancipate us from the balances of nature. This enduring pattern of human demography – if it does endure, for in closing I must stress how faulty demographic prophecy remains, despite all the numerical sophistication of the experts – ought to remind us of those limits.

That, indeed, has been my central purpose here. I have emphasized the role of demography in human affairs and tried to show how politics rides on currents of biological ebb and flow. Only by recognizing these levels of human life and the constraints and possibilities they offer to conscious and deliberate management can we expect to become more nearly able to navigate successfully amidst the tumult of our times.

Such thinking will not eliminate the fallibility of foresight. Fallibility remains essential to the human condition. One cannot really wish for its elimination from our lives. Yet as more or less rational persons we also wish to extend the domain of understanding and deliberate control. Poised between these antimonies, human beings remain unique in the balance of nature, because we use words and ideas to organize our behaviour and to change it. Thus, awareness of demographic trends we dislike may permit us to change them.

Assuredly, demography has affected behaviour – always. Even a partial understanding of that dimension of the past ought to increase the precision and grace with which we respond to ebbs and flows of the future. And that is why population and politics are worth thinking about.

REFERENCES

Bahr, Jurgen and Hans Gans (1986) 'The Federal Republic of Germany', in *West European Population Change*, ed Allan Findlay and Paul White, London: Croom Helm.

Bohannan, Paul and Philip Curtin (1988) *Africa and the Africans*, 3d ed, Prospect Heights, Ill: Waveland Press.

Castles, Stephen, Heather Booth, and Tina Wallace (1984) *Here for Good: Western Europe's New Ethnic Minorities*, London: Pluto Press.

Champion, Anthony (1986) 'Great Britain', in *West European Population Change*, ed Allan Findlay and Paul White, London: Croom Helm.

Chazalette, André and Pierre Michaud (1977) *La deuxième génération d'immigrants dans la région Rhône Alpes*, Lyons: Groupe de sociologie urbaine.

Coale, Ansley J, Barbara A Anderson, and Erna Härm (1979) *Human Fertility in Russia since the 19th century,* Princeton: Princeton University Press.

Franke, Lutz and Hans W Jurgens, eds (1978) *Keine Kinder, Keine Zukunft?* Boppard-am-Rhein: Boldt.

Kalbach, Warren E and Wayne W McVey (1971) *The Demographic Bases of Canadian Society,* 2d ed, Toronto: McGraw-Hill.

LaBarre, Weston (1971) 'Materials for a history of studies of crisis cults: a bibliographic essay', *Current Anthropology* 12 (1971), pp3–42.

McRae, Verena (1981) *Die Gastarbeiter: Daten, Fakten, Probleme,* Munich: Beck.

Ogden, Philip and Hilary Winchester, 'France', in *West European Population Change,* ed Allan Findlay and Paul White, London: Croom Helm.

United Nations, *Demographic Yearbook, 1985,* New York.

Chapter 31

Medical Science, Infectious Disease, and the Unity of Mankind

Joshua Lederberg

The ravaging epidemic of acquired immunodeficiency syndrome has shocked the world. It is still not comprehended widely that it is a natural, almost predictable, phenomenon. We will face similar catastrophes again, and will be ever more confounded in dealing with them, if we do not come to grips with the realities of the place of our species in nature. A large measure of humanistic progress is dedicated to the subordination of human nature to our ideals of individual perfectibility and autonomy. Human intelligence, culture, and technology have left all other plant and animal species out of the competition. We also may legislate human behaviour. But we have too many illusions that we can, by writ, govern the remaining vital kingdoms, the microbes, that remain our competitors of last resort for dominion of the planet. The bacteria and viruses know nothing of national sovereignties. In that natural evolutionary competition, there is no guarantee that we will find ourselves the survivor.

Some of the great successes of medical science, including the 'miracle drugs', the antibiotics of the 1940s, have inculcated premature complacency on the part of the broader culture. Most people today are grossly over-optimistic with respect to the means we have available to forfend global epidemics comparable with the Black Death of the 14th century (or on a lesser scale the influenza of 1918), which took a toll of millions of lives.

Visualize human life on this planet as mirrored in the microcosm of a culture of bacteria; a labouratory test tube can hold 10 billion cells, twice the human population of the globe. More than 70 years ago, Frederick William Twort and Felix d'Herelle discovered that bacteria have their own virus parasites, the bacteriophages. It is not unusual to observe a thriving bacterial population of a billion cells undergo a dramatic wipe-out, a massive lysis, a sudden clearing of the broth following a spontaneous mutation that extends the host range of a single virus particle. A hundred billion virus particles will succeed the bacteria; but their own fate now is problematic, as they will have exhausted their prey (within that test tube). Perhaps there are a few bacterial survivors: mutant bacteria that now resist the mutant virus. If so, these can repopulate the test tube until perhaps a second round, a mutant-mutant virus, appears.

Such processes are not unique to the test tube. The time scale, the numerical odds, will be different. The fundamental biologic principles are the same.

Humans are more dispersed over the planetary surface than are the 'bugs' in a glass tube; there are more diverse sanctuaries, and we have somewhat fewer opportunities to infect one another. The culture medium in the test tube is more hospitable to virus transmission than is the space between people (with the exceptions of sexual contact and transfusion). The ozone shield still lets through enough solar ultraviolet light to hinder aerosol transmission, and most viruses are fairly vulnerable to desiccation in dry air. The unbroken skin is an excellent barrier to infection; the mucous membranes of the respiratory tract are much less so. Our immune defences are a wonderfully intricate legacy of our own evolutionary history. This enables machinery for producing an indefinite panoply of antibodies, some one of which is (we may hope) a specific match to the antigenic challenge of a particular invading parasite (Lederberg 1959). In the normal, immune-competent individual, each incipient infection is a mortal race between the penetration and the proliferation of the virus within the body and the evolution and expansion of antibodies that may be specific for that infection. Previous vaccination or infection with a related virus will facilitate an early immune response. This in turn provides selective pressure on the virus populations, encouraging the emergence of antigenic variants. We see this most dramatically in the influenza pandemics, and every few years we need to disseminate fresh vaccines to cope with the current generation of the flu virus.

Many defence mechanisms, inherent in our evolved biologic capabilities, thus mitigate the pandemic viral threat, Mitigation also is built into the evolution of the virus: it is a Pyrrhic victory for a virus to eradicate its host! This may have happened historically, but then both the vanquished host and the victorious parasite will have disappeared. Even the death of the single infected individual is relatively disadvantageous, in the long run, to the virus compared with a sustained infection that leaves a carrier free to spread the virus to as many contacts as possible. From the perspective of the virus, the ideal would be a nearly symptomless infection in which the host is oblivious of providing shelter and nourishment for the indefinite propagation of the virus' genes (Smith 1934, Burnet and White 1972). Our own genome carries hundreds or thousands of such stowaways. The boundary between them and the 'normal genome' is quite blurred (Lederberg 1952). Not much more than 1 per cent of our DNA can be assigned specific physiological functions; most of it is assumed to be a 'fossil' legacy of our prior evolutionary history, DNA that is today parasitic on the cell (Orgel and Crick 1980, Dulbecco 1987). Further, we know that many viruses can acquire genetic information from their hosts, which from time to time they may transfer to new ones. Hence, intrinsic to our own ancestry and nature are not only Adam and Eve, but any number of individual germs that have crept into our chromosomes. Some confer incidental and mutual benefit. Others of these symbiotic viruses, or 'plasmids', have re-emerged as oncogenes, with the potential to mutate to a state that we recognize as the dysregulated cell growth of a cancer. This is a form of Darwinian evolution that momentarily enhances the fitness of a cell clone at the expense of the entire organism. Still other segments of 'non-functional' DNA are available as reserves of genetic potential for further evolution, in a sense more constructive for the individual and the species.

At evolutionary equilibrium we would continue to share the planet with our internal and external parasites, paying some tribute, perhaps sometimes deriving from them some protection against more violent aggression. The terms of that equilibrium are unwelcome: present knowledge does not offer much hope that we can eradicate the competition. Meanwhile, our parasites and ourselves must share in the dues, payable in a currency of discomfort and precariousness of life. No theory lets us calculate the details; we can hardly be sure that such an equilibrium for earth even includes the human species even as we contrive to eliminate some of the others. Our propensity for technological sophistication harnessed to intraspecies competition adds a further dimension of hazard.

In fact, innumerable perturbations remind us that complex systems often fluctuate far from equilibrium – each individual death of an infected person is a counter-example. Our defence mechanisms do not always work. Viruses are not always as benign as they would be if each particle had the intelligence and altruism to serve the long-term advantage of the group.

Fears of new epidemics as virulent as those of the past have been mollified by the expectation that modern hygiene and medicine would contain any such outbreaks. There is, of course, much merit in those expectations. Influenza in 1918 was undoubtedly complicated by bacterial infections that now can be treated with antibiotics (Kilbourne 1987); vaccines, if we can mobilize them in time, can help prevent the global spread of a new flu. However, the impact of technology is not all on the human side of the struggle. Monoculture of plants and animals has made them more exposed to devastation. The increasing density of human habitations as well as inventions such as the subway and the jet airplane that mix populations all add to the risks of spread of infection. Paradoxically, improvements in sanitation and vaccination sometimes make us the more vulnerable because they leave the larger human herd more innocent of microbial experience.

The opening of wild lands to human occupation also has exposed people to unaccustomed animal viruses, to zoonoses. Yellow fever has sustained reservoirs in jungle primates, and the same source is the probable origin of the human immunodeficiency virus in Africa. It is mystifying that yellow fever has not become endemic in India, where competent mosquitoes and susceptible people abound. We will almost certainly be having like experiences from the 'opening' of the Amazon basin.

Our preoccupation with acquired immunodeficiency syndrome should not obscure the multiplicity of infectious diseases that threaten our future. It is one too soon to start a systematic watch for new viruses before they become so irrevocably lodged. The fundamental bases of virus research can hardly be given too much encouragement. Recombinant DNA, still a scare word in some quarters, is our most potent means of analysing viruses and developing vaccines (Lederberg 1975). Such research should be done on a broad international scale to both share the progress made in advanced countries and amplify the opportunities for field-work at the earliest appearance of outbreaks in the most afflicted areas.

The basic principles of vaccination were established long ago, but practical means of production of vaccines for viral afflictions like polio had to await the cell and tissue culture advances of the 1950s. The most celebrated example, smallpox, also has the oldest historical roots. That success has encouraged other proposals for the eradication of other infectious agents. Rarely do we have the understanding of its natural history needed to calibrate the feasibility of the goal. This will strain our basic knowledge of the genetics and evolution of the etiologic agents.

For example, our stratagems on malaria, gonococcus and human immunodeficiency virus are all confounded by the poorly understood capacity of the viruses to undergo further antigenic evolution. We know a bit more about influenza, but not enough to give us more than a few weeks or months of lead time merely to respond to its perennial variations.

As one species, we share a common vulnerability to these scourges. No matter how selfish our motives, we can no longer be indifferent to the suffering of others. The microbe that felled one child in a distant continent yesterday can reach yours today and seed a global pandemic tomorrow. 'Never send to know for whom the bell tolls; it tolls for thee'.

REFERENCES

Burnet, F M and D O White (1972) *Natural History of Infectious Disease*, Cambridge: Cambridge University Press.

Dulbecco, R (1987) 'The changing DNA', in *The Design of Life*, New Haven, Conn.: Yale University Press.

Kilbourne, E D (1987) *Influenza*, New York: Plenum Medical Books.

Lederberg, J (1952) 'Cell genetics and hereditary symbiosis', *Physiol. Rev.* 32, pp403–30.

– (1953) 'Genes and antibodies', *Science* 129, pp1649–53.

– (1975) 'DNA splicing: will fear rob us of its benefits?' *AMA PRISM* 3, pp33–7.

Orgel, L E and F H C Crick (1980) 'Selfish DNA, the ultimate parasite', *Nature* 284, pp604–08.

Smith, T (1934) *Parasitism and Disease*, Princeton: Princeton University Press.

Chapter 32

A Contradiction in the Argument of Malthus

Fred Hoyle

The prediction of the future is the main concern of science. This is a matter for scientific theories. Experiment exists in science as an aid to arriving at theories, although a casual observation of the facilities provided for experiment on the one hand and theoretical studies on the other, both in universities and in the country at large, might sometimes suggest otherwise.

A theory must always be given some initial information before it can operate. The information usually concerns only the present, but information concerning the past may be used. The idea is to use what has 'already happened' in order to predict what is going to happen. The best physical theories succeed to a quite remarkable accuracy. The eclipse of the sun can be predicted years ahead to within an accuracy of a second or two. The degree of predictive success can be regarded as a figure of merit. Unless the figure of merit is very high indeed, as it is in the case of the gravitational theory, one must obviously be prepared to discard the old ideas in favour of new ones – although it is pointless to discard an old imperfect theory until a better becomes available.

Theories usually become less successful and less precise as we pass from straightforward physical science – such as the case of the eclipse – through chemistry and biology to social studies. The order is one of increasing complexity. Yet a great deal is known about the past history of the human animal. Surely the enormous mass of data must tell us something about the future, if only we have the wit to make a sensible extrapolation? By and large, scientists, physicists particularly, believe extrapolation to be possible, at least to some extent. By and large, the humanities seem to believe that successful prediction is impracticable – the two cultures again.

Because human affairs are directed almost entirely by people trained in the humanities this difference is important. It means that long-range planning never occurs, changes are dictated by circumstances as they arise. An argument in favour of the present system is that planned action based on a wrong extrapolation would undoubtedly give bad results (the results desired at the beginning would not be achieved at the end), whereas a day-to-day pragmatic response to changing circumstances leads to a tolerable situation. Or does it? On the short run, probably yes, but not necessarily in the long run. The present failure of the human species to take long-range action for the future implies that we are almost entirely controlled by our environment; if we include the knowledge that we ourselves create, as a part of the environment.

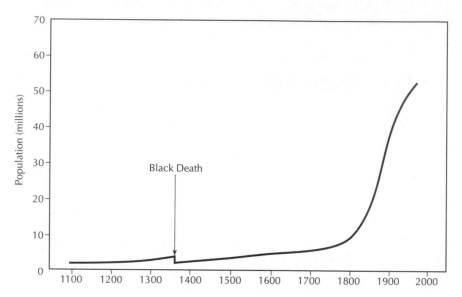

Figure 1: *The population growth of Great Britain*

To anyone who argues that so long as one seeks to take each individual step correctly the whole journey will come out right in the end, I can only say: try walking without a compass across a precipitous mountain in a thick mist.

There are very important things about the future that we can assert with some confidence. A well-known example is shown by Figures 1 and 2, which give the population growths of Great Britain and of the United States. It hits you in the eye that, the Black Death apart, both populations have risen steadily over the centuries. One can make the sensible extrapolation that they will continue to rise in the future. To what extent will they rise? The dotted curve of Figure 2 follows a simple mathematical law, that of the exponential. A similar consideration for the population of the whole world gives a similar exponential rule.

Now, a mathematical rule can easily be extrapolated into the future, and it seems reasonably safe to assume that such an extrapolation will prove tolerably accurate, at any rate for the immediate future – say for the next 50 years. There may be some deviations from one country to another, but averaging for the whole world should be a sound procedure. And we can make the additional statement that *either* the rise will continue into the more distant future *or* conditions different from those experienced in the past must intervene.

The bite in this apparently innocent statement lies in the fact that we can easily prove it is impossible for the rule to continue to hold good indefinitely into the future. Hence different conditions, conditions different in really crucial respects from the past, must arise in the future. What are these differences likely to be?

Before coming to this question, the substance of this essay, how about the proof? One uses the normal mathematical device of a *reductio ad absurdum*. Suppose the rule continues to apply *as at present*. In 500 years or so, the human population will become so enormous that the average ration of standing-room on the Earth's surface will be 1 square yard apiece. In 5000 years or so, the total mass of the species will exceed the mass of all the stars and galaxies visible with the 200-inch telescope on Palomar Mountain.

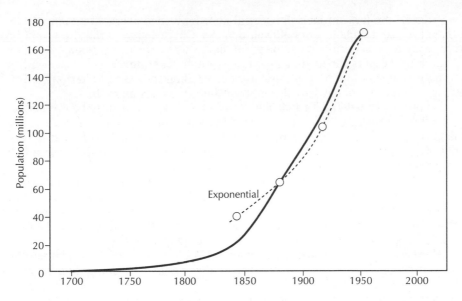

Figure 2: *The population growth of the United States*

Coming now to the question of what is going to change our exponential rule, I would like to follow the argument due first to Malthus, and revived recently in vigorous style by Sir Charles Darwin in his book *The Next Million Years*.

It is no mere chance that the exponential rule fits the facts so well. Write N(t) for the population at time *t*.

Then

$$dN/dt = (b - d)N,$$

where *b* is the birth rate and *d* the death rate defined per person. So long as *b* and *d* are constant, with *b* > *d*, the exponential rule *must* apply. Of course, both *b* and *d* change with time, the introduction of contraceptives decreases *b*, improved medical skill decreases *d*. But such changes only alter the *slope* of the exponential – that is, the steepness of our curves; the exponential character of the situation is unchanged *so long as b remains greater than d*. The changed circumstance in the future must be that *b* will not be greater than *d*. It is impossible to doubt this conclusion. I have stated it in a form free from emotional overtones. Now I will give the overtones. One or other of the following will arise:

- *Either* the death rate *d* will remain substantially unchanged and the birth rate *b* will be reduced to equality with *d* through some form of worldwide social control.
- *Or* the birth rate *b* will remain substantially unchanged and the death rate *d* will increase to equality with *b*.

(A combination of these possibilities could arise, *b* decreasing and *d* increasing, but this 'mixed' case does not seem to introduce anything essentially new.)

The point made so strongly by Sir Charles Darwin was that while we have ample evidence of the occurrence in the past of the second alternative, we have no such evidence for the first. In fact, the second alternative has operated systematically over a thousand million years of evolution. Sir Charles argued that he would be very ready to consider the more 'pleasant' first alternative as a serious possibility if he could be persuaded that new forces might operate in its favour with a strength comparable to that of the forces controlling the second alternative. But so far, he argued, nobody had shown what the new forces might be.

When I first read *The Next Million Years*, I felt this argument to be overstated. The appeal to biological evolution, over a thousand million years, is not entirely fair. It relies on the concept that, if nothing new has emerged over such a large span of time, it is most unlikely that an essentially new situation will arise in the immediate future (the next 2000 or 3000 years). But the emergence and expansion of the human species over the past 5000 years is in fact an entirely new situation. It is true that other species, or groups of species, have acquired dominance in the past, but nothing comparable to the human case in its organization and technology has been known before. We are dealing with a special case and we must obviously be cautious of unsupported generalities.

However, there is one respect in which the human species has shown not the slightest originality – its excessive reproductive vigour. The population growths shown in Figures 1 and 2 are entirely similar to the growths of other entirely different species that have occurred in the past, whenever the environment has permitted them to do so. Imagine a non-human historian of the future looking back over the biological events of the past. Surely he would regard the present-day rise of the human population as one of the best examples of an uncontrolled outburst of a species. If we accept this, as I am inclined to do, we are back at Sir Charles' argument, back with the second of the two alternatives given above. The death rate will rise until it attains equality with the birth rate. How?

Malthus argued that there is a practical limit to the amount of food that can be produced on the Earth. Hence there is a maximum number of people that can be fed. If the population should rise towards this maximum, the death rate must of necessity rise to equality with the birth rate. The population limit is set by starvation.

This argument has had a profound effect on all biological thinking since the days of Malthus. (The original publication, *An Essay on the Principle of Population as it Affects the Future Improvement of Society*, appeared in 1798.) It is well known that Darwin's work on natural selection was in part influenced by Malthus. And his grandson makes a similar use of these ideas in *The Next Million Years*, forecasting that the human society of the future will be limited by starvation, that the men of the future will look back on the present day as the golden age of the species.

Yet I do not now believe the Malthusian argument to be at all correct. I was influenced in my thinking on the matter by a conversation I had some four or five years ago with Sir Charles. I found him to be perhaps most strongly influenced in *his* thinking by the argument that nobody had produced any serious alternative to Malthus; it was the uniqueness that appealed to him so strongly. This set me wondering whether a serious alternative was indeed possible, an alternative that still followed the 'strong' second possibility, in which d increases to equality with b, not the 'weak' first possibility of b being reduced to d; I found such an alternative, and in doing so came to realize that the Malthusian argument is very probably wrong. It can be disproved by a strict *reductio ad absurdum* provided we accept two propositions that seem to me almost self-evident, and which are certainly supported by present-day evidence. Because my conclusions are in some ways more horrible, in some ways more hopeful, and certainly in all ways less dull, than those of Malthus, I state these two propositions rather carefully.

I take it that a starving man cannot work effectively, either physically or mentally. There may be hagglers who will dispute this statement, but if so I propose to disregard them. At a somewhat less trivial level, I take it that a complex technological society cannot be maintained by starving people. Although I recognize argument to be possible here, I think it only serves to convince one that the probability of the proposition being true is very high indeed. Evidence is already available in plenty to show how hard it is to develop technology in the malnourished countries of the East, where we must remember the technologically competent are not starving, and where assistance and know-how is being received from affluent countries. We must also remember that the societies of the future will very likely be much more complex than present-day society. The proposition which I believe to be true is that a world community, intensely complex in its organization and technology, will collapse if food begins to run short and it will collapse *before actual starvation point is reached*. Physical lethargy and mental indifference, the necessary concomitants of starvation, are qualities entirely inconsistent with technological efficiency.

My second proposition is that a technologically efficient community can support more people *well above the starvation level* than an inefficient community can support *at the starvation level*. In fact, the reason why the human population has risen so sharply in recent centuries lies exactly here. Five thousand years ago only a comparatively tiny number of people were maintained in conditions which we, today, would regard as extreme poverty. Although this second proposition is more or less obvious, one may wonder how the changes have, in fact, been brought about: Through the co-operative action of people together, as well as through the use of tools and powered machines. Today we cultivate regions that would have been hopeless only a century ago. We do this through irrigation dams, the tractor, and so forth. The processing and preserving of food is also by no means an unimportant activity, and in the future we may look to more and more use of the factory – do not ignore this even today – remember your vitamin pills. It is not inconceivable that a large fraction of the human food requirements may ultimately be synthesized. But of course this does not destroy our argument about the limitation of standing room on the planet.

The acceptance of these propositions leads immediately to a contradiction in the argument of Malthus. Once the population of a technically complex, adequately fed society exceeds the level permitted by primitive starvation conditions – the Malthusian state of affairs – then the Malthusian argument becomes invalid. It becomes invalid because a decrease of population is required to reach the Malthusian state, whereas all our expectations are that the population will *increase*. Something entirely new is needed.

Before I come to what I think must be the solution to the problem, I should point out that the above discussion of the importance of the birth and death rates was not intended to be mathematically complete. In particular, it is obviously not necessary that the population N should attain a precise steady value. It could oscillate about some average value, $\bar{N}$ say. This is not forbidden by our standing-room argument. So it is not necessary for d to come exactly into consonance with b at all times. There could be epochs in which d was less than b, as at present, provided there were corresponding epochs in which d exceeded b.

With this in mind, let us come to the problem of the future, on the likely assumption that our technological development has already lifted us above the population level corresponding to the Malthusian starvation state. The population rise of the future will only lift the level still further above the Malthusian state. But we know that the rise cannot continue indefinitely. My point is that the factors that will of necessity intervene to prevent the rise from being maintained can have nothing to do with the Malthusian state. We are already beyond it. We are already beyond the normal form of biological control, the control that has directed evolution over the past thousand million years. However, I must emphasize that this is not to say we are beyond all control, rather that a new control is going to come into operation. My view is that the control will be so strong, so overwhelming, that within 5000 years a new species will have taken the place of the human species. It will still be human in shape, but its genetic make-up, its mental processes, its behaviouristic patterns will be so different from present-day norms as to justify the title of a new species.

Now what is to produce the necessary increase of d? The ultimate overloading of a technological complex with too many people. The concept here is that a highly organized society can collapse through a population overload, even though the people themselves are not starving. It is the organization that ultimately becomes overloaded and collapses. For instance, it would be impossible to maintain the organization necessary to support hundreds of thousands of millions of people if the ration of standing room really were reduced to 1 square yard per person.

It is well known in the physical world that organizational structures are subject to discontinuous change. Suppose you heat some ice. As the temperature rises, a definite precise temperature is reached at which the organizational structure of the ice can no longer take the strain of the increasing motions of its constituent molecules. At that precise temperature, the ice melts and becomes liquid water – it takes on a new organization. The point I am making is that the organization does not change continuously with rising temperature, there is one definite temperature at which the whole thing alters decisively. And I suspect that something rather similar will prove to be true of human organization: that as the population rises, there will be a level at which the organization is disrupted. I am not simply invoking an analogy here. Organizations themselves have common properties, irrespective of the individuals that happen to be organized. The melting of ice into water at a critical temperature is not a special property of this one substance. Other substances, composed of quite different molecules, have exactly the same property. I suspect that discontinuous change is a common property of all organizations, irrespective of whether the individuals happen to be humans or chemical molecules.

One can speculate on the immediate 'cause' of disruption. Even today we are becoming familiar with a new concept, that total war could produce a 'collapse of civilization', which is just another way of describing the disruption of the organization of society. Methods of warfare are certain to become more efficient, and it can hardly be doubted that total war a century or two hence would be capable of producing just such a discontinuous change as must arise. This is not to say that war must of necessity be the immediate 'cause' of the ultimate breakdown of civilization, but that it is an entirely possible cause. However, I want to stress that warfare itself never significantly increases the death rate. This might seem callous but it happens to be true. Between AD 1480 and 1941, Great Britain was involved in 78 wars. Inspection of Figure 1 shows no serious influences on the population curve, none to compare with the Black Death.

With the effectively discontinuous collapse of society there will be an effectively discontinuous rise in d, simply because the very organization that permitted vast numbers to be fed and kept alive will have disappeared. At this stage we are, to some extent, forced to make an effort of imagination rather than of logic. There have been plenty of imaginative stories written on the basis of a hypothetical disruption of present-day society. For the most part, it is thought that the effects would be pretty grim, much grimmer than I myself would subscribe to. While only a fool, and apparently there are plenty of these, can contemplate nuclear warfare with equanimity, I do not think the effect would approach the picture painted by Nevil Shute in his novel *On the Beach*, for instance. But the more complex human society becomes – and it will perforce have to become much more complex in order to accommodate the steeply rising populations of the future – the greater will the disaster be. Yet even at its worst, I do not think the utter débâcle visualized by Shute will occur. I think the disaster will be similar in its effect on the population to an event in British history, one we have already noted, the Black Death. I expect a sudden discontinuous drop in the population, analogous to the downward step shown in Figure 1.

In fact, the downward step produced by the Black Death, followed by the subsequent rise, seems to me to be exactly what we must expect to take place in the future. The numbers involved will of course be enormously greater, but the disastrous drop, followed by a slow re-expansion, will be the same. The tattered remnants of humanity will slowly re-form and re-establish themselves. Once again the tendency to overpopulate will assert itself, and the process will be repeated. My prediction, therefore, which I make with a fair measure of confidence, is that the population curve of the future will possess the saw-tooth shape shown in Figure 3. The population levels and the time intervals shown in the figure are not intended to be taken literally, although they are based on reasonable estimates.

I come now to an issue of great interest. In Figure 3 I have marked the beginnings of the re-expansion phases as being subject to evolution. Some care is needed here. Selection during the catastrophic drop is unlikely to be biologically important, since who lives and who dies in a catastrophe is largely a matter of chance. Nor is the selection that must take place in the chaos following the catastrophe of really deep genetic significance. Selection there must be, of course. If I myself were a survivor, I would live in constant terror of breaking my glasses. Such a simple event would almost certainly make further survival impossible for me. But the type of selection that would occur under conditions of extreme chaos are entirely similar to the conditions which have operated in the past over the whole history of the species up to the last century or two. Hence, chaos can hardly produce any crucial change in the genetic make-up of the species. It would simply serve to remove regressions, such as bad eyesight, that had accumulated during the preceding centuries.

The beginning of the re-expansion phase is something different, however. Re-expansion demands reorganization and there would be a heavy selection in favour of those who were most capable of developing the reorganization, just because an organized society is capable of maintaining a much larger population than a chaotic one – the 'biological reward' to those who got the rebuilding of civilization under way would be very great. Repeated oscillations of the population, such as I have indicated in Figure 3, exponentiates the selection, and after ten or more cycles a different creature begins to emerge. I must emphasize that mutations are not involved here;

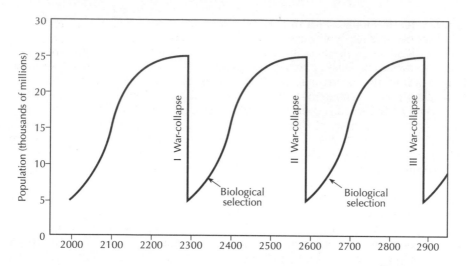

Figure 3: *The future*

all the characteristics of a new creature are to be found in the present-day population, but only among a small section, perhaps a very small section. With respect to certain characteristics, something like the biologist's 'pure line' will have been produced from an initially mixed population. The human gene pool will have been sieved through a mesh which permits only certain genes to pass.

Rather obviously, the new creature – or new species as I prefer to call him – will be much more socially minded than we are. Selection of course is essentially synonymous with rejection. It will be the unco-operative elements that will be rejected. Such individuals prefer to exist in chaos and will finally be submerged. A species much better adapted to the whole phenomenon of social organization will have emerged. Indeed, one can say that even at the present day the human environment has become much more organizational than physical or biological in the ordinary sense – other animals no longer present a serious challenge to us. After perhaps a score of the cycles of Figure 3 the organizational environment will itself, through its own properties, have produced a far better adapted species. And because the new species will be significantly more socially minded than we are, it is possible that the cycles of Figure 3 will eventually terminate. In mathematical terms, the oscillations will be damped and will die away.

A second important characteristic of the new species will be a much higher intellectual standard. Once again, the level will not be higher than *some* individuals possess today, but the average level will be much higher. Put in terms of the rather imprecise concept of the IQ, I would expect that the average level of the whole population might correspond to what we to-day would describe as 150.

To understand why this should be so, consider in more detail what would be required to establish a re-expansion phase. It would be impossible to re-expand, at any rate after the first one or two cycles, if the whole of technology had to be rediscovered independently in every cycle. The first expansion, the one we are now living in, has important assets – coal, oil, high-grade metallic ores – that will not be available in later cycles. On the other hand, the later cycles will have the advantage of information from earlier times. Experience shows that knowledge dies very hard once it has been obtained-the acquisition of knowledge is essentially irreversible, a truth already recognized in the Garden of Eden. Not all of the multitude of libraries would perish in the moments of catastrophe. Remnants would remain to be consulted by the survivors, or rather by the survivors with the wits to consult them. Here is the selective factor. A serious re-expansion would not be possible except to the highly intelligent. Reading in a library is today merely the innocent pursuit of the scholar. In the future the ability to puzzle out the knowledge of the past will be decisive. Knowledge, organization, the library, these are the environmental factors that will determine the future. It may seem strange to the biologist to think of the library as a major environmental factor, but I think the strangeness comes from the newness of the concept rather than from any new principle. So far as the principle of selection is concerned the nature of the 'sieve' or 'gate' is irrelevant. Only when we ask *what* selection does the precise nature of the sieve become important.

Some may question whether a rise of the IQ from the present 100 to as much as 150 could be produced in this way. My belief is that it could, because the effects of succeeding cycles are cumulative. With 20 cycles only a rise of 2.5 points per cycle could be needed, which seems quite modest. Rather the reverse; the selective mechanism is so strong that the ultimate effect is really determined by the highest existing present-day level. Obviously, the processes I have described cannot produce something not already present in the human species – at any rate, without mutations it cannot, and the mutational mechanism I regard as being too slow in its effect; it would require a longer span of time in order to be effective.

Let me then outline in a few words, by way of conclusion, what the broad history of our species is going to be over the next 5000 years, give or take a millennium.

I think that at the present day we are in the first big expansion phase. The first phase is specially important. It possesses assets – coal, oil, etc – that will not be repeated again. In return for the consumption of these assets it must establish a body of knowledge around which future civilizations will be able to build themselves. Without the establishment of this body of knowledge I do not believe our species will have more than a few centuries of existence ahead of it.

I think there will be a series of organizational breakdowns, or catastrophes, occasioned by over-population. This will lead to the saw-tooth-shaped population curve of Figure 3. During the beginnings of the re-expansion phases there will be selection for greater sociability and higher intelligence. The degree of selection in any one cycle need not be dramatically large because the effects of the repeated cycles are cumulative. Indeed I expect the number of cycles, the number that occurs before they are damped away, to be determined by how much selection occurs per cycle. If this is large, the number of cycles will be small, and vice versa, the net effect being the same.

The ultimate outcome, I believe, will be a highly sociable, highly intelligent creature. With this, I would consider a new species to have arrived. It will have its own problems no doubt, but they will not be as elementary as those with which we are faced today.

REFERENCES

Darwin, Charles Galton (1952) *The Next Million Years,* London: Hart-Davis.

[Malthus, Thomas Robert] (1798) *An Essay on the Principle of Population as it Affects the Future Improvement of Society,* London.

SUBJECT INDEX

human capital investment 11, 38, 40, 89–90
human rights 314, 320, 323
hunter-gatherers 28

I=PAT 259, 280–1
ideational change 70, 166–7
ideology and population policy 236
immigration, *see* migration, international
income distribution
  and fertility 13, 16
  and population growth 296
increasing returns 90, 295, 298–9
India
  agrarian change 162
  education 44–6
  fertility determinants 171
  gender inequalities 105–8
  sex ratio 105–6
Indonesia, fertility determinants 173
induced innovation 58–9, 151–3
induced institutional change 151–3
inheritance 128
intergenerational transfers 48–9, 88, 92–5,
    130–1, 166, 177–9, 181
international relations, demographic
    aspects of 214–8, 315–21
international trade 321
investment in human capital, *see* human
    capital investment
Ireland 64n
irrationality 74–5
irrigation 307–8
Islam and fertility 50, 224
isolation paradox 100–3
Italy, demographic transition 204

Japan
  fertility regulation 169, 203–4
  population growth 67
joint family 145–6, 155, 159

labour force
  growth 215–6
  women in 132, 186–95
labour migration, international 10, 220–1,
    322–3, 331–6
land, population carrying capacity of, *see*
    carrying capacity
land use 239, 307–8
Latin America 170–1
life expectancy 28–34, 253
limits to growth 214–5
literacy 43, 109n
local administration 156–8, 160–1
low fertility

causes of 134
  policy responses to 134, 331–7
low-level equilibrium trap, *see* equilib-
    rium-trap models

malaria 30
malnutrition, *see* nutrition
Malthusian theory 1, 58, 59n, 85–6, 151,
    227, 236, 244–6, 295, 345–8
marriage 128, 145, 205n
marriage policy 182–3
Matlab Surveillance Area 168
Mexico 171
micro-economics of fertility 73–82, 124–5
migration
  and disease transmission 206, 330–1
  illegal 221
  international 220, 317–21
  see also labour migration; rural-urban
    migration
migration policy 210, 219–21, 323
millenarianism 330–1
momentum, demographic 182–3, 327
moral economy 160
morbidity, *see* diseases
mortality
  differentials 31–3
  historical trends 6, 28
  in cities 330
  prehistorical 28
  wartime 66
  see also child mortality
mortality decline
  consequences 34
  determinants 15, 29, 31
multiculturalism 314, 320
multiple equilibria 90, 166

Nash equilibrium 103–4
national identity 320
natural capital 272–8
natural resources 245–6, 249–50, 272–8
  and population growth 227, 234, 239
neoclassical growth model 86–8
new growth theory 90
new household economics 69–70, 73–4
North-South differentials 215, 282–4,
    321–2
nuclear family 143–4, 155, 158–9, 165
nuclearization, *see* family structure,
    changes in
nutrition 309–11

old-age security 88, 92–5, 155
optimum population 237, 241, 267–8, 280

INDEX OF NAMES

Note: Page references in **bold type** refer to chapters in this volume.